THE EARHART
ENIGMA

Amelia Earhart. (Courtesy of the Estate of Ben Pinchot)

Courage

Courage is the price that Life exacts for granting peace.
The soul that knows it not
Knows no release from little things:
Knows not the livid loneliness of fear,
Nor mountain heights where bitter joy can hear
The sound of wings.

How can life grant us boon of living, compensate
For dull gray ugliness and pregnant hate
Unless we dare
The soul's dominion? Each time we make a choice, we pay
With courage to behold the resistless day,
And count it far.

—Amelia Earhart

THE EARHART ENIGMA

Retracing Amelia's Last Flight

By Dave Horner

Foreword by Ronald T. Reuther

PELICAN PUBLISHING COMPANY
Gretna 2013

*The word "Pelican" and the depiction of a pelican are
trademarks of Pelican Publishing Company, Inc., and are
registered in the U.S. Patent and Trademark Office.*

Library of Congress Cataloging-in-Publication Data

Horner, Dave.
  The Earhart enigma : retracing Amelia's last flight / by Dave Horner ;
foreword by Ronald T. Reuther.
      pages cm
  Includes bibliographical references and index.
    ISBN 978-1-4556-1781-4 (hardcover : alk. paper) — ISBN 978-1-
4556-1788-3 (e-book) 1. Earhart, Amelia, 1897-1937. 2. Women
air pilots—United States—Biography. 3. Air pilots—United States—
Biography. 4. Aircraft accidents—Investigation—Howland Island. 5.
Aircraft accidents—Investigation—South Pacific Ocean. I. Title.
  TL540.E3H67 2013
  629.13092—dc23
  [B]

                                                            2012043312

Back-cover image: *Airmail postage stamps from the Marshall Islands
from 1987, honoring the fiftieth anniversary of Amelia's crash-landing there.* (Courtesy Dave Horner)

Printed in the United States of America
Published by Pelican Publishing Company, Inc.
1000 Burmaster Street, Gretna, Louisiana 70053

Contents

Foreword

Dave Horner is a nautical treasure hunter and maritime historian, former US Naval assistant navigator, nationally certified SCUBA instructor, author of several popular books on marine exploration, and an excellent writer of fascinating non-fiction. He has been researching the enigma of Amelia Earhart's disappearance for years and has invested considerable time and his own money to do so. •

I came to know Dave and his wife, Jayne, in 2002, when they attended the second Amelia Earhart Symposium at the Western Aerospace Museum, which I had founded near the Oakland Airport.

My own research of Amelia's disappearance began in 1981 due to the influence of my friend Fred Goerner, noted author on the subject and television anchor. The Oakland Airport had been a landing and departure point for Earhart. From there, she set a number of flight records, including the first transcontinental flight across the United States in an autogiro and the first solo flight by anyone from Hawaii to the US. Oakland was also the point of departure for her two attempts to fly around the world near the equator. Both attempts failed: the first attempt because of a ground loop at Luke Field, Pearl Harbor, Hawaii, as she was heading westbound; the second try when she and her navigator Fred Noonan disappeared on July 2, 1937, while flying eastbound, attempting to reach Howland Island (a very small, isolated island in the mid-Pacific). Gradually, I came to the conclusion that she and her highly acclaimed navigator had survived their last flight, were picked up by the Japanese in or near the southeast Marshall Islands, and were held captive until their deaths. History reveals that the US and Japan were both very suspicious of the intentions of one another and that Japan had been aggressively expanding its empire since the turn of the century. Only five days after Earhart's disappearance, the Japanese formally invaded and declared war on China. Four years later, the US and Japan were waging violent war on each other.

Anyone who becomes involved in serious research about the mystery soon becomes aware of the mass of conflicting data published about Earhart and Noonan's last flight. Her friendship and involvement with President and Mrs. Franklin Delano Roosevelt and many other notables; numerous books and magazines; official reports by the US Coast Guard, Department of the Treasury, US Navy, US Army Air Corps, Department of State, US Marine Corps, and US Bureau of Aeronautics; professional and ham radio logs; reams of correspondence; and the wealth of information on the internet and rapid-fire digital communication all are available for study and consideration. However, some data has been buried in the chaos of war or under the security of government intelligence.

To uncover hidden and little-known Earhart information requires people such as Dave Horner, who has the rare, bird-dog ability to smell and sense where to look and persevere until he finds what he is seeking. His knowledge of archival research gained from his excellent work on the Spanish treasure galleons has proved to be of great benefit in developing unique and previously unciphered data about what really happened to Amelia. I endorse this book as a scholarly contribution to the Earhart enigma.

Dave Horner's overall position is that there are so many indicators—some whispering silently, others screaming loud and clear—that Amelia Earhart and Fred Noonan survived past their disappearance of July 2, 1937, and for some time afterwards. He is the first person to develop the details and unravel the amazing story of the French message in the bottle. This little known incident goes a long way in confirming the destiny of Amelia and her navigator, yet it would require pursuing the details of the rare drama around the world to bring the matter to conclusion, as he has done.

Over the years, others also have contributed to the wealth of data and information we now have about Amelia Earhart, and Dave Horner gives credit where credit is due, carefully certifying references and sources. Some may not agree with his views, but there are sufficient citations, theories, and quotations to support his positions. While there is important history within these pages, some of it never before published, the author has purposely avoided the "textbook syndrome." Even with all the valuable details and information contained herein, the chapters are presented in an easy-to-read, honest format and informal style. Whether or not they have a serious interest in Amelia Earhart, men and women of all ages should find this exciting narrative an informative, fun, and fascinating read. In a captivating style, Dave Horner has brought a fresh viewpoint that most definitely must be considered when evaluating the mystery.

Ronald T. Reuther, USAF lieutenant colonel, ret.

Preface

Amelia disappeared in 1937. Yet her soul still captivates me, just as her pleasant smile, personality, and indomitable spirit enchanted millions during her day. There were other female aviators who competed in cross-country races, set speed records, and performed airborne stunts at county fairs, but Amelia is the one who is best remembered. She is as popular today as she was in the 1930s, a tribute to her celebrity and enduring charm as America's sweetheart of the air.

For me, climbing into the cockpit of a vintage 1937 Lockheed Electra brings on an exhilarating sensation. Visiting the home where Amelia was born in Atchison, Kansas, gives me goose bumps. Prose from her several books causes me to reflect upon my own life and my own efforts as an author and to try and do better. Her words about courage, adventure, and impulsive desire will affect me until I die, because I have always felt the same way that she did.

My interest in Amelia Earhart began quite innocently with Dave Jourdan, president of Nauticos, LLC, an underwater exploration company with noteworthy successes. Jourdan invited me to participate in his planned expedition to the far Pacific to locate Amelia's lost airplane. Earhart researcher and renowned pilot Elgen Long convinced Jourdan that the missing airplane, a Lockheed Electra, crashed in the vicinity of Howland Island and today rests quietly on the Pacific floor some three miles deep. If I became an investing partner, Nauticos would award me the book contract covering the historic project.

Recognizing that the likely risk-versus-reward ratio was considerable, the attractive lure of an exciting book offer helped me make a positive decision. The US Navy and Coast Guard always had stated that the likely cause of Amelia's disappearance was that she simply ran out of fuel while searching in vain for the tiny Howland Island landing strip near the Equator in the Pacific Ocean. That seemingly logical conclusion has been generally accepted for multiple generations, haunting friends and family members alike. If the airplane truly could be located on the bottom of the ocean floor, the mystery finally would be solved.

So, as the saying goes, I put up my money to take my chances. Let's get on with the great adventure! After raising the funds, the project began. The research vessel *Davidson* along with its captain and crew was leased to conduct the time-consuming ocean floor survey. The magnificent undertaking departed Honolulu in March 2002. Aboard were the elite Nauticos reconnaissance crew and a National Geographic photographic team. It took a week to reach the location of the secretly designated site.

Utilizing a three-mile-long cable, the ship towed a high-tech sea sled reverently referred to as NOMAD. This sophisticated rig, loaded with customized side-scan sonar and state-of-the-art fiber-optic data telemetry imaging systems, was directed by remote control from a special operations room aboard *Davidson*. After having searched some six hundred square miles of ocean floor never previously viewed and with nine thousand meters of cable out, a serious equipment breakdown occurred. A burst hose resulted in the loss of hydraulic pressure, causing the brakes to fail and the cable drum to spin out of control, "screaming like a maniac," as Jourdan described it. The cable and its tethered undersea vehicle with its state-of-the-art gear settled to the ocean floor. The skilled Nauticos technicians managed to rebuild a brake motor and were able, at great effort and time, to inch the sled and equipment back to the surface. Repairs could not be made at sea, forcing a joyless retreat and cancellation of the expedition.

Every great adventure should begin with planning and research. While Nauticos did this, their target area was based primarily on Elgen Long's views as to where Amelia came down at the time of her fatal ditching. There were also technical studies by Rockwell-Collins radio experts measuring distance/wave-strength transmission ratios as well as other data. Though frustrated over the expedition failure, I diligently continued with my research on Amelia and her navigator, Fred Noonan, probing into all possible scenarios. I read every book and magazine article I could find, and their numbers amazed me. Many of these volumes brought out pertinent points, raised meaningful questions, and offered either good archival research or quoted interviews in the field with credible witnesses, many of whom were no longer around.

I scoured the Internet late into the evenings. I visited endless archives and libraries in many countries. I perused voluminous Coast Guard and Navy records and reports. I made contacts with people who had been researching the Earhart mystery much longer than I. The sheer number of wonderful people I met, many of whom shared their views and theories and became friends, was amazing. When considering the vast assortment of these voluminous news articles, government files with Coast Guard radio transmissions, and naval search reports and logs, the resulting effort to categorize and organize all the information became a mind-boggling nightmare of migraine proportions.

I wondered how one wades through a massive compilation of material to reduce the pile of data to manageable and constructive documentation as I struggled with the quantity of files and my information system.

Slowly but surely, I began to get up to speed. The puzzle started to fit together. One major hypothesis began to stand out and stare at me above all others. Though I tried to reject it, the thought kept returning. *Maybe Amelia didn't crash and sink!* Maybe she and Fred Noonan survived the flight to live another day. The possibilities of proving this were considered, but the realities kept staring right in my face: time and circumstances would have none of it. The dramatic evidence for which I yearned was fragmentary at best. About all I could do was separate the reliable witnesses from the less reliable ones, and many of those were no longer on this earth. Although much of the testimony given by well-meaning people was hearsay and some of the witnesses were children or grandchildren of the person who experienced the event, the facts developed are boundless and compelling. I offer these oral traditions in good faith because the people who faithfully offered them to me did so in order that we might know the truth as they and their forbears did.

In the research archives, occasional bits and pieces of data provided a hint; other researchers and Earhart aficionados who had visited certain Pacific islands and talked with local inhabitants shared their findings. Some views were ridiculous, but others had signs of definite credibility. I was introduced to some amazing people in the Marshall Islands and on Saipan who provided mind-boggling information. Extremely capable professional archivists worked with me but warned that "the road would not be easy. Others have tried to find the answer and have come away disappointed. Most of them finally gave in to accept the government's view: *Amelia ran out of gas while trying to locate Howland Island. She, her navigator Fred Noonan, and her Lockheed 10E NR16020 are resting peacefully three miles down on the bottom of the Pacific Ocean"* (author's emphasis).

When one works on a given project for a long period of time, it is easy to become enamored with it. Sometimes, it is even difficult to accept the views of others, especially if they are contrary. More than one person has told me that I might be considered a little crazy to take the subject so seriously. On any given night, I might watch old movie footage of Amelia. The day after, I'm sure I see her image on the street or at the supermarket. She was an explorer, an adventurer, and those traits unite people. At the very least, we could have been good friends. I'm surprised that my wife, Jayne, doesn't ask me on a regular basis, "Well, what are you and your other woman going to be doing today?"

She has every right to ask that question. She knows that the mystery of Amelia's disappearance has had a profound effect on me. She is aware that my years of searching for the answer has been hard work and cost a lot of money. Yet she shares in the glow of the accomplishments and the many friends made. She has observed each of the discoveries, rumors, clues, hearsay, and stunning witness testimonies that cumulatively provide an answer to what likely happened to the missing fliers. With friends, we watched Mira Nair's movie *Amelia* and were especially delighted with the movie's ending as viewers watched the Electra splashing into the sea. It's too bad that Nair didn't have the benefit of our research!

If the two Americans did crash into the sea near Howland Island, the question remains as to who sent the garbled SOS calls on their radio frequency. These transmissions were logged for several days by the Coast Guard, Navy, Pan American Airways radio operators, and others. The Electra's radio would not have been operative if the airplane had been in the water. Their location, 281 degrees north of Howland, would be on the neighborhood of Mili Atoll. Why would then-Secretary of State Cordell Hull have requested permission of Great Britain to search in their Gilbert Islands? What about those Pan Am radio direction finder reports? Was it just a coincidence their bearings intersected in the southeastern section of the Marshall Islands near Mili Atoll? From Howland Island, 281 degrees on a magnetic compass would lead toward the Mili Atoll region, especially if the Electra's drift had set the plane considerably north. At the time of the US invasion of the Marshalls and Saipan in 1944, consider the orders issued to all military Intelligence Officers "to be on the lookout for any word concerning Amelia Earhart." Why would those orders have existed if the US Government truly was convinced that the fliers crashed, sank, and died in 1937?

One poignant official record continues to fascinate. Now located in the Franklin D. Roosevelt Presidential Library, a letter from Paul Mantz, Amelia's technical adviser, sent to Eleanor Roosevelt is a testament to the unsettling nature of the government's official statements. Mrs. Roosevelt had received the letter dated April 26, 1938, requesting her assistance in getting him a copy of the official report of the *Itasca* about the Earhart disappearance. The Coast Guard in San Francisco had told him that the report was on file in Washington and it could not be released. If this amazing declaration from then-Secretary of the Treasury Henry Morgenthau Jr., who had supervisory responsibility for the Coast Guard, causes you to reference it while reading this book (as I have referenced it while researching), then the twelve years of research and writing of this work truly will have been worthwhile.

On May 13, 1938, ten months after Amelia and Fred disappeared, in the midst of a Treasury Department meeting in Morgenthau's office, a telephone call from the White House interrupted the group. Because Morgenthau was conducting an official Treasury Department meeting, all commentary was transcribed. When the call came in from Mrs. Roosevelt's office and the Secretary of the Treasury took the call, the transcription continued.

Malvina Scheider, Eleanor Roosevelt's personal secretary: Oh, hello Tommy. How are you? This letter that Mrs. Roosevelt wrote me about trying to get the report on Amelia Earhart. Now, I've given a verbal report. If we're going to release this, it's just going to smear the whole reputation of Amelia Earhart, and my . . . yes, but I mean if we give it to this one man we've got to make it public; we can't let one man see it. And if we ever release the report of *Itasca* on Amelia Earhart, any reputation she's got is gone, because . . . and I'd like to . . . I'd really like to return this to you. Now, I know what the Navy did. I know what the *Itasca* did, and I know how Amelia Earhart absolutely disregarded all orders, and if we ever release this thing, goodbye Amelia Earhart's reputation. Now really—if we give the access to one, we have to give it to all. And my advice is that—if the President ever heard that somebody questioned that the Navy hadn't made the proper search, after what those boys went through—I think they searched, as I remember it, fifty thousand square miles, and every one of those planes was out, and the boys just burnt themselves out physically and every other way searching for her. I mean I think he'd get terribly angry if somebody—because they just went the limit, and so did the Coast Guard. And we have the report of all those wireless messages and everything else, what that woman—happened to her the last few minutes. I hope I've just got to never make it public, I mean—OK—well, still if she wants it, I'll tell her. I mean what happened. It isn't a very nice story. Yes. There isn't anything additional to something like that. You think up a good one. Thank you.

Morgenthau [to an aide]: Just send it back.

Aide: Sure.

Morgenthau: I mean we tried—people want us to search again those islands, after what we have gone through. You, Gibbons [Stephen B. Gibbons, Under Secretary of the Treasury] know the story don't you?

Gibbons: We have evidence that the thing is all over, sure. Terrible. It would be awful to make it public.

Thus, we have for posterity an official US Government record documenting the fact that there were some officials within the White House establishment who knew that something "terrible" happened to Amelia. Was it because her airplane had crashed in the Pacific? Or was there more to the story because of "all those wireless messages and it would be awful to make it public"?

Unraveling the Earhart mystery through heretofore undiscovered records and new witness testimonies has been a highly motivating adventure. The results of that remarkable adventure have convinced me that Earhart and her navigator, Fred Noonan, did not crash and sink in the cold, deep Pacific on July 2, 1937. There are simply too many clues to indicate the contrary. I genuinely hope that you will share that conviction by the time you have finished my book. But, even if you don't, I would hope that you will find the story of Earhart's disappearance and death, and my trials and tribulations to understand what actually happened, every bit as compelling as the very public and heroic life that she led right up to the very end.

Let me share with you the facts, fantasies, and suppositions that have come to light since 1937.

Acknowledgments

This book began six decades after Geneviève Barrat found the historic message that washed ashore on the beach at Soulac-sur-Mer near Pointe de Grave and the entrance to the Gironde estuary within the fabulous wine-growing region of Bordeaux. If I knew the name of the Frenchman who wrote the brief message and observed a very alive Amelia Earhart as a fellow captive of the Japanese, I would certainly share author credits with him. After thirteen years of my own research, writing, and following in his footsteps, I would hope to merit his acquaintance. As I read and reread original copies of the small pieces of paper that Geneviève had carefully lifted from the capsule, the enormous significance of the message began to sink in. Other researchers likely had seen the file at the National Archives, but no one had seemed to recognize the magnitude of what the few hand-printed pages represented. Perhaps they felt a deterrence because the note was written in French.

Until now, there has never been a completely accurate translation of the French message and its stenography—not even the translations by the US Embassy in Paris and the State Department in Washington, DC, were one hundred percent correct. Because of the message's historical significance, I believed it was extremely important that every word and shorthand symbol be interpreted correctly and have gone to great lengths to do so.

My narrative of Geneviève's discovery is as remarkable as it is honest. Its time-consuming research around the world certainly makes it one of this book's most valuable assets, for it relates an amazing story never before given such significance. Most importantly, it defines in its own way what Navy Commander John Pillsbury meant when he told Fred Goerner, author of *The Search for Amelia Earhart,* to never give up, for he was on to something that "would stagger one's imagination." Though Goerner followed his advice and never gave up, cancer claimed him before he could finish the job.

This work has benefited from Goerner's additional notes, correspondence, and opinions. It is only right and proper that I

15

recognize him. Though much of his research is now preserved in the San Francisco Public Library and the National Museum of the Pacific War in Fredericksburg, Texas, his personal relationship with former Amelia Earhart Society moderator and foreword writer, Ronald T. Reuther, has further enhanced this book with numerous revelations, many of which are noted herein. It was Ron Reuther who wrote Fred Goerner's obituary. When cancer was about to claim Reuther as well, he urged me never to give up. I have not. Though the complete story behind Amelia's disappearance may never be known, thanks to our message in the bottle and the time, money, and dedication of many Earhart researchers following in the footsteps of Goerner and Reuther, we now know much of Amelia and Noonan's story, especially details not shared by the US Government.

It is therefore only natural that this book be dedicated to the Amelia Earhart Society of Researchers (AES). This is a free-thinking group of enthusiastic individuals committed to knowing the truth about the disappearance of America's sweetheart of the air, many of whom have become good friends. Among the leaders of this elite research force are, and were, the following visionaries:

Bill Prymak, successful businessman, engineer, researcher, and pilot with more than seven thousand flight hours. Bill was the founder of AES and served as president from 1989 to 2000. He funded numerous research trips, seminars, and expeditions to Pacific islands formerly mandated to Japan. In the Marshall Islands, he worked tirelessly to develop an amazing accumulation of new information on the Earhart disappearance, which he has graciously shared with AES. I have always been impressed with the passion Bill displays in discussing his trips to these isolated islands and his memory of the children and the people. The many stories he has picked up about the "white female pilot with hair cut short and wearing pants like a man" in custody of the Japanese represent unique testimonies that should not be discounted or overlooked. I can't thank Bill enough for his assistance, guidance, and permissions for this book.

Ronald T. Reuther, USAF lieutenant colonel, ret. Ron flew B-26 bombers and C-119 flying boxcars in Europe, North Africa, and the Middle East. An aviation enthusiast, he founded and served as Executive Director of the Western Aerospace Museum in Oakland Airport, California, and held many other aviation and exploration leadership positions. Ron was the dynamic moderator of the AES from 2000 to 2004. He believed that Amelia and her navigator came down in Japanese mandated territory, were taken captive, and died in prison. A proven leader and great American, he kindly and gallantly persevered through the pain and complications of colon cancer to complete the foreword of this book just prior to his death.

Joseph Gervais, USAF major, ret., veteran pilot of three wars with sixteen thousand flight hours flying B-24 bombers during WWII, B-29 bombers during the Korean War, and C-130 combat transports during the Vietnam war. Joe spent twenty-four years with the Las Vegas School District. While researching Amelia, he conducted fourteen expeditions to interview witnesses of Earhart's survival. Joe thoughtfully shared key information with me and encouraged me to follow certain paths to undertake further research.

Rollin C. Reineck, USAF colonel, ret., flew in combat in Europe and North Africa and later was chief navigator for Gen. Curtis Lemay and all B-29s on Saipan. The author of *Amelia Earhart Survived,* Rollin guided my early Earhart research and showed me files with volumes of data he'd developed from more than thirty years of being in love with Amelia.

Joe Klaas, USAF lieutenant colonel, ret., with twenty-five decorations. Joe flew Spitfires in the RAF and managed to crash four times in North Africa (none were attributable to pilot error). Returning to the USAAC in 1942, Joe was shot down in the Tunisia Campaign and captured by Arabs who sold him to the Germans for twenty dollars. He spent two years starving in a Nazi POW camp. He authored a number of screen scripts and books about Amelia Earhart based on Gervais's research. His presence and wisdom has been an enduring factor in the AES.

Ann Holtgren Pellegreno courageously retraced Amelia's flight in a Lockheed 10A Electra, a journey that she detailed in her book. A former English teacher, she has graciously critiqued several chapters of this book and made helpful suggestions. An active pilot for many years, she is a former member of the Ninety-Nines, recipient of the Amelia Earhart Pioneering Achievement Award, and an inductee in both the Iowa and Michigan Aviation Halls of Fame.

Paul Rafford Jr. has followed in Amelia's footsteps and air routes for many years. As a former Pan American World Airways radioman, he flew with and befriended many of Fred Noonan's former associates who shared their thoughts and reflections about what probably happened during the fatal world flight. Paul very kindly looked over my shoulder to guide me through the technicalities of understanding radio carrier waves and the transmission of radio communications over different distances.

His friendship and experience has been a valuable ingredient that is reflected in several chapters.

Jo Ann Ridley wrote a number of articles about aviation-related subjects and edited a book about Earhart and Noonan. She personally indexed the multitude of AES Newsletters, a real task. A journalist and professional publicist, she wrote about the arts, travel, aviation, and sailing. I shall always be appreciative for her suggestions and advice.

Michele Cervone has been an admirer of Amelia since the early 1960s and especially enjoys supporting the Amelia Earhart Birthplace Museum in Atchison, Kansas. I'd like to thank her for the many kindnesses she's shown me.

Alex Mandel, PhD, associate professor of biophysics at the Odessa Medical University, Ukraine, is a key player on the AES team. He also is a walking encyclopedia on Amelia Earhart and has authored various papers and reports on Amelia's life and disappearance, including a timeline that covers almost every day of her public life.

Gary LaPook has presented numerous illustrations, examples, and suppositions to AES about why Amelia and Noonan did, or didn't, do certain things that contributed to their disappearance. His experienced analyses add meaning, depth, and detail to the accumulation of what we know and don't know about our heroes. I thank him for his advice on this work.

Ron Bright, former Office of Naval Intelligence investigator, has used his background and professional experience to seriously accumulate Earhart research details over many years. It was Ron's unrelenting pursuit for the answer on who might have sent the Weihsien telegram to G. P. Putnam that provided the answer to settle that mysterious question that had laid low and remained out of sight for a decade.

Dave Bowman, former Navy petty officer and enthusiastic Earhart author, keeps an eye focused for old Earhart photos or souvenirs from days gone by and knows within a heartbeat when any kind of Amelia related item might appear on the internet for auction.

Ian Mann has produced interesting Earhart reference tidbits from sources in Australia and New Zealand from which researchers in America have gleaned new data on previously unknown citations.

Mike Campbell, author, is a former Department of Defense journalist and public affairs officer who shares my view of Amelia's last days as being on Saipan.

Glenn and Irene Plymate are aviation enthusiasts who have devoted much time and thought to the exploits of Amelia Earhart and her mysterious disappearance.

Louise Foudray took over day-to-day management of the Amelia Earhart Birthplace Museum and shows guests the wonderful old home and answers their questions about Amelia.

The rank and file of the AES past and present also are represented by many talented individuals. This group includes pilots, navigators, ship captains, divers, archaeologists, historians, attorneys, educators and many others who share a mutual interest and love for Amelia. They are listed alphabetically:

Dirk Ballendorf, Jim Beeby, David Bellarts, Don Bernitt, Daryll Bolinger, Rebecca Chaky, Dan Cheatham, Jackie Ferrari, Patrick Gaston, Steve Gaston, Lily Gelb, Jim Hanford, Don Iwanski, Bonnie Jacobson, Don Jordan, Chris Kennedy, Julias Laviano, Jean Lewis, Laura McLaughlin, Ed Melvin, Don Newman, Tom Northrop, Carol Osborne, Art Parchen, Adrienne Parks, Bob Payne, Woody Peard, Linda Pendleton, Lisa Cotham Pizani, Debra Plymate, Michael Real, Gerry Elkus Reuther, Phil Rider, Matt Rodina, Harold "Doc" Ross, David Smith, Gene Tissot, James Trautman, Donald Treco, Pat Ward, Cam Warren, Rick Washburn, and Donald M. Wilson.

In addition to some of the above referenced AES members, there are many others who contributed or assisted in this work. My wife, Jayne, and daughter, Julie, helped with numerous typing, filing, editing, research trips, and drudgery details that often get overlooked. Julie single-handedly undertook long-distance research projects and made outstanding accomplishments at such illustrious institutions as Purdue University Library, Lafayette College, Indiana University, and the National Museum of the Pacific War in Fredericksburg, Texas. Julie also was responsible for organizing my many photos.

Tara Lewis provided much needed assistance in systematizing my computer files, photos, and illustrations chapter by chapter, as did Lynda Robinson-Bergen and Susan Viviano. Janice Willett took charge of editing chapters before I got in over my head, as did freelance editor Jeanne Pinault. She also introduced me to editor Judy Reveal who stopped work on her own book to professionally process my index. These talented ladies contributed an assortment of specialized skills in their approach to shifting sections of script for better placement and improving organizational structure of the manuscript.

Julie Imirie came to my rescue after Pelican Publishing gave me a contract. She took charge with a tremendous can-do effort. Thank you Julie! Gratitude is also expressed to talented artist Elizabeth Whelan for her great illustrations. David Wagner was of considerable assistance in prepping and structuring audio-visual works related to this book. I sincerely thank these talented friends so very much for their quality assistance. They all are truly accomplished individuals and their friendship and dedicated commitment to delivering a professional, well-structured book is sincerely appreciated.

Professional researchers and archivists Cliff Callahan, Greg Murphy, and the late John Taylor assisted at the National Archives and Records Administration (NARA). Sammie Morris, archivist and assistant professor of library science at Purdue University was her usual helpful self, as was Carl Snow. Abby Gilbert of the Treasury Historical Association in Washington, DC, was very helpful in researching old Coast Guard documents as we looked for the missing files of former Secretary of the Treasury Henry Morgenthau Jr.

At the Franklin D. Roosevelt Presidential Library and Museum in Hyde Park, New York, I'd like to thank Raymond Teichman, supervisory archivist; Robert Parks; and Virginia Lewick for answering my many questions and providing numerous copies of archive documents.

Robert Stenuit, a Belgian historian and friend of many years, came through as usual when there was difficult archive research to be undertaken. He left no stone unturned of libraries and repositories that might have held some clues and answers to the Earhart/Noonan disappearance. For two solid years, he persevered through repositories of four countries seeking answers to my questions about the French message in the bottle. He used his varied contacts to reach people at all levels of government and society from France to Tahiti to Nauru Island to Australia. He also produced exact literal translations in English from French or other foreign languages.

Neither Stenuit nor I could read shorthand, a key ingredient of the SOS message that washed ashore at Soulac-sur-Mer. His daughter, Marie Eve, precisely transcribed and translated the message in the bottle's extremely important stenography. This very able, intelligent lady learned stenography from scratch to accommodate the difficult translation of the complicated shorthand notes. My sincere thanks to these good friends who worked hard to develop material never before published to make this work a success.

Many others contributed in substantial ways. Peggy and Louis Salmon provided names and introductions in New Jersey that aided my research on the Right Reverend Monsignor James F. Kelley, who alleged to have been involved with Earhart. The Monsignor's nephew, the late Adrian "Red" McBride, and niece, Marilyn Munson, also provided much personal information about their uncle that cleared up a number of earlier questions. Father Stephen F. Duffy; Reverend Monsignor Francis R. Seymour, archdiocesan archivist of Newark (New Jersey); and Reverend Monsignor Thomas P. Ivory, pastor of St. Joseph's Church of West Orange, New Jersey, all provided personal views and observations on Monsignor Kelley for which I am most appreciative.

Long time friend Bob Colombo's introduction of his former CID associate, Fate John Kirby, was a timely favor, as Fate's handwriting analysis of Irene Bolam proved that she was not Amelia Earhart, as others had claimed. Bolam's son, Larry Heller, also privately confirmed that his mother was not Amelia Earhart, and his candor was especially appreciated. Fate Kirby also helpfully analyzed the fingerprints of the bottle message. His analysis later was confirmed by experts from the Federal Bureau of Investigation.

Appreciation is expressed to the Pacific Scientific Information Center and the Bernice P. Bishop Museum of Honolulu, Hawaii, for assistance in providing colonization information and photos of Howland, Baker, and Jarvis Islands and numerous pictures of the outstanding group of young colonists who were the real heroes of the colonization undertaking. Leah Caldiera is recognized for providing information and kind assistance.

My friend Bruce Crawford introduced me to Vice Adm. Al Burkhalder, USN, ret., and Capt. James E. Wise Jr., USN, ret., who spent time trying to assist me break through undefined barriers that appeared to block my efforts to identify the disposition of captured WWII classified material such as Amelia's personal briefcase recovered from the bombed-out building on Saipan by marine Bob Wallack. I thank former FBI agents Clint Van Zandt and Terry Neise, who used their experience and connections to encourage specialists to analyze fingerprints on the message in the bottle. Appreciation goes also to former Marshall Islands ambassador to the United Nations, Alfred Capelle, who kindly provided his frank and personal opinion about Amelia and Fred Noonan being captives of the Japanese in the Marshall Islands. Thank you, Alfred.

Dr. Antoinette Theron introduced me to Mrs. Norma Knaggs, wife of deceased South African author Oliver Knaggs, who was among the first to interview witnesses in the Marshall Islands and Saipan. Norma very kindly gave me permission to quote from selected pages in Knaggs's book and shared with me his key discoveries in the Marshall Islands and selected photos from the

Knaggs collection. Thank you Antoinette and Norma!

Jim and Gin Hannon always will be remembered for their friendship and long hours of discussions detailing Jim's wartime adventures, especially his heroic rescue of the prisoners of Weihsien, China, during August 1945. The secret mission of Operation Duck and its exposure of the POW telegram to G. P. Putnam to Jim's amazing story of intrigue involving a semi-comatose female detainee whom he came to believe was a very ill Amelia Earhart. She was mysteriously flown out of the prison camp confines at the end of World War II prior to the departure of other internees. Former prisoners of the Weihsein Detention Center whom Jim and his small contingent of paratroopers liberated included author Pamela Masters, the late Langdon Gilkey, and New Jersey legislator Mary Taylor Previte, each of whom kindly helped with my questions and research (although they were united in disavowing that Amelia was in that internment center).

Other friends who critiqued chapters and provided personal input for which I am appreciative are: USAF Col. Ed O'Connor, ret.; Knute Bartrug; John Brehmer; Jeff Grandy; David Higgins; H. Davey Hamilton; Pat Walsh; Allan and B. J. Blair; Barry Reardon; Dick Kurtz; Lou Ullian; Paul Perry; Tim McIntire; Guy and Phyllis Fritts; John Kenefick; Shar McBee; Mako Sirota; Rene Hitziger; and long-time friend and adviser Kelly Smith. Former CIA agent Bart Bechtel critiqued several chapters and provided advice on that agency's responsibilities after World War II. Thanks go also to Pam and Jim Harris, who introduced me to Tommy Brennan III in Houston, who graciously related his father's experiences on Saipan attempting to recover Earhart's remains. Judy and Tim Gow introduced me to Mike Case on Majuro, Marshall Islands, which led to my friendship with Matt Holly, who had been searching for Amelia for thirty years. It was Matt who told me to "follow the ring and learn the truth." I believe that I have done just that.

William H. Stewart deserves special credit for his tremendously important interest and assistance. The former deputy director of Development of the Trust Territory of the Pacific Islands, as well as author, economist, military historical cartographer, and raconteur extraordinaire, kindly shared his experiences and friendships of more than a quarter-century on Saipan. His suggestions and introductions opened many doors. Thank you, Bill!

Saipan businessman Dave Sablan related his memories and experiences working with Buddy Brennan in the mid-1980s, helping Brennan to discover what was believed to be the blindfold worn by

Amelia prior to her execution. Sam McPhetres helped me find local Saipan research assistants. Marie Castro directed me to locals who might have seen or heard something about "the American fly-lady." Escolastica T. Cabrera and daughter Olinka C. Chaudhry patiently answered my many questions and made significant contributions to my ultimate determination as to what likely happened to Amelia on Saipan. "Esco" was born in 1930, and though only seven years old when Amelia was brought to Saipan by Japanese military, she told me, "according to testimony of family and close friends who either saw the Caucasian woman flier, or knew people who did see her, she was here. My family would not lie!" My thanks go also to the Bishop of Saipan, Tomas Camacho, for his courtesy and thoughts about the Earhart episode in Saipan's history.

Mr. N. Horiguchi provided considerable historical details about pre-war Saipan under the Japanese. His depth of contacts and intense interest in Chamorro local lore proved to be extremely helpful. I benefited from names of potential witnesses he provided who "were still with clear heads." His time, energy, and research are very much appreciated.

Also to be singled out is David Sablan Celis, retired dental lab technician, who went out of his way to help me double check the accuracy of his family's memories, which led to the recovery of his mother's 1986 momentous taped statement to the Saipan Division of Historic Preservation. My thanks go to David and his extended family for their dedicated assistance in this work.

I'm appreciative also of the thoughtful contribution of the late Dr. Leonard Kaufer and his wife, Connie Tenorio Kaufer, for their assistance. Connie told me that for many years she wore the ring originally given to her aunt and namesake, Consolacion, by the "foreign white female" who was in custody of the Japanese military on Saipan. That little pearl ring represents a beacon of truth confirming Amelia's presence on Saipan.

Scott MacIntosh and Dr. Ralf Birken of Witten Technologies, Inc., contributed to my research documentation through their technical assistance with ground penetrating radar technology. The late Ross Game of the *Napa (CA) Register* enthusiastically answered my many questions about his 1960s Earhart research with Fred Goerner. Ross provided extremely relevant leads and shared valuable documentation of the Game-Goerner combined studies of what happened to Amelia and Fred.

Other friends who offered suggestions and varying views on the

Earhart subject were Sally Putnam Chapman (granddaughter of G. P. Putnam), who gave me direction, provided encouragement, and kindly allowed me to share the original copy of Amelia's pre-nuptial agreement with G. P. and other phrases from his published works. I also thank Dave Jourdan, Tom Detweiler, Gary Bane, Elgen Long, Carol Osborne, Alex Coutts, Doug Westfall, Don and Vernajean Wilson, G. P. Putnam Jr., Amy Kleppner, and Barbara and Dale Earhart for their varying degrees of kind participation.

Additionally, my appreciation goes to Smithsonian Air and Space Museum curator, Von Hardesty, for his helpful direction and chapter structure recommendations and to my very qualified editor-friend, Michael Briggs, for his coaching, encouragement and belief in my work.

Last but not least, I thank Nina Kooij, Editor in Chief; Kathleen C. Nettleton, Publisher; Abi Pollokoff, Assistant Editor; the Calhoun family team; and the many Pelican Publishing Company specialists for bringing this extraordinary new book to life.

Dave Horner

THE EARHART
ENIGMA

Part One: Amelia's Airborne Adventure

Chapter 1

The Final Flight

Please know I am quite aware of the hazards. I want to do it because I want to do it. Women must try to do things as men have tried. When they fail, their failure must be but a challenge to others.

—Amelia Earhart[1]

June 29, 1937: Lae, New Guinea

Having traveled twelve hundred miles from Port Darwin, Australia, in seven hours and forty minutes, Amelia Earhart and Fred Noonan reached Lae, New Guinea, during the afternoon of June 29. The large, heavily forested island of New Guinea is north of Australia and just south of the equator. Guinea Airways, Ltd., under the direction of General Manager Eric Chater, operated the airport in this rough-and-tumble town, whose principal reason for existing was to service the nearby gold fields at Bulolo, a mountain camp some forty miles southeast, in difficult terrain at an altitude of seven thousand feet.

Guinea Airways and its pilots had been very successful in transporting heavy mining equipment, parts, and supplies to the remote mining territory of the jungle. The profitable gold-producing operation was the result of the entrepreneurship of Australian Cecil Levien, the prospector who first located gold nuggets in the gravel of the New Guinea mountain streams. He later teamed up with two other mining engineers, Charles A. Banks and Frank A. Griffin, who had designed a high-yielding dredge. The dredge could be dismantled for shipment into the mountains and then rebuilt at the mining site. The first dredge brought into Bulolo was operational in 1932. Their company was known as Placer Development, Ltd. It grew by acquiring other profitable start-up gold operations and became known worldwide as Placer Dome. In 2006, Placer Dome was acquired by Barrick Gold.[2]

The arrival of Amelia Earhart at the small town and airport of

Lae was big news for that community. Accordingly, Guinea Airways organized a party honoring the arrival of the Earhart-Noonan flight. In addition to their own pilots, Guinea Airways invited the management of the various dredging companies and their wives to come down and celebrate at the airport on the coast by the Gulf of Huon.

"The reception was spectacular," stated Mrs. Louis Joubert, wife of the general manager of Bulolo Gold Dredging Company. "It was a banquet. Local natives even came to join in the welcome given Amelia. The crowd was very excited as the 'large silver bird' circled the airport through the clouds and finally landed. The response Amelia received was quite heartwarming. She appeared very confident and happy."[3]

June 30, 1937

Amelia asked Eric Chater to make sure that her Electra had a careful check-up. From the report of the chief engineer, it appeared that a thorough servicing was performed. A letter written by Chater to Mr. M. E. Griffin of Placer Management, Ltd., dated July 25, 1937, (hereafter referred to as the Chater report), noted the following:

A happy Amelia exiting the cockpit of the Electra in her leather jacket at Lae, New Guinea. (Courtesy Smithsonian Institute)

Report of E. Finn, Chief Engineer:
Clean set of spark plugs fitted to both engines.
Oil drained from both tanks.
Oil filters inspected and cleaned—both engines.
Petrol pump removed from starboard engine on account of fluctuation of pressure at cruising revolutions. Spare petrol pump fitted.
Thermo coupler connection on No. 4 cylinder, starboard engine, repaired.
Air scoop between Nos. 2 and 3 cylinders on port engine repaired.
Propellers greased.
Batteries inspected for level and charge.
New cartridge fitted to exhaust gas analyzer—starboard side.
Spare adapter plug fitted to carburetor air scoop for temperature gauge line.
Sperry Gyro Horizon (lateral and fore and aft level) removed, cleaned, oiled and replaced, as this reported showing machine in right wing low position when actually horizontal.
Engines run up on ground. Petrol pressure on starboard engine too low. Petrol pump removed. Original petrol pump valve and seat ground in to remove unevenness. Pump fitted to engine.
Engines run up on ground and tested in air. Both engines okay. Petrol pressure port engine 4½ pounds, starboard engine 4¾ pounds.
Engines, instruments and aircraft approved okay by Miss Earhart.

Earhart and Noonan were busy cleaning out the airplane while Lae mechanics did their service checks. The fliers removed any personal items and gear not essential for the remainder of the flight over water. Some items were mailed home. Others were given away to airport locals. Their two parachutes had been shipped home from Port Darwin, Australia. Amelia gave Guinea Airways's radioman, Harry Balfour, her Very pistol (flare gun) and a few books. Harry later reported: "One important factor you ought to know is that she handed me her radio facility book plus a lot of papers and her pistol and ammunition. Now, inside that facility book were all her radiograms concerning her communications arrangements with the *Itasca* and suggested frequencies to be used. She could not have remembered all the information these papers contained . . . However, I can guarantee that her radio equipment was in good order when she left."[4]

Amelia was well known to have been concerned about weight. She had left her trailing antenna—an invaluable device for locating her position—in Miami, although the entire rig weighed only about nine pounds, or less than two gallons of gas.[5] She said, "Fred and I have been working very hard in the last two days repacking the plane and eliminating everything unessential. We have discarded as much personal property as we can decently get along without and henceforth propose to travel lighter than ever before."[6]

Satisfied that her plane was sufficiently lightened, Amelia busied herself shuttling between the wireless station and the hangar. She kept a careful eye on what the mechanics were doing. At noon, with Balfour's help, Amelia tested the long-wave radio receiver while the plane was being serviced in the hangar. During this period, the Lockheed receiver was calibrated for reception of Lae radio telephone. That afternoon, the oil tanks were drained and refilled with sixty gallons of Stanavo 120-weight engine oil. Fred Noonan tried without success to obtain a radio time check for his chronometers.

Amelia sent two cablegrams that afternoon. The first was to Richard Black on board the *Itasca*, asking for a Howland Island weather report. Black, a US Department of the Interior field representative, had been engaged by Amelia's husband, George Putnam, to coordinate communications and other logistical requirements necessary for the long flight over water from Lae to Howland and then to Hawaii. Black was a logical choice to assist with the Earhart flight since he was in charge of the Pacific colonization project and thus familiar with the territory. She then sent a cablegram to her husband: "RADIO MISUNDERSTANDING AND PERSONNEL UNFITNESS PROBABLY WILL HOLD ONE DAY HAVE ASKED BLACK FOR FORECAST FOR TOMORROW YOU CHECK METEOROLOGIST ON JOB AS FN MUST HAVE STAR SIGHTS STOP ARRANGE CREDIT IF TRIBUNE WISHES MORE STORY."[7]

The "personnel unfitness" comment has been discussed at great length by Earhart aficionados. To this day, no one can agree whether the comment refers to Noonan or to Amelia as being unfit to fly. Certainly, they both must have been exhausted after pushing themselves during the stress-filled twenty thousand miles of the previous four weeks.

After tending to the wireless messages, Amelia made some notes in her daily log, which she subsequently mailed to her husband prior to her takeoff from Lae. "Tomorrow we should be rolling down the runway, bound for points east. Whether everything to be done can be done within the time remains to be seen. If not, we cannot be home by the Fourth of July as we had hoped, even though we are one day up on the calendar of California. It is Wednesday here, but Tuesday there." Putnam, ever the promoter, had scheduled a celebratory party at Oakland Airport upon his wife's anticipated return on July 4.

Black arranged for a large quantity of aviation gasoline along with an assortment of spare parts to be brought aboard the Coast Guard cutter *Itasca* before its departure from Honolulu on Friday, June 18, 1937. On board the vessel were numerous military personnel, Department of the Interior colonists being rotated to relieve staff at Howland and Baker Islands, mechanics, journalists, photographers, and other invited guests.

The Naval tug *Ontario* had been assigned to a guard station along the anticipated course of the Electra. It was positioned at longitude 165° east, a little south of Nauru Island. If a problem arose with the airplane, however, it remained to be seen as to how effectively this guard ship could deal with it. *Ontario* was one of the oldest tugs in the fleet. It only could communicate on 500 kilocycles per second (kcs), and without the trailing antenna, Amelia could not utilize this frequency. The tug's location was twelve hundred miles from Howland Island, and the coal-burning vessel barely carried enough fuel to make it back to its home port at American Samoa. Amelia had requested that the Navy have *Ontario* send the letter *n* in code on the half-hour on 400 kcs or upon request and its station call letters (NIDX) repeated twice at the end of every minute. This was not an unusual request, but she would first have to contact *Ontario* by code on 500 kcs. That frequency was virtually useless for transmitting over any distance without a trailing antenna. There is no indication that the tug ever received this order. In fact, *Ontario*'s captain, H. W. Blakeslee, told Amelia Earhart Society researcher Paul Rafford Jr. that he had no knowledge concerning a transmission schedule between *Ontario* and KHAQQ (Amelia's radio call sign). In any case, *Ontario* did not have the transmitting capability to communicate on the Earhart frequencies.

The tug was only equipped with a 1920s standard ship-to-shore radio using the primary calling channel of 500 kcs. Once contact was made, the operator would switch to a lower frequency such as 450 or 400 kcs. *Ontario* was unable to communicate on 3105 or 6210 kcs, Amelia's other frequencies. Richard Black had sent a message earlier to Amelia at Bandoeng, Java, informing her of *Ontario*'s call sign, NIDX, and of that vessel's frequency range of 195 to 600 kcs. Black clearly stated that *Ontario* "had no high-frequency equipment on board" and asked Amelia to let him know the frequencies she desired from each guard ship, including *Itasca*, "that were best suited to your homing device."[8] Knowing that *Ontario* was not as technologically advanced as the other ships, it also should have been apparent that it would have been less able to assist during a crisis situation.

The small Navy seaplane tender *Swan* (AVP-7) also had been

ordered to take a guard station position approximately midway between Hawaii and Howland Island in case of a problem on the next leg of the planned flight from Howland to Hawaii. The *Swan* had been asked to transmit by voice on frequencies of 9 megacycles (9000 kc). An important note is that *Swan's* fifty-watt transmitter would be subsequently reduced to about thirty-five watts of power when transmitting by voice. This would considerably reduce the radio's range during the daytime.[9]

The *Itasca* had been requested by Amelia to transmit the letter *a* along with its call letters on the half-hour on 7.5 megacycles (7500 kcs). According to the Chater report, "Miss Earhart and Captain Noonan advised they depended on radio telephone reception as neither of them were able to read Morse at any speed, but could recognize an individual letter sent several times."[10] In addition, Amelia "would give a long call by voice on 3105 kcs on the quarter after hour and possibly quarter to."[11]

USCG cutter Itasca. (Courtesy Purdue University Libraries)

July 1, 1937

Rising early, Amelia took the Electra up for a thirty-minute test flight at 6:30 a.m. She was particularly anxious to check the direction finder, as she had replaced a bad fuse on this piece of equipment at Port Darwin and wanted to make sure it was properly functioning. Balfour sent a long dash while Amelia attempted to obtain a minimum, or null, on the radio signal by rotating her loop antenna. However, she was unable to get an adequate bearing on Balfour's signal. Upon landing, she casually remarked that the reason was probably because the Lae station was "too powerful and too close," and let it go at that.[12]

In response to her question about the overall state of the Electra's radio, Balfour told Amelia that the transmitter seemed fine, but the carrier wave was rough on 6210. He suggested that she pitch her voice higher to help offset the distortion.

After the direction finder test, the ground crew began filling the plane's tanks with fuel:

> Vacuum Oil Company's representatives filled all tanks with 87-octane fuel with the exception of one 81-gallon tank which already contained 100-octane for takeoff purposes. This tank was approximately half full, and it can be safely estimated that, on leaving Lae, the tank contained at least 40 gallons of 100-octane fuel (100-octane fuel is not available in Lae). A total of 654 imperial gallons was filled into the tanks of the Lockheed after the test flight was completed. This would indicate that 1100 US gallons [were] carried by the machine when it took off for Howland Island.[13]

Bob Iredale was the manager of Vacuum Oil in New Guinea. He confirmed that the Electra's tanks were full at takeoff:

> I fueled the Lockheed and did it personally. Fred [Noonan] had arranged 20x44 gallon drums of AVGAS 80-octane shipped out to us from California months before. I can assure you all tanks were absolutely full—the wing tanks and those inside the fuselage. After she had done a test flight, I topped them up again before her final take off. I think she took somewhere around 800 gallons all up. Fred Noonan was with me at the fueling and checked it out. He was also with me when we changed the engine oil, as was Amelia.[14]

There have been numerous references by other authors to the possibility of Fred Noonan's having gone off to Bulolo on a drinking binge prior to the flight. After the Electra's disappearance, Harry

Amelia looking through her direction finder. (Courtesy Purdue University Libraries)

Balfour stated that he understood that Noonan had been at Bulolo on a drinking spree the evening before their departure and did not arrive back in Lae until the morning of takeoff. Consequently, he had little time to do any flight planning. This comment is inconsistent with other reports, which confirm that Noonan was actually quite busy trying to obtain radio time checks in order to set his chronometers. Even Amelia confirmed in *Last Flight,* published by her husband after her disappearance, that "Fred Noonan has been unable, because of radio difficulties, to set his chronometers. Any lack of knowledge of their fastness or slowness would defeat the accuracy of celestial navigation. Howland is such a small spot in the Pacific that every aid to locating it must be available."[15]

Alan Vagg, radio operator at Bulolo, stated that neither Noonan nor Amelia visited Bulolo while they were at Lae.[16] While at Lae, Amelia stayed with the family of Eric Chater. Noonan resided at Voco House with Bob Iredale and Frank Howard of Vacuum Oil Company. Iredale claimed:

> As was our custom, we had a drink in the evening—90°F and 95% humidity made it that way. We asked Fred if he would join us the first night and the comment was, 'I've been three parts around the world without a drink and now we are here for a couple days. I'll have one. Have you a Vat 69?' I did happen to have one so the three of us knocked it off. He confessed to Amelia the next morning he had a bit of a head. Her comment was, 'Naughty boy, Freddie.' That was the only drink session we had, and to suggest he was inebriated before they took off is mischievous nonsense. I can assure you or anyone he had no drink for at least 24 hours before take off.[17]

Noonan's happy hour occurred the evening of their arrival, June 29. The following evening, June 30, he was again invited to meet the locals at the bar. Noonan declined, however, saying he had had quite enough the night before.[18]

During the afternoon of July 1, after the Electra had been filled to capacity with gasoline and oil, Amelia and Fred did a little sightseeing around the Lae countryside.

> We commandeered a truck from the manager of the hotel and with Fred at the wheel, because the native driver was ill with fever, we set out along a dirt road. We forded a sparkling little river which after a heavy rain, so common in the tropics, can become a veritable torrent, and drove through a lane of grass taller than the truck. We

turned into a beautiful coconut grove before a village entrance.

The village was built more or less around a central open plaza. All huts were on stilts and underneath the dogs and pigs held forth. We were told that the natives train pigs as 'watchdogs.' Fred said he would hate to come home late at night and admit being bitten by a pig![19]

After trying for two days to obtain time signals for his chronometer synchronization, Noonan was getting frustrated over the static and local interference that undermined his efforts. Thanks to help from Lae radio operator Harry Balfour, Noonan finally was successful. Eric Chater described the effort:

During the rest of the day constant watch was kept for the reception of time signals with no result until 9 p.m. when the Sydney signal was heard, though with considerable interference. Meanwhile, the Lae operator had advised Rabaul of our lack of success in picking up a time signal owing to local interference. At 10:20 p.m. a message was heard from all Australian coastal stations requesting all shipping to keep silence for a period of ten minutes during the transmission of the Adelaide time signal which was being awaited by Miss Earhart. Complete silence prevailed during this period and a perfect time signal was received by Captain Noonan, and the machine chronometer was found to be three seconds slow.[20]

More from the Chater report: "On July 2nd a further time signal was received from Saigon at 8 a.m. when the chronometer checked the same as the previous night. Both Captain Noonan and Miss Earhart expressed their complete satisfaction and decided to leave at ten o'clock."[21]

July 2, 1937: The Takeoff from Lae

Not much more than a month ago I was on the other shore of the Pacific, looking westward. This evening, I looked eastward over the Pacific. In those fast moving days which have intervened, the whole width of the world has passed behind us except this broad ocean. I shall be glad when we have the hazards of its navigation behind us.
—Amelia Earhart[22]

The airport runway at Lae was one thousand yards of hard-packed dirt. This runway ended at the edge of a cliff that fell off some twenty feet into the Gulf of Huon. At the cliff's edge of the runway was a small perimeter road, cresting slightly higher than the runway itself. Alan E. Board of Guinea Airways, Ltd., was among the small crowd that gathered to witness the historic takeoff. He watched in fascinated awe as Amelia gunned the big Wasp engines using full throttle. The heavily laden Electra began moving ever so slowly, then gradually picked up speed as the plane made its way down the strip. The morning was still and hot with no breeze. A wisp of dust hung limply behind the track of the Lockheed and its whirling propellers. The airplane had never been so heavily loaded with fuel—it was literally a flying gas tank. Would the big bird fly? Amelia surely had one eye on the air speed indicator and the other on the fast-approaching cliff edge. She could see the green water of the Huon Gulf below and just ahead. Almost too soon, she was at the end of the runway and barely airborne.

> At the time of the final, and near fatal takeoff, it looked as though the machine was not going to leave the ground. At the last possible moment Amelia jumped the plane over a slightly raised road running across the seaward end of the "drome." We all had a sick feeling, and I really mean it, when it looked as though it was simply going to flop on to the sea about 20 feet below the shore level. And in fact it was so close that the two slip streams sent up wakes of salt spray for a considerable distance, and when disappearing from sight about 20 miles out, was just beginning to rise from sea level.[23]

Bob Iredale reported later, "Their final take off was something to see. We had a grass/dirt strip some 900-1000 yards long, one end the jungle, the other the sea. Amelia tucked the tail of the plane almost into the jungle, brakes on, engines full bore, and let go. They were still on the ground at the end of the strip. It took off, lowered toward the water some 30 feet below, and the props made ripples on the water. Gradually they gained height, and some 15 miles out, I guess they may have been at 200 feet."[24]

Bert Heath, chief pilot for Guinea Airways, was approaching the Lae airport in his tri-motored Junkers plane. From his altitude above the field, he watched the Electra's progress as it gained speed, using every yard of runway and then some. He noticed the Lockheed bounce in the air as the plane bumped over the perimeter road and then appeared to fall over the cliff as the propellers clawed the sea water until almost out of sight.

A report from James A. Collopy, aviation superintendent for the Lae District of New Guinea, stated, "After taking every yard of the 1000 yard runway . . . the aircraft had not left the ground 50 yards from the end of the runway. When it did leave it sank away but by this time was over the sea. It continued to sink about five or six feet above the water and had not climbed to more than 100 feet before it disappeared from sight. In spite of this, however, it was obvious that the aircraft was well-handled and pilots of Guinea Airways who have flown Lockheed aircraft were loud in their praise of the takeoff with such an overload."[25]

Navigator Fred Noonan knew that it was important for the flight to begin at a time that would place them nearing their destination in daylight hours after having flown 2,556 statute miles all night over the open ocean to a fly-speck of an island called Howland.

At the time of the planned 10 a.m. takeoff from Lae (0000 Greenwich Civil Time), Amelia had been unable to obtain an up-to-date weather report. As fate would have it, this report was received by the Lae wireless station just as she taxied down the runway for liftoff:

EARHART, AMELIA
ACCURATE FORECAST DIFFICULT ACCOUNT LACK OF REPORTS YOUR VICINITY. CONDITIONS APPEAR GENERALLY AVERAGE OVER ROUTE NO MAJOR STORM. APPARENTLY PARTLY CLOUDY WITH DANGEROUS LOCAL RAIN SQUALLS ABOUT 300 MILES EAST OF LAE AND SCATTERED HEAVY SHOWERS REMAINDER OF ROUTE. WINDS EAST SOUTHEAST ABOUT TWENTY FIVE KNOTS TO ONTARIO THEN EAST TO EAST NORTHEAST ABOUT 20 KNOTS TO HOWLAND.

FLEET BASE PEARL HARBOR[26]

This weather information was supposed to have been forwarded to KHAQQ by Harry Balfour during his hourly radio contacts. Because of extreme static interference, however, he was unable to make contact with the plane for the first few hours. Radio specialist Paul Rafford Jr. reported that Balfour had not been able to forward the meteorological data to Amelia.[27] She and Noonan did not know in advance about the 25-knot headwinds ahead until they were in them.

It was Noonan's intention to hold a course of 078° true. However, as the flight progressed, so did the easterly headwinds and accompanying heavy rain. Pilot and navigator soon found themselves being bounced around by consistent 25-knot gusts pushing torrents of rain.

An understanding had been reached with Balfour that the Electra would initiate a call at eighteen minutes past each hour. The first such call came in at 2:18 p.m. Balfour reported receiving the following message from Amelia on 6210 kcs: "Height 7000 feet. Speed 140 knots. Everything ok."[28]

Lae radio then called the plane and requested to report its position, but there was no response.

An hour later Balfour received another transmission from KHAQQ: "Height 10,000 feet. Position 150.7 East, 7.3 South. Cumulus clouds. Everything ok."

The last radio contact with Balfour was in the late afternoon at 5:18 p.m. on 6210 kcs. Sunset was only a half-hour away at 5:55 p.m. At this time, Amelia gave her latitude and longitude position as "4°33.5' south, and 159°.07' east." This would have placed her near the Nukumanu Islands and indicated that she was on course to her destination of Howland Island. She had covered about 785 statute miles since takeoff. Amelia also stated she was flying "at a height of 8,000 feet over cumulus clouds against a wind of 23 knots."

Given the heavy fuel load and the strong headwinds, she was averaging only about 112 miles per hour speed over the ground (SOG). She should have been able to see the nearby islands, which would have provided a good visual fix. The precise measurement of the plane's location that she provided to Balfour likely came from a visual sighting of a Nukumanu landmark. The relatively slow ground speed reflected the lengthy struggle to increase altitude during the Electra's long climb to 12,000 feet altitude.

It was at this time when Amelia notified Balfour that she planned to change to her nighttime frequency of 3105 kcs. She had used that frequency on her previous flight from California to Hawaii with good results. Furthermore, she had been told in earlier communications that the Coast Guard cutter *Itasca* would be contacting her by voice on 3105.[29]

Bulolo radio operator Alan Vagg said that he and Balfour spelled each other during half-hour shifts at Lae throughout the morning and afternoon of July 2. He noted: "KHAQQ would call giving their position, height and airspeed, and we would answer. Our last contact with the airplane was between 5 and 6 p.m. at which time Miss Earhart stated she was switching frequency to 3105 kcs. Since we never heard from her again, we assume this is what she did."[30]

The most interesting part of Vagg's commentary is that he was not equipped for radiophone communication by voice. All of his contact with KHAQQ was by Morse code. It was Vagg who also commented about his Morse communication with the Earhart plane en route from Port Darwin to Lae, New Guinea. He confirmed that Noonan's Morse ability was slow but very clear and easy to read.[31] The Electra "had a telegraph key and provision for plugging in headphones at the navigator's table" in addition to either side of the cockpit forward; it is likely that Noonan handled some of the radio communication from his aft cabin station.[32]

Because Amelia's signals were being received extremely well in the late afternoon, Balfour urged her not to switch frequencies. "Her signals were getting stronger and we should have no trouble holding signals for a long time to come," stated Eric Chater. "We received no reply to this call, although the operator listened for three hours after that on an 8-valve super-heterodyne short-wave receiver and both wave lengths were searched."[33]

It was likely that, after sunset, Noonan recommended a slight course change that would have taken them near Nauru Island. Earlier, Nauru radio had wired Lae the following message and weather information prior to the Electra's takeoff:

NEW NAURU FIXED LIGHT LAT. 0.32 S LONG. 16.55 E. 5000 CANDLEPOWER 5600 FEET ABOVE SEA LEVEL VISIBLE FROM SHIPS TO NAKED EYE AT 34 MILES. ALSO THERE WILL BE BRIGHT LIGHTING ALL NIGHT ON ISLAND FROM PHOSPHATE FIELD WORKINGS. WEATHER 8 AM BAROMETER 29.908 TEMP 84 WIND SE3 CLOUDY SEA SMOOTH TO MODERATE. PLEASE ADVISE TIME DEPARTURE AND ANY INFORMATION RE RADIO TRANSMISSION WITH TIMES.[34]

A good navigator would not miss an opportunity to confirm his or her position after darkness. Identifying the Nauru lights would be a reassuring, defined position, and the modest amount of added mileage would not consume very much fuel. A number of area stations were monitoring Amelia's historic flight, some maintaining continuous radio watches. Radio Sydney, New South Wales, reported in a wireless relayed from Nauru radio via Tutuilla, Samoa: "Message from plane when at least 60 miles south of Nauru received 8:30 p.m. Sydney time, July 2nd, saying, 'ship in sight ahead.' Since identified as steamer *Myrtlebank* which arrived Nauru daybreak today. No contact between *Itasca* and Nauru radio. Continuous watch being maintained by Nauru radio and Suva radio."[35]

Amelia's reference to "ship in sight ahead" could also have been about the US Navy tug *Ontario*, which was stationed midway between Lae and Howland to guard the Earhart flight. Its position was some one hundred miles southeast of Nauru at a latitude of 3°10' south and a longitude of 165°9' east. *Ontario*'s skipper, Captain Blakeslee, told Earhart researcher Paul Rafford Jr. some years later, in October 1988, that the weather was miserable that night: "The wind was howling and rain came in torrents. It was questionable we could do anything to benefit Earhart so I went to bed early and told the radio crew not to try and contact the airplane."[36]

Rafford later said of that conversation:

Captain Blakeslee was 85 and feeble. He was living in an Orlando retirement home, but his memory about his duty station in the Pacific at the time of Amelia's flight appeared intact. His vessel was a vintage coal-burning tug, probably the oldest in the fleet. *Ontario*'s radio receivers did not cover the Electra's frequencies, so they could not have followed Earhart's progress after her Lae departure. It was strange that Blakeslee told his crew not to be concerned about contacting the airplane.[37]

Amelia Earhart Society researcher Paul Cook reported that *Ontario* radioman Clarence S. Snow was on deck for a cigarette break that night when he thought he heard the sound of the Electra's engines overhead and nearby. Although no airplane lights were visible, the time was noted at 11:45 GCT.[38]

T. H. Cude, Nauru director of police, reported that the mining lights were turned up all the way and were brilliant. He was listening to the progress of the flight on his own Atwater Kent short-wave receiver at home. Cude later reported, "Between 10 and 11 p.m. as she approached and passed the island, I distinctly remember her saying, 'lights in sight ahead.'" Cude had been listening on 3105 kcs and figured Earhart and Noonan must have been within sight of the loom of the phosphate lights of Nauru Island, having heard her so clearly.[39]

The Cude time and report from Nauru is an additional confirmation of Amelia and Noonan's progress and location—half the distance to their Howland Island destination. The Electra's speed also appeared to be improving as the plane now had burned off much of its fuel weight.

Amelia and Fred reached the next island to be passed over, the British Gilbert Island of Tabiteuea, at about 3:30 a.m. local time and 15:30 GCT. A Tabiteuea native later confirmed hearing the airplane pass directly overhead. There also would have been a crescent moon, if visibility permitted, at an altitude of 14° and an azimuth of 76°. If Noonan were able to get a moon shot before daybreak, he would have had a Line of Position (LOP) virtually perpendicular to his track, by which he could have verified his ground speed.[40]

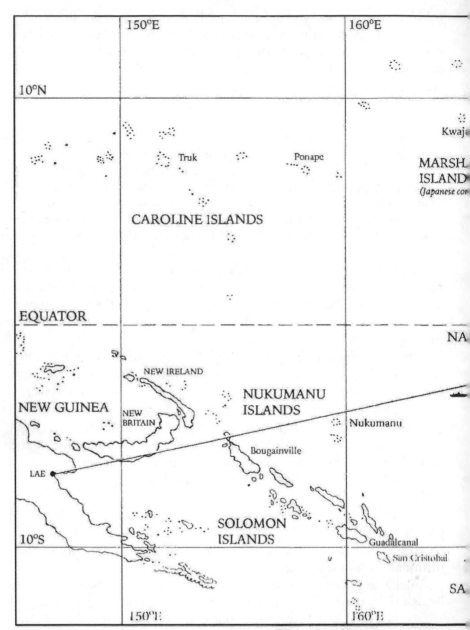

Flight path of final flight from Lae, New Guinea, to Howland Island. (Chart by author)

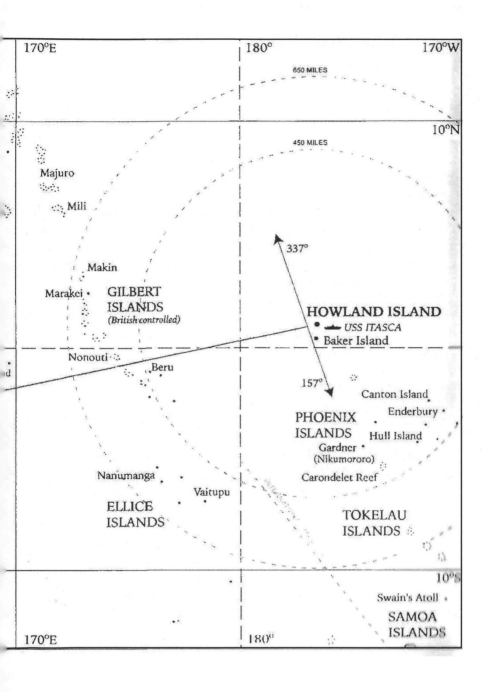

Radio Room, Coast Guard Cutter *Itasca*

As the day of July 2 began for the *Itasca* and those stationed on Howland Island, two radio watch stations were operating. Both of these positions were instructed to maintain logs. Radioman Frank Cipriani, on temporary duty from the Coast Guard cutter *Taney,* was positioned on Howland Island to man an experimental high-frequency radio direction finder there. He also was ordered to keep a log as to the time and bearings that were received from the Electra. *Itasca* radiomen Bill Galten and Thomas O'Hare were assigned to maintain the normal Coast Guard and Navy incoming and outgoing messages. As Amelia neared the *Itasca,* Galten and Chief Radioman Leo Bellarts alternated in monitoring communications with the airplane and the cutter's radio direction finder. George Thompson, another radioman, rotated between watch positions as a relief operator.[41]

It was 2:45 a.m. Howland Island time when *Itasca* picked up Amelia's first voice contact. Her signal was barely audible, a strength of one to two (on a scale of one to five, one being low). Bellarts logged, "CLOUDY AND OVERCAST"

An hour later, at 3:45 a.m., the men recorded a slightly stronger signal (strength two). "OVERCAST. WILL LISTEN ON HOUR AND HALF HOUR ON 3105."

Throughout the early morning hours, *Itasca*'s radio log reflected efforts to contact KHAQQ.

The 4:00 a.m. report read, "Broadcast weather on phone 3105 [voice] and key 3105 [Morse code]." *Itasca* continued trying to contact the airplane. "What is your position? When do you expect to arrive at Howland? We are receiving your signals. Please acknowledge this message on your next schedule."

At 4:54 a.m., the radio watch recorded "PARTLY CLOUDY" as barely readable (strength one).

The next contact from Amelia came at 6:14 a.m. with a signal strength of three, readable with difficulty. Amelia said, "WANT BEARING ON 3105 IN AN HOUR. WILL WHISTLE IN MIC."

6:15 a.m. (sunrise): "ABOUT 200 MILES OUT. WHISTLING NOW."

6:42 a.m.: *Itasca*'s log reported that KHAQQ came on air with fairly clear signals calling *Itasca.* "PLEASE TAKE BEARING ON US AND REPORT IN HALF HOUR. I WILL MAKE NOISE IN MICROPHONE. ABOUT 100 MILES OUT." The log reflected a signal strength of four with the note, "On air so briefly bearings impossible." For the next hour, all attempts at contacting KHAQQ received no response.

7:00 a.m.: *Itasca* sent a weather report and maintained contact on 500 kcs for homing on their radio direction finder, with no success.

7:18 a.m.: *Itasca* again called to KHAQQ: "Cannot take bearing on 3105 very good. Please send on 500 or do you wish to take bearing on us? Go ahead please."

There was no answer. Bellarts sat shirtless, sweltering in the early morning humidity. Bill Galten, who had gotten a few hours of sleep, took over for Bellarts.

Bellarts headed for the bridge to monitor *Itasca*'s direction finder.

At 7:30 a.m., *Itasca* again called the aircraft. "Please acknowledge our signals on key." No answer. There was much anxiety in the radio shack.

Finally, at 7:42 a.m., Amelia came on at strength five. The radio room loudspeaker was turned on. The room was crowded and the doorway to the shack was packed with perspiring people. Amelia's voice boomed over the speaker. Even those out on deck could hear her. "KHAQQ CALLING ITASCA. WE MUST BE ON YOU BUT CANNOT SEE YOU. GAS IS RUNNING LOW. BEEN UNABLE TO REACH YOU BY RADIO. WE ARE FLYING AT ALTITUDE 1000 FEET."

Itasca responded: "Received your message. Signal strength 5. Go ahead."

No answer.

With two logs being maintained in the radio room, this last transmission from Amelia was reported differently on the log not being maintained by Bellarts. Someone added the additional phrase "only half hour fuel remaining." This notation originated from Tom O'Hare's station, also staffed by Bill Galten. It is possible that the log was influenced by the two newspaper reporters present, Howard Hanzlik of the Associated Press and James Carey of United Press International. The resulting confusion as to whether there truly were only thirty minutes of fuel left would confound future researchers and lead to much speculation as to why so little fuel remained. Years later, Fred Goerner learned in a letter from former *Itasca* radioman Bill Galten that perhaps thirty minutes' worth of fuel wasn't the case at all.

Another point of contention regarding this communication planning and setup is that no one in the radio room knew that Amelia could not read Morse code. Though Noonan had earned a second class radio operator's license, his practical skills were limited. This was the Coast Guard ship's primary method of radio communication, and the radio watch had been transmitting by Morse code to the airplane throughout the early morning hours. What's more, because the radiomen on watch were trained to send and receive Morse code telegraphy, they were accustomed to recording the "hard copy" received from incoming Morse transmissions. They were not accustomed to writing notes in longhand that came in by voice. Jotting down words, though abbreviated, took time. Surely, the stress-filled radio room during that final hour was hardly conducive for remembering and noting each and every word that might have been shouted over the plane's microphone, especially if an exhausted and frustrated Amelia was beginning to panic. This breakdown in communications had to be shared by both sides and ultimately contributed to the confusion and conflicting messages between the Electra and the ships below.

Bellarts, along with radioman George Thompson, monitored the aircraft watch position ready to handle all traffic from Earhart. Radioman Bill Galten began the day of July 2 by staffing the *Itasca*'s ship-to-ship position. He was relieved at about 2:00 a.m. by Tom O'Hare. Other than Bellarts, the other *Itasca* radio operators were third class radiomen. Frank Cipriani, who manned the high-frequency portable radio direction finder on Howland Island, was a second-class operator. None of these men were accustomed to voice communication. They always transmitted and received in Morse code.

Cipriani's portable DF had been acquired by Army Air Corps lieutenant Daniel Cooper, who carried it aboard *Itasca* without prior knowledge of the cutter's radio crew. It was a newly developed high-frequency, portable radio direction finder to be positioned on Howland Island during Amelia's flight to assist in homing in on her radio signals. This was an experimental unit known as a model DT (XAB/HRO) high-frequency device that operated on storage batteries. According to Capt. August Detzer Jr., USN, ret., who was in charge of OP-20-GX in 1937, it was loaned by Navy Intelligence.

> We were using every opportunity to run comparison tests against direction finders at the time. We were trying to come up with a direction finder that was both portable and could provide reasonably accurate bearings. We had been saddled with a monstrosity called the CXK which had been developed several years before. It weighed several tons and needed to be housed in its own building. It also was agonizingly slow and inaccurate. The Japanese had a string of HF/DF stations running from the home islands down through the Bonins, Marianas, Carolines, and into the Marshalls. They were monitoring our fleet movements. None of the HF/DF's we had circa 1937 were accurate at any considerable distance to within five to ten degrees.[42]

Richard Black had sent a telegram to Amelia on June 29 when

she was at Lae, New Guinea, stating *Itasca*'s radio frequencies and requesting Amelia's planned time of transmissions:

AMELIA EARHART, LAE
ITASCA TRANSMITTERS CALIBRATED 7500 6210 3105 500 AND 425 KCS LAST THREE EITHER CW OR MCW. ITASCA DIRECTION FINDER FREQUENCY RANGE 550 TO 270 KCS. REQUEST WE BE ADVISED AS TO TIME OF DEPARTURE AND ZONE TIME TO BE USED ON RADIO SCHEDULES. ITASCA AT HOWLAND ISLAND DURING FLIGHT. BLACK ITASCA

Amelia responded the next day at 6:15 a.m.:

COMMANDER USS ITASCA TUTUILLA RADIO
PLAN MIDDAY TAKEOFF HERE PLEASE HAVE METEOROLOGIST SEND FORECAST LAE-HOWLAND SOON AS POSSIBLE. IF REACHES ME IN TIME WILL TRY LEAVE TODAY OTHERWISE JULY FIRST. REPORT IN ENGLISH NOT CODE ESPECIALLY WHILE FLYING. WILL BROADCAST HOURLY QUARTER PAST HOUR / GCT FURTHER INFORMATION LATER. EARHART

Amelia made it clear that she wanted voice communication in English and not code, especially while flying. She also stated very clearly that she would transmit at quarter past the hour. None of this should have caused any problem for Richard Black or Commander Warner Thompson, skipper of the *Itasca*—except that they were unaware she could not effectively use 500 kcs, because she had no trailing antenna. The cutter's low-frequency direction finder channel was calibrated in the 500 range. It later appeared that *Itasca* radio personnel were unaware that Amelia wanted voice transmissions until she was virtually on top of them (within fifty miles, based on the signal strength readings).

Itasca called again at 7:47 and 7:49 a.m.: "Your message ok. Please acknowledge with phone on 3105."

At 7:58 a.m., Earhart came back. Her voice was extremely loud. (The cutter's log indicated volume S-5.) "WE ARE CIRCLING BUT CANNOT HEAR YOU. GO AHEAD ON 7500 EITHER NOW OR IN HALF HOUR."

Itasca sent a constant string of *a*'s on 7500 by Morse and said by voice, "Go ahead on 3105."

8:00 a.m.: "KHAQQ CALLING ITASCA. WE RECEIVED YOUR SIGNALS BUT UNABLE TO GET A MINIMUM. PLEASE TAKE BEARING ON US AND ANSWER ON 3105 WITH VOICE."

8:05 a.m.: *Itasca* responded, "Your signals received ok. We are unable to hear you to take a bearing. It is impracticable to take a

DATE-TIME-ELAPSED TIME
Lae to Howland Segment

Elapsed Time GMT	Lae Time Zone 10E	Time Zone 11E	Time Zone 12E	Howland Time Zone 12W	Itasca Time Zone 11.5 W	Hawaii Time Zone 10W	PILOT RADIO PER ITASCA & LAE
7/1 - 7/2 0:00	7/2 10:00 AM	7/2 11:00AM	7/2 12:00 Noon	7/1 12:00 Noon	7/1 12:30PM	7/1 2:00PM	TAKE OFF
7/2 5:00	7/2 3:00PM	7/2 4:00PM	7/2 5:00PM	7/1 5:00PM	7/1 5:30PM	7/1 7:00PM	E = "At 10,000 ft. but reducing altitude because of bank of cumulus clouds."
7/2 7:00	7/2 5:00PM	7/2 6:00PM	7/2 7:00PM	7/1 7:00PM	7/1 7:30PM	7/1 9:00PM	E = "At 7,000 ft., making 150MPH."
7/2 7:20	7/2 5:20PM	7/2 7:20PM	7/2 7:20PM	7/1 7:50PM	7/1 9:20PM	7/1 9:00PM	E = "Position Latitude: 4° 33.5' South, Longitude: 159° East."
7/2 8:00	7/2 6:00PM	7/2 7:00PM	7/2 8:00PM	7/1 8:00PM	7/1 8:30PM	7/1 10:00PM	E = "On course for Howland Island at 12,000 ft."
7/2 10:30	7/2 8:30PM	7/2 9:30PM	7/2 10:30PM	7/1 10:30PM	7/1 11:00PM	7/2 12:30AM	E = OVERHEARD BY NAURU RADIO: "A ship in sight ahead."
7/2 14:15	7/3 12:15AM	7/3 1:15AM	7/3 2:15AM	7/2 2:15AM	7/2 2:45AM	7/2 4:15AM	I = "Heard Earhart on 3105, but unreadable through a "Cloudy and overcast."
7/2 15:15	7/3 1:15AM	7/3 2:15AM	7/3 3:15AM	7/2 3:15AM	7/2 3:45AM	7/2 5:15AM	E = "Itasca from Earhart, overcast. Will listen on hour half-hour on 3105."
7/2 16:24	7/3 2:24AM	7/3 3:24AM	7/3 4:24AM	7/2 4:24AM	7/2 4:54AM	7/2 6:24AM	E = "Partly cloudy."
7/2 17:44	7/3 3:44AM	7/3 4:44AM	7/3 5:44AM	7/2 5:44AM	7/2 6:14AM	7/2 7:44AM	E = "(Went) bearing on 3105. On hour, will whistle in m"
7/2 17:45	7/3 3:45AM	7/3 4:45AM	7/3 5:45AM	7/2 5:45AM	7/2 6:15AM	7/2 7:45AM	E = "About two hundred miles out, approximately. Whistling now."
7/2 18:15	7/3 4:15AM	7/3 5:15AM	7/3 6:15AM	7/2 6:15AM	7/2 6:45AM	7/2 8:15AM	E = "Please take bearing on us and report in half hour make noise on microphone, about 100 miles out.
7/2 19:12	7/3 5:12AM	7/3 6:12AM	7/3 7:12AM	7/2 7:12AM	7/2 7:42AM	7/2 9:12AM	E = "KHAQQ calling Itasca, we must be on you, but c see you but gas is running low. Been unable to re you by radio. We are flying at 1,000 ft."
7/2 19:13	7/3 5:13AM	7/3 6:13AM	7/3 7:13AM	7/2 7:13AM	7/2 7:43AM	7/2 9:13AM	E = "I received your message signal strength 5 (sent etc. on 500 and 3105) Go ahead."
7/2 19:28	7/3 5:28AM	7/3 6:28AM	7/3 7:28AM	7/2 7:28AM	7/2 7:58AM	7/2 9:28AM	E = "We are circling but cannot hear you, go ahead o either now or on the scheduled time on half hour
7/2 19:29	7/3 5:29AM	7/3 6:29AM	7/3 7:29AM	7/2 7:29AM	7/2 7:59AM	7/2 9:29AM	I = "Volume is S-5." [very loud, maximum strength on I = "AAAAAAAAAAA (on 7500) Go ahead on 3105."
7/2 19:30	7/3 5:30AM	7/3 6:30AM	7/3 7:30AM	7/2 7:30AM	7/2 7:30AM	7/2 9:30AM	E = "KHAQQ calling Itasca, we received your signal, unable to get a minimum, please take bearing on answer 3105 with voice."
7/2 20:14	7/3 6:14AM	7/3 7:14AM	7/3 8:14AM	7/2 8:14AM	7/2 8:44AM	7/2 10:14AM	E = "We are on the line of position 157-337. We are n North and South." I = "On 3105 volume S-5."
23:46:55					12:16:55 PM Itasca		

Chart of compiled radio logs, time, and time zones, Lae to Howland flight. (Reprinted, by permission, from Weisheit, The Last Flight of Frederick J. Noonan and Amelia Earhart.)

bearing on 3105 on your voice. How do you get that? Go ahead."

8:06 a.m.: *Itasca* again called: "Go ahead on 3105 or 500 kilocycles."

No answer. The ship continued to send the letter *a* on 7500 in code, as Earhart's only radio acknowledgment requested signals on 7500.

8:12 a.m.: "*Itasca* to Earhart. Did you get transmission on 7500 kcs? Go ahead on 500 kcs so that we may take a bearing on you. It is impossible to take a bearing on 3105 kilocycles. Please acknowledge."

8:15 a.m.: From *Itasca*. "Do you hear my signals on 7500 or 3105? Please acknowledge receipt on 3105. Go ahead." No answer.

Either Amelia was having radio receiver problems, or transmissions from *Itasca* were occurring at the same time and were blocking her out. She could not transmit and receive simultaneously.

8:18 a.m.: From *Itasca:* "Would you please acknowledge our

signals on 7500 or 3105. Go ahead with 3105." Still no answer.

It is likely that Amelia and Noonan initially were very close to Howland Island. Based on the radio signal strength measurements, Leo Bellarts said that he literally bolted from his chair when Amelia's voice came in—so loud and clear that he thought she was on top of the ship. "It is my recollection her signals were on the increase up to her last transmission when she was really good and loud. Considering her signal strength, and the increase each time, it is hard for me to believe that she over-shot the island. But, Itasca was unaware she could not send on 500 kcs due to not having the trailing antenna. Amelia was careless in not informing Itasca she was unable to transmit on 500. This prevented the ship from taking DF bearings on her."[43]

Suddenly, it was recognized in the radio room that the morning was slipping away, and no airplane was in sight. There had been no word from Amelia since eight o'clock that morning.

At 8:33 a.m., *Itasca* called KHAQQ: "Will you please come in and answer on 3105. We are transmitting constantly on 7500 kcs and we do not hear you on 3105. Please answer on 3105. Go ahead." No response.

8:44 a.m.: After an interminably long three-quarters of an hour, Amelia's voice resounded over the loud speaker without a call sign or warning. The strength of her voice signal was still ranked at a five, but it was not quite as strong as before. She was on 3105 and talking fast. Her voice was high-pitched and shrill—possibly because Balfour had instructed her to do so, to avoid distortion, but more likely because she was dog-tired and frightened. "WE ARE ON LINE OF POSITION 157-337. WILL REPEAT THIS MESSAGE ON 6210 KCS. WAIT. LISTENING ON 6210. WE ARE RUNNING NORTH AND SOUTH."

These were Amelia Earhart's last recorded words. At this critical point, her transmission appears to have been lost, either because she just stopped in the middle of her sentence, perhaps to change frequency to 6210, or because something happened to distract her.

"We had receivers on 6210 and 3105 but never heard another signal from the plane," stated *Itasca*'s chief radioman, Leo Bellarts. "No distress signal was heard or any word of immediate trouble was ever heard from Earhart. If she were actually out of gas at the time and crashed as a result, leaves me no explanation as to just why she ran out of gas at that early hour unless she was traveling at a higher speed due to head winds and actually covering less ground."[44]

At 8:47 a.m., the radio room on the ship was in a dither. They were calling Earhart on 3105 by voice and transmitting by code on 7500. "We heard you ok on 3105 kcs. Please stay on 3105. Do not hear you on 6210. Maintain QSO [radio jargon for transmit and receive] on 3105." No response. *Itasca* kept trying to reestablish contact. "KHAQQ come back. KHAQQ come back to us baby." They were losing her and they knew it. "KHAQQ. KHAQQ. *Itasca* calling KHAQQ on 3105."

Every man who heard her voice that fateful morning sensed in their gut the stress and alarm in her last message. As they sweltered on the Coast Guard ship on that stultifying day, they also felt Amelia's fatigue. They were conscious of the cotton dryness in her mouth, and their eyes most surely were burning, along with Amelia's, as she squinted into the piercing morning sun, trying desperately to spot Howland Island.

Part Two: Impending Destiny

Chapter 2

Clandestine Colonization: Howland, Baker, and Jarvis Islands

Our companions were the birds. All we had were the four of us and nothing else.

—Abraham Piianaia

In the summer of 1934, while returning from a shakedown cruise to Sydney, Australia, the new US cruiser *Astoria* stopped to reconnoiter two small, off-the-beaten-track islands in one of the most remote regions on earth. Just north of the equator and only 214 miles from the International Date Line, Baker and Howland Islands were separated by only 36 miles. Neither had a protected anchorage, fresh water, or any other desirable resources other than guano from thousands of sea birds. Howland Island, 1½ miles long and ½ mile wide with a featureless elevation of between 15 and 18 feet, occupies 455 acres. Baker lies 12 miles north of the Equator, and comprises 340 acres. Jarvis Island, largest of the group, is a distant 1,000 miles east of Howland.

Six months later, in February of 1935, the US Chief of Naval Operations notified the commandant of the Fourteenth Naval District in Honolulu to make preparations to investigate the advisability of developing Howland, Baker, or Jarvis Island as a possible refueling station. Proposed air routes between Hawaii and Australia were being actively planned by major commercial airlines. Private discussions in the White House also targeted strategic locations in the Central Pacific for possible defense purposes. Howland and Baker Islands were situated about two thousand miles south of Honolulu and twenty-four hundred miles from New Zealand.

Many of the islands in this region had been claimed by American companies mining guano deposits under the Guano Act passed by Congress in 1856. When most of the guano was gone, the fertilizer companies went too, and the islands were abandoned. By the mid-1930s,

55

there were no other islands nearby that the United States realistically might have claimed. Pres. Franklin D. Roosevelt and his advisers knew that the islands had to be occupied to ensure the US claim. It was decided to quietly colonize Jarvis, Baker, and Howland Islands.[1]

Pan American Airways was in the process of developing stations at Midway and Wake Islands to service its clippers on their trans-Pacific route to Manila, Hong Kong, and Singapore and then to Indonesia. They also were planning air service from Hawaii to New Zealand and expressed interest in looking at Howland and Baker Islands as a possible base.[2]

Pan Am found an interested partner in the US Navy, whose nautical charts, tide and current information, and piloting knowledge were woefully out of date in the distant Pacific. Juan Trippe, Pan American's chief executive officer, actively courted Navy top brass as he planned strategic air routes to opportune destinations across the Pacific. At the same time, his able-bodied private investigator Harold Gatty personally checked out selected islands for landing sites. It did not take much convincing for the US Navy to visualize the mutual benefits that might be realized.

Roosevelt's logistical interest in these islands suddenly became

Franklin D. Roosevelt and Henry Morgenthau. (Courtesy Franklin D. Roosevelt Library)

multifaceted. He and his advisers had been concerned for some time that Japan was secretly using its Nanyoo Kaihatsu Kaisha (South Seas Development Corporation), responsible for overseeing the cultivation of farming and fishing activities throughout their mandated islands, as a guise to buffer their military preparations. Why shouldn't the US be similarly planning landing facilities for both sea and air craft on selected islands that could serve both colonization and military goals?

The sharing of information and resources promised commercial success to Pan Am and its fleet of clippers and provided vital mapping and navigational facilities to the US Navy. Years later, following the Japanese attack of December 7, 1941, all Pan Am installations were transferred to the Navy, marking an end of an important phase in civilian-military cooperation.[3]

In November 1935, Harold Gatty of Pan American Airways boarded the schooner *Kinkajou* in Honolulu for a cruise to determine which islands would make the best stopovers for the airline's planned route from Hawaii to New Zealand. The *Kinkajou* sailed first to Kingman Reef, then to nearby Palmyra Island, next to Jarvis, Howland, and Baker Islands, and finally to American Samoa. Gatty recognized immediately that neither Howland nor Baker nor Jarvis had a protected harbor or lagoon suitable for seaplane landings, so they were not considered further. Canton Island had been previously inspected and was the preferred choice, but Canton was claimed by Great Britain. The British would not concede landing rights unless the United States would allow them entry to Hawaii. Kingman Reef was then chosen as the initial Pan Am Pacific clipper stopover, although the executives recognized that takeoffs and landings would be difficult, if at all possible, when heavy seas were at hand.[4]

A servicing vessel, the *North Haven,* was scheduled to be anchored at Kingman Reef when flights began. The Pan Am China Clipper, a Martin M-130 flying boat, would complete the first ever trans-Pacific flight.[5]

Meanwhile, as the colonization of Jarvis, Baker, and Howland Islands was being organized, William T. Miller, then superintendent of airways in the Bureau of Air Commerce, was given complete authority for the sizeable undertaking. The priority of the mission was indicated by the high-level support he received.[6]

Located twenty-two nautical miles south of the equator, Jarvis occupies an area of 1,024 acres. At the time it became interesting to the US Navy, its primary claim to fame was a large sooty tern population numbering more than one million birds. There were also large concentrations of frigate birds and blue-faced boobies. The camp that subsequently would be established on Jarvis was located on the highest point (twenty-three-foot elevation), on the northwest side near the designated landing site. It would be named Millerville, to honor William T. Miller, the expedition leader of the first four cruises.

The little settlement established at Baker Island in 1935 was named Meyerton, to recognize the leadership of Harold A. Meyer. This camp was located above the ridge of the favored western landing place. The Howland camp was named Itascatown because of the contributions of that Coast Guard ship and its crew.

The US Army agreed to handle details of setting up tents on the three islands. They also provided cooking equipment, lanterns, kerosene and charcoal, blankets, and clothes. Then-infantry lieutenant and later colonel, Harold A. Meyer, aide to Gen. Halstead Dorey at the Schofield Barracks in Hawaii, coordinated the Army's task and proved to be a valuable assistant to Miller. The Treasury Department agreed to provide support ships to transport and re-supply the colonists. The Coast Guard cutter *Itasca* provided transportation for the first expedition and would make seven subsequent trips. The Navy provided fuel, water, and other supplies. The Medical Corps prepared and equipped four medicine chests, one of which was lost in the surf while offloading at Baker Island.

The Army furloughed twelve soldiers to assist young Hawaiian students, selected from Honolulu's Kamehameha vocational school, who were to be the official colonists. The Kamehameha graduates were between the ages of nineteen and twenty-four. They were expected to spend from six weeks to several months on the islands.

The requirements to be selected for colonization were an age of more than eighteen years, the ability to fish in the native manner, excellent swimming skills, the ability to handle a boat, a strong self-discipline, friendly and unattached character, and a proven sturdy disposition—in short, the colonizers were boys who would be able to handle any obstacles, no matter what might come.[7]

After the participants had been identified, Lieutenant Meyer began planning and organizing the operation. He and Miller were aware of some of the difficulties they would face, but because of the degree of isolation of the islands, they wanted to be sure that they were sufficiently prepared. They knew that bringing their equipment (some of which was extremely heavy and cumbersome) through breaking surf would be a challenge. By dismantling the heaviest gear, the colonists were able to float the equipment to the coral beach on pontoons.

They also were aware of the absolute necessity of bringing sufficient quantities of fresh water. It was determined that each island should have an initial allocation of nine hundred gallons of fresh water. Miller acquired fifty-four fifty-gallon drums from a chemical company to fulfill this requirement.

Pvt. Leonard A. Duff of the Thirty-Fifth Infantry was selected to be in charge of the food supply for the three-island expedition. He planned to supply five men on each island for a minimum stay of forty-two days, even though it was likely that their diet also would be supplemented with fresh fish caught in the shallow waters of the islands. Consequently, the military also supplied fishing rods, reels, hooks, nets, and spears.

The opportunity to visit and live on an uninhabited South Sea isle offered visions of excitement and adventure to many of the Kamehameha students and recent graduates. Many volunteered immediately. George West, one of the original Jarvis Island colonists, described their historic assignment:

> Captain Meyer assembled us together. Staring at us for about five minutes he finally said, "Boys, some day you're going to be mighty proud that you made this trip. Your names will go down in history. You're going to colonize and help establish claim of these islands for the United States Government. These islands are going to be famous air bases in a route that will connect Australia with California."[8]

Original Kamehameha Colonist Group

Jarvis	Howland	Baker
Henry Ahia, Leader	James Kamakaiwi Jr., Leader	Abraham Piianaia, Leader
Daniel Toomey	Killarney Opiopio	William Kaina
Frank Cockett	William Anahu	Archie Ching
George West	William Toomey	Samuel Kalama

The Kamehameha colonists were encouraged to maintain daily diaries of their activities, accomplishments, and psychological challenges of existing and working together on an isolated desert isle. The Bishop

Museum in Honolulu provided materials and directions for collecting scientific specimens of flora and fauna together with a supply of books for study purposes. The colonists' reports are housed there today. These logs reflect extremely busy days of chores and activities ranging from spearing lobsters and fish to building more permanent quarters than the initially provided tents. They worked on the island in preparation of long-term settlers.[9]

The organizers hastily planned the colonization venture and acquired supplies and equipment. "Due to the extremely confidential nature of the mission, it was not possible for me to confer with individuals who might have certain and definite knowledge of the problems," noted Harold A. Meyer.[10]

By late March 1935, the *Itasca* was loaded and ready. Cdr. W. H. Derby was skipper of this historic first Coast Guard colonization cruise. *Itasca* was a 250-foot ship built at Oakland, California, in 1929. She cruised at fifteen knots, had a maximum speed of seventeen knots, and was staffed by twelve officers and eighty-five crew members. On board were both Miller and Meyer. *Itasca* dropped five colonists at Jarvis Island, six at Howland, and five at Baker, along with their proportioned allocation of tents and supplies.

Itasca then proceeded to American Samoa to be refueled before coming back to the newly colonized islands to check on the fledgling colonists. When the Coast Guard cutter returned, the men had plenty to report.

Far from a tropical paradise, Howland more realistically resembled a nightmare. The island's vegetation consisted of coarse, brown, tough pigweed with occasional stunted and leafless Kou trees. After the third expedition, the Kamehameha colonists attempted to plant other species with little enduring success. But Howland's meager flora was not keeping them awake at night—its fauna did that.

Given the scarcity of plant life, it is surprising that the island had such abundant wildlife. In addition to the thousands of gooney and frigate birds as well as an assortment of terns, the boys found colonies of hermit crabs, gecko lizards, and snake-eyed skinks.[11] Though the crabs and reptiles were relatively harmless, thousands and thousands of rats made up the warm-blooded mammal population—they dominated the island. More than once a colonist woke up at night to find a rat in his face. The hardy Hawaiians were determined. They had taken the oath to hang tough, and that is just what they did.[12]

The leaders of each island group maintained daily logs. The Kamehameha boys on Jarvis, Baker, and Howland also kept

Itascatown. (Courtesy National Archives)

individual diaries. These records reflect scientific and meteorological data such as temperature, rainfall, tides, sunrise and sunset, and flora and fauna. More importantly, the diaries document a wide range of personal traits of the young men themselves. On almost every page, the reader can sense the depth of character, personality, and individuality of those young men growing into responsible adults as they went about their daily duties and struggled with the natural elements of their surroundings:

Jarvis Island, July 31, 1935

We took a monthly inventory of ourselves. Our physical condition is good. We live in a spacious cottage made from pieces of a shipwreck. Air and sunlight are abundant; ventilation is perfect. Nights are cool. Everyone feels fine each morning. The dining room, parlor and bedroom are under the same roof. The dining room extends on to the lanai. During meals the whole expanse of the ocean can be seen. The kitchen is out of doors. The stove is a few feet away from the cooking table. Garbage cans, piles of firewood, etc. are handy and arranged systematically. We ran out of potatoes two weeks ago. Onions will be used up in two or three days. One can of ham has spoiled. We have enough poi for the month of August. Rice will last two weeks more. We have half a bag of sugar and enough cream to last until the end of August. We have lots of corn, peas, and corned beef; sausages will be exhausted soon, and so will **peaches** and pineapples. Canned apples are good for weeks to come. Kerosene and water will last for months. There should be a ship on the horizon soon. A chop suey [sic] dinner will be given to the first to sight it.[13]

On Jarvis, lumber and other items retrieved from the beached wreck of the *Amaranth,* which sank there in 1913, was a treasure trove for the colonists. The boys built shacks for shelter to use in lieu of the Army tents. They also constructed beds and tables as well as surfboards and a raft from which they fished. As soon as the raft was finished, three of the colonists went fishing on the reef. Dan, Louis, and Bill found two lobster holes and collected a total of 25 lobsters, eaten for supper and breakfast. The crudely fashioned shelters weren't always satisfactory, as reflected by one log entry: "It rained disgustingly toward midnight, and our roof leaked so badly that we had to move our beds down to the tents for the rest of the night."

Colonist logs vividly indicate how the boys coped with the irritations of an outdoor life: "A bug crawled into George's ear and made him feel very uncomfortable. We flushed the ear with coconut oil and warm water. . . . [The following day:] George's ear has not bothered him today, although he believes the bug is still inside."

There often appear reflective paragraphs confirming a definite awareness of and appreciation for the abundance of life and beauty provided in each and every day:

> There was a change in the way dawn appeared this morning. The sea was calm, glassy. Out on the ocean white flashed, fishes leaping and breaking the smooth surface.
>
> Booby birds skimmed the surface, catching fish. Some would fly high, nose dive, scoop up the fish and fly away. The calmness of the sea made these antics easy to watch. Toward sunset the entire ocean within our view from the cottage was covered by porpoises. They seemed to be passing in review. We estimated seeing as many as 800.

At the same time there was a conscious recognition of the very real need to feed the crew with something other than canned food:

> August 23.
> Today was turtle day on Jarvis. An enormous turtle was found just above the beach crest on the west coast. Henry and George captured

it. It was stubborn and refused to move. It took five and a half hours to move it 150 yards in our direction. At noon Henry got a knife and pan, killed it and brought back a pan full of meat. The turtle meat was good. Some of it was fried, and some was put out to dry. Dan spent the afternoon cleaning the shell.

All of the Hawaiians were excellent swimmers and adept at free diving and spearing fish. Some even developed other special skills sometimes necessary to handle sudden and unique situations, as indicated by the Jarvis log of January 7, 1936:

> Henry speared 15 aholehole and two uhu. While Henry was cleaning the fish a shark came up near the beach. Henry yanked it by the tail, clear out of the water and up on the beach. Half the aholehole were eaten for lunch, the rest for supper.[14]

The Baker Island log entry of November 25, 1935, described local sea conditions and the difficulties heavy surf gave the tender of the yacht *Kinkajou* as it attempted to approach that island shore:

> At about 8:45 the first boat load ashore was caught in one of the huge waves that have been pounding on the reef since midnight. The boat was caught about 200–250 yards off shore and turned over. Four occupants of the boat were Captain Flink, Harold Gatty, Joe King and Toa Hall. Flink is master of the Kinkajou; Gatty, member of Coman's expedition; King and Hall, Samoan boys, members of the crew. All men were saved and none seriously injured. Also saved the mailbag, some onions, and lemons. The sea is getting rougher. Finally, at 2:15 p.m. the sea unleashed one gigantic wave that swept over the whole west ridge of the island. It wrecked our terrace, swamped our campsite, taking everything in its way as far as 300 yards inland. At 4 p.m. another wave of similar proportions swept up and over the west ridge again. The four men from Kinkajou are remaining with us as our guests until the sea calms down. We spent the rest of the day fortifying camp against more onslaughts of colossal waves.

A few days later, November 28, was Thanksgiving, and the *Kinkajou* crew still were sitting out the foul weather.

> This is Thanksgiving Day, but the sea doesn't seem to know it. It is still angry and rumbling like a spoiled tiger. Having no turkey, chicken or pig did not spoil our Thanksgiving Day party a bit. We caught two booby birds and introduced them to the cook. The cook curried one and stewed the other. Believe me, when dinner was over there was no

booby bird left on the table. Everybody enjoyed it and was surprised it tasted so good. That was something to be thankful for.

Booby meat may have been fine for the Baker Island crew, but the colonists on Jarvis regarded it differently: "Chopped meat from a bachelor booby was fried for supper by Anakalea. Spices had to be used to take away the fishy smell. It may do for emergency rations, but as a regular dish . . . I am anti-booby."

The young colonists, being excellent free divers, looked forward to opportunities to dive the reef area with masks, fins, and a long, thin spear known as a Hawaiian Sling. This was an approximately six-foot, sharp-pointed spear, to which was affixed a flexible rubber tubing that, when stretched, could propel the spear several feet into a nearby target. They took advantage of every chance to go diving when wind, seas, and current cooperated. Here is a typical report of their efforts:

> Supper was served at six, with pea soup, sliced ham, fried spuds, beets, corn, rice, coffee, cocoa, and pears for dessert. Leaving Henry with the dishes, we three saw to it that our spears and torches were made ready. We lighted our torch and headed for the beach, toward north point. Within an hour's time we had enough fish and lobster to feed a breadline. Coming back to camp we collected shells that happened to be in our way. With the fish and lobster taken care of we returned to our quarters and sang songs. We had enough fish and lobsters to last us a week.

On this deserted tropical island, every day brought new delights, experiences, and special opportunities. Every meal was special for the young colonists. But, on holidays, the festive dinner meal was extra special. On February 22, 1936, each of the Howland Island colonists was looking forward to celebrating George Washington's birthday in a big way. After an extremely low tide, the water was beautifully clear. Within an hour of diving they had brought up a huge number of lobsters and fish.

> Henry and Alex took care of the fish and lobsters while Joe and I [James Kamakaiwi Jr., Howland crew leader] had the meat and bakery departments. I had a 10 lb. Hormel ham cut in slices (using half of the can) boiled with jelly and then baked apples added. Joe, having his special built oven in heat had his prize cake ready to be placed, only to be called back when I asked him if he had the baking powder in it. With 45 minutes of cooking we had something like a hard bread . . . or petrified

cake. Not satisfied with it, he made apple and chocolate pie. While working on the chicken-ala-king [sic], an odor of something burning came direct from the oven. Lifting the cover we had a magnificent sight . . . seeing two pies and being unable to tell which one was apple.

We set the table and everything was ready. So we all went for a swim to freshen up. Joe wanted to eat at 4:00, but the old tummy just couldn't wait so we had breakfast, lunch and supper at 3:30 on the dot. Besides the other things I mentioned, we had fried and steamed fish smothered with onions, mashed potatoes, beets, lobster salad and plain lobster, fried ham mixed with pineapples, peaches, coffee and fruit cocktail.

Judging from the above dinner menu, it appeared that the boys were very well fed. With their necessary daily chores, water sports, and other diversionary activities, they were able to maintain trim bodies and great physical fitness. In fact, they considered many of these duties as sort of recreation. The word "entertainment" for five or six young men in their early twenties on a desert isle thousands of miles from movie theaters, juke boxes, and soda fountains took on new meaning with little effort. Other than books to read, sunsets to watch, and diaries to maintain and the everyday necessity of fishing and lobstering, they had little to do for entertainment that wasn't of their own devising.

After their newly developed sport of drowning rats in a buried water drum became tiresome, the colonists devised a new game dubbed "aerial polo."[15] Because of the great abundance of rodents available, this new recreational activity involved the rats:

Two rats were tied at both ends of a cord and thrown into the air. The frigate birds' attention was attracted by this act and they would come swooping for the rats. One bird would swallow one rat and the other rat would be dangling, when suddenly another bird would grab it. The two birds, swallowing their rats, would fly in different directions, and one rat would come dangling out of the other's throat. Then other frigates would chase the bird with the rats, and the same thing would happen.

The boys found the aerial trick worked just as well with fish. So, when rats weren't readily available they would tie two fish to the cord ends and toss it in the air: "We had the time of our lives watching the birds, and I never laughed so much since landing on the island. After dinner we still could see the birds fighting for the fish."

The second expedition to the islands took place on June 9, 1935. This voyage replaced the soldiers from the first trip with additional

Kamehameha students, because the Roosevelt administration did not want an observing public to think that the colonization was a military effort. In the end, it took four expeditions to establish and end the initial colonization project. The fourth expedition returned the colonists to civilization after giving them some rest and recreation in American Samoa.

Just a few months after Meyer returned to duty at Schofield Barracks and Miller returned to Washington, President Roosevelt decided to proceed with annexation of Jarvis, Baker, and Howland Islands. He ordered that they be re-colonized. Meyer, now a captain, was put in complete charge of the expedition. Again, haste was the order of the day.

This expedition, the fifth, was organized along the same lines as the previous ones. Before the day was over, Meyer had secured the services of former enlisted personnel, and all the Kamehameha boys volunteered to return to the islands. Sergeant Collins took charge of the group going to Jarvis on the USCG *Tiger* under command of Lt. H. J. Doebler. The USCG cutter *Itasca,* under Cdr. F. T. Kenner, took the groups at full speed to Howland and Baker. They arrived one day ahead of a friendly nation's warship also interested in colonizing the islands.[16]

As the islands began to be reoccupied, the Department of the Interior took control of governmental jurisdiction. Both Department of the Interior Field Agent Richard B. Black and the Bureau of Air Commerce's William T. Miller were aboard for the sixth expedition. As the Interior representative, Black assumed responsibility from Miller. He would be involved in the next eight expeditions, and he wanted to make sure that other countries could not question the United States' claim to these small parcels of real estate in the vast South Pacific. Under his direction, men built more permanent structures on the islands and established radio communication facilities. Black later served as George Putnam's personal representative in coordinating the requirements of Amelia Earhart and Fred Noonan on their flight from Lae, New Guinea, to Howland Island in July 1937.[17]

> As to my association with the Earhart flight, it was all a matter of orders from the Division of Territories and Island Possessions—Interior under Ernest Gruening, Director, and Mrs. Hampton, Assistant Director. I was first told to try to use Jarvis Island, and this later was changed to Howland. Bob Campbell, an engineer with Bureau of Air Commerce, was in Hawaii on location of airfields for commercial aviation in the Islands. I recommended to my Division that he might be ordered to do

the field job on Howland but don't think Bob appreciated my "kindness."

He said later that the constant scream of the seabirds, plus the interminable Kamehameha School jargon of the colonists, plus the incessant strumming of guitar and ukulele were enough to drive a man to distraction.

There were many imponderables in the situation I found myself: Orders to build a scratch-grade airport at Howland; failure to get any additional appropriation for the extra and unexpected work; orders to the local Navy (Admiral Murfin), Army (General Herron), and the Territorial Government (Governor Poindexter), secretly sent by my Division, to assist me in any way possible. One message later, which I should have kept for framing, said something like this: Please point out to the Army, Navy, and Territorial Government that, while we are willing to cooperate in every way, we have no funds for this purpose. That, from my Division, AFTER we had started the whole thing![18]

Another important achievement by *Itasca* on this cruise was a navigational determination of a more precise latitude and longitude of the islands of Howland and Baker. After a number of celestial observations had been taken, navigators determined that Baker Island was 4.5 miles east of its previously charted position and Howland Island was 5.5 miles east of its previous position. Whether this rather significant discrepancy affected the navigational calculations of Fred Noonan eleven months later as he and Amelia Earhart aimed their Lockheed Electra for Howland Island will never be known. It certainly could have spelled the difference between life and death.

Latitude and longitude measurements in the Howland Island sketch reflect the sextant readings and calculations by Coast Guard officers aboard *Itasca*. Data available from our global positioning satellites now calculate the official geographic position of Howland Island as latitude 0°48'20.48" north and longitude 176°37.8'.55" west.

Cruise number eight began on January 13, 1937, when the *William K. Duane* (WPG-33) departed Honolulu loaded with bulldozers, graders, a concrete and steam roller, a harrow, axes, plows, cane knives, and other construction equipment necessary to build the air strip requested by Amelia Earhart, endorsed by FDR, and funded by the Works Progress Administration. Robert L. Campbell of the Bureau of Air Commerce had been assigned the job and was responsible for the men and materials needed to construct the landing field on Howland. Just getting the array of heavy equipment ashore was his first challenge.

There was no harbor or safe landing place at this island. A suggested landing area had been recommended by some of the administrative experts behind desks in Honolulu, primarily because it was located midway on the island, where a small bight existed and reef concentrations seemed minimal. There still were plenty of sharp, jagged coral formations with heavy ocean waves rolling in. There was no way that a large vessel could anchor closer than a half-mile. Sensible captains would lay offshore a mile.

The solution for moving the heavy equipment ashore was pontoons assisted by small boats, and even then it was nerve-wracking. Securing a tractor to a pontoon and then surf-riding it through the breakers was a heart-pounding experience. Beneath the breaking waves were poisonous sea urchins, sea snakes, and razor-sharp coral waiting to cut and infect any hapless foot, leg, or body careless enough to make contact. Wounds from any of these hazards could have left life-long scars. Richard Black summed it up this way: "I had some scary and wild surf-boating while attempting to get ashore at both Howland and Baker Islands, especially during winter months."[19]

Once the equipment was safely on the island, a small cadre of soldiers and workers began clearing and grading what would become known as the James C. Kamakaiwi Jr. Airfield. Kamakaiwi was the first Kamehameha colonist leader at the Howland Island camp, serving for over two years from the original landing in 1935 to July 1937. As fate would have it, this has become the only named airport that never saw an airplane through the time of this writing.[20]

The Department of the Interior expected Amelia Earhart to need the airstrip to be completed in time for her March flight westbound from Honolulu. Seven of those who labored on the runways were WPA workers and four were Kamehameha boys. They worked, sweated, and bled during every long, broiling hour of daylight to get the work completed in time for Amelia's arrival. They built three runways at an amazingly rapid pace in view of the tropical heat and difficult working conditions.

Each runway was 150 feet wide. The longest, facing north and south, was 5,200 feet long. Another runway of 3,022 feet intersected the first, as well as a 2,440-foot east-west cross connector. The base of the landing strips consisted of guano, crushed coral, and sand. When rolled, compacted, and toasted by the hot sun, this combination of local, natural material gave off the "most awful rank and foul-smelling pavement ever created," stated one of the crew. Worst of all—and most dangerous to the workers—was the poisonous guano dust, sent up in great clouds by the graders. It was so putrid and intolerable it forced the men to run for a swim in the sea every couple

USCG Taney *offloading supplies.* (Courtesy National Archives)

of hours to rid themselves of the stinky white powder clinging to their skin. Even so, some developed bad boils.

> The field was all ready and waiting for Amelia and we were standing by in a Coast Guard cutter when we received word of the ground loop accident in Honolulu, Black stated.
> The first I knew of the second, or west to east attempt, was a telephone call from a Honolulu representative of a gasoline company who said, "where shall we deliver the 1800 gallons of 87-octane gas for the Earhart flight?" When I checked with my office in Washington it was confirmed that another attempt would be made, and we began to prepare for our quarterly cruise in June aboard the USCG *Itasca*.[21]

Lt. Daniel Cooper and two enlisted men of the US Army Air Corps were assigned the duty of making sure conditions of the air strip were satisfactory for Amelia's Electra to land and that sufficient markers lined the runway to mark the safe ground. The night before Earhart's anticipated arrival at Howland, a case of dynamite was exploded near the runways to chase away the assortment of sooty terns, gooney birds, and other water fowl that made the island their home.

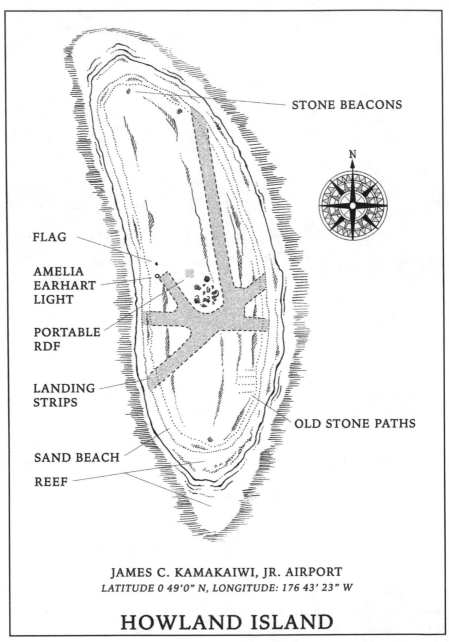

STONE BEACONS

N

FLAG

AMELIA
EARHART
LIGHT

PORTABLE
RDF

LANDING
STRIPS

OLD STONE PATHS

SAND BEACH

REEF

JAMES C. KAMAKAIWI, JR. AIRPORT
LATITUDE 0 49'0" N, LONGITUDE: 176 43' 23" W

HOWLAND ISLAND

Map of Howland Island. (Map by Elizabeth Whelan)

One of the colonizers, Yau Fai Lum, later told Earhart researcher Paul Rafford, "When that dynamite went off its only effect was to cause the birds to jump into the air, flutter around for a brief time shrieking and screaming, and then settle back down into their nests." He indicated that some of the birds were as large as fully grown roosters. Paul also mentioned a comment by *Itasca*'s chief radioman, Leo Bellarts: "Although Amelia might be able to land ok, I don't see how she'd ever get off again because of the dangerously large numbers of birds on the runways." As it turned out, Amelia would not have to worry about the birds.

The United States was not alone in its interest of staking claim to little-known offshore islands. Colonialism had long been a natural instinct of English seafarers. If guano was being retrieved or copra harvested, rights could be argued justifiably to claim islands where that work was being undertaken. Since the British were on Christmas Island growing coconuts, they naturally claimed rights to that piece of land.

Such claims became more complicated in 1937. On May 16 of that year, the American seaplane tender *Avocet* departed Honolulu en route to Canton Island. A three-and-a-half minute total eclipse of the sun was forecast for June 8, and Canton was geographically designated to provide a front-row seat. Aboard *Avocet* was a host of scientists, astrologers, meteorologists, and journalists looking to view this solar phenomenon. However, it also happened that the HMS *Wellington* also showed up at the island loaded with New Zealand scientists. The press later billed this event as the Canton Island Affair.

They found the *Avocet* happily anchored in the choice spot. The New Zealanders immediately cried foul. Claiming a violation of international law, they pointed out that HMS *Leith* had visited Canton in January earlier that year and left a marker signifying Great Britain's claim to bragging and territorial rights. US Navy Captain J. F. Hellway refused to concede his position in the anchorage. He ordered some of *Avocet*'s crew to take ashore a stainless steel American flag and plant it in a conspicuous spot near the British marker. Both the English and American press had a field day over this little brouhaha. The British argued that the American mission was not so much for scientific purposes but for the surveying of Canton Island as a potential base for both seaplanes and land-based aircraft.

The British were correct. US Navy officials aboard the *Avocet* recognized from the moment that the vessel's anchor was lowered that this was an ideal place for both land- and water-based aircraft. Its hard sand beach at low tide and attractive, protected lagoon offered the best combination of landing and take-off terrain, regardless of the type of aircraft landing or taking off. A few bottles of rum brought the dispute to a more relaxed conclusion and in time led to a cooperative joint development with Pan Am.[22]

A month after the Canton Island scuffle, the cutter *Itasca* was on station at Howland Island, waiting for the Lockheed Electra carrying Amelia Earhart and Fred Noonan. The three runways, carved and graded out of the coarse coral, guano, and thick brush of the island by the weary construction crew, were ready and waiting. The Howland Island camp site had been cleaned and neatened. The thoughtful Kamehameha boys had constructed a private outdoor shower featuring solar heat to be exclusively for Amelia's personal use. Under the direction of Army Sgt. "Pop" Summers, the boys had constructed the shower using a fifty-gallon water drum, pieces of scrap lumber, and strategically placed vertical-cut strips of canvas to provide a degree of privacy. Colonist ham radio operator Yau Fai Lum aired his blanket and put clean sheets on his bunk in case Amelia might want to rest after the exhausting flight. Even some landing lights had been placed along the main runway, in case the Electra arrived early. To the dismay of all who labored on Howland, the Electra never arrived.

In March 1938, the government delivered colonists and supplies to Canton and Enderbury Islands in the Phoenix Group. Richard Black described it this way: "Under confidential orders from the Director of Territories, and backed by a Presidential Executive Order, we moved under darkened lights and radio silence to claim Enderbury and Canton Islands in the Phoenix Group, against passive resistance of the British Deputy Administrator and his small staff in residence on Canton.[23]"

In May of that year, the tug *Ontario* delivered Pan Am officials to Canton to assess the location as a base to service their clippers flying from Hawaii to New Zealand. It did not take Pan Am long to initiate a deal for both seaplane and land plane facilities at Canton. Shortly thereafter, in April 1939, both Canton and Enderbury came under joint American and British control for a period of fifty years. The mutual agreement could be continued afterward "until such time as it may be modified or terminated by mutual consent."[24] The Hawaiian colonists were recalled in October 1940, after a reciprocal deal was worked out with the Pan Am station manager answering to the US Department of the Interior.

This was the first indication of a permanent US Government role in the joint development of the island. It also was the first use of a US Navy ship in support of either Pan Am or the colonizing expeditions, although the oiler *Ramapo* (AO-12) provided fuel to Pan Am at Wake and Midway Islands in 1936. Thus, with the Navy's participation, the convergence of national policies regarding commercial aviation and defense in the area was becoming even more apparent.[25]

From 1935 to 1942, vessels of the US Coast Guard made twenty-three voyages to Jarvis, Baker, and Howland Islands. *Itasca* was responsible for eight round-trip voyages. *William J. Duane* (WPG-33) made one voyage; the *Shoshone* made one; the *Tiger* made one; and the *Roger B. Taney* (WPG-37) made twelve round-trips.[26]

The Japanese attack on Pearl Harbor preceded by one day fourteen twin-engine bombers approaching Howland at twelve thousand feet from the northwest. "All four of us were down on the beach cleaning fish," reported Thomas Bederman. "Acting on a hunch that something was wrong, we all ran to the high spot in the center of the island. There was a low grove of dead and decaying kou trees which partially camouflaged us. Joe and Dick Whaley went together, while Alvin Mattson and I stayed together."

The boys crouched in the brush as they watched the big Japanese planes approach them, descending lower and lower. Suddenly, bombs fell with deafening concussions that made the ground quiver. "They

Howland Island Lighthouse Ceremony to commemorate Amelia on November 17, 1937. Left to right: Joseph Anakalea; Solomon Kalama; Richard B. Black, Field Representative, Division of Territory and Island Possessions, US Department of the Interior; William Kaina; Cdr. E. A. Coffin, skipper of the Taney; *Kenneth Lum King; Dr. Ernest H. Gruening, Director of Territory and Island Possessions; Yau Fai Lum; William Tavares; and Jacob Haili.* (Courtesy National Archives)

dropped about twenty bombs, then turned and came back over the island, dropping ten more. Smoke concealed almost everything from our view. Mattson thought he heard a scream."

The boys lay on the ground partially hidden by clumps of bushes. Mattson and Bederman were about one hundred feet from where the other two were hiding. They held their breath as several planes came in extremely low, firing machine guns at the small headquarters known as Itascatown and at the radio station. When the planes finally went away they called to their friends but got no answer. Both Richard "Dicky" Whaley and Joseph Keliihananui had been badly hurt and were found with gaping wounds and massive blood loss. They soon were dead. Dazed and grief-stricken over the sudden and untimely fate of their schoolmates, the two remaining colonists grabbed shovels and began digging a grave in which to bury their friends. Just before darkness, they took blankets and slept out in the open, not wanting to be caught inside their flimsy shelter should the Japanese return early in the morning.

Two days later, the Japanese did come again, but this time with a submarine. Both boys discovered it at two in the morning. "It was a dark night with a light rain and no moon. We could see this dark gray shadow, looking big and sinister, just outside the reef. We knew at dawn we were in for trouble. We fled that night to the other side of the island, away from the buildings, and there dug a dirt trench two and a half feet deep, camouflaged with grass. At seven in the morning the sub started shelling."

Shells crashed into what was left of the buildings. The radio station was totally devastated, its antenna toppled to the ground. Another shell put the weather station out of business. The boys expected sailors from the sub to land but they never did. By noon, the submarine had left and they were alone again.

The survivors trapped rain water and scrounged a few scattered canned goods from the debris of the demolished buildings. They continued to spear fish around the shallow reef and stalked young terns on the beach, grabbing them by hand when the birds least expected the move. Before the bombing there were five chickens on the island, but now only two remained alive. They saved them for Christmas and New Year's.

A month later, the boys figured they had been abandoned and would have to stay on what was left of Howland for the duration of the war. It was not a pleasant thought. The death of their friends still freshly on their minds and the utter isolation of being so far from civilization made them homesick. Just after dawn on January 31 they spotted a gray destroyer on the horizon. The boys figured it was the Japanese coming to officially seize the island. They decided to turn themselves in, hoping their lives might be spared.

"When the landing party was within 100 feet my heart gave a terrific jump," stated Tom Bederman. "They were Americans! Mattson and I were taken aboard the American destroyer."

It was the *Helm* (DD-388). By noon that day, the destroyer was off Baker Island. It, too, had been battered and shot up by the Japanese but had suffered no loss of life. In spite of heavy surf, the four boys who had been marooned there were picked up and tucked away safely on the American warship. These included Walter Burke, colonist leader, Blue Makua, James K. Pease, and James W. Coyle. "All six of us were thirsty, hungry, and almost naked," Bederman later wrote. "When we finally landed in Hawaii, our families thought we were risen from the dead."[27] "We found those guys living like Robinson Crusoe," recalled Victor Dybdal aboard the *Helm*.

The bodies of the two dead colonists were left buried on Howland. About ten years after the war, they were exhumed and reburied in the old military cemetery at Schofield Barracks, Hawaii.[28]

In September 1943, Howland was occupied by a Marine Corps battalion. The camp was known as Howland Naval Air Station until May 1944. Baker Island became an Army Air Force base. Richard Black, then a US Navy officer, was on the scouting mission to determine the use of Baker as a temporary military stopover for land aircraft.

A letter dated March 18, 1968, from Richard Black to Fred Goerner stated: "I was with the Task Force under Admiral Willis Lee which built the pierced-plank runway for the attacks on Makin and Tarawa. Our bombers took off from Canton, and refueled and loaded bombs at Baker. We used the entire width of the island, some 3800 feet, for the strip."

Why the US Government did not use Howland with the already-constructed landing strip is questionable. On July 10, 1944, a US Navy Martin flying boat piloted by William Hines made a forced landing at Howland. The plane landed in the water and was beached as a result of an engine fire. The crew escaped unharmed and was rescued by the USCG Cutter *Balsam*.

Although these particular landing fields did not have a lot of activity, they were welcome safe havens for US aircraft headed for the South Pacific. "These uses alone justified the long and sometimes unclear venture that the colonization project had represented."[29]

The Amelia Earhart Lighthouse (actually a day beacon), which had been broken up by Japanese shelling during the war, was restored on Howland Island by the Coast Guard in 1963. This effort was part of a nationwide recognition dedicated to Amelia's sixty-fifth birthday. From 1935 to 1942, more than 130 young Hawaiian men served on the islands, including Canton and Enderbury, under the colonization program. In 1979, Canton and Enderbury became part

Howland Island lighthouse, circa 1942. (Courtesy United States Coast Guard)

of the Republic of Kiribati. Howland, Baker, and Jarvis remained possessions of the United States and were designated as National Wildlife Refuges. It was not until May 13, 2011, that the US House of Representatives acknowledged the accomplishments and sacrifices of the young Hawaiian colonists, of whom only six were still alive.

Joseph Keliihaninui, Richard "Dickey" Whaley, and colonist Elvis Mattson. (Courtesy Bishop Museum)

Chapter 3

The Pilot, the Plane, the Plan

This book is not a biography of Amelia Earhart. Exhaustive accounts of her life have already been written admirably by others. The narrative that unfolds here covers primarily only the last ten years of her foreshortened life. However, this was her most significant decade—these are the years that will be remembered. This was the Golden Age of Aviation.

During the 1920s and 1930s, men and women from many of the industrialized countries were caught up in the excitement of aviation's newly developing world. The realization that people could actually fly through the air in an assortment of new-fangled machines, previously reserved primarily for military purposes, had taken over the heart, mind, and adventurous spirit of thousands. Sleek "stressed skin" fuselages and later aluminum replaced wood and wire bodies. Barnstormers and aerobatics at county fairs competed for attention, each year adding new tricks to their trade. Both countries and individuals began vying for a place in the growing competition. This unfettered flying excitement encouraged new aviation start-ups. Cessna, Stearman, Beech, Piper, Taylorcraft, and Stinson attracted the attention of individual pilots and pilots-to-be. Of course, the military also was scrambling for a position in the newly developing industry. The first nonstop flight across the United States from New York to California was made in 1923 by two Army pilots. Army pilots also accomplished the first mid-air refueling the subsequent year.

In May of 1927, Charles Lindbergh startled the world when he flew the Atlantic alone from New York to Paris. A year later, Amelia Earhart entered the early flying spotlight by becoming the first female to fly the Atlantic as a passenger. Four years later, she rivaled Lindbergh's limelight by becoming the first woman to fly the Atlantic solo. The fast-growing world of aviation became one of great competition among individual egos as well as international prestige. The "flying boats" of Pan American Airways were mapping a fast track across the Pacific. Aviation records were established and broken in the same week.

One of the early flying greats was Jimmy Doolittle, who pioneered the need and development of instrument flying in 1929. He was an avid race-pilot and in 1932 won the Thompson Air Trophy in his technologically-advanced Gee Bee Racer. After the Japanese attack on Pearl Harbor, he further immortalized himself by leading the raid to bomb Tokyo in 1942, when the aircraft carrier USS *Hornet* launched sixteen B-25 bombers. All of his pilots knew that they would not have sufficient fuel to return to any US friendly base. This heroic effort gave the Japanese a taste of American in-your-face determination as the United States struggled to organize and retaliate after the surprise attack on Hawaii.

In 1931, Wiley Post and Harold Gatty set an around-the-world flying record of eight days, fifteen hours, and fifty-one minutes. Also in the 1930s, Howard Hughes entered the scene with the development of his Hughes H-1 Racer, which set an air-speed record of 352 miles per hour in 1935. During this time, the helicopter also was being developed and refined by men such as Igor Sikorsky. This specialized flying equipment eventually filled a special-needs category by the military.

Although not all of the heroics and record attempts were successful, the courage, commitment, and skill of the early fliers will be remembered, especially the fearless determination and can-do attitude of Amelia Earhart, who increasingly accepted higher risks to break down social barriers.

The Pilot

In the heyday of the 1920s and 1930s, Amelia was a classic, all-American girl. Her quiet, charming style, wholesome good looks, and down-to-earth Midwestern persona made her unique in the eyes of an adoring public. What were the special qualities of this modest woman who was viewed by most as a true heroine? Her determination to master basic piloting skills and courage to take on higher risks to achieve greater feats inspired many across the country to dream bigger and reach further. Having earned her certification as an aviation pilot a mere twenty years after Wilbur and Orville Wright first flew their heavier-than-air machine off of a sand dune at Kill Devil Hills, North Carolina, Amelia proceeded to become the first woman to cross the Atlantic by plane.

Her aviation career was launched by chance when publisher George P. Putnam asked a friend, Hilton H. Railey, to investigate the rumor that a wealthy Englishwoman was planning to fly the Atlantic and had recently purchased a three-engine Fokker. The plane was reportedly being fitted with floats at the East Boston Airport.

The next evening, at Boston's Copley Plaza bar, Railey encountered Wilmer "Bill" Stultz and Lou "Slim" Gordon, who served as pilot and co-pilot respectively on Amelia's first transatlantic flight. Both were well on their way to inebriation and were quite talkative. Railey learned that Mrs. Frederick Guest, with residences in both London and New York, was the Englishwoman with the Fokker. Her husband, who had served as Secretary of State for Air in the English cabinet, was greatly concerned about his wife's adventurous plan. Putnam convinced her that if the "right sort of girl" could be found, he would continue to fund the project, but Mrs. Guest would have to forgo the stunt.[1]

Shortly thereafter, a retired Navy friend recommended that Railey telephone Denison House in Boston, where an aviation enthusiast named Amelia Earhart was doing social work with immigrant children. He made the call and a surprised Amelia cautiously expressed interest. According to Railey, "When Miss Earhart came on the wire, I inquired whether she'd like to participate in an important but hazardous flight. I had to come out with it because she declined an interview until I stated the nature of my business."[2]

Later, in Railey's office, where Amelia had been accompanied by Denison House's head worker Marion Perkins, Railey startled Amelia by asking the question, "How would you like to be the first woman to fly the Atlantic?"

When she heard this out-of-the-blue proposal, Amelia did her best to appear calm. "Only a flicker in her cool eyes betrayed the excitement this question must have aroused," related Railey.[3]

As the breathtaking but dangerous plan was laid out before her, surely Amelia must have been wondered, "Why me?" How could her simple but sincere aviation interests possibly have merited such flattering recognition? What hidden dangers might lie in such a stupendous undertaking? How long would it take to cross that huge expanse of ocean? Would this flight be attempted by a land airplane? She wanted as many details as possible.

"With intense interest I observed and appraised her as she talked," wrote Railey. "Her resemblance to Colonel Lindbergh was so extraordinary that I couldn't resist the impulse to ask her to remove her hat. She complied, brushing back her naturally tousled, wind-swept hair, and her laugh was infectious . . . Lady Lindy!"

"Most of all I was impressed with the poise of the boyish figure at my desk. There was warmth and dignity in her manner, her speech. Mrs. Guest had stipulated that the person to whom she would yield must be 'representative' of American women. In Amelia Earhart I felt that I had discovered not their norm but their sublimation."[4]

Railey and Putnam then met with Mrs. Guest, outlining with a flourish what they anticipated would be a dramatic ocean crossing under their management. Putnam especially relished the thought that he would be not only a producer of this great quest but manager of a new leading lady as well. He had published Charles Lindbergh's book, *We,* following that first historic airborne Atlantic crossing. Now, he envisioned the acclaim and money from another successful aeronautical title.

In early June 1928, the Fokker—named Friendship by Mrs. Guest—flew to Trepassey, Newfoundland, in secret, so as not to alert the press and media. After an agonizing two weeks of bad weather, the Friendship and crew took off around noon on June 17, about a month shy of Amelia's thirty-first birthday. The news flashed around the world. Early the next morning, the SS *America* sent a wire announcing that the Fokker had circled the ship. When word came that Friendship had landed safely at Burry Port, Wales, hundreds gathered to welcome the crew.

In a chartered seaplane from Imperial Airways near London, Railey arrived at the scene. He found swarms of people crowding the shore and dozens of boats bunched together in the harbor, their horns and whistles blowing.

"I caught my first glimpse of Amelia, seated Indian fashion in the doorway of the fuselage and with Indian composure indifferent to the clamor ashore. 'Congratulations!' I sang out, as our dory drew near. 'How's it feel to be the first woman to fly the Atlantic? Aren't you excited?'"

"Excited? No," replied Amelia. "It was a grand experience but all I did was lie on my tummy and take pictures of the clouds. We didn't see much of the ocean. Bill did all the flying—had to. I was just baggage, like a sack of potatoes. Oh well, maybe someday I'll try it alone."[5] Though a licensed pilot, she had never touched the controls and accordingly gave full credit to the two men. The public loved her lack of pretention.

Amelia spent ten days on Newfoundland while waiting for the weather to break. She was hosted by two locals, "Aunt" Fan and Bess. (Courtesy Ellie Turner)

Little did Amelia know that the outcome of the casual conversation between George Putnam and Hilton Railey would determine her career, fame, fortune, and fate. It would transform her from an unknown social worker in Boston to a world-famous, pioneering record holder in aviation. She would be honored by kings, queens, presidents, and prime ministers. She would become an officer and key shareholder of National Airlines, a faculty member of Purdue University, an author in her own right, and an editor of *Cosmopolitan*. She would design her own fashion and luggage line, become in-demand on the lecture circuit, and end up one of the most famous women of the twentieth century.

To capitalize on his famous new prodigy, George Putnam moved Amelia into his home in Rye, New York. This enabled her to write her book under his trained and watchful editor-publisher eyes. Putnam published her book *20 Hrs., 40 Min.* in 1928. Amelia became a close friend of Putnam's wife, Dorothy Binney Putnam, and dedicated the book to her. However, almost coincidently with the release of the book, Dorothy moved out of the house, divorced George, and headed for Florida with their two sons, David and George Jr.

Recognizing her dependence on George Putnam for the wherewithal to participate in the many aviation events in which she was so vitally interested, Amelia accepted his proposal of marriage in 1931. But on their wedding day she extracted from him an interesting and unique pre-marital agreement to release her after a year if there was no happiness.[6]

Dear Gyp,

There are some things which should be writ before we are married—things we have talked over before—most of them.

You must know again my reluctance to marry, my feeling that I shatter thereby chances in work which mean most to me. I feel the move just now as foolish as anything I could do. I know there may be compensations, but have no heart to look ahead.

Letter to G. P. from Amelia, in her handwriting. (Reprinted, by permission, from Sally Putnam Chapman, *Whistled like a Bird.*)

On our life together I want you to understand I shall not hold you to any medieval code of faithfulness to me, nor shall I consider myself bound to you similarly. If we can be honest I think the difficulties which arise may best be avoided should you or I become interested deeply (or in passing) with anyone else.

Please let us not interfere with the other's work or play, nor let the world see our private joys or disagreements. In this connection I may have to keep some place where I can go to be myself now and then, for I cannot guarantee to endure at all times the confinement of even an attractive cage.

I must exact a cruel promise, and that is you will let me go in a year if we find no happiness together.

I will try to do my best in every way and give you that part of me you know and seem to want.

AE

The marriage not only solidified her flying ambitions but also enabled her to become the first female to make a solo flight across the Atlantic Ocean. The feat was accomplished in 1932 in a single-engine Lockheed Vega. From Harbour Grace, Newfoundland, to a cow pasture near Londonderry, Ireland, the flight of 2,026 miles took fourteen hours and fifty-six minutes.

After descending from the clouds and having spotted some relatively smooth farmland, Amelia brought her plane down, landed, and cut the engine. She asked a solitary cowhand where she was, and the man yelled, "At Gallegher's pasture. Have you traveled far?"

"From America," answered the female pilot.

"Holy Mother of God," was the amazed response.[7]

In England, Amelia dined with royalty. Back in America, she was given a ticker tape parade in New York and was presented with the Distinguished Flying Cross by an admiring Congress.

Reflecting on that historic flight and the dark night over the Atlantic in which she encountered extreme turbulence, Amelia noted: "Of the five hours of storm, during black midnight, I kept right side up by instruments alone, buffeted about as I never was before. And then seeing flames lick through the exhaust collector ring, I wondered, in a detached way, whether one would prefer drowning to incineration."[8]

Another difficulty arose when her plane developed icing on its wings and began a downward spiral. "How long we spun I do not know. I do know that I tried my best to do exactly what one should do with a spinning plane, and regained flying control as the warmth

Amelia's Vega in the meadow at Ballyarnett, County Derry, North Ireland, where she landed. Photograph by the local pharmacist, just hours after the landing. (Courtesy Ballyarnett Museum)

of the lower altitude melted the ice. As we righted and held level again, through the blackness below I could see the whitecaps too close for comfort." Her plane's barograph recorded a vertical drop of more than three thousand feet.[9]

After her conquest of the Atlantic, Amelia became the first woman to fly solo across the United States, from Los Angeles, California, to Newark, New Jersey. In 1935, she became the first person to fly from Hawaii across the eastern Pacific to California.

Having arrived at Honolulu just after Christmas in 1934, Amelia, G. P., the Paul Mantzes, and trusted mechanic Ernie Tissot disembarked the Matson steamship *Lurline* on which Amelia's gold and red Lockheed Vega had been carefully stored. By the forecasted good weather of January 11, 1935, Tissot and Mantz carefully checked the Vega and fueled it with 520 gallons of gasoline contained in tanks placed where six passengers could usually sit. On this flight, Amelia had the luxury of being equipped with a two-way radio telephone and delighted in communicating with radio stations as well as with her husband. Because of the radio broadcasts, thousands met at Oakland Airport to greet the first person ever to have successfully flown from Hawaii. Her flight time was eighteen hours and fifteen minutes.

Unlike Amelia's difficult Atlantic crossing three years earlier, the

Historian Robert Stenuit in the Ballyarnett Museum, in front of the wall mural of Amelia's red plane landing on the meadow. (Photograph by author)

Pacific flight was a pleasurable one. "Stars hung outside my cockpit window near enough to touch. I have never seen so many or such large ones. I shall never forget the contrast of the white clouds and the moonlight and starlight against the black of the sea . . . After midnight the moon set and I was alone with the stars. I have often said that the lure of flying is the lure of beauty, and I need no other flight to convince me that the reason flyers fly, whether they know it or not, is the esthetic appeal of flying."[10]

Later that year, Amelia set a new 1,700-mile record from Burbank, California, to Mexico City, having been invited by the Mexican government to fly to that country. She took part in an eight-day fiesta, and on the day of her departure she "had breakfast in Mexico City and supper in New York—a very early breakfast to be sure, and a decidedly late supper, for it was 10:30 p.m. when I landed at Newark, 2,185 miles to the north."[11]

Regularly scheduled stunt races, combined with long-distance records and the resulting publicity, made Amelia a household name. She was a delightful and refreshing role model in the male-dominated world of aviation. Her overnight status as a legendary aviatrix had a mesmerizing effect that drove her ever onward. Amelia's ultimate goal was to circumnavigate the globe, as no woman or man had ever flown an airplane all the way around the world at its circumference, using routes paralleling the equator. Amelia Earhart's dream was to add this adventurous bold stroke to her already impressive list of aerial accomplishments.

The Team

Paul Mantz, Technical Adviser

Amelia had known Paul Mantz for several years. She was impressed not only with his flying ability but also with his thorough knowledge of aeronautics in general. He had a special touch for engines and diagnosing engine problems, fuel management, safety precautions, and overall flight dynamics. He was a flamboyant, success-driven, and spectacularly daring flier. Amelia saw in him many of the personal traits she desired herself, not so much the grandiosity, but the fearlessness, the intensity, and the knowledge. Though her husband, G. P., was not all that keen on him, Amelia selected Mantz as her technical adviser.[12]

Earhart and Mantz made a good team. They became close friends and had mutual respect for each other. Both pilots raced airplanes, set speed records, and competed fiercely. Before the start of the

Paul Mantz, Amelia Earhart, Harry Manning, and Fred Noonan. (Courtesy Purdue University Libraries)

around-the-world flight, they signed an agreement to form the Earhart-Mantz Flying School upon Amelia's return. It would be a natural success, they thought: he, the handsome Hollywood pilot, and she, the lovely Lady Lindy, a label the press bestowed upon her because of her resemblance to the famous Colonel Lindbergh.

Because of his association with Hollywood's elite, Paul Mantz considered himself to be an actor, too. His brown eyes, prominent Roman nose, black hair, and Clark Gable-esque mustache allowed him to look the part. Because of undependable bookings in the stunt flying business, Paul established an air charter company to make ends meet. His Honeymoon Express specialized in champagne flights for the stars to quick weekend getaways without a press-driven fanfare. On other occasions, the Honeymoon Express plane was converted to an air ambulance. One time, Mantz rushed a hard-hat diver with the bends to a Navy decompression chamber, saving his life. Always the opportunist, he offered himself and his plane where needed—airdrops to firefighters, flying heart patients to hospitals, and even pioneer rainmaking in Arizona.

As Amelia's technical adviser, Mantz prided himself in analyzing every aspect of the new Electra's equipment. He strategically planned the placement of additional fuel tanks in the Lockheed: three tanks in each wing and six stacked in the fuselage between the cockpit and the aft navigation station. This provided a total gasoline capacity of 1,150 gallons. One of the wing tanks was reserved exclusively for 100-octane fuel, to be used solely for takeoffs. The Electra would have a range up to four thousand miles and between twenty-three and twenty-four hours of flying time, depending on flight conditions and appropriate fuel management. With the assistance of his friend and aeronautical engineer Clarence Belinn, they designed a fuel cross-feeding system to provide a controlled and balanced flow between the fuel tanks to the engines, operated by means of one master valve in the cockpit floor. Mixture controls on the big Pratt & Whitney 550 hp Wasp engines, normally automatic, were replaced with manual handles to conserve fuel when needed. After a number of flight tests, Paul determined the throttle setting and propeller pitch he felt best for the aircraft. He estimated that Amelia would be flying at an average altitude of between six thousand and ten thousand feet. To achieve an efficient average airspeed of 150 miles per hour, he taught Amelia to use a device known as a Cambridge analyzer in order to conserve and burn as little fuel as possible on longer trips.

Mantz also recommended installing a Sperry autopilot, because he knew that the "robot pilot" would considerably reduce pilot fatigue. Having flown with Amelia on several lengthy flights, he was aware of her stamina level and was concerned about how she would hold up under stressful conditions day in and day out. When he wasn't customizing equipment and instrumentation, Paul helped Amelia to practice blind-flying tactics on the Link apparatus installed in his airport hangar. He knew that there would be many times when her life might very well be determined by her ability to fly only by cockpit instruments. The absolute necessity of steering good compass courses and correcting properly for over- or under-steering was an unwritten code of pilot conditioning when bad weather prevailed and there was zero visibility.

On the leg of the first flight attempt from Oakland to Honolulu, Paul Mantz sat in the co-pilot's seat on the right side of the cockpit. He was at the controls on takeoff and later on landing in Honolulu. He planned to deplane in Hawaii, but at least he would be assured that everything was working properly.

After reaching a cruising altitude of eight thousand feet, Amelia took over the flying and Paul maintained the radio log and monitored fuel consumption. He also worked with Amelia on rotating the radio direction finder loop. Mantz later related to Don Dwiggins, author of *Hollywood Pilot,* a biography of Mantz, that he was pleased with Amelia's knowledgeable use of the RDF equipment. This compliment to Amelia later proved irrelevant. In her desperate search for Howland Island, she abandoned everything that Mantz had taught her on rotating the RDF loop and was unable to obtain any kind of direction finding fix.

Paul Mantz did not consider himself to be a stunt pilot, although that is the direction in which his career led him.[13] "I'm a precision flyer and I'm here to prove it," he once said to Don Dwiggins. Two months later, he met his fate in a filming accident at the Buttercup Valley desert near Yuma, Arizona. He was sixty-two years old.[14]

Harry Manning, Navigator

For the original around-the-world flight, Amelia signed Capt. Harry Manning to handle the navigating responsibilities. He had just been named captain of the United States SS *President Roosevelt* when that ship returned Earhart, Stultz, and Gordon to New York after their historic Atlantic crossing in the Friendship in 1928. Captain Manning and Amelia had become friends during this voyage, and he spent time teaching her his specialty, navigation.

When Amelia asked Manning to participate in her grandiose plan to fly around the world, he requested and received a leave of absence from his company.[15] At this time, he took the test to obtain his third-class radio operator's license, having proven his ability to send and receive Morse code at the required speed of sixteen words per minute. Because Manning's total experience had evolved around navigation at sea, the pair brought along Fred Noonan, a former noted Pan American Airways navigator, as assistant navigator in order to ensure an orderly crossing over the wide expanse of the Pacific. Just as Mantz was to leave the crew at Hawaii, Noonan was to deplane at Howland Island and return on the Coast Guard ship assigned to that distant station.

Manning would then get Amelia to Lae, New Guinea, where he would hop off, leaving Amelia to her own devices for the rest of the journey. Amelia's publicity-minded husband suggested this schedule to make sure that she received full credit for the around-the-world undertaking.

Fred Noonan, Navigator

Frederick Joseph Noonan was born in Chicago in 1893. His mother,

Catherine, died when Fred was only four. At the tender age of twelve, he left Chicago and headed for Seattle, Washington, where he signed up as an apprentice seaman on a sailing ship. He worked in various seafaring capacities on a number of ships, obtaining ratings as Boatswain's Mate and Quartermaster. In 1910, he served aboard the largest square-rigger of the day, the bark *Crompton,* and was at sea for 152 days travelling from Washington State to Ireland. In 1912, he served aboard the American barkentine *Aurora,* sailing from San Francisco to Honolulu in seventeen days. When World War I broke out, he served on a munitions carrier between New York and England. He later attended the London Nautical College and served in the Royal British Naval Service. Enemies torpedoed his ships on three different occasions.

After the war, on a voyage from London to Montreal, he spotted and rescued five French sailors adrift on an ice floe. On another cruise, he helped save the crew of a sinking Portuguese fishing schooner. By the time his seafaring days were over, he had been licensed as a Master Mariner unlimited and as a Mississippi River Pilot and had rounded Cape Horn seven times: three times on windjammers and four on steamships.

Tall, slender, and resembling the movie star James Stewart, Fred was a handsome, blue-eyed seafarer. In 1930, he earned a limited commercial pilot's license (single-engine rating), and in 1931, he became rated as a second-class radio operator in Morse code from the US Department of Commerce.

Noonan joined the New York, Rio, and Buenos Aires air trajectory shortly before Pan American Airways acquired it. With Pan Am, Fred first served as an instructor in Miami and later managed his company's airport operation in Port-au-Prince, Haiti. It was not long before Fred's navigational skills placed him in the forefront of Pan Am's early survey flights across the South Pacific. He figured prominently in determining course recommendations and developed flight plans from Hawaii to Midway Island, Wake, and Guam in a Sikorsky S-42 flying boat. He navigated the round-trip Pan Am clipper flight in 1935 between San Francisco and Honolulu with Capt. Ed Musick, which earned him a place in aviation history prior to his historic flight with Amelia Earhart. In time, Fred knew the routes, islands, and Pacific Ocean better than anyone in his day.

As Pan Am grew, Fred trained junior officers on the fine points of air navigation techniques: bubble octant for celestial observations, pelorus for checking drift with smoke bombs tossed overboard during the day and flares at night, the art of RDF to search a known station that could pick up a signal, and the last case scenario of dead reckoning to obtain an estimated position of latitude and longitude. Noonan's long hours and vast navigational experience at sea, enhanced by his gentle nature, made him a natural as a patient instructor giving on-the-job training to his airborne students. He gained their immediate respect and confidence.

But being an accomplished navigator and revered instructor could not offset Fred's addiction to alcohol. After having been literally "assisted" into his plane a few times during early morning flights, his affinity for drink cost him his job at Pan American Airways. Although Noonan's reputation had been lessened, one colleague endorsed his credentials: "In critical situations Fred never left his desk. I never witnessed any irregularity. True, at layovers, Fred retired to his room, and we saw nothing of him till departure time. Th[at] was his business."[16]

Amelia recognized that good, open-ocean navigators were hard to come by. In Fred Noonan, Amelia had one of the great navigators, if not the greatest, of her day and time. His experience on the long flights of Pan Am flying boats across the Pacific served her needs better than any other person. While his previous alcohol situation had been a problem for Pan Am, he had obviously convinced the Putnams that the problem was under control and behind him. Though Harry Manning was skipper of a steamship and also had a pilot's license, he had no air navigational experience. Amelia felt that she needed Fred's proven familiarity as a backup. At forty-three years old, Fred knew that a positive association with Amelia offered him a second chance. The flight around the world with the renowned Miss Earhart would have reestablished his navigational credibility. It would have been one more endorsement for the navigation school he hoped to open upon completion of the world flight. "Fred, at that time," stated Pan Am friend Marius Lodesen, "was the world's most experienced aerial navigator, in any sense a brilliant one."[17]

The Plane

During the mid-1930s, Amelia's prominence as a female flyer led her to accept guest lecturing invitations as a part-time faculty member of Purduc University in Lafayette, Indiana. Through

Amelia with her "Flying Laboratory." (Courtesy Purdue University Libraries)

her connections there and in the aviation industry, professionals supplied her with a new twin-engine Lockheed Electra, which was ultra-customized for long-range flight and had all the latest equipment. Knowing of Amelia's plans for an around-the-world attempt, many manufacturers within the industry wanted to be represented. Amelia dubbed the plane her "flying laboratory," and it truly was one of the finest of the day.[18]

Amelia's Electra was powered by two Pratt & Whitney R-1340 Wasp S3H-1 engines (serial numbers 6149 and 6150) each of 550 horsepower. These engines were equipped with two-bladed, constant-speed Hamilton Standard propellers.

The Electra 10E was delivered to Amelia on her thirty-ninth birthday, July 24, 1936. Its registration number was X16020 while the plane was being flight tested, R16020 during the Bendix race that September, and finally NR16020, which the Electra carried during the world flight. The last number indicated that the plane was restricted to carrying up to four crew members for aeronautical tests and experimental purposes.

Electra's Primary Specifications:

Aircraft Type:	Fixed-wing monoplane, twin engine transport
Wing Span:	55 feet
Height:	10 feet, 1 inch
Length:	38 feet, 7 inches
Fuel Capacity:	1150 US gallons
Cruising Speed:	150 miles per hour
Range:	4000 miles

Filler access panels for the six fuselage fuel tanks were on the port side of the aircraft, where the windows would have been in the normal transport model. These fuselage tanks increased the Electra's gasoline capacity to 1150 gallons, much greater than the normal 250 to 350 gallons of the transport prototype.

In the aft navigation area, engineers added two windows: "One in the entrance door and another opposite in the fuselage for a total of four. These two added windows were larger than normal and were optically flat, permitting the navigator, whose desk and station was positioned there, to obtain accurate celestial observations. Later for Amelia's last flights, the starboard large window was removed and the fuselage skinned over."[19]

The Electra's radio was a fifty-watt Western Electric with three crystal-controlled channels. Transmission usually was by voice with a hand-held microphone. Morse code could be sent by utilizing a telegraph key. While Morse was the preferred method of communicating among most commercial planes and pilots, Amelia was not proficient in using code. She could recognize simple letters sent slowly, such as A (dot, dash) or N (dash, dot). Regrettably, she showed little interest in practicing or studying the Morse code process, always digressing to vocal radio-telephony. Her navigator, Fred Noonan, did have a second-class radio operator's license and could send and receive messages slowly by code. There was a variable-frequency receiver with four bands, ranging from 200 to 10,000 kilocycles (today kilohertz). The Electra also was equipped with an early version of a manually operated direction-finder loop antenna situated on the roof of the airplane and manipulated by a handle to rotate the loop from inside the cockpit.

The frequency of 6210 kilocycles was best used during daylight hours. For night communications during darkness, Amelia used the

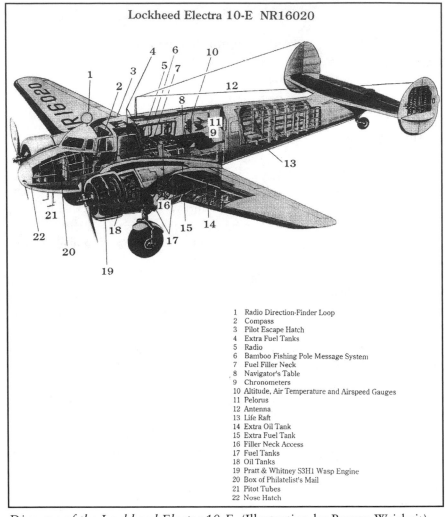

Lockheed Electra 10-E NR16020

1 Radio Direction-Finder Loop
2 Compass
3 Pilot Escape Hatch
4 Extra Fuel Tanks
5 Radio
6 Bamboo Fishing Pole Message System
7 Fuel Filler Neck
8 Navigator's Table
9 Chronometers
10 Altitude, Air Temperature and Airspeed Gauges
11 Pelorus
12 Antenna
13 Life Raft
14 Extra Oil Tank
15 Extra Fuel Tank
16 Filler Neck Access
17 Fuel Tanks
18 Oil Tanks
19 Pratt & Whitney S3H1 Wasp Engine
20 Box of Philatelist's Mail
21 Pitot Tubes
22 Nose Hatch

Diagram of the Lockheed Electra 10-E. (Illustration by Bowen Weisheit)

3105 kilocycle frequency. Both of these frequencies were standard for aircraft of this era. A low-frequency 500-kcs channel was available for hailing, emergency, and ship-to-shore stations. This lower frequency also was effective for direction finding but required a 250-foot trailing antenna. The antenna wire included a several pound weight at the end. The entire apparatus was let out and reeled in electronically from the tail section of the airplane.

This 500-kcs transmission capability was probably the most important and most reliable feature of the aircraft's radio equipment. Both ship and shore stations could obtain a bearing on Amelia's

Form 108A   500 Sets 5-36 W.P.Co.   SELLER'S COPY

LOCKHEED AIRCRAFT CORPORATION
ORDER BLANK

To:
LOCKHEED AIRCRAFT CORPORATION,
BURBANK CALIFORNIA.

March 20, 1936.

I
~~We~~ hereby purchase....1..(One)..Lockheed Electra 10-E.................
　　　　　　　(Quantity)　　　　　　　　　　　　　　　　　　(Model)

I
..2..(Two)..Pratt.&.Whitney.Wasps.SEH1.....................for which ~~We~~ agree to pay as follows:
　　　(Engine)

Flyaway price at........Las.Vegas,.Nevada.................................	$..55,910	00
Extra Equipment as follows:—		
......Gasoline.capacity.to.provide.range.of.4500.miles.in.		
accordance.with.our.letters.dated.2/21/36.and.3/5/36	8,500	00
	64,410	00
............Less.equipment.to.be.furnished.by.purchaser.per.		
attached.sheet.as.outlined.in.our.letter.dated.2/21/36-$19,263.90		
............Less.special.rebate.according.to.our.letter.		
dated.2/21/36	3,136.10	
................Total.deductions............22,400.00	22,400	00
............The.airplane.shall.correspond.with.standard.Electra.Model.		
10E,.specifications.covering.which.are.attached.hereto,.except.		
as.modified.in.our.letters.dated.2/21/36.and.3/5/36		
California State Sales Tax....................		
Delivery Charges...................		
Boxing or Crating................................Total	$..42,010	00
Initial deposit herewith of(Check.on.Fifth.Avenue.Bank.of.N.Y.dated.3/24/36	$.10,000	00
Balance due on delivery......................	$..32,010	00

Delivery of the personal property ordered shall be made on or about the....first......day of....July.............
193.6. at...Las.Vegas,.Nevada...; and the price herein specified
includes all charges by Seller for such delivery. Change in point of delivery after execution of this order
will necessitate appropriate adjustment of said price and if applicable shall be subject to the provisions of
paragraph 9 of the conditions on the reverse hereof. Title to said property shall not pass until said delivery
at said point and until full payment of balance due therefor shall have been made to Lockheed Aircraft
Corporation by Cash, Cashier's Check, Bank Draft, or Money Order calling for payment in funds and
exchange of the United States of America. Payment in foreign exchange will not be accepted.

I
We have read the conditions and warranty printed on the reverse side hereof and agree to and accept them
as part of this order.

This order contains the entire agreement affecting this purchase, and no other agreement or understanding
of any nature concerning same has been made or entered into or is a part of this transaction, except such
additional agreements as may be specifically noted herein and made a part hereof.

I
We hereby acknowledge receipt of a duplicate copy of this order.

Dated Signed.....March 23,...............19.36..　　Purchaser...._[signature]_
　　　　　　　　　　　　　　　　　　By....................................
Seller: Lockheed Aircraft Corporation.　　Street Address...60...W.45th.St.-
　　　　　　　　　　　　　　　　　　City......new.york...........
By.._[signature]_ Sec'y　　　　　　　State...N.Y...................

The original order form for the Electra in the name of Amelia Earhart.
(Courtesy Lockheed Martin)

transmissions and then relay bearing fixes and other information back to her.[20]

At the time of departure from Miami on her second around-the-world attempt, Amelia chose to discard her trailing antenna along with the Morse code telegraph key. Neither Amelia nor her husband, George Putnam, ever satisfactorily explained this decision, and it is known that her technical adviser, Paul Mantz, was very upset about the decision. The most likely reason was that Vincent Bendix, one of her sponsors, had convinced the Putnams that his newly developed High Frequency Radio Direction Finder was superior for long-range navigation, compared to the low-frequency equipment in standard use at the time. This subject will be discussed later in more detail.

The Plan

Amelia's around-the-world flight would require extensive planning, much of which was undertaken by her husband, G. P. He communicated almost daily with US State Department personnel for assistance in obtaining fly-over permissions and visas from numerous foreign countries. Landing rights and aviation fuel caches had to be arranged in advance, as did lodging and meals. The selection of airports along the anticipated route was based on their ability to service the Lockheed Electra and provide reserve gas and oil.

G. P. took advantage of Amelia's friendship with Eleanor Roosevelt and solicited her assistance as a "go-between" with State Department connections. In a letter from June 19, 1936, to the President's wife, he wrote, "Our wish is to be put in touch with the proper person in the State Department whose aid can be enlisted in connection with Amelia's proposed world flight. We want appropriate guidance in securing the required permissions, etc."

Mrs. Roosevelt didn't hesitate to contact Richard Southgate, Chief of the Division of Protocol, thanking him in advance for taking care of the things Putnam requested, and urging Southgate "to be very nice to him." Not only did Putnam avail himself of State Department assistance but also consulted noted pilots in other regions of the world as to recommended airports and facilities. English flyer Jacques de Sibour was associated with Standard Oil of New Jersey. Amelia had met him and his wife, Violette, while being entertained in England after her Friendship flight. They provided valuable assistance in identifying landing sites and supplies in Africa and Asia.[21]

Because of the extensive distance in flying over the Pacific Ocean, consideration initially was given to the possibility of in-flight refueling. In a letter dated November 10, 1936, Amelia wrote to President Roosevelt, reminding him of her planned flight and soliciting his assistance of having the Navy's support of the plan. "I am discussing with the Navy a possible refueling in the air over Midway Island . . . and am asking you to help me secure Navy cooperation."

FDR apparently endorsed this mid-air refueling request. However, after Amelia and G. P. received word on the Navy's requirements, they began to rethink the matter. The Navy's assistance would be provided subject to the successful "completion of preliminary preparations and trial . . . and the matter of expenses should be borne by Miss Earhart."[22]

On January 8, 1937, Amelia wired the President after learning of the Howland Island colonization program: "I hope to land on tiny Howland Island where the Government is about to establish an emergency field . . . which [would be] permanently useful and valuable aeronautically and nationally," she stated.

Several days later, the White House responded: "An allocation of Federal Funds has been made by the President to the Works Progress Administration to enable the Bureau of Air Commerce to carry out the construction of such a field."

Retired Navy Commander Clarence Williams, along with some volunteer aeronautical students, helped "swing" the three compasses on the Electra. The swinging process ensured that each was exactly coordinated and synchronized. Williams also assisted in plotting and laying out strip sheets as a guide for hypothetical courses to be steered, distances calculated, and time-of-flight estimates between specific points, based on predetermined cruising courses and speeds. It is not known whether Amelia ever used them. A listing of these strip charts can be found at Purdue University Library.

G. P. shipped and stored fuel and oil supplies in fifty-gallon drums bearing Amelia's name to more than thirty locations on the twenty-seven thousand-mile route. He ordered extra engine parts and sent them to carefully selected airports where mechanics who were familiar with the Lockheed and its Pratt & Whitney Wasp engines would be able to work on them.

Emergency items aboard the Electra included a small hand compass, a waterproof match box, a knife, a small ax, and a canteen. In the airplane's aft fuselage was a two-person rubber life raft, inflated by carbon dioxide capsules. There was also a Very pistol for firing distress signal flares and an orange kite. "If we sit down somewhere in the Pacific and stay afloat, I'd like to be noticed," Amelia stated.[23]

As for food, Amelia carried a large quantity of cans of tomato juice, her old standby. She also stored thermos bottles of hot cocoa, a supply of concentrated food, malted milk tablets, raisins, chocolate, and canteens of water. In addition to carrying an assortment of sunglasses to help reduce eye strain, there were also engine and propeller covers made from green felt cloth as well as tie-down line and stakes to anchor the airplane on the ground when necessary.

Helpers made efforts to supply Amelia with the best of everything, but the aircraft's internal communication system was shockingly primitive. Shouting back and forth between the forward and aft sections was impractical because of the engine noise. Instead, Earhart and Noonan passed notes clipped on a bamboo fishing pole between the cockpit and the navigator's desk behind the assortment of gasoline tanks in the fuselage. Another alternative to the pole system was a pulley system, but the pole system seemed easier.

At that time, radio direction finding (RDF) navigation was in its beginning stages and was being tested. Few land or sea navigators had experience in the technique, which involved slowly rotating the loop antenna toward a radio signal coming from another station. When the signal strength reached its minimum, or null point, a bearing could be taken revealing the direction from which the signal was being transmitted. Western Electric recommended a trailing wire antenna of at least 250 feet for obtaining the best results in airplanes. Amelia disliked the chore of having to reel this wire out and, later, back in. At Miami, prior to the second world flight, she removed the entire rig, probably because of her extreme concerns about excess weight.

Noonan devised an arrangement in which the cabin door could be opened and secured about four inches while the Electra was in the air. This enabled him to use his Pioneer drift indicator. Looking through the small doorway opening, he could check the degree and direction in which the wind caused the airplane to drift. In daylight, he would drop smoke bombs, and at night he would use flares. At his chart table mounted three chronometers. He also had an altimeter, air speed indicator, and temperature gauge. It is likely that he also had a spare radio telegraph key.[24]

Of paramount importance to Earhart and Putnam were the financial rewards of a successful flight. They hoped to receive $25,000 from marketing of sixty-five hundred philatelic covers by Gimbel's department store. Gimbel's offered four thousand colorful envelopes autographed by Amelia for sale at a price of $5 each. They also sold twenty-five hundred unsigned covers at $2 each. Amelia dutifully managed to have these covers hand cancelled at Karachi, Pakistan, and Lae, New Guinea. "In Karachi I visited the post office to get the covers I was carrying cancelled. The Director of Post and Telegraph and the Postmaster were very courteous and cooperative, permitting me to select the stamp I wished used. Of course, I chose the Karachi airmail type [stamp] which, I hoped, would look well on the already decorated envelopes."[25]

Harry Balfour, the Lae, New Guinea, radioman, was responsible for removing the flight covers, having them postmarked and returned to the airplane after it landed on June 29.

Amelia had signed a book contract with Harcourt Brace and maintained high hopes for what should have become a very successful author's tour upon her return. She also had an exclusive agreement with the *New York Herald Tribune* that committed her to regularly scheduled submissions and progress reports along the way. Amelia wired these brief narratives from selected ports of call and likely would have formed an outline for her forthcoming documentary. The *Tribune* already had begun a series of features leading up to the start of the world flight.

As to the bigger picture, the mid-1930s witnessed a maturation of the Golden Age of aviation and the advent of intercontinental activity. In addition to Amelia and Fred's around-the-world adventure, 1937 represented a climax in world-wide mania for long-distance air records. Valery Chkalov successfully flew over the North Pole. His record flight soon was repeated by another Russian aviator, Gromov, who set a new world record. In August, another Russian, Levanevsky, disappeared during his transpolar flight attempt. As in Amelia's case, Levanevsky's aircraft was never recovered, another reminder of the perils of long-distance flying, especially in uncharted and sparsely populated regions. If these adventures were meant to prove anything, it confirmed that as far as crossing oceans was concerned, seat-of-the-pants stunt flying was no longer the trending phenomenon. As the world began to assess the matter of these disappearances more carefully, scheduled logistics and careful, long-range navigational planning became key factors in future long-distance flights overseas.

Huge airplanes with fuselages like the hulls of ships were just beginning their series of adventures in crossing the great oceans of the world. They could take off and land on the water, moor to a buoy or floating dock, or taxi up a gently sloping ramp to a safe and secure air strip where cargoes and passengers could be unloaded. Airlines made great strides in transporting both people and freight.

Valery Chkalov. (Courtesy V. P. Tchkalov's Memorial Museum)

Sigizmund Levanevsky.

Mikhail Gromov.

Floyd B. Odlum. (Courtesy Library of Congress)

Jackie Cochran.

German and Japanese plans of conquest interrupted aviation's peaceful Golden Age. After the war, America led the world into the exploration and development of Outer Space.

A lot more was riding on that great globe-circling flight than Amelia and George Putnam had imagined. Upon the successful conclusion of this world attempt, they planned to form their own airline along with Eugene Vidal, Floyd Odlum, and other notables. Furthermore, with her flight completed, Amelia would have proven that land airplanes could cross wide expanses of water on an equal basis as the flying boats. For Amelia and G. P., the future looked promising. If their good fortunes held, it "would be fun to grow old," as Amelia once stated.

Chapter 4

The Around-the-World Flights

The Luke Field Crash

Amelia's first effort to circumnavigate the globe along the Equator began on March 17, 1937. With 947 gallons of fuel in the Electra's tanks, Amelia and her team of Paul Mantz, Harry Manning, and Fred Noonan took off from Oakland Airport in California bound for Hawaii. The flight of 2410 miles took fifteen hours and forty-seven minutes and set a new record by more than an hour, beating the previous time of a Pan Am clipper flight.

As the airplane neared the island of Oahu and descended from the clouds, the weary fliers saw Diamond Head directly in front of them, confirming the perfect navigation of Noonan and Manning. Amelia, being especially fatigued, asked Mantz to handle the landing at Wheeler Field. When the famous stunt pilot took the wheel, angling the plane downward in a sharp, steep bank, Amelia shouted, "Don't, don't!" Mantz later stated, "She calmed down when I made a normal approach and we landed."[2]

The weather reports for the next couple of days were favorable. The distance from Hawaii to Howland Island was approximately six hundred miles less than the distance they had just covered. However, Mantz suggested that Amelia rest for a day before undertaking the journey across the vast Pacific to a flyspeck of an island. The only navigational aid would come from a Coast Guard ship maintaining its position there. The cutter *Shoshone*, commanded by G. T. Finlay, had departed Honolulu on March 10, 1937, to deliver colonists and supplies and to stand by for the Electra flight. Also on board was Department of the Interior agent Richard B. Black, serving as expedition leader and assisted by the Army's H. A. Meyer.

Mantz also determined that the plane's propeller bearings needed lubricating and that Manning had managed to burn out a radio generator fuse by excessively depressing the Morse telegraph key in a long dash to aid the Hawaii Direction Finder station in taking a bearing on the inbound plane.

This shorting of the generator fuse was forever etched in the back of Amelia's mind. The likelihood of such a problem occurring in the future gave her constant cause for worry as her long-distance flight progressed. When transmitting, she stayed on the radio for very brief periods. If a long count or long dash was requested, she never provided one of sufficient duration to enable a bearing to be taken or a signal acknowledged by the receiving station.

The planned schedule was for Mantz to return to California by steamship, for Noonan to disembark at Howland and return aboard the waiting Coast Guard ship, and for Manning to handle the navigation to Australia and deplane at Darwin. This would enable Amelia to complete the remainder of the globe-circling flight and receive full credit upon its conclusion.

In preparation for the next day's early morning departure, Paul Mantz moved the aircraft to the Army's Luke Field, with its paved three-thousand-foot runway. He saw that the Electra's tanks were filled with nine hundred gallons of gasoline and made certain that the one hundred-octane wing tank, reserved exclusively for use during takeoff, was totally full.[3]

It was just after sunrise at 7:35 a.m. Honolulu time when Amelia pushed the throttles forward and the Electra began moving down the runway, gaining speed for liftoff to Howland Island. There had been some rain during the early morning hours. Paul Mantz watched the plane's progress down the runway with a group of Army Air Corps officers standing beside him. Many times, he had cautioned Amelia to be sure she controlled the heavily loaded plane on takeoff with the rudder pedals and not the throttles in order to keep the aircraft straight and steady. He was thinking about the aircraft's weight when he saw the plane yaw to the right. He heard the left engine being throttled down, and then watched with concern as the airplane began a wild, uncontrollable swing to the left, sliding on its belly in a spark-showered skid of several hundred yards.

Fire and rescue equipment rushed to the scene. Miraculously, there was no fire. A shaky and pale-faced Amelia emerged from the airplane as Fred Noonan casually folded his navigational charts. Harry Manning was visibly shaken. Having occupied the copilot's seat, he saw and felt the plane veer off to the right and then slide precipitously to the left. He recognized that the occupants were extremely fortunate to be alive. Manning recognized that it would take time to repair the airplane and his ninety-day furlough from his steamship company would not cover the delay for rebuilding the Electra. Returning to his ship was a reasonable excuse for him to abandon the project. In discussing the matter afterwards, he was generally critical of Amelia. "Amelia was responsible for the crash," he told Vincent Loomis, an Amelia Earhart researcher and author. "She overcorrected to the left, then to the right, gas leaking and lots of sparks. We were all just damn lucky it didn't catch fire. Amelia was something of a prima-donna—had an ego and could be tough as nails. I got very fed up with her bullheadedness several times. That's why she brought Noonan into the picture—in the event that I gave up on the flight."[4]

Amelia was not the only one upset over the Luke Field incident; a few minutes after the crash, her husband in Oakland was equally shaken. George Putnam told it this way:

The telephone rang. I put the receiver to my ear. Putnam, have you heard? They crashed . . . the ship's in flames . . .

I could not listen further. I moved out into the cold morning trying to walk steadily. In just a few minutes, they came racing after me. No fire . . . no fire at all. False report! No one hurt. The naked metal of the undercarriage grinding on the concrete threw up such a shower of sparks someone had called the word "Fire," but miraculously, despite all the spilled gasoline, there had been no fire.

G. P. immediately sent a telegram to Amelia: "SO LONG AS YOU AND THE BOYS ARE OKEH, THE REST DOESN'T MATTER. IT'S JUST ONE OF THOSE THINGS. WHETHER YOU WANT TO CALL IT A DAY OR KEEP GOING LATER IS EQUALLY JAKE WITH ME."

An hour later both were on the telephone, she in Honolulu and he in Oakland. "Will you try again?" He asked. "Of course," she said quite simply. Her voice was weary with sadness as she realized more fully what problems lay before her.[5]

Probably the best explanation of the accident comes from the Accident Report of the Luke Field Board of Inquiry:

As the airplane gathered speed it swung slightly to the right. Miss Earhart corrected this tendency by throttling the left hand motor. The aircraft then began to swing to the left with increasing speed, characteristic of a ground loop. It tilted forward, right wing low and for 50 or 60 yards was supported by the right wheel only. The right hand landing gear suddenly collapsed under the excessive load, followed by the left. The airplane spun sharply to the left sliding on its belly and amid a shower of sparks from the mat came to rest headed about 200° from its initial course.[6]

The damaged airplane was shipped back to California on a Matson steamship. After being unloaded, the airplane parts were laid out on the hangar floor. It was there that Art Kennedy's expertise came into play. As he studied the assortment of wreckage, Art immediately noticed the badly burned right brake, the left brake being normal.

Art Kennedy first met Amelia when he was working for Pacific Airmotive Corporation in 1934. She asked him to carefully check over the single engine of her Lockheed Vega as she prepared for the first leg of the around-the-world flight from Hawaii to California. For several nights a week, he moonlighted as Amelia's mechanic, fine-tuning every aspect of the motor. She was often in the hangar watching him work late into the evening.

Amelia confided in Art that she was a little afraid of the Vega's 450-horsepower engine. She explained that sometimes it ran so rough that she wasn't sure who was shuddering more, she or the motor. When the overhaul was completed, Amelia took the plane up for a short checkout flight. Kennedy described her reaction to his mechanical efforts: "On landing she jumped out of the pit, threw her arms around me, and gave me a kiss that forever will be burned into my memory. She was ecstatic that her engine now hummed, as smooth as glass. If that kiss was an indication of her gratitude, she was so grateful I didn't think I would tell my wife about it."[1]

Art wrote a book, *High Times—Keeping 'Em Flying,* after fifty years of servicing aircraft engines and working with some of the outstanding pilots of those early flying days. During WWII, he was involved with the training of RAF mechanics in maintaining their B-14 Hudson reconnaissance planes. He later held a variety of airline maintenance posts and retired in Portugal after performing military contract work there for the US Air Force and Navy.

In his chapter titled "Amelia," Kennedy brings to light some amazing revelations, mostly centered on the crash at Luke Field and the wreckage that he surveyed back in the States.

> The right wing and right gear had suffered all the damage, as was ex-
> pected for a left ground loop, but the right gear was collapsed outboard.
> In a normal accidental ground loop to the left, when the right brake was
> scorched, the right gear would have collapsed inboard. The left propeller

blades were only slightly scuffed but the starboard props were severely bent forward, indicating a high-powered contact with the ground."[7]

He later asked Amelia, "What's going on? This couldn't have been a normal ground loop. It was forced. Why?"

Amelia was strangely noncommittal, but she encouraged Art to reposition the gear with an eight-foot crowbar so as to appear normal. She knew that the accident investigator would be looking at the situation in the morning. Later that evening, she took Art and his wife, Polly, to dinner and opened up about the situation.

She told them that as she was doing her crosschecks inside the Electra prior to takeoff at Luke Field en route to Howland Island, she received information that the flight needed to be aborted. Kennedy never indicated just where these instructions originated.

> Unfortunately for posterity I didn't have sense enough to ask, but I don't think she'd have told me. Nor did she directly admit to deliberately faking a ground loop.
>
> Yet the evidence then, and now, was clear to me. My analysis is that she decided to abort by faking a last-minute ground loop on takeoff, but forgot to consider her high speed and the extra weight of the fully loaded aircraft . . . either way, it was no accident.[8]

During dinner, Amelia reiterated that Art must remain quiet about having bent the right gear back to its normal position and to never discuss the necessity of aborting the Luke Field takeoff. She stunned the Kennedys with the comment that her flight plan *had* to appear to be an around-the-world record-setting effort, but the facts were she was really undertaking a "special mission."

"Can you imagine me being a spy?" she asked. Art and Polly looked at each other in amazement.

"I never said that!" Amelia changed the subject.

Later, they dropped off Amelia at her hotel. After a "goodnight" to Polly and generous hug to Art, Amelia said to him, "Remember we are friends, and friends are faithful." Art reminisced: "She then gives me another faithful-friends kiss and slipped a fifty-dollar bill into my hand. Polly and I were shocked. It was more than half my monthly salary."[9]

It is likely that Amelia, being embarrassed about the ground loop and subsequent damage to the aircraft, sought solace in talking about other purposes of the flight to her close friends in order to diffuse the fact of the difficult-to-swallow crash. This special mission that Amelia mentioned actually was conceived by FDR and some aides, when they recognized that Amelia's needs provided the civilian excuse to construct an airfield on Howland Island that might have had additional future uses, such as military benefits. United States Navy Capt. Bruce Livingston Canaga, ret., served as an Office of Naval Intelligence aide to President Roosevelt and also headed the US Island Government Office. He had a hand in convincing FDR of the hidden benefits of Howland, Baker, and Jarvis Islands. Amelia would be serving her country in making the long Pacific hop by testing the Howland airstrip and proving that the venture could be achieved in a land airplane. Pan Am's clippers had been successfully island hopping since 1935. This committed plan, along with some occasional white spying (civilian unofficial observation) when there were opportunities to observe certain foreign airfields, probably comprised her special mission, according to Fred Goerner in a letter dated February 20, 1988, to his friend, Theodore Barreaux.

Harry Manning told Fred Goerner in *The Search for Amelia Earhart,* "The Luke Field take-off crash was the result of Earhart jockeying the throttles as she was having problems controlling the fuel-heavy airplane." Manning was in the copilot's seat on the right and in perfect position to observe what happened.

Alex Coutts, a young Navy seaman who was the first to arrive at the crash scene on a fire and rescue truck, related, "The plane's tail had been up the last hundred yards down the runway. The aircraft was moving fast and was poised for lift off."[10]

The Bendix Corporation not only supplied the radio direction finder on Amelia's Lockheed Electra but also furnished its generator, magnetos, and brakes. A Bendix technician was sent to Honolulu to ensure that the company's equipment was in good working order prior to takeoff. Upon his return to Burbank, he described to Art Kennedy Amelia's crash:

> I was half way down the runway when the accident happened. She had her tail high, and I thought she was about to lift off when she ground looped.
>
> I was the first to get to the plane. The brakes were our responsibility, so I borrowed some tools from a Navy truck and removed them. The right brake was badly burned and the left was absolutely normal. I heard only one engine reduce power.
>
> You know Amelia is one damn fine pilot, and how she could have had this accident is beyond belief. All we could get out of her was that she just didn't know how it happened. Something's fishy![11]

When considering what really happened in the Luke Field ground loop, it is important to weigh what Kelly Johnson, senior vice president of Lockheed, thought, as he had worked extensively with Amelia to make sure that she was completely familiar with the peculiarities of that aircraft. He verified that "Miss Earhart did practice full load takeoffs and actually had an incident of a minor ground loop on one test when flying with a full fuel load."[12]

Amelia told her husband that she did have the airplane under control at the time of takeoff.

> Then something gave way on the right side. It may never be known whether the tire exploded first, or the oleo strut of the landing gear gave way. The collapse of one almost instantly would follow the failure of the other. The plane, then with a speed of probably sixty or seventy miles an hour with its very heavy load, started a vicious swing to the right. Uncontrolled, it doubtless would have gone into a complete crack-up, ending on its back, quite possibly with results fatal to the occupants.[13]

Amelia's reaction was to throttle down the left motor in an attempt to straighten the now uncontrollable direction. This move caused the Electra to ground loop to the left, shearing off the entire landing gear. After a thousand feet of sliding, grinding, and bumping, the plane came to a swinging halt, showering sparks all the way. Amelia had the quick thinking to shut down all switches. A wing tank ruptured, spilling gasoline. There was no fire. Amazingly, none of the three occupants were injured, but the airplane was a mess.

The late Col. Rollin Reineck, Amelia Earhart Society researcher and author of *Amelia Earhart Survived,* had pictures of the wrecked airplane from the *Honolulu Star-Advertiser.* They showed the right gear and tire completely separated from the aircraft and lying twenty feet in front of the plane. The left tire and gear were still partially attached but thoroughly smashed and lying under the port engine. Propellers on both engines were severely bent forward.

Following the Luke Field ground loop, Fred Noonan ran into his old Pan Am associate whom he had trained, Capt. Marius Lodesen. Lodesen had just arrived at Honolulu inbound from Manila in the China Clipper. Following a couple of beers at the Hawaiian Hotel, Noonan took him to the airport hangar to view the wrecked Electra, which was being dismantled for shipping to Lockheed at Burbank.

"The Electra looked as if she had been in a fight with a concrete mixer," stated Lodesen. "The wheels were sheared off, the under carriage smashed, the right wing crumpled, the starboard engine mount was bent and both propellers were twisted askew."

In Lodesen's summary of the accident, he made several important comments regarding the ground loop:

> For takeoff and landings, this plane's tail wheel had to be fixed in the fore and aft position. If you forgot to do this, you had a tiger by the tail. It had been raining and ground around the tarmac was soft and somewhat muddy. There was a possibility the Electra's tail wheel could have picked up some mud and was not locked in a straight forward position.

"The airplane's equipment was piled on the hangar floor. I noticed the lack of a life raft," Lodesen reported. "The life raft purportedly was stowed in the plane's tail section." At that point, Noonan explained, "We couldn't carry everything."

If Lodesen was correct and they didn't carry a life raft during that first attempt, maybe they didn't have a raft on board for the second round-the-world effort.

Lodesen proffered an added thought: "The two 550-horsepower

Wrecked Electra following the ground loop accident at Luke Field, Hawaii. Note the crushed starboard engine and bent propeller. (Courtesy A. Coutts)

engines afforded a false sense of security. The plane could not remain aloft on one engine above the standard gross weight of 12,500 pounds, upped for this flight to 16,500 pounds."[14]

Whether Amelia purposely or accidentally ground looped will never be known. It seems hard to believe that she would have risked her life and the lives of the two navigators aboard just to stop the airplane at the last minute. The reality of the Luke Field Crash will never be known.

As a consequence of the spark-laden crash, the Electra's repairs came with a hefty price tag. Amelia and G. P. needed to find the funds so that Amelia could have a second attempt. As it stood, the Putnams and Purdue University were in a small budget deficit for the costs of the original airplane and trip preparation. They had been planning to cover the shortfall by a $5,000 commitment from the *New York Herald Tribune* for rights to the world flight story, to be paid upon completion of the trip. After the Luke Field shenanigan, it looked like the cost of repairs was going to be in the neighborhood of $30,000. Where was the money coming from? G. P. headed back to Purdue with his hat in his hand.

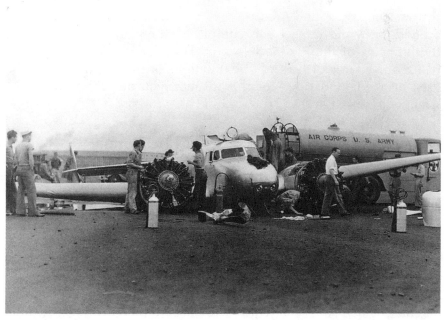

Loading the broken Electra at Luke Field, Hawaii. (Courtesy National Archives)

Putnam attempted to explain to Stanley Meikle of the Purdue Research Foundation: "I am expecting revenue of about $5,000 from stamp covers. An additional $10,000 is forthcoming from Miss Earhart and myself. I believe that between $5,000 and $10,000 additionally will be available from several friends. This will leave a balance to be raised probably not less than $5,000 and not more than $10,000."[15] Putnam actually was anticipating gross revenue from the decorative stamp envelopes of $25,000 from Gimbel's Department Store.

Some of the original contributors stepped in again, and with Putnam and Earhart, scraped together the much-needed funds. The Purdue Research Foundation dug deeper into their coffers, and Amelia and George came through with their $10,000 by borrowing on their Valley Spring Lane home. Amelia was quoted as saying "We are mortgaging the future, but that's what futures are for."[16]

When the steamship transporting the disassembled Electra docked at Burbank, Lockheed engineers and mechanics immediately began analyzing the damage in order to reassemble and rebuild the aircraft. They made stronger landing struts and tested heavier rubber tires. Lockheed employees worked overtime—with no overtime pay—to get their favorite female flier back in the air.

Although the Purdue Research Foundation had come through with the financing, G. P. and Amelia owed them more in return. After the around-the-world project was completed, the plane was to become the property of the Purdue Research Foundation, and any income realized from book royalties or exhibitions of the airplane would be used by the Foundation "for the advancement of pure and applied scientific research in the aeronautics field."[17]

Take Two: A Successful Beginning

Two months after the ground-loop crash in Hawaii, Amelia and navigator Fred Noonan were ready to give the world flight attempt another try. A cross-country flight from Oakland to Miami would serve as the flight test, and the fliers would leave from Miami on June 1, 1937.

In Miami, Pan American Airways mechanics were efficient and helpful. Various adjustments were made to the radio and auto-pilot. One important change concerned the 250 feet of trailing wire antenna, which Amelia discarded because it was too much trouble to let it out and reel it in. She was concerned about the additional weight it placed in the tail section of the aircraft. The entire assembly weighed less than nine pounds and was electronically operated, but Amelia was fanatical about excess weight. She also decided to leave behind her Morse code key, because Harry Manning had shorted a generator fuse by depressing the key too long on the flight to Hawaii. Amelia was overly sensitive about doing likewise. Pan Am technicians recommended putting appropriate crystals in her radio, permitting their stations in the Pacific to track her when she was within range of their radio direction finders. Amelia unhesitatingly rejected that idea.

A curious question is why Fred Noonan, a highly rated former Pan American Airways navigator, agreed—or backed down—with Amelia's decisions on these important communication and navigation matters. The lack of this antenna would make the 500 kcs ship-to-shore calling and receiving frequency virtually unusable, would greatly hinder direction-finding capability, and would further reduce signal strength on the other primary frequencies.[18]

It was still dark on that early morning of June 1, when the great adventure began in Miami. Amelia momentarily delayed take-off in order for mechanic Bo McKneely to make a last-minute repair to a thermocouple lead that registered the cylinder head temperature of the port engine. Amelia and her husband walked into the rear of the hangar. Putnam later wrote, "There in the dim chill we perched briefly on cold steps, her hands in mine. There is very little one says at such times. When Bo called that all was ready, Amelia's eyes were clear with the good light of the adventure that lay before her. But as she walked out to the airplane she seemed to me very small and slim and feminine."[19]

Just before 6:00 a.m., the Electra roared down the Miami runway and took off. The first stop was San Juan, Puerto Rico. Next would be Caripito, Venezuela; Paramaribo, Dutch Guiana (Surinam); and then Fortaleza and Natal, Brazil, before the big hop over the Atlantic. After a nineteen-hundred-mile flight across the South Atlantic, they made it to Africa, landing at Saint-Louis, Senegal.

The next day, Amelia and Noonan flew to Dakar to have the engines inspected. From Dakar, they traveled to Gao, on the upper reaches of the Niger River in French Sudan. From there, they struggled for one thousand miles with the winds and glaring sun over the great, monotonous Sahara Desert to Fort-Lamy in Chad. It was so hot that the plane could not be refueled until after sunset for fear of gasoline igniting on hot metal.[20]

Their next stop was El Fasher, Sudan, before Khartoum on the Nile, and then Massawa, Ethiopia. They arrived on June 14. In two weeks, they had covered fifteen thousand miles.

They next flew along the Red Sea to Assab. With a full load of gasoline, they reached Karachi, Pakistan—a flight of 1,920 miles— in thirteen hours and ten minutes. It was here that Amelia visited the post office to have her special envelope "covers" stamped for a marketing campaign by Gimbel's in New York.

On June 17, Amelia and Noonan flew to Calcutta. After a day of fierce rain and wind, they made it to Rangoon, Burma. Battling defiant monsoons, they finally struggled into Bangkok. "The airport was one of the best we encountered," Amelia noted.[21]

Ever onward they flew, next to Singapore. "From aloft, we saw ships of all kinds from every port. Below us, an aviation miracle of the east, lay the magnificent new nine-million dollar airport, the peer of any in the world . . . From the standpoint of military strategy, Singapore is pre-eminent in the Far East."[22] It is significant that Amelia commented on "military strategy," which should have had no bearing on her many airborne responsibilities on this monumental flight.

From Singapore, Amelia and Fred navigated to Bandoeng, Java, where Royal Dutch Airlines (KLM) mechanics gave the Electra a thorough going-over. Because of pesky problems with some malfunctioning engine gauges, it was five days before they were able to head for Port Darwin, Australia, and from there to the gold-mining community of Lae, New Guinea, which they reached on June 30.

The two fliers had covered some twenty-two thousand miles in their around-the-world quest, which had thus far taken one month. Only seven thousand miles remained. But they both knew that the next leg of their historic journey, an approximate twenty-five hundred miles over the mostly uncharted Pacific Ocean to a tiny speck of land called Howland Island, would be the most dangerous part of all.

Because of the strange nature of her ever-so-brief radio communications, and being unable to locate Howland Island with such a qualified navigator on board, many Earhart aficionados question whether Amelia had anything to do with some kind of spy mission. Those who knew her would have difficulty believing this, because such a purpose did not belong in her personal character and beliefs. She always made it clear that she was a pacifist.

But years after Amelia disappeared, it was learned that at the time the Electra was being repaired following the ground-loop accident, Amelia had two visits from high level Washington dignitaries. Bernard Baruch, adviser to President Roosevelt, and Gen. Oscar Westover, chief of the US Army Air Corps, met privately with her at March Air Force Base in Riverside, California. This information was passed on to Amelia Earhart Society researcher and USAF Maj. Joe Gervais, ret., by Amelia's secretary, Margot DeCarie.[23]

Had these close friends of the President traveled all the way to California just to have tea with Amelia? Or were they asking her to take some liberties with her flight schedule to obtain some badly needed intelligence observations?

Art Kennedy related, "I would have been among those (who might disagree she was a spy) had it not been for what she told me about the aborted take off in Hawaii . . . I think Amelia's 'spy mission' was simply to provide an excuse for the Navy to do their spying."[24]

Nobody will ever know for sure, but Art Kennedy may have been correct in his view on this subject. Amelia may very well have been convinced by the Navy to put down on some island other than Howland and cause the Navy to come and search for her. In doing so they could take their pictures, update their charts, study islands, reefs, channels, and currents, and note what preparations the Japanese had in the Marshalls. Afterward, they would find the missing aviators, and all would live happily ever after. Unfortunately, it did not go exactly to plan.

Part Three: Beyond the Horizon

Chapter 5

KHAQQ Calling *Itasca:*
"We Must Be On You but Cannot See You"

*She was notoriously lazy about learning to use the radio properly
... I remember Paul Mantz telling her that she must be up to speed
on frequencies for daylight and night transmissions. She flippantly
replied that if she couldn't get what she wanted she'd just keep trying
until she got a response. That failure to learn radio procedures may
be significant in light of the apparently frantic transmissions before
she disappeared.*

—Art Kennedy

After twenty hours of flying through daylight haze and then the black
of night, buffeted by heavy wind and driving rain and sighting no
landmarks or navigational aids since the Nauru phosphate lights the
previous evening, Earhart and Noonan still had not found Howland
Island. Both of them must have been frantically thinking about their
need to make a decision and land the plane. The Electra could not
land on water, so their options were very limited.

From our vantage point more than seven decades later, there are
two possible scenarios: either they crashed in the Pacific Ocean and
sank in water about three miles deep, or they managed to land in a
reasonably dry place, where they might have had a chance to survive.
The outcome depended on a decision—presumably Amelia's—
influenced by factors that now can only be surmised or, more
promisingly, gleaned from documentary evidence.

Flight Fatigue

Fatigue and near exhaustion had to be a major complication for
Earhart and Noonan as daylight came before them that fateful
morning. Having successfully flown twenty thousand miles during
the past month through numerous time zones with little rest, they
most likely were hardly aware of just how exhausted they truly were.

The unfamiliar and sometimes unsatisfactory airports and sleeping quarters, let alone the strange foods offered to them by well-wishers, had to have taken a toll on their mental and physical strengths.

The extent of a pilot's weariness in flight varies from the pilot's physical fitness and energy level as well as the monotony of the flight itself. Fatigue might manifest as an absolute, physical exhaustion or as impaired judgment—neither consequence very helpful for flying an airplane. Considering the size of the cockpit (four feet, six inches wide, four feet, six inches deep, and four feet, eight inches high) into which Earhart folded her five-foot, eight-inch frame, the incessant vibration and deafening roar of the engines, and the never-ending assault of fuel fumes, we can only marvel at Earhart and Noonan's ability to have made it as far as they did. Communication was exhausting, both with each other and to the ground.

The modern airline industry claims that its rules limit the hours a pilot can work in a given day, but it is often up to the pilots themselves to determine whether they are too tired to fly. Many of them feel that they can take the risk of overworking themselves, hoping they can pull off an above-par flight. Of course, commercial airlines generally have copilots to share the load. In Amelia's day, the larger planes carried a radioman and a navigator. Amelia, the sole pilot, had only Fred's assistance.

Fuel

Earhart enthusiasts have religiously debated Amelia's fuel capacity when she was documented as saying, "Gas is running low." This was part of her transmission logged at 0742: "KHAQQ CALLING ITASCA. WE MUST BE ON YOU BUT CANNOT SEE YOU. GAS IS RUNNING LOW. BEEN UNABLE TO REACH YOU BY RADIO. WE ARE FLYING AT 1000 FEET."

This quote was recorded in Radio Log No. 2, maintained by Leo Bellarts and Bill Galten. It is very clear that Amelia reported that her gas gauge was pointing toward low. However, at 7:40 a.m., there is a notation in radio log No. 1, originated apparently by third-class radioman Thomas O'Hare: "EARHART NOW SAYS RUNNING OUT OF GAS, ONLY HALF HOUR LEFT, CAN'T HEAR US AT ALL—WE HEAR HER AND ARE SENDING ON 3105 AND 500 SAME TIME CONSTANTLY, AND LISTENING ON HER FREQUENCY." Where did that ominous detail originate? If Amelia and Fred really had only thirty minutes of gas left, they were in big trouble.

Could the newspaper reporters who came aboard *Itasca* in Honolulu, Hanzlik and Carey, have had anything to do with this "30 minutes" reference? They and others were listening to the radio room speakers and could hear the incoming communication. Could they have inserted their own interpretation of "low fuel" to achieve a more dramatic editorial effect in their daily radio reports submitted to their home newspapers?

On the Coast Guard cutter, men maintained two radio logs. The copy of radio log No. 1 indicates that the "30 minutes" reference came from that station, which was monitoring *Itasca's* other basic ship and shore communications.

O'Hare assumed the radio watch at 1:59 a.m. on July 2. He staffed that position throughout the early morning hours until relieved by Bill Galten at 10:35 a.m. This was about the time that *Itasca* took off to search for the plane, believed to be down in the water. Galten appears to have been the primary radio watch stander at station No. 2 during the time frame in which most of the action occurred between Earhart and *Itasca*. He relieved Chief Bellarts at 7:19 a.m. and held his post until 10:35 a.m. Bellarts rotated in from the ship's direction finder on the bridge to the radio room. The No. 2 log indicated that Bellarts tuned up a transmitter in preparation to communicate with the San Francisco Coast Guard (call sign NCM) at 8:42 a.m. This was about the time of Amelia's last transmission from 8:43 a.m. to 8:44 a.m.

Earhart's schedule for contacting the Coast Guard ship was fifteen minutes before and after the hour. Why did the chief radioman tune up the T-16 transmitter to call NMC at that particular time? At the very least, his action raises the question whether the *Itasca* radio crew was aware of Amelia's radio call schedule or if they knew something about Amelia's intended disappearance.[1]

From this information, we must interpret that O'Hare, on Radio Station No. 1, was diverted from his ship's watch at this particular time just when communications between the cutter and the airplane became more frantic. (Bellarts had turned on the speakers in the radio room so that bystanders could hear.) The record about the level of gasoline has to be attributed to O'Hare, because it does not show up in Galten's log No. 2, the primary log recording the plane's messages with the cutter. The gas note is the No. 2 log record. There is no further comment made about low fuel. KHAQQ continued to send fragmentary transmissions by voice for approximately an hour after Amelia's comment. She never again referred to being out of gas or made any kind of mayday call or plea for help, according to either of these radio logs.

When flying an airplane, fuel planning becomes a virtual sixth sense. Certainly, a careful navigator such as Fred Noonan would have known exactly how much fuel they had left. A pilot must know what his or her fuel reserve is at all times and have contingency plans for changes in weather, such as clouds or fog, that might reduce his or her chances of putting the plane down. Of course, the situation that confronted Amelia and Noonan offered no alternatives. Other than Howland Island, there were no pit stops or places to land. If they couldn't find Howland, their only chance for safety and rescue would have been an isolated island beach where they would have had a fighting chance to make a wheels-down landing—except that there were no nearby islands.

Noonan and Amelia both were involved in fueling the Electra. All tanks in the aircraft were totally full except for the special 100-octane tank reserved for takeoffs. This tank was between forty and fifty percent full upon leaving Lae, according to Jim Collopy, who also oversaw the fueling there and regretted that there was no additional 100-octane available. The Electra had 1,100 US gallons of 87-octane gasoline on board, which was all the plane could carry.[2] At takeoff, the Electra was truly a flying gas tank, weighing more than fifteen thousand pounds.

Wind, Weight, and Stars

The US Coast Guard and the Navy satisfied themselves with detailed reports stating unequivocally that the Electra ran out of fuel while attempting to locate Howland Island and came down somewhere to the northwest of Howland. Given the documented data available at the time, nothing seemed wrong with this estimate. Earhart and Noonan had struggled against extremely difficult headwinds that they had not anticipated (26 mph eastern winds for almost half of the flight versus an expected 15 mph winds). Their aircraft was overweight with its heaviest fuel load. The weight strain, coupled with the serious headwinds, slowed their ground speed more than they ever previously had experienced on long flights.

Noonan's initial estimate of flight time from Lae to Howland was an optimistic eighteen hours. With extreme headwinds slowing the Electra's speed and heavy cumulus clouds at twenty thousand feet limiting most visibility, their best hope was for an early morning sun line and a direction finding bearing from *Itasca*.

With his expertise, it may have been possible for Fred Noonan to have gotten a star sight that long, dark, squally night. US Navy Capt. Ernest W. Humphrey, ret., was assistant navigator on the aircraft carrier *Lexington* during the 1937 search for the Earhart plane. In 1971, he told Earhart researcher Paul Van Dyke that, according to his information, Noonan "reported a poor fix was obtained through a hole in the weather at midnight." Humphrey guessed this meant accuracy within thirty miles.

Kelly Johnson, former senior officer of Lockheed, stated that "The Electra was equipped with oxygen which would allow flight to about 24,000-25,000 feet altitude for at least several hours. This would be at gross weight with about half the fuel. It could not attain this altitude with more than that amount on board." With the benefit of oxygen aboard, it could have been possible for Amelia to have climbed through the heavy cumulus cloud cover for Fred and get a shot at a star.[3]

Charts and the Pacific

To further complicate their navigation, the actual geographic position of Howland Island in the Pacific Ocean was miscalculated by about five nautical miles on the charts of that era. The island's actual geographic position had just recently been reported about a longitude of 5' east of its original measurement. This new and corrected location had been determined by a previous visit by the Coast Guard cutter *Itasca* eleven months earlier. Whether navigator Fred Noonan had received this information in time to correct his own chart is unknown. No charts have been recovered showing the course plotted for this final flight. However, the charts used for the westward flight attempt, only two months before, show the earlier uncorrected coordinates for the islands.[4]

Today, the Coast Guard issues *Notice to Mariners* on a frequent basis, allowing seafarers to have access to the most updated nautical information and to make corrections on their own charts. However, it takes the US Hydrographic Office and other map makers much longer to print new charts with new data. This position problem relating to Howland's location should not have affected Noonan's navigation very much. With good visibility in the Howland area and light winds at 8 mph on the morning of July 2, he or Amelia should have been able to spot either Baker or Howland Islands on their approach. The *Itasca* had been "blowing smoke" since first light to assist the pilots in seeing the ship. Unfortunately, with hardly any breeze, the dark smoke just hung along the surface of the sea instead of rising in the sky.

In his interview with Van Dyke, Captain Humphrey also stated, "Noonan reported he got an excellent fix at 4:45 a.m. flying at 12,000 feet." The navy captain interpreted this to mean accuracy within three to five miles. The position was not reported, but Humphrey made a determination of within sixty miles by star deduction—that is, by knowing which star could be used for a fix from a given position. Captain Humphrey also said that "Noonan reported a course change to 090. They would fly that course until intersecting the Howland sun line at a reported speed of 120 knots." Upon intersecting the sun line, they would follow it to Howland.

> Voice transmissions reporting letdown from 12,000 feet were heard. Between 6:42 and 7:42 a.m., a descent to 10,000 feet was accomplished. This was erroneously copied by Itasca as 1,000 feet.
>   Humphrey indicated he immediately recognized the discrepancy. The message was corrected to read 10,000 feet. Finally, in error, changed again to read 1,000 feet when the final report was reviewed by a non-flying desk jockey at 14th Naval District.[5]

Humphrey also stated that KHAQQ transmitted on various frequencies day and night, both MCW (Morse code, with Noonan's key) and voice. He said the calls were received by *Ontario, Itasca,* and Frank Cipriani, who was staffing the Howland radio direction finder.[6]

Paul Van Dyke indicated that Captain Humphrey placed great stock in the accuracy of Cipriani's estimate that Amelia was thirty-five to forty-five miles northwest of Howland at her last transmission. This statement from Captain Humphrey is especially interesting, since Cipriani's batteries were almost totally discharged at that point of Earhart's flight. His log indicated that he was unable to get any kind of accurate fix on Amelia's last transmission.

Captain Humphrey told Van Dyke that he had come upon some critical information about the Earhart flight while serving at the Naval War College in Newport, Rhode Island. The retired captain didn't elaborate because details were still under wraps, as they could potentially snuff out some careers. Humphrey threw out a few more tidbits without qualifying the sources, such as:

> Amelia and Noonan faced headwinds of 20 knots shortly after takeoff from New Guinea, and these winds averaged 22 knots for the first seven hours of flight. [Noonan] knew they were under heavy cloud cover at sunset. Later, they flew into an equatorial front with heavy rains from 8 to 12 p.m. Instead of the expected tail wind during the last half of the flight, they actually encountered a 7 knot crosswind (southeasterly).[7]

Humphrey also commented that Noonan took several drift sights before 8 p.m. and knew that he was being set to the north.[8]

Humphrey's final comment was that "KHAQQ's last transmission consisted of a keyed microphone and a woman's scream." Humphrey believed emphatically that this was the moment when the Electra splashed into the ocean.

Humphrey's boss, Adm. Felix Stump, was the navigator aboard the USS *Lexington* during the Earhart search. The Admiral told author Fred Goerner, "If there was anything unusual about the Earhart flight, no one he knew of aboard the *Lexington* was aware of it." However, notes taken during Van Dyke's interview with Humphrey stated that Admiral Stump gave some papers to Captain Humphrey relating to Amelia saying, "Here, keep these. They will come in handy some day."

Could these papers possibly have had anything to do with another piece of information that Fred Goerner gleaned, namely that Laurance Frye Safford, OP-20-G Naval Intelligence Communications, also was on board the aircraft carrier during the search for Earhart and Noonan? Safford could have been monitoring a special emergency telegraph system that a classified State Department file mentions as having been installed in the Electra at Port Darwin, Australia.[9]

Frederick J. Hooven, inventor of an early radio-compass, commented to Goerner,

> The several references to a wavering note and to a frequency slightly above 3105 does support the emergency transmitter idea, since I think it very unlikely that the plane's 50-watt transmitter would put out such a note.
>
> You could ordinarily not obtain a null on frequencies higher than the 200-1430 range using a loop antenna. At night, the upper frequency limit is much lower than 1430, except for short ranges. With a loop receiver (which Amelia had) there is simply no minimum to be had, it just doesn't work at all. Amelia's ignorance of this fundamental limitation of radio navigation is clearly the reason why she was lost. . . . It seems to me that Amelia was using the same receiver for communication as for Direction Finding. The reason she didn't hear very much of what they said to her was she used the DF loop all the time, instead of switching to an appropriate antenna for the high frequency communication signals. The loop simply would not tune to the higher frequencies, and it is not a very good receiving antenna even when it is set on maximum instead of near the null point. The reason Amelia couldn't get a null on this HF was not only owing to the poor directional characteristics of loops at high frequencies, or the vagaries of HF waves in general, it was because her loop wouldn't tune to the HF signals. It didn't even function as a loop on those frequencies.[10]

Before Amelia attempted her world flight, Hooven had installed one of the first prototypes of an aircraft radio direction finder in her Lockheed at Purdue University's airport. This device was later removed because one of the key sponsors of the aircraft, William Bendix, convinced Amelia that his high frequency model direction finder would give her greater signal range. It later became apparent that the Navy was very interested in testing this high-frequency equipment, as the Radio Research Company of Washington, DC, was a division of Bendix that manufactured standard navy aircraft direction finders.[11]

Quite naturally, Hooven was upset that Bendix had outmaneuvered him. His views on the consequences for the Earhart flight were clear:

> Installed in her plane in place of my more modern equipment was an old fashioned null type DF. My instrument would have given her a heading on the transmitter of the cutter *Itasca* at Howland Island even under poor reception conditions. It would have shown her without ambiguity that her destination was still ahead. My DF used a conventional antenna in addition to the directional loop. This made it possible to listen to the station at the same time a bearing was being taken. It was so much more sensitive that it was possible to use a much smaller loop. Most importantly, by using the signal from the non-directional antenna as a point of reference, the modern instrument is able to indicate the true direction of the distant transmitter. The null type indicator could do no more than tell that the transmitting station was somewhere along the line that passed through the center of the loop antenna. To obtain a useable null with the old system the signal must be several times louder than the background noise. With my system (known as a radio-compass) a useable bearing may be taken on a station that is not readable through the noise. All of these things combine to convince me that Miss Earhart would have reached Howland Island if my radio compass had still been in her plane.[12]

Lockheed aircraft executive and design engineer Clarence L. "Kelly" Johnson spent considerable time indoctrinating Amelia on flying the Electra 10E. He stated that the all-out range of her airplane with the extra fuel tanks carrying 1,150 US gallons was 4,500 miles with an average wind speed of zero. "Miss Earhart should have had ample fuel to fly at least 1,500 miles more than the distance to Howland Island."[13]

Fuel consumption tests on the normal model 10E burned an average of 56 gallons per hour at a maximum gross weight of 10,500 pounds at a speed of 188 mph at 5,000 feet. Amelia's airplane exceeded the normal gross weight when fully loaded by more than 50 percent. On a long flight, Amelia's Electra would not have achieved the average fuel burn rate until well over halfway, when much of the fuel overload had been burned. She would not have been able to reach her objective of an average 150 mph cruising speed until late in the flight because of the initial weight overload coupled with the adverse head winds. These facts of the flight stretched Noonan's anticipated eighteen hours of flying time to closer to twenty hours.

If they didn't know this before leaving Lae, they certainly would have figured out the flying-time facts after encountering the heavy weather as they made their way eastward.

Lae radio operator Harry Balfour was in hourly contact throughout the daylight hours. He most likely forwarded the weather forecast from Pearl Harbor, which he received just as the Electra was taking off. "It is inconceivable that they would have ventured forth with just a half-hour or so of extra fuel. By almost any measure, this would be too slim a margin between success and complete disaster."[14]

Kelly Johnson worked with Amelia in flying different weight loads, balance conditions, power settings, and varying altitudes. He showed her how to use the Cambridge Analyzer to assay exhaust gas, permitting adjustment of mixture controls to lean engine fuel for maximum miles per gallon. He felt that Amelia was well versed in this technique. He coached her in practicing takeoffs with heavy fuel loads and wrote procedures covering the best possible takeoff technique. "I flew with Miss Earhart and trained her in the use of various items of equipment to obtain maximum range with the model 10E. I wrote her specific directions on how to get the most out of the Electra. Amelia was a very careful pilot and followed instructions precisely."[15]

"It has been implied that Amelia may have been a poor pilot," stated Johnson. "She was a good one when I knew her. She was very sensible, very studious, and paid attention to what she was told."[16]

At the time they reached the Nukumanu Islands in late afternoon, they had a definite position fix and knew the weather conditions ahead. This would have been the point in their flight to consider whether to continue or to turn back. Under adverse conditions in other flight segments, Amelia had turned back, so that decision was not something she was hesitant to make. After the disappearance, Fred Noonan's wife, Mary Bea, mentioned that Fred had told her he would turn back if he had any trepidations.[17]

Capt. Almon A. Gray was one of the notable radio operators of his day, and he flew with Fred Noonan on several occasions. In terms of what happened to Amelia and Fred, he thought the following.

> I envisage that Earhart was homing with the DF in a general westerly direction on the signals from the broadcast radio station at Jaluit. Her gas tanks were virtually empty. She sighted land close to her track and made an emergency landing. Beyond reasonable doubt the land was in the Marshall Islands. The landing was made about mid-afternoon of July 2, 1937, Howland time. The radio equipment in the aircraft was started up later in the afternoon and was used intermittently for at least three days without molestation. Many radio listeners at numerous sites reported hearing distress signals from the plane but were not taken seriously. (In retrospect I believe that most of them were genuine.) The quality of the transmissions was very poor and virtually no useful information was passed in all that time. However, the peculiar characteristics which made the transmitted voice signals unintelligible were unique and served to identify the signals as coming from the Earhart plane whenever they were heard.
>
> With what I have here plus what I consider as very good bearings from the PAA Adcock RDFs at Wake and Midway, I feel quite comfortable in believing that Earhart landed in the Marshalls. The homing track to the Jaluit Radio Station makes me believe that the most likely locale would be the very northern part of Mili Atoll.[17]

Bill Prymak, former president of the Amelia Earhart Society of Researchers, spent time with Capt. Al Gray in 1993. Captain Gray told Bill that he had flown in several flights over the pacific with Fred Noonan when they were employed by Pan American Airways. Gray was the radio operator and Noonan was navigator. "Many times Fred would monitor the radio when I needed a break," he told Prymak.

> His Morse was pretty good, 15-16 words a minute. Fred also liked to dial in on the 50-thousand watt high powered radio station on Jaluit. Station JRX began operating in 1928. It was the first Japanese transmitter in the Marshall Islands. The station generally was operational from early morning to well into the evening. They listened to its music, but more importantly Fred would get a direction finding fix on its transmission. Then he would take an intersecting fix on Wake Island to check his navigation.[18]

With this solid information from Captain Gray, it is highly likely that Noonan, probably in the heavy cloud cover that existed north of Howland, would naturally do what he did best. Knowing about where he was and exactly how much fuel remained in the Electra yet still unable to spot Howland Island, he and Amelia would pursue

Plan B. He would home in on Jaluit Radio, setting a course in that direction in order to bring the sight of dry land to their weary eyes— if they had enough fuel to hold out.

Gene Vidal, former head of the Bureau of Air Commerce, was a good friend of Amelia's. He helped her with foreign airport selections, long-range fuel planning, and many other preparations for her world flight attempt.

> We discussed her route and studied maps. She always sat on the floor with friends, so maps were all over the rugs. Her only worry on the entire world flight was not to miss Howland, a very small island in the southwest Pacific. From Lae, New Guinea, to Howland is about 2,500 miles. During the flight she would cross the Gilbert Islands, a chain running some 1,500 miles perpendicular to her course. This chain is about 2,000 miles east of Lae, or 500 miles west of Howland.
>
> We know she passed the Gilbert Islands since messages indicated she was near Howland, working back and forth, north and south, trying to find Howland. The radio compass, a homing device, was new and apparently not properly receiving the transmissions from the *Itasca*. Her plan had been to hunt for Howland until she had some four hours of gas left. If she had not located it by that time she planned to return to the Gilbert Islands, which she felt she could not miss, and land on a beach.
>
> She finally radioed her gas was running low at the time when she should have had four hours remaining. So one can assume she then turned back and landed on one of the Gilbert Island beaches as planned.
>
> Mantz claims she did not run out of gas, because she was a very thorough, capable person and planned in great detail all flights, taking into consideration all alternatives. She must have turned back to the Gilberts when she had about four hours of gas remaining as she had planned to do, and landed on a beach.[19]

Plan B

When Amelia called *Itasca* and gave her line of position at 8:44 a.m. Howland time, she and Noonan had been flying for twenty hours and fourteen minutes. An hour earlier, they knew they had accomplished their dead reckoning objective for distance flown when Amelia said to *Itasca*, "WE MUST BE ON YOU BUT CANNOT SEE YOU." They then spent an hour of precious time flying up and down the course determined by Noonan's early morning sun line, 157° to the southeast, and then 337° toward the northwest.

At that time, they certainly could have calculated that they had only 149 gallons of fuel left based on Kelly Johnson's fuel burn rate chart. This would translate to 3.92 flying hours remaining at 38 gallons per hour. When considering the unknown quantity of 100-octane left in the takeoff tank, this amount of remaining flying time agrees almost precisely with the Plan B alternative that she related to Gene Vidal. Her plan B was to turn and retrace her flight path "back to the Gilberts" when she was down to four hours of gasoline.

The British had established several radio stations in the Gilberts on Beru, Tarawa, and Butaritari. One must wonder why no contact was made with officials there for radio checks or a possible emergency landing plan. There also is the question as to why Amelia and Noonan did not delay their Lae departure time to enable them to over fly the Gilberts—a pivotal checkpoint—during daylight hours.

Of course, these considerations are based on the assumption that Amelia did, in fact, have 149 gallons remaining. Kelly Johnson's fuel burn rate calculations included a range of a twenty-five percent margin assuming zero wind conditions. After the first leg of her original efforts, from Oakland to Honolulu, Earhart had reported, "We arrived at Hawaii with more than four hours supply of gasoline remaining, which would have given us over 600 miles of additional flying, a satisfactory safety margin." However, that estimate did not necessarily apply to the reverse journey.

As a responsible pilot, Amelia was conscientious about her fuel usage and the precautions she needed to take on her journey: "We are throttled down to 120 indicated air speed so not to arrive in darkness. We are burning less than 20 gallons of gas at 10,000 feet."

As an afterthought, she added, "The element of speed is far from uppermost in such a flight as this. It can't be. Quite truly, I'm in no hurry . . . As for this present venture, I just want to progress as safely and sanely as day to day conditions make possible . . . and with good fortune get back with plane and pilot all in one piece."[20]

In his book, Elgen Long admirably discussed fuel usage and navigation technology of that day and time. He spent years studying the details of Amelia's final flight, committing themselves to the theory that Amelia and Noonan exhausted their fuel supply while searching for Howland Island and crashed into the Pacific Ocean just after her last radio message at 8:44 a.m.

A professional pilot with forty thousand hours of flying time, much of it over open ocean, Elgen's fuel consumption and time estimations certainly should be considered. But his theory is only based on the

Itasca radio log entry about low fuel levels. If this really were the actual scenario, Amelia and her navigator were in deeper trouble than anyone could have thought, both in terms of her flight and her piloting estimations and decisions.

Both Lockheed's Kelly Johnson and Amelia's friend Gene Vidal confirmed that she was a careful planner and endeavored to consider every possible aspect of flight time and potential logistical difficulties. It was Vidal who related, after the disappearance, that Amelia planned to turn and head back to the Gilberts if they had not located their safe haven at Howland when they were down to four hours of remaining fuel. Certainly, her navigator Fred Noonan would have endorsed this plan.

I believe that Amelia's half-hour warning was her reference to implementing Plan B and turning around. A fine navigator such as Noonan would never have agreed to a planned fuel burn rate to coincide with their anticipated arrival time at Howland. That would have been equivalent to planned suicide.

Long-distance flights such as the one Earhart and Noonan were attempting are host to a range of difficulties and scenarios, so having a sufficient reserve of gasoline is paramount. Fuel tanks have been known to leak, but there was no indication there was a problem of this type. Excess fuel was definitely burned in climbing to the ten thousand-foot altitude she reported by radio to Harry Balfour, who was monitoring her flight from Lae. In light of the training she had received from Kelly Johnson and the experts at Lockheed, together with the relentless fuel management coaching from Paul Mantz, Amelia's "fuel is running low" comment did not necessarily mean she had only a half-hour left. While much has been made over the thirty minute notation in *Itasca* radio log No. 1, Amelia never gave any further mention to this subject. There was never any indication that she sincerely was running out of gas.

The likelihood that Vidal did help develop—and thus was aware of—Amelia's Plan B, is further indicated in the following note to President Roosevelt from his personal assistant, Marvin McIntyre, dated July 29, 1937: "Gene Vidal has been in very close touch with the Earhart story, talking several times a day to her husband, Mr. Putnam. He has some very interesting sidelights and some speculations, which are probably true, as to what actually happened. You might find it interesting to spend 15 minutes with him." FDR scribbled on McIntyre's memo, "Mac, I would like to see him for 5 or 10 minutes."

According to the President's calendar, Gene Vidal and Pres.

July 26

file

THE WHITE HOUSE
WASHINGTON

7/20/37

MEMORANDUM FOR   THE PRESIDENT

Gene Vidal has been in very close touch
with the Earhart story, talking several times
a day to her husband, Mr. Putnam. #

He has some very interesting sidelights
and some speculations, which are probably true,
as to what actually happened. You might find
it interesting to spend 15 minutes with him,

P.P.F.
960

M. H. M.

*I would like to
see him for 5 or
10 minutes*

*will be back
July 26*

Memo to FDR, including his request to speak with Gene Vidal. (Courtesy
Franklin D. Roosevelt Library)

Franklin D. Roosevelt discussed the fate of Amelia Earhart on July
26, 1937, from 10:45 a.m. to 11:00 a.m.[21]

There is no known recorded documentation reflecting the
conversation that morning in the White House. FDR didn't like to keep
notes, and he urged his top advisers not to as well. It is likely that Vidal
conveyed to the President exactly what Amelia told him she would
do if she were unable to locate Howland Island. The Gilberts lie 450-
500 miles from Howland, just beyond the International Date Line.

However, because Amelia and Fred were farther north of Howland than they anticipated, when they turned and headed northwest for the Gilberts, their direction pointed them more toward the Marshall Islands. If Fred Noonan had the Electra following a direction-finder bearing on Jaluit radio as Capt. Almon Gray suggested, the first land they would have found would have been the lower southeastern end of the Marshalls.

Gene Vidal recommended to the President that the search for the missing plane needed to focus on the Gilbert Islands. The ensuing days found the State Department scrambling to obtain the necessary permissions required for entry into those waters. In fact, the Coast Guard cutter *Itasca* already was headed in that direction and arrived before clearance had been received.

Just a few days afterward, on July 30, Secretary of State Cordell Hull telegrammed the American Embassy in London noting that Amelia may have been on the ground and requesting assistance in the search for the missing fliers and aircraft. He also specified a monetary reward for definitive evidence regarding their situation.

This message is written confirmation that at least some of the top people in the Roosevelt hierarchy knew that Amelia Earhart and Fred Noonan did not crash and sink in the Pacific Ocean, as they claim that "Amelia Earhart (Mrs. Putnam) was on land." The telegram lends further credence and subsequent legitimacy to the faint KHAQQ radio carrier waves and SOS calls intercepted during the first few days after the disappearance as originating with Earhart and/or Noonan. It also endorses the Pan American Airways DF bearings obtained from Wake, Midway, and Makapuu Point, Hawaii.

Even before this, Lieutenant Johnson, a Coast Guard communications officer at Fort Funston, told the *Oakland Tribune,* "We picked up signals from the plane on Friday night, Saturday and Sunday—three days running. There is no questioning their authenticity. As the plane could not broadcast even carrier signals from the water, they must have originated from land."[22]

Despite evidence that the Electra did not fall from the sky and sink in the Pacific, many well-placed people in aviation, the military, and government advanced the opinion that it did.

Stewart A. Saunders, former airport manager for Pan American Airlines at Midway Island, was a close friend of Fred Noonan. On the evening of July 2, 1937, he was having dinner with Pan Am chief pilot, Ed Musick, who had just arrived from Honolulu. A messenger from COMPAC Cable Relay Station brought Musick a request to

TELEGRAM SENT

LMS   GRAY

                                       July 30, 1937

                                       7 p. m.

AMEMBASSY

    LONDON (ENGLAND).

    328.

    Evidence which to many sources seems positive indicates
that Amelia Earhart (Mrs. Putnam) was on land the two nights
following her disappearance. In the circumstances we should
appreciate your getting in touch with the Colonial Office
or other appropriate authority and telling them: (1) that
if the authorities could send a boat from the Gilbert Islands
to continue a thorough surface search in those Islands Mr.
Putnam would be glad to defray the expenses involved, and
(2) that word might be circulated that there is a reward
of $2,000 offered for any evidence leading to a solution
of her disappearance whether in the nature of wreckage or
more positive indication of what happened.

                                       HULL
                                       (SW)

EU:PM:A   SD

*Telegram sent from Cordell Hull, Secretary of State, to the American
Embassy of London.* (Courtesy Franklin D. Roosevelt Library)

re-open his radio operation immediately and comment on the following
message: "Get Ingram to open up your radio." Ingram had succeeded Fred
Noonan as chief navigator at Pan Am. Saunders said that Musick's boss
at Honolulu had cabled: "WHAT DOES INGRAM MAKE OF THIS MESSAGE
FROM FRED NOONAN? EARLY MORNING SUN LINE . . . — . . . REPEAT . . . — .
. . 80 MILES SE HOWLAND . . . 30 MINUTES GAS . . . NOONAN."

Saunders couldn't remember the coordinates given in the Noonan
message, but it was likely the 157°-337° pattern that KHAQQ
gave to *Itasca* in Amelia's last broadcast. This wire does, however,
confirm that Noonan did get a sun line, and if in fact they were, at

that moment, eighty miles southeast of Howland, they had initially chosen to run down the 157° course to try and find the island. This probably took a half-hour. Shortly, they would have turned and run on 337°. They obviously had overshot their destination and would attempt to correct when they turned northwesterly. This also explains the approximate one hour of no calls to *Itasca* from 7:42 a.m. to 8:43 a.m. Noonan was busy trying to reach a Pan Am operator to let his former friends and associates know of his plight. Saunders and Musick considered this bearing and its reciprocal and plotted the position on a chart. It did correlate with Amelia's last words—they were running on a line of 157°-337°.

Saunders believed that Amelia ran out of fuel and crashed in the Pacific while trying to locate Howland Island. "They probably didn't even have time to deploy their life raft," he told Leo Bellarts, *Itasca* chief radioman, in a letter written in 1968.[23]

Another hypothesis of the destiny of Earhart and Noonan came from the letter of Lt. Cdr. Frank T. Kenner, former skipper of *Itasca,* who was on board for this cruise as a watch-standing passenger to assist Cdr. Warner Thompson in his first voyage on the cutter. Upon the unsuccessful conclusion of the search for the missing fliers, *Itasca* returned to Honolulu. In port, Kenner wrote his sister, Eve, an important letter:

> It was some cruise to say the least. In spite of the tragic events that took place it was filled with interesting moments. I did enjoy getting back in the South Pacific with the old *Itasca* crowd. Our cruise lasted 36 days and we cruised nearly 9,000 miles.
>
> As to Amelia losing herself, she had only herself to blame. We all admired her nerve and pluck to attempt such a flight, but we cannot admire her good sense and judgment in her conduct of it. She was too sure of herself, and too casual. She devoted no effort to the details at all. When it was too late and she was going down she hollered for our aid but that was too late. We did all we could. She never gave us any of her positions as we repeatedly requested of her. She never answered or acknowledged any of our messages. She gave us no information as to her plans. What plans she had for communications she changed in the middle of the flight. All in all it was a mess.
>
> I heard her last broadcasts myself. She realized too late that she was in trouble, then she went to pieces. Her voice plainly indicated that fact, by the desperate note in her transmissions. She asked us to do the impossible, knowing ahead of time that we could not furnish her with the services she wanted. She clearly indicated throughout the flight that she was not familiar with her radio equipment. If she had only answered our messages earlier in the flight we might have had

some idea where to look for her, and might have been able to save her.

It would take hours to write the whole story. Some day I'll tell it all to you for it is interesting. There is so much that we had to assume, that we really cannot find all the answers . . ."[24]

Leo Bellarts, aboard *Itasca* on that historic voyage, ended a letter of his own in a similar manner: "Considering the increase in her signal strength from her first to last transmission there leaves no doubt in my mind that she now rests peacefully on the bottom of the sea, no farther than 100 miles from Howland. If you could have heard the last transmission, the frantic note and near hysteria in her voice, you also would be convinced of her fate."[25]

Several of the Coast Guardsmen, as well as Captain Humphrey, assistant navigator on the *Lexington,* refer to a frantic voice, even a scream, during Amelia's last transmission. However, the official Coast Guard radio log does not give any indication of "hysteria in her voice," as cited later by Bellarts. Were the *Itasca* radio operators so busy copying pertinent data from the ever-so-rapid voice transmissions that they missed this detail? Or was it later deleted for Coast Guard editorial purposes? In studying the log of radio station No. 2 (covering transmissions between the plane and the ship) around 8:45 a.m. after Amelia's last statement of her location, there was a gap of twenty-one minutes in the log with no meaningful copy other than *Itasca* calling the Electra. From 8:47 a.m. to 9:08 a.m., there were just the most basic log entries, such as: "KHAQQ FROM NRUI, ANSWER ON 3105 KCS. . . . UNANSWERED . . . GO AHEAD WITH YOUR POSITION ON 3105 OR 500 . . . UNANSWERED . . ."

These extremely important twenty-one minutes were filled with useless garble. If there was hysteria in Amelia's transmission as Chief Bellarts and other authorities have noted, this most likely would have been the time for it to have been logged. The fact that it was not logged does raise the question whether *Itasca*'s radio log was modified or rewritten beyond standard smoothing or whether the hysteria in her voice was added by the media for emotional reactions. Bellarts did state that some of the log information was written later when time permitted. Bellarts's personal hand-written log did not reflect anything remarkable in Earhart's tone of conversation, other than that her last three transmissions were very loud and clear.

Charles Hill also raised several questions about the accuracy of the *Itasca* radio log and the actual time certain transmission copy was recorded. He inferred that "an attempt was made to 'reconstruct' the

David Bellarts (left), *son of chief radioman Leo Bellarts, with author Dave Horner at the 2006 Amelia Earhart Festival.*

transmissions after the fact." Hill also said that from 8:55 a.m. to 9:07 a.m., "all of this final transmission was left out of, or expunged from, the official records. There was a long broadcast series from Amelia between 8:55 a.m. and 8:56 a.m. and between 9:07 a.m. and 9:08 a.m., with a clearly disturbing content and little pertinent data."

Dr. David J. Zaugg, medical officer of the Merchant Marine Hospital in San Francisco, was on *Itasca* to service the Coast Guard men and colonists and to be of assistance if needed when Earhart and Noonan arrived. He later reported, "She was flying right into the rising sun. She might not have seen Howland at all. The Coast Guard cutter Itasca began putting out a big cloud of black smoke to help her see the island. We started picking her up quite clearly on our radio. But the difficulty was she persisted in using her voice when we needed Morse dots and dashes to triangulate her position. I think she just went into the drink."[26]

Donald B. Beery, executive officer of the battleship *Colorado* (later vice admiral) stated, "The weather was bright and clear during the 10-day search. It is my guess that Miss Earhart ran out of fuel, crashed and drowned."

0245 – first heard plane – unreadable due to static
0345 – AE stated she would listen on hour
         and half hour on 3105 KC.
0453 A E heard – recognized "part cloudy"
0614 A E "wants bearing on 3105 on the hour – will
         whistle in mic")
0615 A E stated "about 200 miles out approximately"
         (now whistling in mic) actually it was
         a high pitched note.
0645 A E " Please take bearing on us and report
         in half hour" – "I will make noise in
         mic (microphone) about 100 miles out"
0742 " we must (be) on you but cannot see you
         but gas is running low been unable to reach
         you by radio – we are flying at 1000 ft."
0758 " We are Circling but cannot hear you go ahead
         on 7500 (KCS) with a long count either now
         or on the skd (schedule) time on 1/2 hour".
         (A E was very loud and clear on this transmission
0803 " We received your signals but unable to get a
         minimum (bearing) please take bearing on us
         and answer 3105 with voice".
0846 " We are on the line 157 337 will repeat message
         this on 6210 – Wait".
         Nothing was heard again on any frequency. AE
         was very loud and clear on these last 3 transmis

Handwritten summary of Itasca radio log by Chief Radioman Leo Bellarts.
(Courtesy David Bellarts)

The aircraft carrier *Lexington* launched all of its sixty-three planes and searched an ocean corridor 800 miles wide by 250 miles long each day. GO (later Rear Adm.) Kenneth M. Hoeffel reported, "I've always believed Miss Earhart and Noonan crashed and drowned. I've never accepted the idea that she might have been captured by the Japanese and executed. As far as her landing on some other island—there just aren't any."

Lockheed executive Clarence L. "Kelly" Johnson was convinced that Amelia was badly disoriented, far north of her proper course. "My computations on her flight time and fuel consumption indicate that she ran out of fuel completely while many miles from Howland Island."[27]

In the Aftermath . . .

While there are many views on what happened to Amelia and Fred, most Navy and Coast Guard personnel are of the opinion that the pair "crashed and sank." But a translation of a Japanese Government telegram dated July 13, 1937, puts some new light on all the theories:

> JULY 13, 1937   11:20 AM
> TO AMBASSADOR YOSHITA, ENGLAND
> FOREIGN MINISTER
> HIROTA
> # 270 (MOST URGENT)
> RE: RESCUE OF THE EARHART PLANE
> THE ADVERTISER HERE REPORTS THAT THEY RECEIVED A LONDON
> INTERNATIONAL NEWS DISPATCH AT 2:00 AM TODAY TO THE EFFECT
> THAT A JAPANESE FISHING BOAT HAD RESCUED THE EARHART PLANE.
> PLEASE VERIFY THIS AND CONFIRM BY RETURN.

Here you have the Japanese Foreign Minister in Tokyo asking his ambassador in London to find out what's going on. Could British intelligence on Beru in the Gilbert Islands have picked up a radio message being transmitted by the Japanese survey ship *Koshu*, which had been dispatched from Ponape to the Marshall Islands to find the Earhart airplane?

The date of the telegram, July 13, is most interesting also. That was the date the *Koshu* arrived at Jabor harbor on the atoll of Jaluit. *Koshu* was a coal-burning vessel of slightly more than two thousand tons. Its captain was a career Imperial Japanese Navy officer named Hanjiro Takagi. Late that afternoon, a coal barge came alongside *Koshu* at Jabor. One of those laboring to load coal that evening was Tamaki Mayazo. Years later, he cemented himself in Earhart history by telling his very simple, direct, and short story to numerous researchers: "The Japanese crew told us we had to hurry with the coal because they had to rush to Mili Atoll to pick up two American fliers who had crashed near there."[28]

The *Koshu* chugged off to Mili. It returned six days later on July 19. Two medics were summoned to the harbor and rowed out to the anchored vessel. One of them later said that seated on the main deck in the waist of the ship were two white people, a man and a woman. The woman was pale and tired but unhurt. The man had a cut on his forehead above his right eye. There was a deeper wound above his right knee which was infected.[29]

Chapter 6

The Howland Direction Finder

The Portable High-Frequency Direction Finder

One or two things should never be published as long as anyone on the Itasca remains alive.

—Leo Bellarts[1]

Itasca Cdr. Warner Thompson began his official report on the Earhart disappearance as follows: "This report has been made confidential due to the fact that it contains a large number of personal messages and that it further discusses, frankly, certain matters which might be considered as controversial . . ."

The Coast Guard commander's use of the word "controversial" apparently applied only to his opinion of Amelia's radio behavior: "Viewed from the fact that Miss Earhart's flight was largely dependent upon radio communication, her attitude toward arrangements was most casual, to say the least."

Leo Bellarts remarked in a 1973 interview, "Thompson was just a little bit more than disgusted with Amelia."[2]

Commander Thompson's report "Earhart Flight," dated July 29, 1937, raised more questions than it answered. After reviewing the 8:40 a.m. entry of Amelia's last transmission "of being on the line 157°-337° and running north and south, no reference point given, reception excellent," Thompson then reported, "0900, signaled shore party to return to ship as by this time fears were felt that the Earhart plane had probably landed wide of the island."

In only twenty minutes, the *Itasca* commander determined that the plane was down after just reporting that reception was excellent. Next, he said, "Landing party returned at 0912." The fact remains that *Itasca* was drifting on the lee side between a half-mile and a mile offshore of Howland. It seems illogical—impossible, even—that a motorized launch could mobilize, efficiently retrieve personnel, struggle through the breaking surf, and return to its mother ship in twelve minutes.

Next, Thompson added in his report: "As soon as the plane had indicated that it was still aloft at 0843 and possibly on a line which would provide a land fall it was deemed advisable to retain homing position at Howland with the vessel for some time, on the possibility that the plane might still come in. Frank Cipriani, radioman second class, USCG, was left ashore in charge of the high-frequency radio direction apparatus to obtain bearings, if possible, on the plane."

Cipriani already had reported that his batteries were discharged and he was unable to obtain any bearing on the Earhart plane. The "if possible" insertion by Thompson indicates that he was nonetheless attempting to cover all his bases in the case that his report might be reviewed in depth at some future time by his superiors. Thompson's actual report would not be finalized for three weeks, after numerous problems and challenges were dealt with. In all probability, he likely did not know that the portable direction finder operated by Cipriani was a secret, experimental high-frequency unit being tested for Naval Intelligence.

Commander Thompson continued in his report, "The following Department of Interior personnel were left on Howland in excess of normal personnel for the purpose of assisting the plane if, by any chance, it neared the island during the absence of the *Itasca*: Ah Kin Leong; Albert K. Akana, Jr.; William Tavares; Carl Kahalewai and Henry Lau."

Here, again, Thompson follows the same modus operandi: "if, by any chance" is his subtle indication that his report was finalized long after the fact with the unquestioned knowledge that the high-frequency direction finder did not perform. This entire report was structured to place the best possible light on his preparation and performance, although his mission failed to safely assist Amelia in reaching Howland Island. In this situation, he had the benefit of being able to look back on all that happened and to implement the best possible spin on the situation, shifting as much blame to Amelia's implied incompetence.

In an article, John P. Riley Jr., a radio technician of that era, described his correspondence with Yau Fai Lum, the ham operator on Howland at the time of the Earhart flight. Riley reminded Lum that *Itasca*'s communication officer, Ens. W. L. Sutter, had signed off on the radio logs, authenticating their contents. Lum then stated to Riley, "I have never met W. L. Sutter and don't know who he is, so I can't say if he is part of the cover up. But Ah Kin Leong and Henry

Lau were definitely not on Howland with me during the Earhart search. I have a letter from Leong saying he, Lau, and Cipriani were aboard the *Itasca*. I don't remember Akana, and Kahalewai, but Bill Tavares was with me for we went fishing together."[3]

It was this reference to a cover up by the colonist Yau Fai Lum that caught my eye and compelled a more thorough review of *Itasca*'s logs.

Before the search for the Earhart Electra was launched (around half an hour to two hours after its disappearance), the officers and crew of the *Itasca* evaluated their situation:

• Flying conditions within a radius of forty miles of Howland were excellent, with wind on the surface east 8 to 13 mph, unlimited ceiling, and a smooth sea.

• Visibility south and east of Howland was excellent and unlimited as far as could be observed. The sun was rising clear and bright on the island; ship and smokescreen in the glare thereof.

• Visibility north and west of Howland was excellent to the horizon. Beyond the island were banks of heavy cumulus clouds.

• Plane transmissions indicated cloudy and overcast skies over the course of the night and early morning, with dead-reckoned distance accomplished.

• Plane signal strength was high and unchanged during last hour of transmission.

• Stellar navigation possibilities south and east of Howland and close to Howland were excellent that night.

After analyzing the above information, *Itasca* finally proceeded to a designated search area, between forty miles and two hundred miles off of Howland Island and between bearings 337° and 45° true. The shore party was recalled at 9:00 a.m.; the cutter actually departed from its Howland Island position at 10:40 a.m., according to Thompson's report. This would have allowed plenty of time for anyone on shore to make it back to *Itasca*.

Frank Cipriani was one of eleven Coast Guard men assigned to Temporary Additional Duty (TAD) aboard *Itasca* from the Coast Guard cutter *Roger B. Taney*. These men not only supplemented the *Itasca* roster but also reinforced logistical activities on Howland Island. There were several Navy petty officers from Fleet Air Base, Honolulu. Lt. Daniel A. Cooper from the US Army Air Corps at Luke Field, Hawaii, was in charge of three USAAC staff sergeants, one from the Eleventh Photo Section, and two from the Fourth Observation Squadron. Army Capt. A. M. Neilson of the Third Engineers had been at Howland along with Staff Sgt. Joseph Knopping to make sure that the landing strip was ready for Amelia's arrival. There is a question as to who was directly responsible for all of these extras and their assorted duties once they boarded the Coast Guard ship and while the various groups were on Howland Island.

Howard Hanzlik, a young journalist-recruit, was on board *Itasca* representing the United Press, as was James Carey, a University of Hawaii student apprenticing with Associated Press. Albert K. Akana of KBS radio was on *Itasca* with radio tech Henry Lau of the Army Signal Corps, and welcomed aboard his son, Albert Jr., who had been colonist leader on Baker Island since October 26, 1936.[4]

According to the organizational chart issued by the cutter's communications officer, Ens. W. L. Sutter, Cipriani was responsible for the high-frequency direction finder ashore. His orders were "to keep in direct contact with the ship by means of the portable transmitter as to what time and frequency to take bearings, keeping a log as to the time and bearings received from the plane." Unfortunately, there is no date on this directive, but it most likely was written as part of the plan to assist Amelia in reaching Howland. Cipriani was asked to familiarize himself with the operation and calibration of the direction finder prior to the flight. We know he did this, because *Itasca* reported cruising around Howland Island at a ten-mile range and at a twenty-mile range in order to calibrate the portable DF. This particular radioman was the only person who had been trained on this new equipment. According to Richard Black, the agent responsible for the colonization effort, once Cipriani had been selected for this responsibility, Navy radiomen spent several days working with him in Honolulu, training him on this newly developed unit that was presently under testing by Naval Intelligence.

Having set up his new DF station under a tent in the center of Howland Island near the living quarters, Cipriani officially opened his watch and began his documentation at 10:00 p.m. that long night of July 1, 1937, and into the early morning hours of July 2. The first page of his log is dated July 2, 1937, which is ahead by one day.

This first page of the direction-finder log appears standard. Cipriani's original entry stated that he was "STANDING BY TO TAKE BEARINGS ON 3105 KCS ON THE EARHART PLANE." Shortly after midnight (the date read July 3 but should have read July 2) at 12:15 a.m., he logged, "WEAK FONE ON 3105 (I AM USING A LONG VERTICAL ANTENNA FOR RECEPTION OF SIGNALS ONLY) UNABLE TO GET BEARINGS." He noted that *Itasca* was giving weather to KHAQQ on 3105 at 6:30 a.m., 7:00 a.m., and 7:15 a.m. Then, at

1. This organization will be followed at all times while Amelia Earhart's plane is in the air.

BELLARTS CRM -- Handle all plane communications, and log the same. Keep all interested parties informed of the position of the plane and all pertinent data connected with the flight, (the Commanding Officer and the Officer of the Deck, the latter will plot the plane positions) In the event of a casualty in either take-off or landing make proper steps to assure the Itasca, handles all imformation relative to the casualty, and allow no other station to assume responsibilities of communications or dissemination of imformation, if necessary use the proper transmitter to block out any superfluous transmission from any unauthorized sources. Prepare a message for action to Headquarters, imformation to Com fran Div and ComHawsec giving the extent of the casualty and requesting action to be taken , this message to go in Code A.

CIPRIANTI Man high frequency direction finder ashore, keeping in direct contact with the ship by means of the portable transmitter as to what time, and on what frequency to take bearings, keep a log as to the time and bearing received from the plane. Familiarize self withoperation and calibration of direction finder previous to flight.

O'HARE Take over watch and handle all incoming and outgoing messages to NPU, NPM and NMC in such a manner as not to interfere with plane traffic. Keep Swan, Ontario, Com Fourteen, ComFan Div and ComHawsec informed.

GALTEN When plane comes within a 1000 miles of Howland Island Man the ship's direction finder and listen in on five hundred k.c. for the plane and when it is heard take a bearing record same with the proper time in a suitable log.

THOMPSON Relief operator, ~~also send out all homing in signals on the frequency as requested by the plane.~~

W. L. SUTTER

Lt. W. L. Sutter's organization of radio personnel with instructions. (Courtesy National Archives) that very same time, his log reflected, "PICKED UP EARHART USING LONG ANTENNA S-3 HARDLY ANY CARRIER, SHE IS OVER MODULATED, SWITCHED OVER TO LOOP FOR BEARING, S1 TO 0. SHE STOPPED TRANSMISSION, BEARING NIL." This should have been stated as "S-0 to 1," meaning weaker than S-1 or barely discernible. Radioman Paul Rafford Jr. said that the signal pickup on a loop is almost 100 times weaker than a long antenna.

At 7:35 a.m., Cipriani's log entry read, "(AM USING THE D/F AND RECEIVING SET SPARINGLY DUE TO HEAVY DRAINAGE ON BATTERIES. THE BATTERIES ARE OF LOW AMP HOUR CAPACITY) EARHART ON THE AIR, S-4, 'GIVE ME A BEARING.' EARHART DID NOT TEST FOR BEARING." This means that she did not provide a series of Morse Code dashes or a long count to give the receiving operator enough time to obtain a minimum, or null, which would provide a bearing. "HER TRANSMISSION TOO SHORT FOR BEARING, STATIC X5, HER CARRIER IS COMPLETELY MODULATED. COULD NOT GET A BEARING DUE TO ABOVE REASONS."

For the next hour, Cipriani noted that *Itasca* was sending *A* to KHAQQ as well as calling on "fone." This comment could confirm that *Itasca*'s constant stream of *a*'s were blocking Amelia's incoming calls to the Coast Guard ship.

At 8:45 a.m., his entry reads "BATTERIES WEAK." At 8:59 a.m., "VOICE ON 3105. CAME IN AT END OF TRANSMISSION." This is probably when Amelia was stating her line of position, 157°-337°. Cipriani apparently picked up the end of her message, but, because of the low battery problem, he couldn't get a bearing. Also, his logged time of 8:59 a.m. is sixteen minutes after the *Itasca* log, which recorded 8:43 a.m. for the 157°-337° course headings that Amelia pursued. Regardless, this was Amelia's last message.

At 9:26 a.m. his log stated, "RECEIVED INFORMATION THAT ITASCA BELIEVES EARHART DOWN. LANDING PARTY RECALLED BACK TO VESSEL." Then, at 10:00 a.m., his log indicated, "ALL BATTERIES ON THE ISLAND ARE DISCHARGED. COMMENCED TO CHARGE THEM." There is no other entry for this entire day, or the next one, July 3, other than "charging batteries."

He must have been part of the landing party. According to his log, Cipriani had been on duty all night. Nobody afloat or ashore knew the precise time they might expect to see the arrival of the Electra and its tired crew.

The log entry for the next day continued to show an incorrect date: "4 July 1937." "CHARGING BATTERIES ALL DAY." It ended with a typed signature: "F. CIPRIANI RM2C."

This is the first insinuation of something gone awry. It could not have reasonably taken two days to bring the batteries back to a reasonable charge. Look again at the 9:26 a.m. time noted by Cipriani, indicating the landing party was, or had been, recalled. The Coast Guard Commander's report showed that the landing party was recalled at 9:00 a.m. and all personnel were back aboard at 9:12 a.m. In addition, this log entry was typed after the fact. Cipriani had no typewriter with him on Howland. It provides the first indication that Cipriani did not stay on the island but went back aboard *Itasca* before it sailed off to the search area. With his special watch over and the landing party recalled, there would have been nothing else for him to do but return to the ship, especially as he had been on duty since 10:00 p.m. the previous evening. Cipriani had done the best he could with the test equipment he had been given. Amelia was believed down. His job was over.

USAAC First Lt. Daniel A. Cooper documented his recollections of the Howland Island happenings the morning of July 2, 1937. His report, typed upon returning to Luke Field, Hawaii, is dated July 27, 1937: "When Amelia Earhart failed to arrive by 0900 all hands except a radio operator and several colonists returned to the ship, and by 1000 started out in search to the north of the island." Was the mentioned radio operator Frank Cipriani? Or, since the operator was mentioned along with "several colonists," was he referring to the Howland colonist amateur radio operator, Yau Fai Lum?

Earhart researcher and radio technician John Riley communicated with Yau Fai Lum before Lum's death. In a letter dated June 2, 1995, Riley reminded Lum that Commander Thompson stated in his report that he left Cipriani on Howland on July 2, 1937, and picked him up on July 18, to which Lum responded: "Cipriani was not on Howland but aboard *Itasca* during the Earhart search." Lum also provided Riley with a note from colonist Ah Kin Leong confirming this.

Riley had made the assumption, based on Lieutenant Cooper's comment, that the radio operator who remained on the island with the colonists was Cipriani. Again, Lum corrected him: "I was the only radio operator of K6GNW—no one else. I had schedules with Itasca once a day, usually between 5:00 p.m. and 9:00 p.m. I am not trained, experienced, have the equipment, antenna, or know-how to do DF work."

Lieutenant Cooper's report most likely implied that it was Lum, the colonist ham operator, who remained on the island along with his other colonist volunteers, instead of Cipriani. Both Lum and colonist Ah Kin Leong were emphatic that Cipriani did not remain on Howland but returned to the ship.

This whole affair of the Howland DF log didn't get messy until Yau Fai Lum claimed years later that Cipriani did not stay on the island during the Earhart search. All of this surfaced in the early 1990s, when Lum told Earhart researcher and author Paul Rafford and John Riley, both contemporary radio experts, that he had never even met Cipriani.

Rafford was stunned. "Never met Cipriani? According to the log of *Itasca* you were on that flyspeck of an island for over two weeks with him. How could you possibly not have met him in all of that time?"

Lum responded directly and to the point. Cipriani was only on Howland Island the evening before and early morning of Earhart's anticipated arrival.

> He was quite busy with that portable direction finder device which none of us knew how to operate. I didn't want to bother him. Around ten o'clock the morning of the airplane's disappearance, the Coast Guard took Cipriani aboard the ship and headed off to search for the missing plane.
>
> Two other Hawaiians who had been on the ship and who had come ashore early that morning were Henry Lau, who was in the Army Signal Corps, and Ah Kin Leong, a colonist who had served on Baker and was destined for service on Jarvis Island after the Earhart flight to Howland. Both of those men were taken back aboard the cutter. That's why I said I had not met Cipriani. I never got to talk with him because he was not on the island very long. No watches were manned because there was no one available to operate the specialized direction finding equipment.[5]

Rafford continued his questions of Lum: "There are daily direction finding reports written until the search was over. Your name is there, along with Cipriani's, Leong, and Lau. You all stood DF watches. Your name is right there in black and white! How can you deny this?"

Lum illustrated this disparity with one immeasurable comment: "If I signed or typed the log, how could I misspell my own name? *Yat* instead of *Yau*. Our names as well as our call signs are typed, not signed by us. It is a counterfeit!"

In researching the background of the DF log and the names associated with it, one discrepancy jumped right out. Whoever prepared this "counterfeit," as Lum described it, definitely was careless in choosing the name of "Yat" Lum, instead of "Yau" Lum, for the hypothetical watch list, which obviously was prepared after the fact. Whoever did this must have been on the Coast Guard ship, because he didn't know the names of the colonists. In typing the name of "Lum," he consistently typed the name of the wrong one. He also continued using the wrong date. Cipriani made the original mistake of dating the first day of his log on July 2 instead of the correct date of July 1. One would think that if there were three others sharing watch-standing duties, sooner or later someone would know the correct date. The date discrepancy was noticed and adjusted in the log on July 5.

Paul Yat Lum (call sign K6INF) was the name of another Kamehameha colonist, but he was not on Howland at the time. He had served three months on Howland Island from October 26, 1936, to January 27, 1937, before being transferred to Baker Island. He was listed as being on Baker at the time of the Earhart flight. It is easy, then, to visualize how someone who did not know the individuals could look at previous watch lists and pick the wrong one to fill the void.

There were several other Lums serving as colonists as well. Kenneth Lum-King served on Howland from November 16, 1937, to March 23, 1938. Harold C. Lum served three months on Jarvis Island from October 22, 1936, to January 18, 1937. So, for a person to clandestinely attempt to re-create a log from July 3 to July 18—a log that had not been maintained in the first place—it is easy to see how the "ghost" writer could have inserted the wrong Lum into the illusory record, especially if he did not know personally the individual supposedly involved in the watch that wasn't staffed.

In defending himself, Yau Fai Lum stated, "Our names and call letters could easily be obtained from Richard Black, our boss, who had a complete file on us. Not only was I never introduced to Cipriani, I was never asked to stand a radio watch on the Earhart frequency on his radio or on mine."[6]

This is an almost unbelievable development. The *Itasca* report from Commander Thompson placed Ah Kin Leong and Henry Lau ashore on Howland Island in order to assist Cipriani staff the high-frequency DF. But Lum asserted, "That is a false report, full of --."

John Riley questioned Lum in a 1994 letter: "You say Henry Lau and Ah Kin Leong, who were supposed to be watch standers, were not even on the island at that time. I have researched this point very carefully and according to the official report of Commander Thompson of the *Itasca*, these two men were left on Howland Island for 16 days while that ship was at sea looking for Amelia. I attach pages from his report. Comments?"

Yau Fai Lum. (Courtesy Paul Rafford Jr.)

Lum responded: "This letter from Ah Kin Leong proves that I am right and Captain Thompson's report is not accurate. If we were watch standers we would have spoken to Cipriani at least 16 times when we changed shifts in monitoring Earhart. This never happened. I have never seen the Coast Guard radio equipment nor did Cipriani come over to look at my equipment. I stand by my previous statement. The radio report is false."

Still incredulous over Lum's comments, Riley asked, "Isn't it possible that your memory is playing tricks on you? It would not be surprising. We are talking about events that took place 57 years ago."

Lum handled the question with honest clarity. "Things that happened more than half a century ago are hard to remember, but what I do remember I tell you the truth as I recall them. As to your research on official reports in the national archives, it turns out too many of them are not true. I think they are written to make a certain person look good, or to gain publicity at the expense of others. How a person can make such wild statements without concrete proof is beyond me. I like to tell the truth, the whole truth and nothing but the truth. So what I tell you is the truth to the best of my memory."

Who won this debate? Both Paul Rafford and John Riley said that they cast their vote on the side of the colonists. "They have no ax to grind," said Riley. "I put my trust in Lum and Leong, both of whom maintain the log was cooked. Leong says he has no idea who wrote the false log. He confirmed he stood no radio watches on Howland Island."[7]

Leong continued, "Cipriani, Henry Lau and me [sic] were on the Coast Guard cutter *Itasca* when it left Howland Island looking for Earhart."[8]

Certainly, one of the most significant factors to be considered in judging whether the cover up of the Howland direction-finder log is fact or fiction is the knowledge that both Yau Fai Lum and Ah Kin Leong confirmed the same story. Each of these men made the same statements. If only one of them had made the accusation, it would have been a different situation. However, both have made their denunciations and carried them to their graves. That two witnesses believe that the log was falsified is not conclusive, but it certainly is persuasive in light of other reported irregularities.

Henry Lau was listed on the *Itasca*'s roster as a radio technician to assist Albert Akana, head of KBS Radio, Honolulu. Henry also had some experience with Morse code, as he was in the Army Reserve Signal Corps. Yau Fai Lum was a friend of Lau's and told Rafford that Lau had been working at his father's grocery in Honolulu just before being invited to participate in the cruise to Howland. Lau later advanced in the Signal Corps to become a lieutenant colonel. Early in the morning of July 2, Lau and USAAC Lt. Daniel Cooper were on the island with Cipriani, awaiting Amelia's arrival.

Yau Fai Lum certified to Paul Rafford that, when word came that Earhart was overdue and the landing party was recalled, "Henry Lau, Ah Kin Leong, Frank Cipriani, and Lieutenant Daniel Cooper hightailed it back to *Itasca*."[9]

Paul Rafford often spoke about the makeup of the Howland DF log and the colonists' accounts of whether or not Cipriani remained on Howland when others had gone back to the Coast Guard ship. Paul, always the gentleman, reminded me to put myself in the position of those young colonists in their late teens or early twenties. It was a privilege to be selected for this duty. They were paid three dollars per day and had no expenses. It was a great way for them to go down in history and save some money, too. Each of these young men had been selected because of his integrity and excellent high school reports. These were some of Hawaii's outstanding former Kamehameha students. It is Rafford's view that "their strong character traits would not allow them to fabricate untrue stories."

Rafford corresponded personally with Yau Fai Lum for some years before Lum died. He considered him a friend. "Lum was a quiet, scholarly type. He tended to be on the shy side, but I always believed he was straight and truthful. He went on to become a captain with the Honolulu police. I have absolutely no reason to doubt him or question his veracity. The real question is, why would someone on *Itasca* go to the trouble of creating such a massive deception?"

Perhaps a deception was not planned originally. Maybe it later became a necessity in an attempt to protect certain officers aboard *Itasca* and government intelligentsia. After those SOS messages were heard, the world began to believe that Amelia and Noonan did not crash and sink. At the time, everyone hoped that the downed fliers could be found and rescued. The radio message that excited everyone was received at 2:42 a.m. on July 5, 1937. The Coast Guard Hawaiian Section sent word to *Itasca* that Naval Radio Station Wailupe had intercepted the following message: "281 NORTH HOWLAND CALL KHAQQ BEYOND NORTH . . . DON'T HOLD WITH US MUCH LONGER . . . ABOVE WATER SHUT OFF . . ." This message was confirmed by three different navy radiomen as coming from the downed Electra with its identifying call letters, KHAQQ. *Itasca* was ordered to proceed to that area and continue its search.

Paul Rafford is emphatic that his old friend, Yau Fai Lum, would not lie about his memory of the events. Rafford related, "I asked Lum why, after some fifty years had passed, did you wait so long to describe this cover up. Why have you never mentioned this to me before?" Again, Rafford was shocked by Lum's response: "Nobody ever asked."

Rafford very plainly stated that there was no reason whatsoever for Lum to create some fictional story about the *Itasca* radio logs being bogus. If anyone had asked him earlier, Lum would have said the exact same thing. Someone aboard the Coast Guard ship created that Howland DF log to cover up the fact that there wasn't one. Rafford was convinced: "Lum swears by it. I believe him. End of story."

Obvious peculiarities surface in the most cursory review of that direction-finder log. First of all, the date Cipriani entered as July 2 was wrong when he opened his station at 10:00 p.m. on July 1. The ensuing dates of the log were not corrected for five days. If all the various watch standers, including Lum—who swore he never stood a DF watch because he didn't know DF and was busy with his own station—had signed their names at the end of their watches, then why didn't they pick up on the wrong date? And, as Lum so vividly pointed out, why would he have continually misspelled his own name?

The reason is obvious. The person who created the log and forged the various names of the supposed watch standers didn't know the Lum boys and picked the wrong one, who was actually on Baker Island at the time.

Another mistake was that Ah Kin Leong had been serving on Baker. When he was replaced in that position by Paul Yat Lum, he was picked up by *Itasca* for delivery to an assignment on Jarvis and was to be taken to that station after the arrival of the Earhart flight. This was to take place when *Itasca* returned to Honolulu. Under these circumstances, Leong certainly could have been asked to supplement the Howland crew while *Itasca* searched for the missing airplane. Yet Leong also stated unequivocally that he stood no watches on Howland Island and that he was on the Coast Guard ship. Why would these two outstanding young men, who volunteered for many months of extraordinary service for the US Department of the Interior, even think about fabricating such a far-reaching falsehood?

The answer is simple: they didn't.

Lt. Daniel Cooper had helped Department of the Interior agent Richard Black obtain the portable high-frequency DF unit and bring it aboard the *Itasca*. The lieutenant was an interested observer, but he certainly wasn't going to remain on Howland Island if his ship—including a warm bunk and ample chow line—was leaving.

When *Itasca* took off to try and rescue the Earhart plane, which Commander Thompson and all on board fully believed had crashed at sea, cranking up that portable high-frequency DF was the last thing on anybody's mind. Their purpose on Howland Island was over. Regardless of what the *Itasca*'s skipper later stated in his report, no orders or instructions for any of the TAD personnel can be located telling them to stay after Amelia failed to land there.

If it is true that the Howland DF log was rigged (and that certainly seems to be the case), who might have been involved in the scheme? Paul Rafford compared the typewriter imprint and reported that it was the same type style as indicated on logs typed from the *Itasca* radio room typewriter. He told me that he had compared the type of Cipriani's log with the type style of other radio logs on *Itasca*. Although identifying the same font is not proof that it was the same typewriter, it certainly provides some clues. It most likely was the only typewriter used to record the DF log, supposedly maintained by Cipriani, just as it was used to record the other *Itasca* radio logs—there was only one typewriter for the entire radio crew. Several *Itasca* radio operators made it clear years later that they had no use for Cipriani in their radio room. Thus, someone within the *Itasca* radio crew must have typed this log after the fact. Rafford added, "Judging from the erasures, smudges, and other marks on the original, it was worked over several times."

When the landing party was recalled to return to *Itasca* in order to find the downed Earhart airplane, deck log entries for July 2, 1937, reflected no documentation as to who returned to the ship that morning from Howland Island when the so-called shore party was summoned. The only reference that exists to indicate whether Cipriani or others stayed ashore with the three colonists—William Kaina, Joseph Anakalea, and Yau Fai Lum—is Commander Thompson's final report, dated July 29, 1937, completed and filed five days after *Itasca*'s return to Hawaii.

Based on the deck log of July 18, when Commander Thompson was in a hurry to depart Howland and head for Honolulu after all the trials of an unsuccessful search, our questionable radio DF operators appeared to leave the island and board the ship at that time—that is, of course, according to the deck log, kept separately from the other radio logs.

The Flip Side of the Coin

David Bellarts, son of the chief radioman aboard *Itasca,* Leo G. Bellarts, said that his father believed that Cipriani did remain on the island with the high-frequency DF equipment until the search was over: "[Cipriani] was not familiar with the Itasca radio room as were the other radio operators, and none of the Itasca radio crew knew how to operate his portable rig."[10]

Chief Bellarts told Earhart author Elgen Long that it was in his recollection that Cipriani spent almost three weeks on Howland Island. Bellarts also told Long that he had a chance to inspect the portable high-frequency DF when the Coast Guard ship returned to Howland after the failed search. The Coast Guard chief radioman was critical of the portable high-frequency DF, saying it came from the Navy but "it was good for nothing."

I took a look at the contraption upon returning from the search. While the receiver wasn't heavy and one man could handle it, the rig depended on a dry storage battery and Cipriani had allowed that to run down during the early morning hours. When the crucial time arrived with Earhart nearby, the battery was almost totally discharged. The unit had a small loop of 12-15 inches diameter, but there were no slip rings or stops. If you turned it the loop would rotate all the way around. Consequently all the wiring was completely twisted. Although Cipriani reported getting some brief bearings on Amelia's frequency I don't think he really did. That DF was an inoperative piece of junk.[11]

Richard Black was in charge of the colonization program. He maintained files on the young colonists, consisting of biographical data, special skills (such as meteorology or amateur radio status and call signs), and other personal information. He took his job seriously and it is doubtful that he would get involved in any chicanery. In fact, he almost refused to bring the portable high-frequency DF unit to Howland Island, and he told Fred Goerner so:

Miss Earhart had specifically stated she did not wish any assistance from shore or any RDF equipment on the ground at the island, but that *she* would home on 3105 and 6210 kcs transmissions from *Itasca*. She even specified the times for the ship to transmit on those frequencies, on the hour and half-hour. She knew of course that the ship (and all ships) are equipped with radio loops on the shipboard emergency frequency of 500 kcs. It is therefore all the more un-understandable that she is reported to have lightened her plane at Miami by leaving behind the trailing antenna and reel which would have allowed her to transmit on 500 kcs. After some hesitation (because of Amelia's instructions) I agreed to take the portable RDF set.[12]

This comment from Black confirms that Amelia had aboard her plane a high-frequency radio direction finder; otherwise, she would not have been able to home on 3105 or 6210 kcs. Regrettably, *Itasca*'s sending dots and dashes on 500 kcs was virtually useless, because Amelia had detached her trailing antenna in Miami. This trailing antenna was not required for receiving short-range airborne bearings on 500, but it was needed in order to transmit on 500, so that *Itasca* could, in turn, take bearings on the plane. In retrospect, if Amelia had been within fifty miles of *Itasca*, even without the trailing antenna, all she had to do was hold down the telegraph key and *Itasca* would likely have picked up her signal on 3105 kcs. Although Amelia supposedly had also left a telegraph key in Miami along with the trailing antenna, Alan Vagg, Bulolo radio operator, communicated earlier with Noonan by code, so there must have been another key on board.

I asked Paul Rafford about the question of the Howland Island DF log. He agreed that many comments in the Howland log are questionable. But he explained that most watch standing was at night. The mysterious radio signals that were heard after Amelia disappeared were picked up on night radio watches—the best time to receive radio signals. "However," he said, "at midnight it would be nearly impossible to get a DF bearing from a distance much more than 50 miles from a downed airplane's modulated signal if there was no antenna."

At this point I asked, "Paul, I understand your theory, but you were with Pan Am for a number of years. Don't you have confidence in those DF bearings obtained by the stations on Wake and Midway Islands with their extremely tall antennas? Remember those curious carrier waves, or at least the overtone of them, reported by the Pan Am operators?"

Rafford responded:

You're right, Pan Am had those huge antennas, and their Adcock DF systems were better than anything the US Government had. And sometimes you can have the benefit at night from what we call "skip." But at midnight you cannot get a steady bearing on 3105 kcs with a loop DF more than just a few miles away. The antenna is the key. In Amelia's case, a trailing antenna would have radiated 95% of the power supplied to it. My guess is that it was also equally convenient for the ghost writer of that Howland log to fantasize over a signal strength of S-3, which the log indicates did not last very long and is the "reason" Cipriani could get only a very general bearing. At least that's what the Howland log reports.

And think about this. Bill Galten, one of the radiomen on watch that day on *Itasca* later came to work for Pan Am when I was there. He told me, "Paul, that woman never planned to land on Howland Island." Whether this comment makes any sense or not, I don't know.[13]

A key factor that makes the Howland DF log suspect is suggested by a radio message sent late in the evening of July 4, 1937, at 10:12 p.m. from *Itasca* to Yau Fai Lum on Howland Island. This message was instigated by several earlier reports of hearing "a rough carrier wave to the northwest but bearings difficult." The message asked Lum if he heard it and if he could get a bearing.

At 2216 Lum responded: "YES. HEARD EARHART CALL ITASCA AND BAKER HEARD EARHART PLANE AT QSA 4 LAST NITE AT 8:20 PM." Lum further stated that he couldn't get a bearing because he was using his antenna to transmit to *Itasca*. The Coast Guard ship comes back to Lum on Howland:

> THIS VERY IMPORTANT. MR BAKER SAYS HONOLULU APPARENTLY GETTING EARHART SIGNALS. HE WANTS HOWLAND TO KEEP LOOP IN USE ESPECIALLY AT NITE. USE CHINESE OPERATORS UNDER YOUR CONTROL. KEEP BAKER ALSO ON ALERT AS TO PLANE DATA AND REPORT TO ITASCA THROUGH HOWLAND.
>
> KEEP LOG. CAPTAIN EXPECTS RESULTS. HAVE YOU BEEN CALLING US ON 3105? RECEIVED OK. NO. HAVE BEEN CALLING YOU ON 24. WE'VE BEEN HEARING CARRIER ON 3105. A MAN'S VOICE FROM 2137 TO 2153. MAKE SCHEDULE WITH US EVERY 4 HOURS STARTING MIDNIGHT. WHAT IS YOUR TIME? NW 2323. NEXT SCHEDULE AT 1 AM YOUR TIME. USE INTERIOR'S BATTERIES IF NECESSARY. MR BLACK SEZ CIPRIANI IS IN CONTROL AND TO KEEP CONTINOUS WATCH ON 3105 AND TAKE BEARINGS.
>
> USE CHINESE OPERATORS HR. IF YOU HAVE TROUBLE HAVING BOYS STAND WATCHES MR BLACK SEZ TELL JIMMY. BAKER HEARD PLANE CALLING NRUI [*ITASCA*] TONITE. GET DIRECTION FINDER IN OPERATION.

Now, if Cipriani was on board *Itasca* and not on the island, there would not have been anybody standing by the Howland DF. And, likewise, the radio room on the Coast Guard ship was most likely distracted and frenetic. The wording of several segments of this message revealed all the cards:

"KEEP LOG. CAPTAIN EXPECTS RESULTS." In this phrase, the executive officer pulled rank to emphasize the necessity of getting a bearing on Amelia's signals. In that moment, it was do or die. The men needed positive results.

"MR BLACK SEZ CIPRIANI IS IN CONTROL." Had Cipriani been on Howland Island, the Coast Guard ship would not have communicated directly with the colonist ham operator. Any message from the radio room of *Itasca* would have been directed to RM2 Cipriani, care of his call letters, NRUI2, the same ones as Itasca but with the number on the end. If signal strength was in question and the Coast Guard ship had to go through the Howland ham to reach Cipriani, any message sent through K6GNW would have stated "FOR NRUI2." Furthermore, there is no question of whether Cipriani would have been in control because none of the colonists knew how to operate the DF. His name was simply being mentioned in the message to imply that he was *supposed* to have been on the island.

"TAKE BEARINGS" and "USE CHINESE OPERATORS HR." The abbreviation "HR" stands for "here." That little slip triggers another clue. The message should have said "there." The radioman who created the wire, and perhaps sent it, momentarily forgot where he was—and that he was creating a message of subterfuge.[14]

"IF YOU HAVE TROUBLE HAVING BOYS STAND WATCHES MR BLACK SEZ TO TELL JIMMY." Jimmy was the popular original Howland colonist leader, James Kamakaiwi Jr. He was to have been relieved by William Kaina and return to Honolulu aboard *Itasca* after having served two years on Howland Island. Obviously, the Kamehameha colonists were going to have difficulty standing watches if Cipriani wasn't there. None of them knew anything about direction finders. What this sentence is implying is that Richard Black knew good and well that none of the colonists had any experience with direction finding and there was going to be trouble getting them to do any meaningful watch standing.

"GET DIRECTION FINDER IN OPERATION." This final order to Howland's hapless colonists virtually confirms that certain *Itasca* officers were now aware of the likelihood that no Howland DF watches were being staffed, because Cipriani was aboard the ship. With SOS calls and mysterious signals now being received by responsible radio stations, including Naval Radio at Wailupe along with authentic Pan American direction-finder bearings being relayed to the Coast Guard and Navy, somebody absolutely had to come through with a positive DF bearing.

Less than an hour after that message was sent, the ghost of Frank Cipriani, RM2 extraordinaire, entered the scene. The log entry immediately reflected: "July 5, 0001, RECEIVED ORDERS FROM ITASCA TO MAINTAIN WATCH ON 3105 AND OBTAIN BEARING ON KHAQQ."

These were Cipriani's orders for the past five days. He originally opened his log with this similar statement. Why was he repeating himself? Because Cipriani didn't write this! The creative ghost writer continued with the Cipriani DF log: "TO OBTAIN BEARING UNTIL CHINESE AMATEUR OPERATORS COOPERATE IN MAINTAINING WATCHES . . . WEAK CARRIER ON 3105. NO CALL SIGN GIVEN. UNILATERAL BEARING IMPOSSIBLE DUE TO NIGHT EFFECT. USING SMALL PACKED [POCKET] COMPASS TO DETERMINE RELATIVE DIRECTION. BEARING ONLY APPROXIMATE SSE OR NNW."

The wording here is also critical. "TO OBTAIN BEARING UNTIL CHINESE AMATEUR OPERATORS COOPERATE . . ." Clearly, there's evidence of a problem and it's confirmed in this statement. The

Chinese operators didn't know DF so they couldn't—or perhaps wouldn't—stand watches. It was not their fault that Cipriani was not around, and none of them were going to cover for him, even if they could. Next, this is the first indication there was any kind of compass on Howland Island—Cipriani was slick enough to have stashed one in his pocket. That was why anyone writing this log had to state "BEARINGS ONLY APPROXIMATE," because that's all one would get with a pocket compass, whether there really was a compass, and whether or not Cipriani actually was truly present.

There are other miscellaneous comments in the log until 4:15 a.m., when Cipriani was supposedly relieved by Yat Fai Lum (K6GNW). The call sign belongs to Yau Fai Lum, but the name of the watch replacement is "Yat." Paul Yat Lum was on Baker Island, not Howland—and their call signs are completely different. After the first page of this DF log—which seems to have been written by Cipriani due to its clarity—the poorly structured remaining pages, with atrocious spelling and grammatical errors, make the log even more suspect. And, of course, the wrong date continued to be carried forward for the first four days along with the wrong name of Mr. Lum. Every page other than Cipriani's page appeared ragged and pressed for time.

The key question that remains is who completed the log and then forged Cipriani's typed name to the document. The entire episode exposes a poorly planned attempt to test this newly developed equipment with little thought and coordination. Correspondence between Goerner and Black years later relate to friction between Bellarts and Cipriani and Black and Commander Thompson. As the newly designated skipper of the *Itasca,* Thompson resented Black, at the time a Department of the Interior representative, bringing aboard his ship the portable Direction Finding equipment with no previous notification by the Navy or any other authority, and then having the gall to utilize an *Itasca* gun battery to power it. The situation obviously escalated when it turned out that the gun battery had lacked charging and was virtually impotent at the very time Amelia was approaching loud and clear and requesting contact by the portable, high-frequency equipment.

Did chief radioman Leo Bellarts have anything to do with the doctoring of *Itasca*'s radio logs? He certainly acted very quickly in making certain he had personal control of the originals. "The original radio log I have in my possession and there it stays," he told author Fred Goerner years later. "Honestly, I thought there was going to be an investigation of the flight and that is the reason I have kept certain logs and papers concerning the flight. There are two or three things that have never been brought to light but they would only tend to degrade certain people and I would rather let them remain buried in my mind."[15] Black attempted to distance himself from the controversy of the failure of the DF system which resulted in *Itasca*'s inability to bring in Amelia to the safety of Howland Island.

In a conversation with David Bellarts, Leo Bellarts's son, he refused to answer the question and let me know that he did not appreciate my second-guessing his father's motives and rationale. It is challenging to comprehend how Coast Guard personnel could take it upon themselves to remove official government documents and take them home "for safe keeping." Bellarts also reported later that certain notes and memos disappeared and O'Hare removed some "souvenirs."

However, the important Coast Guard log records removed by Bellarts finally reached the correct repository. After their father's death, Bellarts's children donated his Coast Guard memorabilia to the National Archives. According to David, the three *Itasca* original log pages of the Earhart Flight are in the Bellarts microfilm section, Records Group 200, National Archives Gift Collection, Leo G. Bellarts. The log pages that were retyped several times in the Coast Guard editing process can be found in Microfilm Publication 272, Amelia Earhart, US Coast Guard Records.[16]

Yau Fai Lum died in Hawaii in 1998. Frank Cipriani was a radio operator on a transport ship and died when that vessel was torpedoed during World War II. Cdr. Warner Thompson died in Ketchikan, Alaska, on September 1, 1939, from a coronary thrombosis. Leo Bellarts's died in 1974 after retiring from the Coast Guard in 1946 as a full lieutenant. Henry Lau is gone, as is Ah Kin Leong. We shall never know every inch of truth about the Howland DF log, but we will have to make do with the papers that remain.

Black Operations

It is probable that a newly developed high-frequency direction finder had been installed in Amelia's Electra compliments of Vincent L. Bendix. Cam Warren, co-author of *Earhart's Flight into Yesterday,* said: "To me the most important part of the story was the new 'secret' Bendix HF/DF that I am convinced was installed in the Electra in Miami. It covered up to 8000 kcs. The most likely instigators were Vince Bendix and G. P. Putnam, with some probable unofficial help from a Navy VIP. Absolutely such a device existed in 1937. And, absolutely the Navy bought 250 from Bendix."[17]

Vince Bendix had long been a supporter of Amelia. He was one of the original Purdue University contributors to the Earhart "flying laboratory" Research Foundation. It was likely that his charm and confidence led Amelia to believe that this new and magical high-frequency direction finder simply had to be turned on, and it would miraculously and automatically lead her to Howland Island and the safety of the waiting *Itasca*.

Was this why it was so important for the portable high-frequency direction finder to be set up, calibrated, and operational on Howland Island? Richard Black said that it was a backup, and if Amelia knew about it, it was not Black who told her. In any event, that direction finder served no purpose and resulted in a completely mishandled testing mission.

In reviewing correspondence years later, Richard Black continued to distance himself from anything to do with that portable high-frequency direction finder. Did he know something then? Was he running from something later? Capt. August Detzer, OP-20-GX, told Fred Goerner, "Amelia Earhart certainly did know that a high-frequency/direction finder was going to be available to her at Howland Island."[18]

There are indications that Amelia was urged by the Navy and nudged by her key sponsor, Vincent Bendix, to test a high-frequency direction finder on this flight. She most likely had been given a few other informal considerations, such as keeping her eyes open in certain designated locations where US military could not reach and noting runway lengths, weather and radio characteristics, availability of fuel supplies and other equipment, which would be of interest to US military.

A retired US Air Force colonel who was very much interested in intelligence activities looked over some of my research. When I told him of the possibility that Earhart had a high-frequency DF on the Electra and relayed the comments of Captain Detzer, who acknowledged that they were testing the Howland Island portable unit in hopes of improving their technology, he smiled and said, "Dave, this has every indication of 'Black Ops.'"

"Black Operations indicate the likelihood of a parallel Navy program going on with no disclosure to the Coast Guard," he explained. "There was probably some outside Navy direction for the purpose of getting this new and unproven equipment tested. This sort of thing was going on all the time."

Maybe that's what those meetings between Amelia, USAAC

Gen. Oscar Westover, and presidential adviser Bernard Baruch were about. That also could have explained what Amelia's assistant, Margot DeCarie, meant when she told Earhart sleuth Joe Gervais, "From that point on the Navy took over and no more bills came across her desk for payment." Perhaps the Navy did agree to help Amelia, and asked her to do likewise.[19]

Radio tech Cam Warren said, "Amelia thought she had the hot setup to DF into Howland, and didn't think she needed to bother with a backup. She could eliminate all the weight and physical complication of a 500 kcs system, which we unequivocally know she did. It's most likely Bendix et al. quickly swept the whole deal under the rug when Amelia and Fred Noonan disappeared."

This also could have been why Amelia was so cavalier about discarding her trailing antenna and why she turned down Pan Am's offer to track her across the Pacific with their strategically placed long-range direction finders. There do not appear to be any previous instances in her entire flight up to the Howland approach when she utilized her high-frequency direction finder equipment. In a preliminary test at Lae, New Guinea, Amelia attempted to obtain a minimum, but was not able to get an accurate bearing. This was on a known target within short range. Her casual comment was that "the Lae station was too powerful and too close." She let it go at that.

Cam Warren summed it up: "She had such an easy time using DF on her flight from Oakland to Honolulu (thanks to the skill and experience of Captain Harry Manning), she naturally expected that with her 'wizard' Bendix HF Direction Finder she would have absolutely no trouble in finding Howland Island. When the critical moment came, and she attempted to locate the *Itasca* by its 7500 signal, she could well have made some simple mistake, such as forgetting to turn off the Automatic Volume Control on the receiver."[20]

For a novice with little experience in using a high-frequency radio direction finder, it would have been very difficult to manually rotate the Electra's loop antenna, tune the incoming radio signal to a null, or minimum, note the compass bearing . . . and have confidence in the resulting DF bearing. As dog-tired as Amelia surely must have been, with very little experience in tuning a direction finder with no supervision, the effort must have been an ongoing nightmare. The act of manually turning the antenna loop from a handle under the cockpit roof is, in itself, a movement requiring sensitivity and feel, working the radio signal as it becomes louder, softer, and then null.

With the null fading in and out, the signal's precise bearing would have been uncertain and difficult to pinpoint.

Pan American Airways had the most accurate RDF facilities at their Makapuu-Hawaii, Midway, and Wake Island stations. Their Adcock systems utilized "four crossed and balanced dipole antennas" that were aligned with true north. The fact that these very tall antennas were accurately plotted geographically essentially eliminated corrections for magnetic deviation and variation. They were considered accurate for five hundred miles and sometimes twice that distance.[21]

Under the circumstances in which Amelia found herself that hot and nervous July morning, obtaining a DF minimum on *Itasca*'s radio transmissions and having confidence in the resulting bearing would have been a miraculous accomplishment. Such an effort would have taken an experienced radio operator several minutes to tune and home in on a radio transmission in order to obtain a reliable compass bearing. Amelia took this important navigational technique far too casually, as Commander Thompson stated in his report. She never really practiced radio direction finding with any degree of seriousness, and it could have been her undoing.

One also has to wonder what specific job occupied Fred Noonan at this crucial time. The former Pan Am professional navigator must have taken a morning sun line and plotted his course and probable offset to what he thought would bring them to Howland Island. As he had a second-class radio operator's license, he should have been able to assist Amelia if she had required it.

"For the last two hours she was plenty loud," Leo Bellarts told author Elgen Long. "I thought she'd be flying into our rigging at any moment she was so doggone close. We were frantic. We were going nuts."[22]

The number of adjustments made to *Itasca*'s radio log entries the morning of July 2, 1937, as well as to the separate DF log begun by Frank Cipriani monitoring the high-frequency experimental equipment on Howland Island could have been to neutralize the fact that the only high-frequency DF operator, supposedly ashore on Howland, actually was back aboard the Coast Guard ship. There was absolutely no one else on Howland who could have held a watch at that station. Surely, if word ever was passed that *Itasca* had blown its mission to safely bring in Amelia's Electra to the custom-built airfield personally ordered by the president of the United States, a lot of careers would have been ruined.

The records indicate that *Itasca* was not that efficient in dealing with some Earhart requests that came in by radio. In fact, we must question whether Bellarts and his crew of petty officers ever received the Earhart message of June 30, 1937, "Requesting that radio reporting be in English . . . and that she would broadcast at quarter past the hour."

Initially, it does appear that the radiomen all were expecting Morse code signals, as they were unprepared to handle voice contact by Amelia. They also seemed to ignore the "quarter past the hour" timetable, as they were transmitting relentlessly to her, which would have blocked her incoming calls or signals. If this was, in fact, the case, the Coast Guard was derelict in their stand-by radio and direction-finding assistance for Amelia. It could have been the reason for their scramble to complete the blank pages of the DF log.

With obvious tensions between Black, Cipriani, and Commander Thompson at the very start of the unsuccessful search for the missing airplane, one can imagine the stress exemplified several days later when Naval Radio in Hawaii picked up SOS calls on the Electra's radio frequency. The resulting pressure on the Coast Guard to get something done by obtaining a direction-finder bearing on the distress signals supposedly emanating from KHAQQ became the top priority of ensuing days and nights. With Cipriani aboard the *Itasca,* there was no person on Howland who could have handled the important assignment.

Itasca's radio crew observed a surprising calmness from Cipriani during that time, but no one was able to report the strange behavior to Commander Thompson until Cipriani was headed back to the *Taney* as soon as *Itasca*'s gangway touched the Honolulu dock.

Other important points eluded Commander Thompson's search summary report. Both Howland and Baker Island colonist radio operators heard and reported transmissions from the missing plane two days after its disappearance.

Yau Fai Lum reported from Howland, "Earhart called *Itasca* the evening of July 4." The Baker Island operator also reported, "Heard Earhart plane QSA 4 last nite at 8:20 p.m." QSA 4 indicated good readability of 4 out of a possible 5.

No reference to this significant development was made in the report submitted by *Itasca*'s commanding officer. Other than his comment "Amateurs reported several messages, all probably criminally false," the *Itasca* commanding officer dismissed the subject and concluded his report with, "Extremely doubtful that Earhart ever sent signals after 0846, July 2, 1937."

The *Itasca* cruise report of June 4 to July 24, 1937, listed the following personnel left on Howland Island "for the purpose of assisting the plane if, by any chance, it neared the island during the

Frank Cipriani's direction finder radio log. (Courtesy National Archives)

absence of the *Itasca*: Ah Kin Leong, Albert K. Akana, Jr., William Tavares, Carl Kahalewai and Henry Lau."

The next paragraph referred to *Itasca*'s daily activities, such as "Searching throughout the day to the northward of Howland Island and during the night with search lights. Extra lookouts posted etc." However, inserted as the first sentence to this paragraph was the following: "Frank Cipriani, Radioman second class, USCG, was left ashore in charge of high frequency direction apparatus to obtain bearings, if possible, on the plane."

Clearly, this insertion was added after the fact perhaps to reinforce Commander Thompson's excellence in planning. But, because it was an afterthought, the insert was inappropriately placed in the cruising log section and not where it should have been, among the previous list of those temporarily transferred to Howland to assist the plane "if by any chance it neared the island." In fact, Ah Kin Leong said that Cipriani was never on Howland. Leong previously had served on Baker Island but was picked up by *Itasca* on June 25 to be returned to Honolulu.

On July 18, the Cruise Log Report noted *Itasca* back at Howland with the list of colonists temporarily assigned there returning aboard. However, similar to the above insert, this was squeezed in the ship's log reflecting *Itasca's* readiness to sail for Honolulu: "CIPRIANI, FRANK (206-314) RM2, USCG, returned from temporary duty on Howland Island . . . 1100 All stores and personnel on board . . . on course for Honolulu."

The Deck Log Report had an entry a half hour before that of the Cruise Log: "1030, Frank Cipriani (206-314) RM2, returned from temporary duty on Howland Island." This entry is signed by L.H. Hines, Gunner, with the same hand-writing as the other 0800 to 1200 watch entries. However, there is a different pencil being used for this entry. It is much lighter than the earlier entries. The fact that the time of 1030 is again repeated un-necessarily, copied with the use of a different writing instrument, makes one wonder if this is another log entry added after the fact. Further, in reviewing other pages of the log where L. H. Hines was on duty, his hand-writing appeared bolder and photocopies are reproduced darker.

Another interesting detail: on July 24, upon reaching Honolulu and docking at Pier 27, the Cruise Report named all Temporary Duty personnel who were leaving the ship. The list appeared complete except for one person. Frank Cipriani, RM2, was not listed.

In the final analysis, Amelia's lack of preparation, practice, and basic knowledge of the Bendix high-frequency direction-finding equipment proved to be not equal to the task. The resulting confusion suggests that the anticipated radio and navigation link to the heroic undertaking unfortunately was poorly planned and coordinated by all concerned. If there was a mission to secretly test that newly developing radio technology, it failed.

After all of these years, the Coast Guard's Summary Report would have had the world believe that Amelia and Noonan crashed, sank, and drowned at 8:46 a.m. July 2, 1937. However, the reality of the situation is a bit more complicated than that.

Chapter 7

Noonan's Navigation

The US Coast Guard claims that Earhart and her navigator Fred Noonan ran out of fuel while searching for Howland Island and crashed in the Pacific Ocean within forty to fifty miles of the island. If that is truly the case, why have so many experts failed in their search to find any sign of the aircraft on the bottom of the Pacific?

A number of accomplished authors and researchers have spent years studying the few facts available and have provided us with their opinions of the outcome—but in each case, questions arise. There has not appeared one conclusive answer to this perplexing mystery. Some believe there never will be. I believe that the answer is staring us right in the face.

Having examined the circumstances surrounding Amelia's last flight I will now endeavor to provide examples of existing data to confirm the probability that Amelia Earhart and Fred Noonan did not disappear near Howland Island. While some of the testimony originated in hearsay and oral tradition, some evidence was derived from decisive military reports by American intelligence officers prepared in 1944 following the invasion and liberation of the Marshall Islands and Saipan. These reports specifically relate to two American fliers—a man and a woman dressed "like a man"—having been picked up by a Japanese fishing boat seven years earlier. Those reports directly correspond with the oral histories of the Marshall Islanders. In addition, as Amelia's own mother openly discussed, Japanese fishermen picked up Amelia and Fred from somewhere in the Marshall atolls expecting the world to laud them as heroes.[1]

In addition to my own research, Fred Goerner's primary investigation during the early 1960s uncovered a wealth of informative testimony, in particular that of Pacific Fleet Adm. Chester Nimitz. South African Oliver Knaggs, who contributed new witnesses from the Mili Atoll region of the Marshall Islands as well as Saipan, reinforced Goerner's position and knowledge base. Bill Prymak, Joe Gervais, and many other researchers and enthusiasts contributed a wealth of information relating to the fate of Amelia and Fred over the decades since her disappearance. After sifting through the layers of data, it appeared that all roads pointed to an ultimate Saipan disappearance.

This thesis is not an original one, but I feel that the data that I have compiled presents the most conclusive body of literature. One of the first mentions of the Saipan-via-Marshall Islands hypothesis came from Roy Blay, former editor of *Lockheed Horizons,* in his article published in May 1988. "Amelia Earhart's Last Flight" ended with the following paragraph:

> At least one solution to the mystery disappearance, which begins with a crash landing on Mili Atoll in the Marshalls, is plausible, if only barely possible. Backed up by considerable research and eye-witness accounts, it is extremely convincing, enough so to prompt the Marshall Islands to issue a series of stamps commemorating the 50th anniversary of Amelia's flight by portraying on the stamps the principal events in this scenario.

Fred Noonan's Challenges

No experienced pilot or navigator would have taken off on a long distance flight such as that of Lae to Howland without a sufficient reserve of fuel for backup and safety. Navigator Fred Noonan was one of the best in the business. He knew their situation better than Amelia did to a certain extent, as he was responsible for knowing their directions and coordinates. On their long-distance flight from Oakland to Hawaii on their first attempt, they planned a fuel reserve of almost four additional hours, and there was room for more. Noonan would not have allowed anything less from Lae to Howland. In fact, he was completely involved in overseeing the fueling of the plane and was obstinate in obtaining not one, but two, time checks to ensure his chronometer was absolutely precise—an extremely important tool for accuracy in determining latitude and longitude positions from celestial observations. So how, then, did his navigation have them wind up in a vastly different location than planned?

There is no question that Amelia did not have an updated weather report at the time of the Lae takeoff. The velocity of the anticipated easterly headwinds was twice as strong as expected, 25-30 mph instead of 15 mph, which had been forecast the day before. As Amelia and Fred taxied down the airstrip for takeoff to Howland, Lae radio operator Harry Balfour received the following weather report: "FROM

FLEET BASE, PEARL HARBOR: DANGEROUS LOCAL RAIN SQUALLS ABOUT 300 MILES EAST OF LAE AND SCATTERED HEAVY SHOWERS REMAINDER OF ROUTE. WINDS EAST SOUTH EAST ABOUT 25 KNOTS TO ONTARIO THEN EAST NORTHEAST ABOUT 20 KNOTS TO HOWLAND."

The Electra reached this squally area before receiving the weather report, if they ever did receive the report. Balfour claimed to have forwarded weather data to the Electra twice that day but admitted that there was considerable static. Certainly, at the time the fliers encountered this heavy weather, they knew that the stronger headwind would increase their fuel burn rate and affect the aircraft's groundspeed, thus delaying their estimated arrival time at Howland. Also, the ESE wind would encourage a significant northerly drift against the plane's average course of 078° to Howland.

Noonan would have known all of these things, but if he were unable to get a star sight during the early morning hours because of heavy cloud cover, it is likely that the last check he obtained would have been the Nauru Island mining lights at about 10:30 p.m. local time the previous evening, which would have been 10:30 a.m. GCT— if he had been able to see them through the clouds at all. The mining lights had been purposely turned up to high intensity as a special aid for his navigation. From the Electra's known position south of Nauru, some one thousand nautical miles west of Howland, Noonan would have adjusted his dead reckoning track toward Howland and the waiting Coast Guard ship *Itasca*.

From his years of navigational experience, first on the old square-rigged sailing vessels and later with Pan American Airways, Noonan knew that reasonably efficient dead reckoning results should have produced an accuracy average within five and ten percent of the distance flown from his last known position. In the case of his likely course from Nauru to Howland, this would have meant an estimated accuracy within the limits of fifty to one hundred nautical miles of the approximate one thousand nautical miles from Nauru to Howland.[2]

Having taken great pride in charting the course and being the lead navigator on Pan Am's original 1935 flight of the China Clipper from San Francisco to Manila and back, Noonan calculated in advance the tables and mathematical correctives necessary for computing star, moon, or sun sights. Having taught pre-flight navigational planning to numerous Pan Am navigators-to-be, he was a highly respected teacher and navigator and considered by many of that period as the most proficient navigator in the world. He would have scheduled the time of the Lae departure to coincide with the best possible arrival time at Howland. In other words, he would have planned the flight for early morning star sights followed by several good sun line shots with his bubble octant in order to be as accurate as possible to his dead reckoned course and planned ETA at Howland.

Even with his expertise and advance planning, a five to ten percent margin of error on the dead reckoning course would have been a serious challenge for Noonan. His dead reckoning could have virtually split the difference between Howland and Baker Islands and he still could have missed the two landmarks, even though they were separated by only thirty-six miles of Pacific Ocean. Noonan had to be right on the money, and that does not even take into account the arduous conditions of cloud and rain.

In a letter to renowned Navy navigator P. V. H. Weems, dated May 11, 1936, Fred Noonan shared some personal preferences and feelings about navigation. He did not hesitate to endorse his Pioneer bubble octant and stated that "an accuracy rating within ten miles was reasonable for aerial navigation." Noonan also emphasized his attention to precision: "I maintained a very detailed log. In addition to recording courses, variation, track made good, indicated and true air speeds etc., a complete meteorological record was kept . . . each hour representing 60 very busy minutes."[3]

What Noonan's expectations might have been on his dead reckoning accuracy on the July 2, 1937, Howland approach versus his "within ten miles" statement on celestial fixes, we will never know. However, it is difficult to imagine the possibility that this outstanding navigator could have been off of his DR track by fifty to one hundred nautical miles and, consequently, missed the safety of both Howland Island and the Coast Guard cutter *Itasca*.

There is no known record of any of Noonan's midnight or early morning astronomical observations. However, his standard operating procedure included routine pre-flight calculations of waypoints or position checks. Along with the confirmation by *Itasca* of the Electra's increasing radio strength, Noonan's background gives credence to excellent navigation. After a twenty-hour flight of 2,555 miles, Noonan could have been within 15 nautical miles of the Coast Guard cutter and missed seeing the ship or the island because of the intense sun glare and tired eyes. Three decades after Amelia and Fred's fatal flight, Ann Pellegreno and her qualified crew nearly missed seeing Howland during her world flight in 1967, and when they finally did spot that elusive piece of land, they were twelve nautical miles north. Finding Howland in the middle of the ocean was no joking matter.

When Amelia reported by radio that they were flying on course 157°-337°, both she and Fred believed that they would have been able to visually sight the *Itasca* or one of the islands. (Baker Island logically might have been easier to see. Although it was smaller in size with a round shape, its elevation was higher than that of Howland by about six feet.) After flying about thirty minutes in a southeasterly direction on 157°, their tired eyes straining in the brilliant morning sunlight and not having spotted anything that looked like a low-lying island or a ship, Noonan likely recommended a northwesterly turn of course to 337°. With the sun now on the right wing tip, visibility would have been better, and they had gained a slight tail wind. Surely, they believed that one of them would see Howland or the Coast Guard ship. The miles and the minutes flashed by. An hour later, both time and precious fuel had been wasted with nothing accomplished. There was no ship or island within their red-eyed sight. Fred Noonan's excellent navigational ability could have been as accurate as possible, given his technology and weather conditions, and spotting the destination still would have been a challenge.

How Much Did Amelia Really Know about Radio Direction Finding?

At 7:58 a.m., Amelia requested a long count on 7500 kcs. Why was she attempting to obtain a high-frequency DF bearing? *Itasca*

Howland Island, as pictured from the Lockheed Electra flown by Ann Pellegreno on July 2, 1967, exactly thirty years after Amelia and Noonan had hoped to arrive at Howland. (Courtesy Ann Pellegreno)

informed her that its direction finder was tuned to the low-frequency range of 270-550 kcs and that they were constantly sending the letter *a* in Morse code, as they had sent her a radiogram on June 28. Why didn't she switch to 500 kcs and request *Itasca* to pick up her dots and dashes on their direction finder and provide a course to their position? She could not get a bearing (a minimum) on *Itasca's* high frequency signal primarily because her loop antenna could not tune to accept high-frequency radio signals. During the checkouts at Lae, no one, including radioman Harry Balfour, realized that the Electra's loop antenna could not tune to radio signals in the upper range. Amelia dismissed the matter, saying that she was probably too close for her loop antenna to pick up the strong signals from nearby Lae.

The fact that Amelia had disconnected her trailing antenna at Miami considerably reduced her ability to communicate by radio with *Itasca* or any other ship or station. In that day and time, if radio bearings were not within range of the plane's ability to receive them during daylight hours over open water, it was generally impossible to get more than one line of position other than that provided by the sun: "The air navigator, having found a position line as he approaches his destination, continues flying on his course until the position line carried forward by dead reckoning passes through the destination. He then turns right or left and follows the line of position. If, after reasonable time, the destination is not sighted, he infers that he has turned the wrong way, and so reverses his track."[4]

Suddenly, at 8:43 a.m. on July 2, Amelia came in on 3105 kcs. Her voice was loud and clear. "WE ARE ON LINE OF POSITION 157°-337°. WILL REPEAT THIS MESSAGE. WE ARE RUNNING NORTH AND SOUTH. WE WILL REPEAT THIS MESSAGE ON 6210. WAIT."

Those were Amelia's last words as recorded in the radio logs on *Itasca*. Nothing more was heard on 6210 or any other frequency, according to official records.

Lockheed officials and a number of navigators theorized later that Amelia and Noonan were flying on the 337° course at the time of their last radio contact. If so, it was estimated that they were probably 100-150 miles northwest of Howland when they made the decision to implement their Plan B. Noonan most certainly had confidence in continuing to head in a northwesterly direction, as he knew he could home in on the high-powered Japanese radio station JRX located at Jaluit Atoll. If he could get a direction finder bearing on the station's signal when within five to six hundred miles, an intersecting bearing on Pan American Airways's radio signal from Wake Island would give him a good navigational position fix, just as he used to when flying for Pan Am. From there, he would be able to determine a resulting course to safety. Almon A. Gray, former captain for Pan American Airways, explained that "the homing track to the Jaluit Radio Station makes me believe that the most likely locale would be the very northern part of Mili Atoll. I feel very comfortable in believing that Earhart landed in the Marshalls. The most likely locale would be the very northern part of Mili Atoll."[5]

He further explained his Mili Atoll landing theory as a result of Noonan homing on the Jaluit radio transmitter:

In early 1937, several weeks before her Oakland-Honolulu flight . . . Miss Earhart met at Alameda, CA, with George Angus, Supervisor of Communications for the Pacific Division of Pan American Airways. She was particularly interested in obtaining radio bearings to augment her celestial navigation. At that time PAA had specially designed versions of the Adcock radio direction finding system in service at Alameda, CA; Mokapu Point, Hawaii; Midway Island; Wake Island; Guam; and Manila, Philippines, to support Clipper operations. These systems were capable of taking radio bearings on frequencies much higher than could be utilized successfully by conventional loop type direction finders, hence were effective over much greater distances. . . . Angus agreed to help her while she was within radio range of PAA stations, and details for doing so were worked out. This was somewhat complicated inasmuch as PAA was not equipped to transmit on either of Earhart's communication frequencies (3105 and 6210 KHz) and could not transmit voice on any frequency. The solution agreed upon was that the plane would request a bearing by voice on the frequency in use . . . and follow the request with a series of long dashes lasting in the aggregate a couple minutes. The PAA DF station would take a bearing and transmit it to the plane on an agreed upon PAA frequency, using CW (telegraphy) sent at such a slow speed that the individual dots and dashes of the numbers could be copied on paper and later translated into numbers. This arrangement was tested on the flight from Oakland to Honolulu with the bearings being taken by PAA on 3105 KHz and sent to the plane on 2986 KHz. It worked out very well."[6]

Obviously, Amelia was unable to get a bearing on the *Itasca*'s 7500 high-frequency signal. Whether this failure originated in the Electra's antenna system or Amelia's inability to obtain a minimum with the Bendix equipment, we'll never know. The basic question that arises is whether she was really that unfamiliar with how her system worked. In her exhausted state, she may have not been able to focus and determine what she needed to do with the new high-frequency radio direction finder. She apparently didn't remember, or know, that her loop antenna was not designed to tune to the higher frequencies. In her apparent disorientation the thought probably never occurred to try her other wire antenna affixed to the twin tails instead of the traditional loop over the cockpit.

During repairs to the Electra following the unfortunate accident in Hawaii, the Electra's Western Electric radio receiver was replaced with an experimental Bendix unit that covered a range of 150 kcs to 10,000 kcs. It could transmit and receive both voice and Morse code signals. A switch allowed the receiver to be connected to the plane's loop or wire antenna, whichever needed to be used.

Another key question is why she or one of the *Itasca* radio crew did not suggest switching to 500 kcs, the basic ship-to-shore calling frequency. Even without her trailing antenna, she should have been able to communicate for fifty miles or so. The Coast Guard ship could—and should—have guided the Electra safely to Howland with their direction finder by insisting that Amelia shift to this basic ship-to-shore frequency and give them some dots and dashes so they could pick her up on their DF.

If Amelia had been better schooled in the use of her radio receiver and transmitter, she would have established two-way communication with *Itasca*. Her difficulties could have been a result of something simple, such as failing to flip the send/receive relay switch. Back in Oakland, radio technician Joe Gurr attempted to review with Amelia specific direction-finding techniques both before the first world flight attempt and later after the Electra had been repaired. Amelia showed little interest in knowing details of this specialized equipment. "We never covered actual operations such as taking a bearing with a direction finder . . ." Gurr reported.[7] Comments such as this one from certified technicians reveal the unfortunate reality that all too often, Amelia was just too busy with opposing demands to adequately develop necessary skills required for her major undertakings.

Signals for a loop antenna are strongest when the antenna is parallel to the direction of the radio waves being received. When the loop antenna is perpendicular to the direction of the radio wave, the signal received becomes minimum or zero. If a pointer dial is attached to the loop antenna, the direction of the antenna itself, as well as the direction of the transmitter, can be determined. When a signal is heard, a sharper reading actually can be obtained from the minimum signal (the null), rather than the maximum. At the time the minimum is received, the heading of the plane must be noted. The true direction of the bearing is then obtained by adding the plane's true heading to the relative bearing of the radio direction finder.[8]

Today, such calculations are automatic, but in Amelia and Fred's day, they were not. We can thus understand how someone like Amelia, untrained in the technique of using this newly developed electronic equipment, could have experienced difficulty trying to fly the airplane and simultaneously handle the DF requirements to any degree of satisfaction. Noonan would have been very busy measuring his degree of drift that would have occurred during the late hours of storm and darkness while simultaneously double-checking his earlier morning sun-line measurement to make certain they were on the 157° heading and noting how long they had been flying that course. With all this going on, it truly was a very busy and nervous time for both pilot and navigator as their eyes frantically searched in every direction for the Coast Guard ship or the island.

The single greatest source of error in obtaining DF bearings originated with the operator. This was especially true in those early days of development and experimentation. Even today, the US Navy's manual *Navigation and Nautical Astronomy* states with regard to direction finder bearings, "Frequent practice is essential if this source of error is to be reduced."[9]

Early Morning Navigation to Howland

As the Electra approached the Howland dead reckoned position, Noonan would have taken one of several sun sights around thirty to forty minutes after sunrise. Aware of the likelihood of a northerly drift during the squally night, he would have flown a short offset course of about 065° before turning on his pre-calculated southeasterly sun line course of 157°. By doing this, Noonan calculated two targets on which to rely. He either could have seen Howland on his left or Baker Island as the plane flew down the sun line.

Throughout the long evening and some of the early morning hours, the Electra had been buffeted with rain and wind from the east and southeast. Noonan surely knew that he likely had drifted north of his course by the time he was able to get a sun shot shortly after sunrise, 5:45 a.m. Howland time (5:45 p.m. GCT). Since he had the benefit of sighting the Nauru mining lights or the navigation lights of the tug *Ontario* the previous evening, he knew his position at that time, and he also was aware of the headwinds buffeting the plane.

With the resulting turbulence, it would have been difficult to hold the airplane's course to within five degrees of the 078° track in the heavy weather as the aircraft was bounced from port to starboard.

The Electra met the sunrise that fateful morning at 067° true. If Amelia's two hundred miles out radio comment was from Noonan's dead reckoning, then her one hundred miles out radio message a half hour later (6:45 a.m. Howland Island time) probably resulted from a sun-line fix from which Noonan would have given her the 157°-337° course to fly.

In its passage from east to west, the sun tracks north of the equator. In that part of the world on July 2, it passed almost 23° north at that time of the morning. As Amelia turned onto her course of 157°, the sun would have been rising to the left of the Electra. For a brutal eighteen hours, both pilot and navigator had been subjected to an exhaustive schedule of demands from flying the plane through darkness and rain. Crammed into tight quarters in the midst of a vibrating engine roar and sickening gasoline fumes, the overall effects on both fliers must have been debilitating. Yet, here they were, nearing their objective of Howland Island and being received loud and clear by the Coast Guard cutter guarding their flight. At 7:58 a.m. Amelia reported: "WE ARE CIRCLING BUT CANNOT HEAR YOU. GO AHEAD ON 7500 WITH A LONG COUNT . . ."

By now, Amelia surely was aware that two hours had passed since sunrise, at which time they were about two hundred nautical miles away from the Howland dead reckoned position. They should have achieved the distance without further difficulty. With two pairs of eyeballs straining, neither she nor Fred recognized anything that remotely looked like a coral island or a white Coast Guard ship. Their hearts must have been pounding in tandem with the deafening noise of the engines as they wearily scanned the horizon.

Why Noonan Never Found Howland: The Circling Dangers

When did Amelia start circling and how long had that been going on? In the last records of her flight path, she had transitioned into a course of 157° to fly. She may have altered her path to do things her way, as she had earlier in her journey. On their trans-Atlantic flight from Natal, Brazil, they found the African coast enshrouded in haze. Noonan recommended a right turn to bring them to Dakar. "But a left turn seemed to me in order, and after fifty miles of flying along the coast we found ourselves at St. Louis, Senegal," Amelia later wrote. Had they turned south as Fred had suggested, they would have found

Dakar in a half hour. It is feasible that with Howland and *Itasca* not in sight, Amelia may have taken directions into her own hands.

When Amelia radioed *Itasca* at 7:42 a.m. that she was at one thousand feet, she should have had a theoretical horizon of thirty-six miles of visibility on a clear day, per elevation and distance calculations. Yet neither she nor her navigator discerned any land or ship that was their target. Whether the full thirty-six miles of visibility or half that distance was available for the weary fliers, we will never know. At one thousand feet, they should have been under the cumulus cloud cover. Visibility at that height should have been good, as reported by *Itasca* logs, and there were considerably less head winds remaining from the stormy weather encountered the night before. In any case, a quarter of an hour later, Amelia reported to *Itasca* that she was circling and requested that they transmit on 7500 so she might get a bearing, which she did not succeed in accomplishing. Not only had precious time been lost, but the circling tremendously complicated matters for Noonan. She now had him completely confounded.

Amelia's circling complicated his planning. There would have been

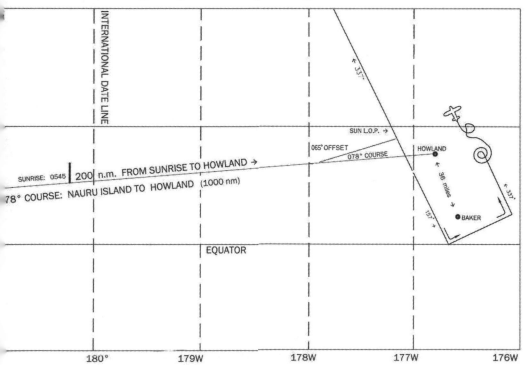

Interpretation of Electra's course approaching Howland and of Noonan's probable squared-sector search (never implemented). (Map by author)

no way to determine whether he had made good on his calculated dead-reckoned course to Howland or if he had over-shot the island. The circling made it virtually impossible for Noonan to accurately recover and use his navigational skills to find Howland. Any direction in which he might have aimed the airplane would have been a huge guess. There was nothing, absolutely nothing, within their line of sight on which Noonan could have fixed a position. Unless this renowned navigator could have pulled some magic out of his hat, the flight of Amelia Earhart and Fred Noonan soon would have become their last, regardless of which way they turned.

Having expended his hour of fuel time allocated for locating Howland and not knowing if or how much they had over-flown the island, Noonan likely would have continued flying his west-northwest course at approximately 120 mph hoping to pick up the radio signal from the JRX transmitter at Jaluit Atoll, which had a range of five to six hundred miles. This dotted line squared-sector search pattern

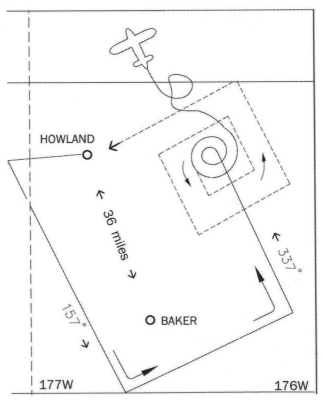

Detail of Noonan's probable squared-sector search (never implemented). (Map by author)

illustrates the organized technique that Noonan would have used to zero-in on either Howland or Baker, whichever was first sighted. However, Amelia's random circling interrupted this maneuver, and because of low fuel, forced the fliers to enact Plan B.

Not having been able to personally sight Howland Island must have been a jarring blow to Noonan's ego and confidence. But the northwesterly direction they likely were heading should have provided a visible string of the Gilbert Islands, with the Marshall Islands still farther northwest. If only they would have enough fuel to find just one small piece of dry land. They needed to do everything possible to conserve every last drop of gasoline, especially the small amount of gas still remaining in the 100-octane takeoff tank.

In looking back on Amelia's mysterious disappearance and the unanswered aspects of her history, there is a tendency to eliminate or forget basic facts as being worthy objects of consideration. After years of collecting pertinent documents, we must do everything possible to engage logic and common sense in weighing what might have happened. Among the credible testaments to Amelia and Fred's fate is an Army intelligence document indicating Earhart's "last" message to *Itasca* may not have been her last:

NOVEMBER 1, 1938
FOR THE ASST. CHIEF OF STAFF, G-2 WAR DEPT.
ATTACHED HERETO IS A LETTER RECEIVED BY ONE OF THE CIVILIANS IN THE INFORMATION DIVISION OF THIS OFFICE, FROM A MAN IN AUSTRALIA ALLEGING THAT THE EARHART PLANE WAS SHOT DOWN BY THE JAPANESE.

IT IS DEFINITELY KNOWN THAT SUCH IS NOT THE CASE. MISS EARHART WAS HEARD ON HER RADIO BY ARMY PERSONNEL STATIONED AT HOWLAND ISLAND, AND JUDGING FROM THE STRENGTH OF THE RADIO SIGNALS RECEIVED, SHE PASSED QUITE CLOSE TO THE ISLAND, SOME FIFTY MILES OR LESS. SHORTLY THEREAFTER SHE STATED SHE WAS TURNING NORTH AND THEY CONTINUED TO HEAR HER AT INTERVALS. HER SIGNALS BECAME FAINTER EACH TIME RECEIVED, UNTIL FINALLY SHE STATED SHE WAS OUT OF GAS. THAT WAS THE LAST HEARD FROM HER. FOR THE CHIEF OF THE AIR CORPS; H.H.C. RICHARDS; COLONEL, AIR LIAISON.

What is meaningful is that G-2 was Army Intelligence. If Army personnel on Howland heard the message indicating the Electra was turning north, the Japanese at Jaluit Atoll in the Marshalls could hear it too. In fact, they were in position to track Earhart and Noonan's every movement. If Amelia was turning north she'd be heading for the

Japanese mandated territory, for which they were given Trust Custody by the League of Nations at the end of World War I. This award was not considered direct ownership, but the Japanese considered it thus. In 1933, they had exited the League and begun denying access to foreign visitors. They considered the Marshalls (and other islands within their Trust Territory) as the Imperial Islands of Japan. Throughout this region, which had been designated for agriculture and fishing purposes, they were busy deepening harbors and building barracks, warehouses, ammunition bunkers, and airfields for both land and seaplanes and the coming war with Western Powers.

Part Four: The Aftermath

Chapter 8

The Search

We were lucky in always reaching our objectives. In all the distance I don't think we wandered off the course for half an hour, although there were times when I couldn't have bet a nickel on the accuracy of our assumed position.

—Fred Noonan[1]

Approximately ten hours after *Itasca* radio operators logged Amelia's last transmission, the British light cruiser HMSNZ *Achilles,* en route from American Samoa to Honolulu, picked up a radiotelephone station calling SOS with the call sign KHAQQ. *Achilles* reported hearing the words "QUITE DOWN, BUT RADIO STILL WORKING."[2]

Two hours later, T. H. Cude, director of police on Nauru Island, reported hearing the unintelligible voice of a woman calling on 6210 kcs saying, "land in sight ahead." He had heard Amelia calling the previous evening and noted, "The voice sounded similar to Earhart's when she passed the Island the night before. However, there was no hum of engines in the background."[3]

Karl Pierson, chief engineer of Patterson Radio Company in Los Angeles, had established radio watches on Amelia's frequencies. During the early morning hours of July 3, Amelia's 6210 frequency picked up SOS calls in a woman's voice.

Since Amelia and Noonan could not have used the Electra's radio if the plane were in the water, these SOS calls implied that the radio and its batteries were dry at the time of transmitting, and therefore there was no way that the aircraft could have been submerged in water.

When Lockheed officials learned that the Electra was missing, they telephoned Walter McMenamy, one of Pierson's associates. They knew that Amelia's radio contact man would be listening on her frequencies. They also knew that this particular operator had been working with Amelia for more than two years beginning in January 1935, when Amelia flew her Vega from Hawaii to California. Cooperating with radio station KFI, which was broadcasting to the

Vega, McMenamy was the only radio receiver in touch with her airplane. Though his set was little more than a laboratory experiment, he was able to receive Amelia's voice transmissions when KFI's equipment could not.[4] He was very familiar with her voice and radio habits, which enabled him to read her messages when static interfered or the carrier faded. According to McMenamy, at 6:00 a.m. on July 3, seventeen hours after Amelia's disappearance, "a steady carrier was picked up on one of Miss Earhart's wavelengths, and was heard intermittently for 20 minutes."[5] The signals were too weak to be understood. However, within a few minutes, McMenamy heard another much stronger radio wave and had no doubts: "I recognized the woman's voice as that of Miss Earhart saying, 'KHAQQ CALLING SOS.'"[6]

During the three minutes in which the SOS continued, McMenamy thought he heard the words "Southwest Howland," although the reception was very faint and with considerable static. He also could hear the sound of an airplane motor running, which could have been the starboard engine of the Electra turning in order to charge the batteries.

By coincidence, Pete Pringle, managing news editor of Station KNX, called McMenamy by telephone to check on his radio reports. Through McMenamy's loudspeaker, Pringle heard the woman's voice calling SOS. When he went on the air a half-hour later at his station, he told his listening audience that he could confirm hearing Miss Earhart's voice requesting help—he had heard her himself.[7]

In the meantime, Washington had received word that the Earhart plane was overdue and had never reached Howland Island. At noon on July 3, the Navy directed the commander in chief of the US Fleet to hold an aircraft carrier in readiness and make preparations to proceed to the vicinity of Howland Island to undertake the search for Amelia Earhart and Fred Noonan.

The aircraft carrier *Lexington* left Santa Barbara, California, at 4:00 p.m. on July 3 and arrived at San Diego at 11:00 p.m. The destroyer *Lamson* had the ready duty for that Fourth of July weekend with a full crew on board. It was directed to join the Earhart search. The destroyer *Drayton* was also assigned to guard the *Lexington* but had to sail with forty men short of her allowance because they were on leave and could not be reached. The destroyers *Cushing* and *Perkins*, then en route from Puget Sound, were directed to proceed at 28 knots to join up with the search team. At 5:30 p.m. on the Fourth of July, however, *Perkins* developed serious vibrations in her port high-pressure turbine and radioed that she was unable to exceed 17 knots. She was directed to cruise alongside the repair ship *Whitney* in

San Diego to have the problem corrected. The rest of the *Lexington* group made an average speed of 23.5 knots, a record at that time, during the passage from Coronado Roads in San Diego to Lahaina anchorage between Maui and Lanai, near Pearl Harbor. By the time all of the ships had been outfitted with fuel and provisions—the *Lexington* alone received 903,784 gallons of fuel—it was 3:15 p.m. on July 9, and the aircraft carrier and its escorts left for Howland Island. Amelia's Electra had been missing for nearly a week. The carrier's speed was set initially at 19 knots in order to reach the search starting point, approximately one hundred miles north of Howland at daybreak on July 13—a full ten days after Amelia's plane disappeared.[8]

The destroyers were sent ahead to rendezvous with the battleship *Colorado.* The *Colorado,* on a training cruise from California to Hawaii, had just secured its lines to Honolulu Pier at the time of Amelia's disappearance. Because this important ship was the closest to the Howland Island search area, it was ordered to take on fuel and supplies and proceed with all dispatch to where Amelia and Noonan likely had disappeared. The *Itasca, Swan,* and *Moorby,* an English steamer that changed course to aid in the search, were patrolling northwest of Howland. The *Colorado* sailed promptly from Pearl Harbor at 1:00 p.m. on July 3 for Howland, a distance of 1,660 nautical miles.

After cruising on a southwesterly course at 18 knots for two full days, at about 9:30 p.m. on July 5, those listening in the *Colorado* radio room were astounded to hear over the loudspeaker: "EARHART FROM ITASCA, DID YOU SEND UP A FLARE? IF YOU DID, SEND UP ANOTHER. PLEASE GO AHEAD." Ten minutes later, the Coast Guard cutter called again: "EARHART PLANE FROM ITASCA, WE SEE A SECOND FLARE. WE ARE COMING FOR YOU. WE ARE STARTING TOWARD YOU." Five minutes after that, "WE SEE YOUR FLARE AND ARE PROCEEDING TOWARD YOU."

Aboard *Colorado* the word spread like wildfire. The excitement and tension of the listeners was contagious. Many of those on board the battleship were Naval ROTC students receiving summer training. They could not have hoped for any more exciting action on a training cruise.

Colorado's written report reflected the subsequent disappointment of all on board: "It was therefore with great sadness that the following was received shortly after. REPORT IN ERROR. OBJECTS SIGHTED ARE APPARENTLY METEORS. HOWLAND REPORTED SAME EFFECT." The *Swan* reported having sighted a meteorological shower at the same time that the *Itasca* thought it was seeing flares from the Earhart plane.

It had been determined that *Colorado* would search to the southeast of Howland, including the Phoenix group of islands; the *Swan* and *Itasca* would do a sweep to the west, including a thorough search of the Gilbert Islands; and the carrier *Lexington* would use its planes to conduct an east-to-west search in the open Pacific northwest of Howland Island.

Also on July 3, at about 6:00 p.m. Honolulu time, a patrol bomber was dispatched from Pearl Harbor to Howland Island to assist in the search. Its flight captain was Lt. Warren W. Harvey. The Navy was aware that there were 1,500 gallons of aviation fuel and 120 gallons of oil on Howland, which were brought by *Itasca* to refuel Amelia's Electra. This could have been used for the big flying boat to return to Hawaii. However, after flying all night to within four hundred miles of Howland, Harvey radioed the following message: "POSITION 06-35N AND 172-00W. LAST TWO HOURS IN EXTREMELY BAD WEATHER BETWEEN ALTITUDE 2000 AND 12000 FEET. SNOW, SLEET, RAIN, AND ELECTRICAL STORMS. IN DAYLIGHT CONDITIONS LOOK EQUALLY BAD. CLOUD TOPS APPEAR TO BE 18000 FEET OR MORE. AM RETURNING TO PEARL HARBOR. NOW HAVE 900 GALLONS OF FUEL ON BOARD 0710."

The patrol bomber returned safely to Pearl Harbor at 7:00 p.m. on July 4.

Two days after the Electra's disappearance, US Naval Radio at Wailupe, Hawaii, recorded the following message: "...281...NORTH HOWLAND...KHAQQ BEYOND...NORTH...DON'T HOLD WITH US MUCH LONGER...ABOVE WATER...SHUT OFF..." Three Navy radio operators confirmed hearing this broken message.

USNR Capt. Almon A. Gray, ret., was in charge of the Pan Am Radio and Direction Finding Station on Wake Island in 1935. He also had flown with Fred Noonan, and noted this in regard to the 281 message:

> Figures are easy to copy and it is likely to have been copied correctly. The "281" is near the start of the message, where Fred normally put the latitude and longitude in the clipper position reports. From Dead Reckoning he may have believed he had made good an overall course of 281° from the Howland Island area to point of landing. The best he could say was he was on a reef (or beach) somewhere on a bearing of 281° from Howland.[9]

The 281 message implied that Noonan knew their general whereabouts. The real question is whether they were 281° from Howland when they ceased looking for the island and proceeded on a course that would take them back to the Gilberts or whether they were 281 miles from Howland, which would have positioned them in open ocean.

They knew that they were considerably north of their intended destination. According to Captain Gray, "It is obvious that Amelia and Fred were much farther north than they realized when they left what they believed to be the Howland area to seek survival in the Gilberts."[10]

The statement "don't hold with us much longer" could indicate that either Amelia and Fred couldn't hold out much longer or that their batteries couldn't last. "Above water" suggests that they were above sea water at that moment. As for "shut off," the radio would have to be shut down if there was any chance of salt water getting to the batteries. Perhaps the Electra was on a beach or tidal reef.

Amelia had told Gene Vidal, then director of Air Commerce, that she would try and find a beach in the Gilberts on which to come down if she was unable to locate Howland Island. "Hopefully," she added, "it will be a place that has fresh water."[11]

If the Electra had crashed in the ocean, the weight of its engines would have caused the nose and forward section to immediately tilt downward at an extreme angle. Water would have seeped through the overhead cockpit hatch and windows. The empty fuselage fuel tanks might have kept the aircraft partially buoyant for a short while until the air vents allowed water in, but the cockpit and batteries (located beneath the cockpit floor) would have been immersed in short order.

Walter McMenamy and Karl Pierson continued their listening vigil. Though nothing of consequence was heard for two days, on July 5 at 4:30 a.m. California time, they picked up the Earhart signals once more. At first, they heard *Itasca* calling the plane, requesting that they send three dashes if on land. Almost immediately, the operators heard three long dashes on the plane's frequency. Fifteen minutes later, *Itasca* repeated its request. Again, the answer came back with three long dashes, ending with a decided sputtering or rippling. McMenamy assessed the sputtering as indication that the batteries were nearly exhausted.

At 3:30 a.m. on July 6, Louis Messier, a Los Angeles ham operator, picked up a weak, unidentified code signal sent very slowly on the Earhart plane frequency, and ending with a pronounced ripple. Messier logged the message as follows: "17 ... MO ... U ... 4 ... SOUTHWES ... I ... 53 ... ARN ... REL ... 13 ... JA ... SO ... NOT ... NX ... CALL ... EQUEN ... 170 ... SOU ... SEC ... WILL ... SON ... MOST ... NEW ... SOU ..."[12]

It appears that Noonan was trying to send the latitude and longitude of their position—but naturally, this depends on interpretation. In any case, it was the last anyone heard from KHAQQ. By July 6, Noonan would have had plenty of time to figure out where they were, especially if he had access to his sextant. One interpretation of the numbers as 171.4° west (longitude), and 5.3° north (latitude) puts them very close to Mili Atoll.

Ham radio operators were not the only ones listening on the Earhart frequencies. Late in the afternoon on July 2, George W. Angus, assistant communications engineer for Pan American Airways, reported from Alameda, California, that some San Francisco newsmen had called him about the recent Coast Guard announcement of the overdue Earhart plane. It was the first he knew that a search had been undertaken. Pan Am immediately established around-the-clock watches at their bases at Honolulu, Midway, and Wake Islands. Two Hawaiian commercial AM stations, KGU and KGMB, with excellent westward airwaves coverage, also established a special broadcast schedule to the Earhart plane.

These Pan Am stations heard definite signals and compiled extremely useful reports that indicated that Amelia and Noonan were calling for help during all hours, especially at night, over the period of July 3-6. The Pan Am reports are summarized as follows.[13]

Saturday, July 3
Makapuu (Honolulu): Nothing heard.

Midway Island: Nothing heard.

Wake Island: Heard an intermittent phone of rather wobbly characteristics—male voice modulated, although unreadable due to static. R. W. Hansen, operator in charge of communications, called this to the attention of Honolulu. Pan Am Honolulu advised all stations that the Coast Guard was requesting every effort to obtain a bearing on KHAQQ, even if only an approximate or doubtful one.

Nauru Island: Operator heard signals on 6210 kcs and was confident they came from the plane. Signal strength was 3 (on a scale of 0-5). The operator noted, "Voice was similar to that emitted from plane last night with exception no hum of engines in background."

Sunday, July 4
Makapuu: At 7:30 p.m. local Honolulu time, Station KGMB arranged

a special broadcast asking KHAQQ to transmit four long dashes on 3105 if they heard the KGMB broadcast. Immediately afterward they distinctly heard four dashes. USN Capt. Almon A. Gray, ret., later reported:

> We are certain of the frequency because the *Itasca* had previously set their transmitter on this frequency in an effort to contact the plane. We had just taken bearings of Itasca on this frequency. On hearing the four dashes we immediately called KGMB by phone and asked them to repeat the test. This was done and we again heard the same signals. Except at this time, only two dashes were received. [Note: While in principle someone other than Amelia and Noonan could have transmitted the dashes, it is unlikely that any other transmitters existed in that isolated part of the world.] The second dash trailed off to a weak signal as though the power supply on the transmitter had failed. We observed an approximate bearing of 213° from Makapuu.[14]

Midway Island: At 2:57 p.m. Greenwich Civil Time (now Greenwich Mean Time), a very weak, wobbly signal was heard which sounded like a phone but was too weak to identify. At 3:12 p.m., a very faint, broad signal, apparently from a radiophone, was heard but was again too weak to take a bearing.

Wake Island: "We were busy with our PAA flying boat. Also, neither 6210 or 3105 kcs are any good here during daylight hours."

Monday, July 5

Makapuu: "Carrier [a radio wave in the ionosphere] heard from Direction Finder close to 3105 but signals so weak it was impossible to obtain even a fair check. Average seems to be about 215°, but doubtful bearing. Once it seemed as though it was a woman's voice, but may have been our imagination."

Midway Island: "We heard the peculiar signal and received a DF bearing of approximately 201°." Station manager G. H. Miller took the bearing and defined it through the following characteristics:

The signal was on 3105. The frequency had been checked against *Itasca* signals.

The carrier was wobbly and cut off, which did not permit refining the bearing.

There was a distinct male voice, but not with sufficient modulation to be understood or identified.

This peculiar signal was only heard once from Midway.

Wake Island:

At 0948 GCT a phone signal of good intensity and well modulated by a voice but wavering badly suddenly came on 3105. While the carrier frequency of this signal did not appear to vary appreciably, its strength did vary in an unusually erratic manner. At 0950 the carrier strength fell off to signal strength S-2 with the wavering more noticeable than ever. At 0952 it went off completely. At 1212, I opened the DF guard on 3105 kcs. At 1223 a very unsteady voice modulated carrier was observed. This transmission lasted until 1236 GCT. I was able to get an approximate bearing of 144°. In spite of the eccentricity of this signal during the entire length of the transmission, the splits were definite and pretty fair. At the time I believed this bearing to be reasonably accurate. And, I am still of that opinion. This signal started in at a carrier strength of 5 and at 1236, when the transmission stopped, it had gradually petered out to a strength of 2, during the intervals it was audible. The characteristics of this signal were identical with those of the signals heard the previous night. While no identification call letters were distinguished in either case, I was positive at that time this was KHAQQ.

Howland Island: On July 5, the log of the portable high-frequency direction finder positioned under a tent in the center of the island indicated a direction finder "fix" was obtained. Around midnight (with Cipriani's battery now completely recharged) the log reported receiving "a fairly strong bearing on Amelia's frequency." The null zone on the direction finder indicated that an SOS was being transmitted either from NNW or SSE of Howland Island. No useful information or other identification was given. In order for this station to receive this message its transmission had to be sent continuously in Morse code. Was it Noonan, still trying to get through to someone? NNW would position the SOS coming from the direction of the Marshall Islands. SSE would probably have the SOS originating from somewhere in the Phoenix group of islands. Nevertheless, on the strength of the Howland Island direction finder bearing and other data, the *Itasca* turned its heading NNW and proceeded at full speed.

Tuesday, July 6
Makapuu: "Our ship was en route to Alameda, therefore all our facilities were in use guarding the flight [the Pan Am clipper flight inbound to California from Hawaii]." There was some later listening on 3105, but nothing heard.

Midway Island: Nothing heard.

Wake Island: A severe electrical storm in the area made it impossible to do anything. Cdr. Warner Thompson of the *Itasca* sent a radio message to Treasury Secretary Morgenthau on July 5:

INTERCEPTS OF RAGGED TRANSMISSION INDICATE POSSIBILITY EARHART PLANE STILL AFLOAT TWO EIGHTY ONE MILES NORTH HOWLAND. BEARINGS RADIO DIRECTION FINDER ON HOWLAND CONFIRMED APPROXIMATE POSITION. WE WILL ARRIVE INDICATED POSITION THIS AFTERNOON ABOUT 1700 PLUS ELEVEN AND ONE HALF TIME.

On July 6, Henry Morgenthau, Secretary of the Treasury and responsible for Coast Guard activities, received a report on the disappointing results: "SEARCHING AREA REPORTED POSITION EARHART PLANE SINCE DUSK YESTERDAY. RESULTS NEGATIVE."

On July 9, K. C. Ambler, Pan Am section supervisor in charge of communication in Honolulu, noted that the watches were being discontinued since none of their stations had lately heard the "peculiar signals." He did add, however, an interesting comment: "If we do hear the signals again, we will advise Alameda, as this would be proof that the signals did not originate at the Earhart plane."[15]

At Wake Island, R. W. Hansen, operator in charge of communications, ended his report on July 9: "There is not the slightest question in my mind that the signals I have reported on could have been those of a maladjusted Coast Guard phone, because (1) the abnormal and unusually erratic characteristics of these signals as compared to the steady operating CG phones, and (2) the fact that no Coast Guard boats were, to the best of my knowledge, anywhere near the line of the Wake DF [direction finder] bearing of 144°." Note that this bearing is consistent with Mili Atoll.

The "peculiar signal" heard by experienced radio operators in California, Hawaii, Wake Island, and Midway Island was, at times, strong enough to provide direction-finder bearings. USN Capt. August Detzer, ret., indicated to Earhart researcher Fred Goerner that direction finder bearings of that period "could not be considered to be accurate closer than five degrees on signal sources over significant distances."[16] While the bearings may not have been precisely accurate, when plotted on a chart of that section of the Pacific, they all point to the southeastern Marshall Islands.

In the end, more than a dozen different radio stations heard SOS messages, long dashes, and carrier waves associated with the Electra and its call letters KHAQQ after the plane was reported overdue and presumed down in the Pacific. These stations were staffed by various professional radiomen and experienced ham operators:

Professional Radiomen and Stations:
  Pan American Airways, Makapuu, Hawaii
  Pan American Airways, Midway Island
  Pan American Airways, Wake Island
  HMSNZ *Achilles*, en route from American Samoa to Honolulu
  SS *Moorby*, changed course to participate in search 281 miles NW
    Howland Island
  Nauru Island Radio
  US Naval Radio, Wailupe, Hawaii
  US Coast Guard cutter *Itasca*
  US Coast Guard San Francisco
  Howland Direction Finder, Frank Cipriani, RM2 on temporary duty

Experienced Ham Operators:
  Walter McMenamy, Los Angeles
  Karl Pierson, Patterson Radio Company, Los Angeles
  Louis Messier, Los Angeles
  Yau Fai Lum, Howland Island, K6GNW
  Paul Yat Lum, Baker Island

The chief significance of all of these radio signals is that the Earhart plane was still broadcasting days after it presumably fell into the sea and when its radio would have been inoperative due to the aircraft being in the water. The fact that these signals were heard by responsible radio operators throughout much of the Pacific, including the *Itasca,* adds credence to the theory that Amelia and Noonan did not simply "crash and sink." It is also worth noting that at no time, even after reporting their low fuel, did Amelia and Noonan indicate that they were lost, in trouble, preparing to ditch, or use mayday calls of any kind.

Of course, if Pan Am radio operators could obtain long-distance direction-finder bearings on a "wavering, wobbly, and erratic" signal, so could the Japanese, for whom the signal would not have been so faint and weak. If Amelia and Noonan were broadcasting from a site in or near the Marshall Islands, they were in the backyard of the Japanese. Their signal would have been loud and clear—easy

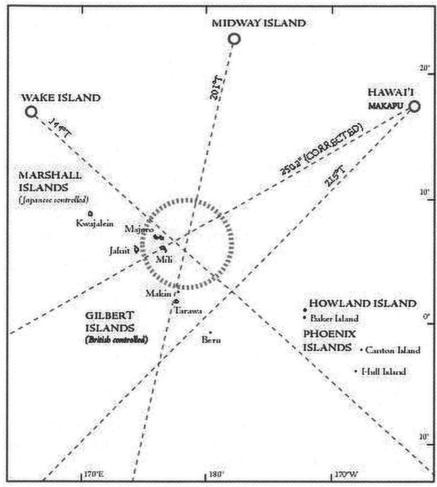

Original RDF bearings taken by Pan American Airways radio operations on signals believed to have come from the Electra were reported at 213.5° from Makapuu Point on July 4 and 215° on July 5. On July 5th, results of known positions found the Makapuu bearing 35.2° off. When the original bearings were corrected, the resulting fix corresponded more naturally with the bearings from Midway and Wake Islands. The three RDF bearings intersected in the vicinity of Mili Atoll. (Map by Elizabeth Whelan)

pickings for the Japanese direction finder at Jaluit Atoll. The Japanese direction-finder bearings would have pointed to the Earhart plane like a well-drawn treasure map.

Japanese radio monitors almost certainly heard the Honolulu commercial stations KGU and KGMB broadcasting to the Earhart Electra. They heard the requests for long dashes and for a response on 500, 3105, or 6210 kcs. They also heard everything that came out from KHAQQ. They would have heard the woman's voice and known it was Amelia. They easily could have read Noonan's slow, steady Morse code telegraphy, which would have been copied and translated.

Joseph W. Ballantine, director of US Far Eastern Affairs, approached Second Secretary Hayana of the Japanese Embassy: "The US Navy had received a faint message which offered a clue that Miss Earhart's plane might be down at a spot about 200 miles north of Howland Island."[17] The director explained that the aircraft carrier *Lexington* was on its way to that destination from distant California, and the battleship *Colorado* was departing from Honolulu. It would take them some days to reach the designated spot from which the faint messages were sent. He added, "If the Japanese Government had any vessels which could reach the spot earlier, any assistance they could give would be appreciated."

This message, dated July 11, answered the request: "The survey ship Koshu, 2500 tons, now somewhere in the South Seas, has been instructed to take part in the search for the airplane of Miss Earhart, and to get in touch with Japanese vessels near the place where Miss Earhart's airplane is reported to have been lost."[18]

The Japanese had the benefit of Director Ballantine's telegram to the Embassy in Tokyo giving general directions to the location where the US believed the Electra came down with his request for assistance. In addition, they had the advantage of strategically placed direction finders tuned in on the Electra's frequencies.[19]

Ballantine confirmed in a telegram dated July 11, 1937, from Tokyo that a senior aide to the Japanese Naval Minister stated that the government ordered Japanese radio stations to be on continuous watch for Earhart signals and instructed Japanese fishing crafts working around the Marshall Islands to be on the lookout.

There is every indication from Japanese newspapers of the day that they followed the Earhart flight with interest. After word came of Amelia's disappearance, Japanese suspicions arose with regard to the situation and expressed via the following telegram, dated July

7, 1937, from Japanese Consul-General Fukuma in Honolulu to Foreign Minister Hirota in Tokyo.

> It already has been five days since the Earhart plane first was reported missing, and the fate of the missing plane is today generally thought to be pessimistic. Despite this, however, the fact that the United States Navy has set up such an exaggerated search plan raises a suspicion that they may be trying to collect materials for strategic study under the pretense of such an air search.[20]

Shortly after the search for the missing Lockheed Electra was called off, on July 18, 1937, US Naval Intelligence officers paid a visit to Pan American Airlines Pacific Communications Headquarters in Alameda. Every station document reflecting direction-finder bearings believed to have been received from KHAQQ was seized. Nonetheless, these documents were not lost forever. Ellen Belotti, a long-time Pan Am employee and secretary in the communications department, kept a complete copy of each station's reports. After her retirement, she made the historic documents available because she "didn't think it fair and proper for the Navy to withhold something that might have helped in finding Miss Earhart."[21]

In its search report, the Navy assumed that the Electra would float with engines nearly submerged, with wings nearly submerged, with fuselage partly submerged, and with tail surfaces out of the water. The Navy also made the initial assumption that the plane had come down within 300 miles of Howland, landing on a reef or island or in the water. These hypotheses may well have been right on the money. The only position report had been given in the late afternoon of the previous day, when the Electra had covered 785 miles after leaving Lae.

The Navy was aware of the strong winds that buffeted the Earhart plane during its approach to Howland. They knew that this would have had a significant effect on the Electra's ground speed and its fuel burn rate. Navigation officers tried to put themselves in Fred Noonan's shoes to determine what his likely plan would have been on that fateful July morning. To the north of Howland Island was a huge stretch of Pacific Ocean. To the southeast was the Phoenix group of islands. With his position in doubt and flying a land airplane, the naval navigators determined that Noonan probably would have flown down a sun line leading to Howland or possibly Baker Island. If he couldn't find either, the possibility of continuing on in that direction would have brought him to one of the islands in the Phoenix group, where he and Amelia could have put the plane down and, hopefully, had a chance to be rescued. With this logic, the navigators aboard the *Colorado* felt that the most likely place to search would have been the Phoenix group, and so that is what they did.

The search groups knew that the prevailing winds were easterly at 10 knots. They also were aware that 4° north latitude marks the boundary between the southern equatorial current, flowing westerly, and the counter-equatorial, flowing easterly, which forms near the Gilberts. They recognized that if the plane was nearly submerged and drifting with the wind, the wind resistance would be small and the underwater drag great, so the resulting current effect would be great. A rubber life raft would drift about twenty miles per day in no wind. Wind conditions could have a strong influence on the daily drift distance, especially if the wind were blowing in the same direction as the current flow. Whether Amelia and Noonan had a rubber life raft remains an unanswered question, however, judging by Amelia's insistence on lightening the aircraft, there is a strong possibility that they did not have one on board. In addition, Capt. Marius Lodesen, former Pan Am pilot and Noonan associate, inspected the wreckage following the Luke Field ground loop of the initial attempt. Noting there was no inflatable raft among the survival equipment, he heard Noonan respond, "We couldn't take everything."

By 2:30 p.m. on July 7, the *Colorado* was approaching the westward charted islands of the Phoenix group. Lt. John Lambrecht recalled the moment: "The Old Man called the navigator and me to the bridge where the navigator broke out the pertinent charts and we looked over the situation. The appropriate search procedure became evident immediately. There were islands (the Phoenix Group) a little south and east of Howland and Baker on which Miss Earhart, having missed her intended landing point, might have landed—in an island lagoon, inside a barrier reef, or, if she was lucky, on a nice smooth beach. Accordingly, it was decided to put the emphasis on a search of the Phoenix Islands."[22]

Colorado carried three aircraft used for observation and scouting purposes. These were open cockpit biplanes that normally cruised at ninety knots. Their only navigational instruments were a magnetic compass, an airspeed indicator, and a turn-and-bank indicator. There was also a Morse code radio transmitter and receiver with a trailing antenna but no voice communications. No photographic equipment was on the observation planes, although some of the observers positioned in the rear seats brought personal cameras and took pictures of some of the islands.

The three observation airplanes, fitted with pontoons and air-cooled Wasp motors, were launched by catapult to search the sandbank north of Winslow Reef. They covered some two hundred miles before returning to the ship, having seen no signs of a wrecked or floating airplane or even Winslow Reef. The next day, two different sets of flights covered a rectangle of some thirty-five hundred miles with excellent visibility, but they found nothing. The weather in the search area was perfect and sea conditions were good. These three scout airplanes from the *Colorado* flew more miles and covered more territory than some of the carrier *Lexington* planes would. "I might say that some of the search flights we made were longer in mileage than most Carrier scouting hops I've ever made," Lambrecht reported.[23]

At 7:00 a.m. on July 9, the *Colorado* launched her planes toward McKean Island. After searching in that vicinity, they moved on to Gardner Island and continued to Carondelet Reef before returning to the ship. They reported these islands to be not in their charted positions, but near enough so that the pilots were able to spot them from a considerable distance. According to the *Lexington* report, "McKean Island was such that a plane could have made a safe crash landing, either on the beach or in the center of the island. McKean also showed unmistakable signs of having at one time been inhabited. On the northwest side of the island there appeared buildings of the adobe type. No one was seen and no wreckage was spotted on either Gardner or McKean Islands. Carondelet Reef was underwater but plainly could be seen from the planes at a distance of 10 miles. If Winslow Reef and the Sand Bank to the northwest of it exist, they are many miles from their charted positions."[24]

The afternoon search was in the direction of Hull Island. As the planes approached the island, natives were seen running out of their huts and waving clothes. Lt. Lambrecht, in charge of the flight, landed in the lagoon for the purpose of asking the inhabitants if they had seen or heard of the Earhart plane. A European Resident Manager came out in a canoe to meet the plane. Having asked where the planes were from and been told Honolulu, he nearly upset the canoe in his excitement. The lieutenant then told him that the planes had arrived on the battleship *Colorado,* relatively nearby. He said there was a radio on the island, but he knew nothing of the flight and had never heard of Miss Earhart. Neither he nor his natives had seen any other airplane.

Lieutenant Lambrecht was senior aviator aboard the *Colorado* and led each day's aerial search utilizing the Navy float planes launched from the stern of the battleship. He added some interesting views of his part in the search effort: "With only three aircraft, and those tired and obsolete, we concentrated our aerial search on the water portions of the Phoenix Islands. We gave each island a thorough search, and I am certain Amelia did not land, crash, or otherwise go down in this area southeast of Howland."[25]

At Gardner Island, now Nikumaroro, search teams spotted the wrecked tramp steamer *Norwich City,* a British freighter lost in 1929, lying just offshore with its hull broken. According to the report from the *Colorado,* "No dwellings appeared on Gardner or any other signs of habitation. A long shallow lagoon extends the entire length of the island and through most of the width. A seaplane could land in the lagoon and it is believed a land plane could make a forced landing there, and the occupants walk ashore. Coral reefs extend out from the shoreline for about 150 yards. Groves of coconut palms grow on the western end and the entire island is covered with tropical vegetation. Myriads of birds cover both Gardner and McKean islands."[26]

Lt. Lambrecht summed up the search effort as follows:

As to the how, why, and when the plane got off track, probably no one will ever know . . . The Gilbert Islands should have provided another good fix, check on the wind, and a final point of departure. However, from the Gilberts on, he [Noonan] would have needed all his navigational skills, a good set of eyes, and an intimate rapport with Lady Luck—Howland is a pretty small dot in a vast ocean.

However, if Miss Earhart and Fred Noonan dealt with their dead reckoning and celestial navigation with the same calm insouciance with which they apparently treated their radio equipment throughout the journey, it is no wonder they never arrived at their intended destination. Lost at sea . . . Why not let it be their final epitaph? After all, it puts them in good company.[27]

He later offered these thoughts on Amelia's disappearance and the historic search for her:

If she was not found on one of the islands (of either the Phoenix or the Gilberts) she had gone down at sea. I think the Skipper felt the same way . . . Their track should have been merely a magnetic course, Lae to Howland, corrected for the wind, and then corrected periodically as they progressed along the flight path by sights and fixes and the then 'guesstimated' wind . . . Noonan's navigation could have been almost perfect and yet Miss Earhart could have missed her destination by as little as ten to twenty miles (depending on visibility and flight altitude) and without a homing device of some sort, she'd have had it. Blowing or whistling into a microphone to produce a homing signal is not my idea of a "homing device."[28]

The aircraft tender *Swan,* previously on station halfway between Howland and Hawaii, arrived in the area to help in the Phoenix Islands search and was directed to check out Canton Island. On July 10, the *Colorado* launched its planes at 7:00 a.m. and proceeded to survey Sydney, Phoenix, Enderbury, and Birnie Islands, in that order. Sydney was the only island that showed signs of recent habitation. It had the usual shallow lagoon, which was large enough to accommodate a seaplane landing. The *Swan,* being low on fuel, came alongside *Colorado* to be replenished and was later ordered to another site while *Colorado* planes carefully searched Canton. This island was the largest of any searched in the Phoenix group. At the western end, the planes spotted shacks and scaffolding erected by the recent eclipse expeditions of June 8, 1937, but found no sign of the Electra.

Colorado then headed for a destination north of Howland, where it met up with the three destroyers of the *Lexington* group, which were in need of fuel. On July 12, after refueling the destroyers, the battleship was detached from the search to return to California. The ROTC students, who had embarked for a month's cruise, saw their voyage extended to six weeks and covered many more miles than expected, twice crossing the equator. From the morning of July 7 through July 12, the *Colorado* steamed 1,240 miles. Her observation planes flew 21.2 hours and 1,908 miles each, and covered a radius of visibility of 25,490 square miles. Alongside the mileage between Pearl Harbor and the search area, the battleship steamed 3,980 miles and 320 hours more than expected when the Navy ROTC training cruise began.

On the morning of July 13, the aircraft carrier *Lexington* arrived at a point about one hundred miles north of Howland Island. Although the weather was squally with a wind velocity of 22-28 knots and undesirable flying conditions, pilots launched twenty-seven planes and searched a 10,000 square mile corridor. Since they were aware of the fairly strong westerly drift, the areas searched were in that direction. On July 14, the search began at latitude 00-00 and longitude 180° with persisting squalls. Two destroyers positioned themselves sixty miles away on the *Lexington*'s flanks. The other one was sixty miles ahead. On July 15, they encountered a current with a definite set to the northwest, so they shifted their search in that direction. By July 18, the most probable areas had been covered, and they received orders to discontinue the search. On average, forty planes were in the air daily for seven to eight hours each from the *Lexington*. They covered 151,556 square miles and were airborne a total of 1,591 hours. In his final report, Capt. Leigh Noyes of the *Lexington* noted, "It was the conviction of the aviators who did the flying that neither the Earhart plane nor the survivors were in the area searched. Although unfortunately the fate of the missing flyers remains a mystery, it is considered that the search made was efficient and that the areas covered were the most probable ones, based on the facts and information available."[29]

With the *Lexington* group searching the waters north and west of Howland, *Itasca* and *Swan* were directed to visually inspect the most eastward of the Gilbert Islands. Commander Thompson had a feeling that the Earhart airplane had been set north of its course to Howland, and its approach was caught up in the continuous heavy clouds to the northwest. Throughout the early morning hours, the Electra's transmissions indicated flight through cloudy and overcast skies. During the last hour of transmission, the plane's signal strength was strong and there was every indication that dead reckoning distances had been accomplished. They should have been in the vicinity of Howland.

Thompson had to assume that the 157°-337° course reported from Amelia's last transmission was from a resulting sun line obtained when they emerged from the clouds early that morning. *Itasca* emitted a smoke trail as an aid to the fliers, but the island and the ship's position were almost directly in line with the glare of the rising sun, partially in the face of the two weary flyers. Because of the strength of the airplane's last radio transmissions, the assumption was that Earhart was relatively nearby. On the way to the Gilberts, Thompson decided to search a sector between forty and two hundred miles off of Howland Island, starting on the line 337° and working northerly to a bearing of 45°.

The Coast Guard cutter *Itasca* was placed under Navy command for the duration of the search. According to Richard Black, who was the Department of the Interior's expedition leader to Howland at the time of the Earhart flight, "We were assigned to the Gilbert Islands chain as our area. Itasca called at every island of the Gilberts, interviewing the natives who came out in canoes. We ended up at

Tarawa where we met with the British administrators to see if they had any sign or report of a plane in trouble."[30]

By July 11, *Itasca* found itself approaching Arorai Island in the lower Gilberts. They questioned the local magistrate but reported nothing. The next stop was Tamana Island, but they did not gain any information there either. July 14 found the *Itasca* close to the lee side of Nauuki Island. No natives came out and the surf was breaking too heavily to attempt going ashore. They then set course for Kuria Island, arriving at 4 p.m. Having lowered the surfboat, a party went to the beach to speak with the magistrate, who knew of no plane or wreckage. On July 15, a frazzled Coast Guard group went ashore at Tarawa, where the resident commissioner "received the party graciously, but declined to receive the visit as official, owing to the fact he had received no notice of the vessel's arrival in the Gilbert Islands. He requested *Itasca* notify the Resident Commissioner at Ocean Island."[31] He did tell the landing party that no information had been received on Tarawa about the passage of the Earhart plane or its wreckage. By July 16, *Itasca* was headed back to Howland to pick up personnel and supplies and set course for Hawaii, having been released from the search effort.

Although the aircraft tender *Swan* was the smallest ship involved in the Earhart search, it made more than its share of Gilbert Island contacts, visiting Nukunau, Beru, Tabiteuea, Nonouti, and Onotoa. This vessel was at sea for thirty-seven days and steamed seven thousand miles. Although no information was forthcoming about the missing Electra, *Swan*'s captain and crew were commended in the final search report: "Despite the onerous operating conditions involving shortage of provisions and supplies, *Swan* carried out all assigned duties in a manner reflecting great credit on the commanding officer, Lieutenant H. F. MacComsey, the officers and crew. During her entire cruise there occurred no machinery failure nor a single sick day."[32] On July 16, this vessel too was released from search duty and directed to return to Pearl Harbor.

Itasca Cdr. W. K. Thompson received a special commendation: "His intelligent and zealous conduct of the initial phase of the search under most trying conditions deserves especial commendation. His reports, together with the wholehearted cooperation of the Commander, Hawaiian Section, US Coast Guard, were of great assistance to the subsequent conduct of operations by the Navy. The performance of the Itasca was excellent in all respects throughout the flight and the search. Careful study of all communications and other information pertaining to the flight, and the preparations, indicate clearly that the Itasca left nothing undone to insure the safe completion of the Earhart flight."[33]

However, not everyone agreed with this assessment of Commander Thompson. Years later, Fred Goerner mentioned to Richard Black his having heard that there was considerable friction between Thompson and Black, emanating from the fact that Black had taken it upon himself to bring a portable high-frequency direction finder unit aboard *Itasca* along with a man to operate it.[34] Thompson's ego had taken a hit, and it showed. Word leaked that Black interfered with the already-established radio watches, and it was none of his business. Goerner asked Black if he had indeed gone over Thompson's head. Black answered,

If I went over Thompson's head I'm not aware of it. In any case it was not much of a head anyway. He was a miserable character and his exec was no better. From the moment I boarded they had a chip on their shoulders ... Thompson resented being ordered to make that particular cruise, and when it extended into a three-week search he was beside himself.[35]

After the search was called off as unsuccessful, there were many backseat advisers. Each had his own view and after-the-fact recommendations. George Putnam, Amelia's husband, got advice from all directions and persons. He even heard from psychics who told him exactly where the Electra wreckage lay. One of the first telegrams to reach Putnam after news of Amelia's disappearance became public was sent from New York to the operations manager, Oakland Airport, California:

PLEASE GET THIS INFORMATION TO GEORGE PUTNAM. EMINENT PSYCHIC SAYS BOTH SAFE ON REEF LESS THAN 200 MILES NORTH WEST HOWLAND ISLAND. PLANE PRETTY WELL CRACKED UP BUT BOTH SAFE. MISS EARHART IN BETTER SHAPE THAN NOONAN. ITASCA WILL FIND THEM IN MORNING. HASTE IS NECESSARY BUT THEY WILL BE RESCUED. PLEASE TAKE THIS FOR WHAT IT IS WORTH FROM A WELL WISHER.[36]

Putnam pushed the government to keep searching. A retired sea captain's telegram referred to an isolated Pacific reef where the natives went to gather turtle eggs, and Putnam had a vision that Amelia might be there. If the government would not help, he would do it himself. The location was near the British Gilbert Islands and happened to be almost exactly where another psychic referred to a similar latitude and longitude where she had visions of Amelia still being alive. Putnam knew Amelia had long been attracted to psychic practices and mystic understandings. Though she never mentioned such phenomena to others, she participated with friends in psychic experiments, including mental telepathy, astrology, and clairvoyant visions. Spiritual directions were coming to Putnam, who was wild with concern over what might have happened to his wife. The clairvoyants were adamant: "Go to the turtle reef!"

He sent numerous telegrams and prevailed himself upon his friends at the State Department. Though it took time to reach the remote British outpost of Tarawa, the government made arrangements for another search about eighty-five miles out, on a bearing of 106° near Makin Island. For a fee of $2,000, a Captain Handley sailed with a small crew in his cutter-rigged sloop to determine if he could find the uncharted reef, where local natives supposedly searched for turtle eggs and where the psychics claimed Amelia would be found. Captain Handley sailed off but returned having failed to find any sign of Amelia or the Electra.

It was all wasted time, effort, and money. Notes in bottles on the shore, letters to the FBI, and strange calls to newspapers and radio stations all pointed the way to the whereabouts of Amelia and Fred. Putnam had received so many telephone calls and telegrams that Western Union delivered their wires to him in huge bundles rather than individually.

Putnam responded to many of those who contacted him. The Ouija Board Women, a group of college women whose fascination with the disappearance of Amelia created an invisible power which moved the wooden finger of their game board to the name of Amelia Earhart, decided to contact George Putnam to discuss Amelia's fate. "We are ordinarily sensible people," they wrote. "But, we found our game turning into something frightening and mysterious. I wish we knew the answer, but are sending the material to you." George Putnam had been contacted by many dedicated psychics, most of whom were just trying to be helpful. His response to the Ouija Board Women was mature, resigned, and empathetic:

> I gather that you regard such manifestations much as I do. That is, with open-mindedness and tempered curiosity. Long ago I became convinced, as did Miss Earhart, that there is much on the borderland of things psychic about which we understand little or nothing. We were both always ready "to be shown." I have had an extraordinary amount of this

kind of communication for many months, coming from sincere people
with no ax to grind, no favors to ask. I have told them what I am telling
you: I honestly do not know how to explain these things.[37]

One of the more vocal players was the US Congress. When it was
discovered that the Earhart search costs had exceeded $4 million (the
equivalent of $75 million in 2012), many voices asked why. In an
attempt to mollify its critics, the Navy stated to the *New York Times* that
Navy crews and ships had been practicing and working, and the attempt
to rescue Amelia provided many opportunities to fly over territory never
before seen and to conduct necessary and functional training.[38]

When the *Itasca* returned to Pearl Harbor upon the unsuccessful
conclusion of the search, Commander Thompson found Treasury
Secretary Henry Morgenthau on the Honolulu pier to greet him. The
secretary, his deputy, Stephen B. Gibbons, and their families were
vacationing in Hawaii. While this impromptu meeting was perhaps
coincidental, there were some raised eyebrows as to why one of FDR's
closest advisers, who also had organizational responsibility for the
Coast Guard, happened to be in Hawaii when the *Itasca* returned.
The *Itasca*'s deck log indicated that Morgenthau and Commander
Thompson had two meetings aboard the Coast Guard cutter on July
28, 1937. There has been speculation by some Earhart sleuths that
Secretary Morgenthau brought the radio log of the *Itasca* back to
Washington with him.

Henry Morgenthau's son, former New York District Attorney
Robert M. Morgenthau, was an executive officer and navigator
on two destroyers during World War II. In a 2003 letter to Earhart
researcher Davey Hamilton, the younger Morgenthau indicated that
he would have been very interested in any information his father had
about Amelia Earhart's disappearance.[39] He quickly added, however,
"I have no recollection of ever discussing the disappearance of Amelia
Earhart with my father." He also confirmed the purpose of the trip
to Hawaii:

> Our family always took a vacation together in the month of August.
> In 1937, we took that vacation in the Hawaiian Islands, which had
> been planned long before the disappearance of Amelia Earhart.
> I cannot shed any light on the minutes of the alleged Treasury
> Department meeting in 1938; I know nothing of the 12 boxes of
> my father's records allegedly stored in the sub-basement of the main
> Treasury Department Building; I doubt very much that he brought
> back the radio log of the Itasca.

A little more than a month after Amelia Earhart and Fred Noonan disappeared, renowned Naval Capt. P. V. H. Weems, inventor of the Weems system of navigation, contacted the Coast Guard requesting copies of *Itasca* radio messages between the Coast Guard cutter and the Earhart Electra. As a distinguished navigator and a friend of Fred Noonan, he wanted to analyze the logs to determine what might have gone wrong on the fatal flight. Rear Adm. R. R. Waesche, Commandant of the Coast Guard, tersely denied access.

Now, if the Lockheed Electra went down at sea after running out of fuel, taking Amelia and Fred with it, as was stated in official Coast Guard and Navy reports, why would Adm. Waesche not allow a renowned navigator, author, and Navy officer to see the *Itasca* messages? And why would it have been "believed inadvisable to submit any of the information for study or publication?"

In any event, there is no denying the magnitude of the US

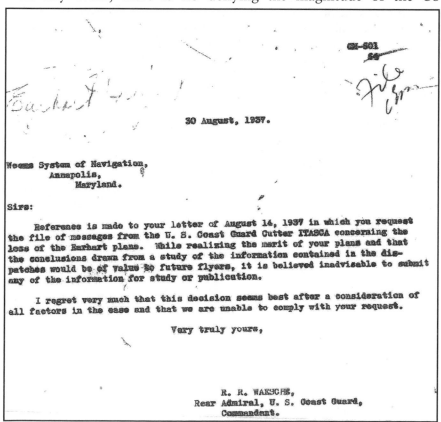

R. R. Waesche's refusal to release documents surrounding Earhart's disappearance, August 30, 1937. (Courtesy National Archives)

Government's effort in conducting what was ultimately a huge Naval search for Amelia, Fred, and the missing Electra, which involved men, ships, and planes from the carrier *Lexington,* the battleship *Colorado,* and the destroyers *Cushing, Lamson,* and *Drayton,* not to mention the Coast Guard cutter *Itasca,* the Navy tug *Ontario,* and the seaplane tender *Swan.* US military men and assets devoted themselves to the search of the Earhart flight for weeks and even months. Whether this reflects concern for America's sweetheart aviatrix and her historic quest or something more significant is left to the judgment of the reader.

We must, however, take a look at one last reference from State Department document No. 1335, Foreign Relations, 1937, Volume IV, dated Washington, September 14, 1937, relative to the Embassy's despatch No. 2523 of August 4, 1937:

> It would be helpful for the Embassy and consular offices in Japan to receive standing instructions in regard to the policy which should be followed in cases wherein the Japanese authorities refuse to permit American consular offices to communicate with American citizens under detention or arrest . . . Discussions have been in suspense for several months because of the failure so far of the Japanese to give satisfactory assurances that American consular officers in Japan shall have the right to visit American citizens under detention or arrest in that country.

Chapter 9

A Powder Keg

Genuinely as a tribute to her sex rather than for her glorification, she accepted the honors that accrued—for the participation of women in aviation, which at all times she strove to encourage and pace, was the obsession which lured her to her death. Why did she attempt that hazardous expedition? She had to. She was caught up in the hero racket which compelled her to strive for increasingly dramatic records, bigger and braver feats that automatically insured the publicity necessary to the maintenance of her position as the foremost woman pilot in the world.

—Hilton H. Railey[1]

After the widespread search for Earhart and Noonan seemed fruitless, the White House was unable to conceal from the public the possibility that America's sweetheart aviatrix had been shot down or forced down by Japanese aircraft, removing all evidence of her plane from the face of the earth. Among those who were convinced of this explanation of Amelia's disappearance was Claude A. Swanson, Secretary of the Navy, who told Congressman William I. Sirovich of New York that, under the circumstances, it was incredible to believe that the Earhart plane could have disappeared without a trace unless every matchstick of it had been deliberately destroyed. According to Swanson,

This is a powder keg. Any public discussion will furnish the torch for the explosion. I firmly believe that Miss Earhart, in trying to reach Howland Island, a speck on the map, lost her directions by a sudden shift in the wind and was brought down over territory she was not supposed to see. We are aware that something is going on there. I am not the only one in this department who feels that she saw activities which she could not have described later and remained alive. That is the only explanation I can reach for the blotting out of her plane and every solitary piece of her equipment. Otherwise, something would have remained. The attention which the Japanese newspapers paid to the smallest details of this sad flight from the time it began shows the peculiar interest with which Japan followed every mile of her progress. To speculate about this publicly would sever our diplomatic relations with Japan and lead to something worse.[2]

Japan's Position in the 1930s

Long before a World Flight was even a glint in Amelia's eyes, the Government of Japan was free-falling into the hands of a militaristic group of radicals bent on controlling the Pacific region of the world. The 1930s saw Japan provoking China and invading Manchuria in September 1931 and Jehol in 1933. Tientsin ceded to them as a result. The year 1936 saw them withdraw from discussions with the United States and England to limit the types and numbers of each country's naval ships. To imply that they had definite long range plans would have been an understatement.

On the other side of the world, America was struggling to overcome its economic depression. It had few funds for military equipment and expansion and an army and navy whose men were trained with World War I weaponry, supplies, and equipment. Its population was busy trying to find jobs and had little interest in faraway happenings or gathering intelligence in a distant and little understood region of the world.

Just a few days after Amelia was to land at Howland Island, Japan attacked Wanping, China, near the Marco Polo Bridge, on July 5, 1937. Five months later, Japanese dive bombers sank the US gunboat *Panay* in the Yangtze River along with a similar craft of Great Britain. Both vessels had been stationed there to protect American and English interests in the region. The United States and Britain protested these incidents and were awarded some damages but did not press the issue in terms of a bigger picture.

Throughout this period, Japan was buying Lockheed and Douglas aircraft in the US. They later were licensed to produce these aircraft in Japan with American engineers re-locating to that country to assist in the process. "This saved the Japanese aircraft industry months of development time and both types [of aircraft] remained in Japanese service throughout the Pacific War as standard military transports."[3]

The Japanese did not appreciate Juan Trippe's flying boat incursions into their territories. Trippe, the president of Pan American Airways, made deals with the US Navy to land at various island bases, including Hong Kong. The Japanese recognized his encroachment, and in their way of thinking, this was an infringement by America into Japan's part of the world. It probably blew their minds when they learned

Juan Trippe, founder of Pan American Airways.

Gen. Claire Chennault, American adviser to CNAC and leader of the Flying Tigers.

of Trippe's involvement with CNAC, the China National Airline, not to mention American Gen. Claire Chennault's association with that group in 1937. Japan certainly took note of the famous Pan American Airways pilot, Capt. Ed Musick, departing San Francisco on a survey route to New Zealand on the same day that Amelia left on her around-the-world flight to Hawaii. We recognize also that Japanese efforts to sabotage Juan Trippe's Pan Am clippers are a matter of recorded history.

Although a closely guarded Defense Department secret, we now know that American aircraft did take some liberties during the search for the missing fliers and did over-fly certain islands within the Japanese held Marshall group. This fact was cited by Francis X. Holbrook in his thesis, *United States Defense and Transpacific Commercial Air Routes 1933-1941*. He noted, "During the air sweeps conducted by the *Lexington*'s squadrons, several of the Japanese islands in the Marshalls were flown over."[4]

To this day, both the CIA and Japanese officials claim to know nothing about Amelia or Noonan having been in the Marshall Islands or Saipan. However, certain realities are now evident with regard to United States and Japanese involvement in Amelia's around-the-world flight.

The Japanese had more than a passing interest in Earhart's around-the-world attempt, which was confirmed by their daily newspaper accounts. They were better prepared and positioned to keep tabs on the

Maj. Gen. Oscar Westover, head of the US Army Air Corps.

Ernest J. King, Fleet Admiral. (Courtesy Library of Congress)

progress of the flight with their high-powered radio direction finders.

We know in hindsight that they were busily engaged in preparing fortifications on key atolls and were extremely sensitive about any outsiders getting near. This sensitivity was confirmed when Japan told America that they would handle any searching for the missing plane and pilots in their territorial seas without any US assistance. There is no question that the Japanese were suspicious of US planes or ships staging any kind of search anywhere near their islands.

The US had no ships along the Earhart track flown other than the tug *Ontario,* stationed south of Nauru Island, and the aircraft tender *Swan,* positioned halfway between Howland and Hawaii. Of course, the USCG cutter *Itasca* was positioned at Howland Island.

The Japanese had better high-frequency radio direction finders on land and at sea than did the US. Whether the large number of Japanese "fishing fleet" vessels was equipped with DF's is not known, but they certainly had marine radios and were better situated to follow the flight and respond to and find any downed airplanes.

Official US references have been cited (Coast Guard, Navy, and Pan American Airways) confirming radio signals from KHAQQ being heard for several days after Amelia's no-show at Howland Island.

The Coast Guard cutter *Itasca*'s radio logs reflected no pertinent calls or messages after the plane was last heard from. But, individual

Allen Dulles, director of the CIA from 1953 to 1961. (Courtesy National Archives)

William H. Webster, director of the CIA from 1987 to 1991. (Courtesy National Archives)

Itasca officers later spoke and wrote of having heard over the radio a woman's hysterical scream during the last radio contact. This information certainly was not recorded in any of the *Itasca* radio logs preserved for posterity. With the many contradictions, it is reasonable to infer that the ship documents and summary reports from officers later were edited to support the official government conclusion of the last known moments of the fateful flight.

If this were not the case, why would the US Navy have sequestered the Pan Am RDF reports that were so conscientiously prepared by their highly qualified station managers? The records of direction-finder bearings on strange signals believed to be from the Electra taken during July 3-5, 1937, and submitted to Pan Am's head office in Alameda, California, contradict the precision indicated in the initial logs and reports. In addition, there is this after-the-fact letter from Frederick Hooven, the inventor of the high-frequency direction finder:

> Considering the stupidity exhibited by Earhart with regard to her navigation and communications, and all the useless strain and work it cost the US Navy . . . the reasons why the military services continue to keep so much of the information classified may at last come to light . . . If it were not for the radio signals received after the flight there would be no reason to believe anything else.[5]

A final thought that should be considered is a letter dated June 7, 1979, from Fred Goerner to Hooven, referencing a native report from Tabiteuea in the British controlled Gilbert group confirming a plane passed over in the early morning hours of July 2 flying eastward. "If so," said Goerner, "Noonan was dead on course at that point, some 14 hours after leaving Lae, assuming 140 mph ground speed average to that time . . ."

Initially, the Japanese probably were unsure as to what to do with Amelia and Fred when they were "rescued" in the Marshall Islands. The small Japanese Army contingent that found the American fliers might have momentarily considered a goodwill gesture to notify our State Department, but communications were difficult in that part of the world. Their location near Mili Atoll was a great distance from Tokyo, some two thousand nautical miles, but only thirteen hundred miles from Japanese regional headquarters at Saipan. Nobody would ever know the American fliers were in Japanese custody in that isolated part of the Pacific.

Frederick J. Hooven, inventor of the radio direction finder.

With increasing military paranoia over maintaining secrecy about their clandestine construction projects in the Marshalls, the longer the American fliers were held there, the more difficult it would be to let them go or even announce their presence. The militaristic Japanese Army clearly did not appreciate America's alliance with Chinese interests and remained arrogant and in a war-mongering mode through their surrender of WWII. It was not their problem that Amelia and Fred made the choice to put their airplane down in Japanese-mandated islands. To Japanese eyes and minds, these newly arrived aviators had to be spies.

Former Pacific Fleet intelligence officer, Cdr. Edwin Layton, noted that the US Naval Intelligence unit at Pearl Harbor had developed data in late 1940 and early 1941 confirming Japanese violations within their WWI mandate agreement. In May 1941, he briefed Admiral Kimmel, head of CINCPACFLT, that evidence had been obtained regarding Japan's violations from monitoring Japanese radio traffic, submarine surveillance, voluntary comments from friendly merchant mariners, and even helpful suggestions from Pan American Airways pilots who purposely passed near to Japanese occupied islands and reported what they saw. "On Kwajalein and Jaluit in the Marshalls there was evidence that seaplane and submarine bases had been blasted out of coral lagoons. At Ponape in the Carolines transmitting towers rose high above the Palm trees. Airstrips capable of handling long-range bombers had been bulldozed across the cane fields of Saipan in the Marianas. A deep-water anchorage at Truk Lagoon offered an advance base big enough to shelter the entire Japanese Combined Fleet." Following the Japanese attack on Pearl Harbor, Truk became known as the Gibraltar of the Pacific.

National Reactions

Gen. Frank Andrews also was convinced that Amelia's Electra had been brought down by the Japanese. "The President," he said, "would not have ordered a fighting naval armada to the scene if the suspicion had not been officially entertained. When we start shedding American blood out there we will find out what all of this means."[6]

Although the Roosevelt Administration was concerned about the possible reasons as to why the Japanese were so protective of what was happening on their islands, little was done about it. Reports from Australia, New Zealand, and other allies noted a level of concern

Adm. Milton Miles, OSS chief, China. (Courtesy National Archives)

over Japan's movement of heavy equipment and construction material to the mandates. On one hand, this raised suspicions for many in the Roosevelt Cabinet. On the other hand, the American people did not want to get involved in another international conflict, having just settled down from World War I. Most US citizens were struggling to emerge from the ravages of recession. Few wanted to involve themselves in a foreign country's business on the other side of the globe. The degree of militarization of Japan's mandated islands remained a huge taboo for the United States.

Four years later, after the infamous nightmare at Pearl Harbor, the United States learned exactly what Japan had been up to during the period of Earhart's around-the-world flight. Air bases had been constructed or under preparation at Jaluit, Maloelap, and Wotje Atolls. Kwajalein, one of the largest coral atolls, saw major construction of housing and support buildings for a huge garrison, and its strategic air base, Roi-Namur, became home to the longest runway in the world at that time. While the US suspected that the Japanese were using the islands as forward naval bases, the extent of their fortifications was unknown until pilots took combat aerial reconnaissance photos as the Americans fought back after Pearl Harbor.

Not long after Amelia's disappearance, the October 16, 1937, issue of *Smith's Weekly* leaked an Australian Defense Department tip about America's naval planes flying over some of the Japanese mandated islands while searching for the lost Electra of Earhart and Noonan. Japan had earlier notified the US State Department that Japan would use its own aircraft and ships to search its territorial waters. In other words, Japan demanded that the United States stay out. The article read, "U.S.A. Does Australia a Secret Service: Amelia Earhart Search Made the Opportunity."

Until now the real story has been withheld of the desperate international intrigue bracketing Australia that went with the search for ill-fated Amelia Earhart, when that intrepid aviatrix crashed into the Pacific somewhere near the Phoenix Islands.

It is a story of military tactics that went hand in hand with the terrific expense of £500,000 spent on American naval planes.

American planes did more than just search for Amelia Earhart. They cut a wide swath over the Pacific and circled near the Caroline and Marshall Islands.

Here Australia comes into the picture. The grim threat of war appears a little closer when it is realized that the groups of islands, and another (Yap), controlled by Japan, lie right at Australia's northern door.

Under cover of the search for the missing aviatrix, America's naval aircraft were anxious to glimpse two of the islands, believed by military experts to have been fortified by the Japanese. The Australian Government now knows more about that search than has been disclosed publicly.

When Japan struck so suddenly at China, and its war machine blackened Shanghai, the doctrine of naked force was revealed. The it-can't-happen-nowadays theory was bayoneted out of existence.

Australia's interest lies in the fact that quietly and with the usual lack of publicity Japan has been working to get closer to the Commonwealth, building Japanese bases admirably suited for an expedition into the Pacific. This knowledge does not add to a feeling of security, when armies march into foreign countries practically without warning and start to "mop up."

This is grim news to the War Department. It means there are military occupation, fortification, bases and war materiel, prying eyes are not permitted to see in cases like these.

So when Amelia Earhart went down and her faint distress signals

Smith's Weekly *article featuring the search for Amelia Earhart and the discovery of Japan's severe fortifications.*

located her plane around the Phoenix Islands, the search for her gave the pretext that was needed. Sentiment comes second to secret service.

U.S. planes swept over the waters around Phoenix Islands and then took a wide turn and went farther. They circled on, covering the areas in which the Caroline and Marshall Islands are to be found. Naval flying men are admirable observers. It is their profession.

America poured out money on this search. Allowing for the human interest, the search was so costly that only those on the inside even guessed at the purpose of the expenditure. It was the opportunity not to be missed, a real excuse to fly over Japan's islands by mandate, to observe what the waters contained. Today the Australian Government has been apprised of some of the knowledge gleaned. With the world situation as it is and with Australia's neglect of defense over the years the knowledge came as a godsend—paid for by the U.S.A.

Word of the *Smith's Weekly* article describing the US fly-over of certain mandated islands soon reached Japanese eyes.[7] In a telegram dated December 6, 1937, to Consul-General Wakamatau in Sydney, Australia, Foreign Minister Hirota requested that he be sent two copies of the newspaper "carrying an article regarding Madame Earhart reported missing in the Pacific this summer."[8]

Few official US Government records indicate whether President Roosevelt was involved in the Earhart around-the-world flight. There are, however, numerous letters and telegrams to him or his wife, Eleanor, from Amelia and her husband, George Putnam. Presidential files at the FDR Library in Hyde Park, New York, are replete with letters and telegrams to the Roosevelts, their assistants, and others involved in the administration. Presidential Assistant Marvin McIntyre received the bulk of these contacts, but he wasn't alone. Amelia and her husband directed requests at the likes of Secretary of State Cordell Hull, Secretary of the Navy Claude Swanson, and Director of Air Commerce Eugene Vidal, to name a few. The Putnams weren't modest in stating their wishes—they requested that the proposed airstrip to be built on Howland Island be expedited so that Amelia might land the Electra there and rest after her long flight from New Guinea; they wanted in-flight refueling to be provided by the Navy as Amelia approached Midway Island; and they requested that State Department personnel should process some twenty requests for clearance into foreign countries, including visas, fuel, food and lodging. Most of these requests were satisfied.

Though he was not directly linked with the Earhart around-the-world effort, there is every indication that FDR in fact followed the logistics and planning of Amelia's flight, even though Mrs. Roosevelt was already involved.[9] As late as April 1945, an aide in the Office of Naval Records stated, "There was no information in the files of the Chief of Naval Operations to indicate there was White House interest in the search for Amelia Earhart." There was, however, a note of clarification: "It would appear that whatever the President did was done by personal conversation or by telephone."[10]

When the Electra failed to reach Howland Island, President Roosevelt didn't hesitate to order a massive naval search. Not only were Fourteenth Naval District fleet vessels and planes at Pearl Harbor involved but also the aircraft carrier *Lexington,* then at Santa Barbara, California, was pressed into action along with an assortment of destroyers based in San Diego.

During that period, the US regularly reviewed Tokyo's diplomatic code and, to a lesser extent, the Japanese naval code. In view of the extensive search for the missing Lockheed Electra, it is a near certainty that the American codebreakers paid considerable attention to the greatly increased numbers of wireless messages originating from the Marshall Islands. Listening from Guam and Cavite and possibly from US Navy ships, specialists very carefully tuned to Japanese radio communications, where they could follow the Earhart search from the Japanese point of view. Wailupe was the US Navy operations station in Hawaii and was staffed around the clock with qualified radiomen. Heeia was the designated intercept center but was staffed with only a handful of men in 1937. Lualualei, Hawaii, became the primary direction-finding location in the islands.[11]

When American code breakers recognized that Amelia's airplane likely had come down near the Japan-mandated islands, it did not take long for word to be relayed to Washington. None of this information could be released to the public without compromising our intelligence capabilities, which further fueled the Navy's paranoia concerning secrecy on the Amelia incident. Though relations with Japan were fast deteriorating, Japan remained America's best foreign trade partner. America sold about $250 million of products to Japan during 1937—the equivalent of $5 billion in 2012.[12]

FDR, who was prone to dabble in intelligence matters, had to figure out what to do about the Earhart dilemma. As time passed, his choices narrowed. He appeared to have ordered some form of Presidential secrecy to be stamped on key documents relating to the unfortunate Earhart episode in order to keep the

Bernard Baruch, presidential adviser.

records of Amelia's fate out of the public's vision. The documents could only be released in the future by another president.

Although no document or report has been found to confirm whether a Presidential Seal was placed on Earhart documents, it is the only possible explanation why the Earhart trail of evidence stops cold—even with regard to verified sources. Though FDR died in 1945, files that existed in the 1950s and 1960s have disappeared. Also gone are key memorandums and references noted by early Earhart researchers.

During the course of Fred Goerner's research, he stumbled across a conspicuous absence of files and documentation. Goerner noted the lack of forthcoming information from people who should have had specific answers. When speaking with his friend Ross Game, who helped with Goerner's research, Fred claimed, "No one laughs at me or puts me down, but every time I begin to follow a lead, those in official places get defensive. . . . From what we've learned, I have to believe Earhart and Noonan were captured by the Japanese and more than a few people in Washington knew about or suspected it long before Pearl Harbor."[13]

Ross Game, of course, shared Goerner's view. In a letter to Utah Senator Wallace Bennett's office, he stated:

> It is fantastic to find that federal officials now deny that certain files exist when those same files were shown to three of us only two years ago. And in a classified Department of the Navy file was an intelligence report indicating that many of the witnesses we had found were checked out by the Navy Intelligence people. This report indicated that there was nothing to indicate that the people talking to us were telling anything but the truth.
>
> We're getting much double talk from the government. It would appear as though the Defense and State Departments are trying to hide something much larger than the Earhart story.[14]

Fred Goerner also believed in the likelihood of a Presidential Seal having been placed on some of the more definitive Amelia Earhart classified files, as indicated in this quote in a letter from 1976:

> We learned that records dealing with the Japanese involvement with Earhart are currently being housed in top-secret files at Fort Holabird, Maryland. They are files of U.S. Army CIC from Tokyo after 1946. The files carry a Presidential classification which can be removed only by another President. We have been trying in recent months through various channels to persuade President Ford to release the material, but nothing so far.[15]

In addition to the clamp-down on government files and papers, FDR also sent his friend and Hyde Park neighbor William Vincent Astor and his yacht *Nourmahal* to cruise the Pacific and see if Astor might gain entry to the Marshall Islands as a private yacht. Even the tiniest bit of information gained would have been helpful.[16]

In the spring of 1938, Vince Astor and an assemblage of close friends, including Kermit Roosevelt, son of Theodore Roosevelt, headed on a cruise in the South Seas. Boarding the *Nourmahal* in Panama, they were to sail first to Honolulu, then to Tahiti and Fiji. Honolulu, however, was not their first stop—it was the last stop before returning home. Astor said that the purpose of the trip was "to collect tropical deep-sea specimens for the Bermuda Aquarium." He turned over thirteen pages of handwritten notes on *Nourmahal* letterhead to President Roosevelt. The notes revealed some interesting points.[17] Astor wrote to Roosevelt:

> I shall make a complete report to O.N.I. However, in the remote possibility of trouble between now and then, you might consider the following conclusions concerning the Marshall Islands. First, I did not visit any Japanese Island. (Sounds fairly cowardly after the arrangements you made!) A letter received at Suva from the Jap[anese] Consulate General in N.Y. led me to believe that an application to visit this territory would be favourably considered. (This was probably a successful leg pull on me.) So I made my application through the N.Y. Consulate to the Minister of Overseas Affairs-Tokyo to enter at Jaluit. Permission was withheld not only for this, but to go anywhere else in the Marshalls. (The radio correspondence is quite instructive.)
>
> I happened to have learned what happened to the two latest British Intelligence efforts, and it seemed evident that any attempt to get in would produce zero in useful results, and about a 100% probability of making serious trouble for you, and the State and Navy Departments. So I spent my time circulating amongst the neighboring Ellice and Gilbert Islands picking up all I could. Here are the results in brief. They are not guaranteed as exact facts, but are conclusions which I believe to be substantially correct.

Astor reported on details he had picked up from British sources in other island groups. His comments covered Eniwetok, which he surmised would become the Japanese principal naval base; Bikini, their "second string" base; and Wotje, where an airplane landing field was being expanded and where six submarines and a tender had been observed in the lagoon. According to the British, who passed along this data, it was their opinion that Wotje would be used as a base for submarines and commerce raiders. Jaluit was the administrative seat of the Marshalls and the port of the greatest importance. Astor reported spotting searchlights and observation balloons but no fortifications. Regrettably, there was no mention of Amelia Earhart.[18]

In a transcript of a 1938 meeting with Treasury Secretary Henry Morgenthau, Under Secretary Stephen Gibbons noted, "We have evidence the thing is all over. Sure. Terrible. It would be awful to make it public." In that same meeting, Morgenthau referred to "the report of all those wireless messages and everything else," presumably obtained from the decrypting of intercepted Japanese radio transmissions.

Not only was the United States reading the Japanese diplomatic code, but so were the Soviets. Although Stalin had signed the German-Soviet Pact in 1939, it was nonetheless a fact that Russia, France, and

England—the old allies of WWI—had been monitoring the recent German-Japanese alliance. By the early 1930s, Soviet decrypting specialists made it their task to develop anti-Japanese intelligence. A decrypting and interception agency headed by Col. Gleb Boky and Colonel Kharkevitch was devoted to the interception of Japanese wireless transmissions.[19]

This activity was well documented by Roger Faligot, a French specialist on international spying efforts, who collaborated with numerous Japanese historians and university professors to document the breaking of the Japanese codes by the Americans, Australians, and Russians. In May 1941, Japan's Ambassador Nomura sent this extraordinary message: "From Washington (Nomura) to Tokyo: #327. Intelligence: Although I do not know which ones, I have discovered that the United States can read some of our codes. To inform you how I obtained this information I will communicate by mail or other safe means."[20]

American cryptologists continued to succeed in breaking the Japanese codes and would do so through the end of World War II. This remarkable message dated December 2, 1941, was stamped KOKKA HIMITSU (State Secret) by Kameyama Kazuji, chief of the Japanese Transmission Center in their Ministry of Foreign Affairs: "NIITAKA YAMA NOBORE 1208." Translation: "To climb Mount Niitaka on December 8." This was the coded message announcing the final decision to attack on Pearl Harbor.[21] December 8 in Japan would have been December 7 in Hawaii because of the International Date Line. In short, FDR and his administration kept tabs on Japanese activity—and Amelia and Fred's story remained a part of those secrets for many years.

Meanwhile, Amelia's husband was dealing with a different set of affairs. In the Los Angeles court of Superior Judge Elliot Craig on January 5, 1939, eighteen difficult months after Amelia's disappearance, George Palmer Putnam was addressed by a judge: "Mr. Putnam, do you believe your wife is alive?"

His answer required several moments. "No, Your Honor."

"Then, with all the evidence before me, I can reach no other decision. Amelia Earhart Putnam died on or about July 2, 1937."[22]

Under normal circumstances and procedure, it took seven years before a missing person could be legally declared deceased by a court of law. However, the extremely well-publicized and documented Navy search and the eminence of the parties involved induced the judge's decision to help G. P.'s mourning and speed the process.

As the months went by and America entered World War II, Amelia Earhart and Fred Noonan faded from the spotlight—but not from America's memory.

In February 1940, a group of Earhart followers attempted to raise funds for another search: "No sufficient search was ever really made, and they either are now alive on land in the lonely, untraveled nowhere of their disappearance, or have since died, praying they would be found."[23] Among the organizers were Amelia's mother, Amy Otis Earhart; Clarence S. Williams, the pilot and navigator who helped chart Amelia's course around the world; Paul Mantz, Amelia's technical adviser and friend; E. H. Dimity, an Earhart friend and parachute manufacturer who founded the Amelia Earhart Foundation (much to the dismay of George Putnam, who had not been contacted); Walter E. McMenamy, a ham radio operator who followed the Earhart flight and heard the SOS calls; Margot DeCarie, Amelia's personal aide and secretary; and Palmer Bevis, a New York investor. Though their search and rescue program never got off the ground, the logic and thinking of the group provides insight into why they believed Earhart and Noonan did not crash and sink:[24]

With little fuel, what would experienced fliers do? They had undoubtedly passed many islands on the course behind them. Any pilot under the circumstances would have gone back to those islands and landed, relying on their radio and on searching parties for rescue.

The Ellice Islands, about six hundred miles southwest of Howland, were never searched, and not all of the Gilbert Islands were searched.

McMenamy stated with authority that he was well aware of the characteristic noise of Amelia's transmitter, which he helped install. He certified that the signals he heard on her wavelength on July 3 came from the Electra. The first SOS message was repeated for about five minutes. Two days later, the morning of July 5, both McMenamy and Karl Pierson picked up the signals. Afterwards, they heard a decided sputtering, indicating the batteries were exhausted. Howland Island also reported hearing KHAQQ that morning.

The morning of July 3, the British cruiser *Achilles* reported hearing an unknown station saying, "Please give us a few dashes if you get us." This was heard on the Earhart frequency of 3105 kcs. The station then reported "KHAQQ" twice before disappearing.

The Earhart plane must have come down on land, as evidenced by its ability to transmit. The possibility that the messages were a cruel hoax was dismissed, because there were no other transmitters in that part of the world that could have sent the signals.

Even after World War II broke out, Amelia's mother never gave up hope that her daughter might still be alive. In response to an Associated Press reference to a Japanese trader who had seen an American woman pilot in custody of the Japanese military prior to the War, Mrs. Amy Earhart wrote in 1944:

> It does happen to fit in with information brought me by a friend a few days after Amelia's SOS who was listening to a former schoolmate's short-wave radio when a broadcast from Tokyo came in saying they were celebrating there with parades, etc. because of Amelia's rescue or pick up by a Japanese fisherman. That was before the war you know, and evidently the ordinary Jap had no knowledge of their military leaders' plans so were proud of the rescue and expected the world to be.
>
> Many other things have come to me from time to time from people interested and who no more believe she crashed into the sea than I did. I have thought for some time she was being kept a prisoner there, because of what she saw and which they knew would be reported if she didn't have an accident happen to her, which did to several sent by the government to see if those islands were not being fortified. It all fell together as small pieces came in and makes a story. I have said very little about much that I have gathered and especially about that connected with the Jap prisoner side of it, except to a very few close-lipped friends, not even telling Muriel [Amelia's sister] for I couldn't check up on it and had no desire to start rumors which would worry Muriel, as it often does me . . .[25]

It seems, though, that Muriel did learn of the possibility of Amelia's imprisonment by the Japanese. In 1961, she wrote to Fred Goerner asking, "Would you please brief me again? Were records of Amelia's death from dysentery given to you by the Japanese Navy or the government in Tokyo? Also, I am not clear about the length of elapsed time between the crash landing of the Electra near Jaluit and the imprisonment of the fliers on Saipan." Goerner responded as follows:

> The possibility of dysentery being the cause of your sister's death was discerned from testimony given by the Saipanese natives to the Navy and Church authorities. To my knowledge, Japan has not released any records to our government. The information concerning the Lockheed Electra landing on or near Jaluit in the Marshall Islands was given to me by the Navy. Commander Paul Bridwell, ComNav Saipan, did not reveal the exact sources of this information, but did suggest the radio logs of several United States vessels plying the far western Pacific in the late 1930s might prove fruitful for further research. I do not know the full extent of the Navy's knowledge or the specific results of the ONI's investigation of

this past year. The Navy did conjecture with me that it might have been several months before Amelia and Fred finally reached Saipan.[26]

Goerner probably interviewed more military officials than any other Earhart author. His CBS radio broadcasting experience along with his ability to talk and meet with people at all levels opened many doors. He was relentless in his pursuit for information on what really happened to Amelia and his passion was contagious. At a retirement party honoring Cdr. John Pillsbury, who had served as public information officer for the Twelfth Naval District and as an aide to Fleet Adm. Chester Nimitz, Pillsbury took Goerner aside and said, "I'm officially retired now, so I'm going to tell you a couple of things. You're on the right track with your Amelia Earhart investigation. Admiral Nimitz wants you to continue, and he says you're on to something that will stagger your imagination."[27] When Goerner asked Commander Pillsbury to encourage Admiral Nimitz to tell Goerner the entire Earhart story, Pillsbury answered: "Even though the Admiral is seventy-seven, he still is on active duty. There's a limit to what he can tell you, particularly if the matter concerns classified information."

Prior to leaving for Washington, DC, for interviews with high-level Marine Corps generals, Goerner received a telephone call from Nimitz. "Now that you're going to Washington, Fred," the Admiral stated, "I want to tell you Earhart and her navigator did go down in the Marshalls and were picked up by the Japanese."[28] Although Goerner pressed the Admiral for more information, he did not receive any more hints, as Nimitz, then an adviser to the Secretary of Defense, was still on active duty. No matter the outcome, Goerner still felt rewarded for his efforts. He had clear proof that all of his research and time had pushed him in the right direction.[29]

The confirmation by Admiral Nimitz that Earhart and Noonan did, in fact, crash in the Marshall Islands was a significant and historic revelation. It may very likely have originated with one of Nimitz's intelligence officers, Rear Adm. Edwin T. Layton, as evidenced by the following quote:

The conversation turned to Fred Goerner's book which I had just recently finished. My admiral had not read it but he told me almost exactly the story hypothesized by Goerner in his last chapter, including that Earhart was first taken by the Japanese to Kwajalein before being taken to Saipan, where she was killed. I asked the source of this information. The admiral said he had been told by a classmate [Annapolis '24] named Leighton [author's phonetic spelling] who had been intelligence chief to Nimitz.[30]

On August 10, 1971, Gen. Alexander A. Vandegrift, who was commandant of the Marine Corps during most of World War II, wrote to Goerner and confirmed that Amelia Earhart and her navigator, Fred Noonan, had perished on Saipan in Japanese custody. Vandegrift told Goerner that he had obtained this information from Gen. Thomas Watson, who commanded the Second Marine Division during the hard-fought assault on Saipan in 1944.[31]

In November 1966, Goerner interviewed Gen. Graves Erskine at WCBS radio in San Francisco. During this discussion, Goerner brought up the subject of Amelia Earhart. General Erskine made an astonishing admission: "It was established that Earhart was on Saipan, but that's all I'm going to say. You'll have to dig the rest out yourself."

Ross Game later confirmed: "Nimitz gave us names of others who knew the story. Still, many of the wartime commanders who might have known something refused to admit anything."[32] Game acknowledged that he and Goerner were allowed to view secret State Department and CIA files in the presence of a senior State Department person and a Navy Intelligence officer (a captain), but they could not take any pictures or make any copies:

> We had access to classified files on Amelia thanks to my friend Pierre Salinger at the White House. In fact, President Kennedy was tremendously interested in our work. Had it not been for his untimely death, both Fred and I believed Kennedy was giving consideration to removing the classified seal from the key Earhart documents. Pierre kept the President informed as to the military leaders with whom we were talking, the questions we were asking, and the information we had developed, all of which kindled the President's fascination. Actually, I think JFK was a little hesitant to be the one to remove fellow democrat Roosevelt's executive privilege classifying Earhart data confidential. But I can tell you, if there was any President who might have accomplished it, Kennedy would have been the most likely one. Lyndon Johnson surely didn't want any part of it.
>
> One of the most significant things we learned from those secret CIA files was the fact that much of the information the Government was keeping under wraps we already had obtained from various private citizens. Probably the most significant revelation was the likelihood Amelia died in September 1937, on Saipan. There was a notation that

Noonan's death occurred about the same time. Other information indicated that George Putnam, an Air Corps major serving in the China theater, was allowed to travel privately to Saipan to view the gravesite of his wife. This was after the remains had been exhumed by the Marine Intelligence officer. It was through the CIA that we were able to learn the names of the Marines involved. The CIA was tremendously helpful.

Captain Tracy Griswold was the Marine Intelligence officer in charge of the detail, although he was not happy about our contacting him, and gave us little or no information. He had asked for volunteers from Company D, Second Battalion, Eighteenth Marine Regiment. The two who were selected were PFC Billy Burks, who we found years later in Texas, and PFC Everett Henson, Jr., whose home location I've forgotten. Both were very cooperative and I'm convinced they told it just like the story played out.

They confirmed that Griswold was an intelligence officer and he seemed to be acting on orders from higher up. The captain drove the privates to a small native cemetery near Garapan. He apparently had some notes and a small map as he was looking for a grove of trees just outside the cemetery. They came upon an old and twisted tree with a large double trunk in front of which there was a slight depression in the ground. In the center of the depression there were several chunks of white bleached coral rocks piled on top of each other. Griswold instructed the two marines to dig there.

Upon unearthing badly decomposed bodies wrapped in rough cloth they moved more dirt as the captain began placing the bones in a container. When no more bones were found the hole was filled. One of the marines asked why they had opened the grave. The captain stared at the private and muttered, "Ever hear of Amelia Earhart?" After being told there'd be no more questions, the privates were ordered not to say anything about the incident. Burks later volunteered to us that he heard the remains were secretly taken to Washington.

We learned Griswold had retired from the Corps in 1963. When contacted on the telephone in 1965 by Fred Goerner, he admitted having come ashore on Red Beach One at Saipan in 1944. Yes, he had served as an Intelligence Officer with the Eighteenth Marines, Second Division. No, he couldn't recall being responsible for exhuming any graves. He was also unable to remember the names of the two privates he recruited to do the digging. He did invite Fred to his home in Pennsylvania where they might discuss the matter. Goerner never made further contact.

On April 16, 1965, after meeting personally with General Wallace M. Greene, Jr., Commandant of the U.S. Marine Corps in Washington, we followed up with a letter reminding the General of our questions:

Basically, we asked him does the U.S. Marine Corps officially confirm or deny that three Marines of the Second Division disinterred the remains of two individuals from a grave outside a native cemetery on the island of Saipan after the island was secured in 1944? And, what was discovered and what was the disposition and subsequent identification of the remains?

The Commandant denied knowing anything.

After Lyndon Johnson succeeded Kennedy as President our access to the CIA went completely downhill. Johnson was adamant that he didn't want to hear any more discussion about Amelia Earhart. He literally slammed the door on us saying he didn't give a damn about the woman. He personally threatened my CIA friend saying he was on thin ice and Fred and I were off limits. We were completely cut off from our previous support and vital Federal sources . . .

From Commandant Green came a clipped and condensed written response: "The Marine Corps takes no position on these questions."[33] Even more interesting is that USMC Tracy Griswold, ret., immediately went on file with Col. Randolph C. Berkeley Jr., assistant chief of staff, G-2, Headquarters, US Marine Corps. In a letter dated May 24, 1965, barely a month after Fred Goerner's letter to the Marine Corps Commandant, Major Griswold notified headquarters of the following:

Specifically, I do not recall any single patrol activity where any investigation was made at the supposed graveyard in question . . . I fully believe therefore that the incident in question, if it occurred, involved the presence of others and the possible use of my name as a cover for the activities. I again reiterate I have no knowledge or remembrance of such a patrol and am so advising both Mr. Goerner and Mr. Game.

The timing of this letter, along with its phrasing, suggests that it may have been written as a result of a request or an order. Its legalistic formality certainly presents the possibility that it was prepared by the Judge Advocate General Corps counsel.

According to Ross Game, "Griswold only admitted to being on Saipan. He never admitted to knowing the privates, having anything to do with that grave, or carrying away the remains. A lot of these intelligence guys still recall taking an oath of secrecy back in their wartime days. Some of them carry it to their graves. But the important point to remember is that Griswold never denied the grave disinterment took place, either."

Although it took almost another twenty years for the two Marine

Randolph C. Berkeley Jr., major general, USMC.
(Courtesy United States Marine Corps)

privates to come clean, Burks and Henson finally stepped forward. Former PFC Billy G. Burks wrote to Col. John G. Miller, USMC, Marine Historical Section, in a letter dated March 27, 1983. In this letter, he stated very positively:

The United States Marine Corps investigated the Earhart disappearance in 1960, and takes the position that there was no involvement by the United States Marine Corps on Saipan in a grave excavation believed to be that of Amelia Earhart. The Marine Corps is not fully informed. There was Marine involvement of a grave excavation on the Island of Saipan in 1944 shortly after the invasion of Saipan. I was part of that involvement.

It was Henson who found the grave, not too far from a very large, forked tree. Captain Griswold gave us shovels that he brought with him and told us to start digging. Henson asked Captain Griswold who we were digging up. The Captain answered, "Did you ever hear of Amelia Earhart?" We said we had. He then told us to keep quiet and keep digging. We found bones. By the looks of it there were two skeletons. We put the bones in a body bag or box, I can't remember which, and then in the jeep. We filled in the grave, got in the jeep, and Captain Griswold drove us back to our barracks. The remains of the grave went with Captain Griswold.

On April 21, 1981, former Marine PFC Everett W. Henson Jr. wrote to Earhart researcher Donald Kothera, who later distributed copies of the letter at a gathering of Earhart researchers in 2000 at Las Vegas:

I ran across two graves outlined with white stone. I called to Captain Griswold and he said, "Let's dig them up." We dug and came upon two skeletons. We put the bones in a canister. On our way from the gravesite I asked Captain Griswold what we were doing there and who were we looking for. The Captain asked, "Did you ever hear of Amelia Earhart?" I said, "Yes," and he said, "Well, enough said." He admonished Burks and me not to talk any more about it. The canister with the bones went with Captain Griswold.

The straightforward statements by Burks and Henson contrast sharply with the carefully worded statement from Griswold.

Former Brig. Gen. Arthur B. Hanson, USMCR, later a Washington, DC, attorney, wrote a memo to the Historical Reference Section, Historical Branch, Department of the Navy, dated November 30, 1967, which said in part:

I was Regimental Intelligence Officer of the Twenty-Fourth Marines, Fourth Division during the battle of Roi-Namur in 1944, and the battles of Saipan and Tinian in June and July, 1944. I was in that position throughout these battles . . . We had briefed our Company Commanders and Battalion Intelligence Sections and Regimental Intelligence to be on the alert for any intelligence on Amelia Earhart . . . We were given the same briefing concerning Amelia Earhart prior to our landing on Saipan on June 15, 1944.

If US Marine Corps Intelligence Officers were ordered to be alert for information on Amelia prior to invasions in the Marshalls and Saipan, why would the Marine Corps later slam the door in the faces of qualified Earhart researchers asking questions about Earhart's fate, unless their information was true? Was it because the Marine Corps already had the answer and they were protecting it for their own purposes? Or had word come from higher authority that such news would do the American people no good at such a late date? Certainly, any word about Earhart's fate other than what the public was told in 1937 would have been explosive news—as former Navy Secretary Swanson had indicated, a "powder keg." Without question, the Marine Corps files on the Saipan exhumations would have to have been kept sealed and off limits, at least until those involved were dead and long gone.

In the late summer and fall of 1944, after Saipan had been taken and secured, Americans witnessed a hard-fought presidential election. It is perhaps understandable that those highly ranked in the government at the time would not want to get involved with the Earhart hot potato.

In February 1999, Ellis Bailey, a sailor on the USS *Vega* (AK-17) during World War II, gave a three-page memorandum to Amelia Earhart Society president Bill Prymak about his experience as a crew member on board the *Vega,* a cargo ship that received four battle stars for its service. The *Vega* moved thousands of tons of equipment and supplies between California and the Marshalls, Carolines, and Marianas. It was scrapped in 1946.

> Our second time to Saipan was the last part of July, 1944. Our Skipper got orders to take on fuel and supplies for a 1,000-mile voyage to Majuro to take a Government intelligence officer and two boxes of human remains that were two Caucasian flyers lost at sea seven years earlier. One was a woman. The officer wanted to talk to two natives who had seen and talked with the flyers. The following morning the intelligence officer came aboard with two boxes, the remains of the flyers. They were taken to the bridge and put under 24-hour guard.
>
> A day after reaching Majuro we were ordered to Kwajalein with all hands topside to search for a 2-engine civilian plane that had crashed on a beach. We found one but it wasn't the right one. After arriving at Kwajalein we dropped anchor and a small boat came alongside with six or seven marines. They told us that the day before one of their group on Roi-Namur found Amelia Earhart's suitcase of clothes and her diary in a barracks. The intelligence officer left the ship at that time with the two boxes of remains.[34]

In July 1944, the island of Saipan was not completely secure. The officials sent the remains to another base, where they were presumably air freighted to the United States. Kwajalein and Majuro had been taken in February.

The Patton Report

Consistent with the date of December 23, 1960, supposedly marking closure on the status of Amelia in Saipan, Special Agent Joseph M. Patton, Office of Naval Intelligence, completed a nine-page report filed at Navy Command, Marianas (ONI-2345-7-b). His report, entitled "EARHART, Amelia; information ref: location of grave of" was delivered to the Commander, Naval Forces Marianas.

The Patton ONI official report began, "One Jesus Salas testified he overheard Japanese military people talking about the crash of Subject's plane at Jaluit Atoll in the Marshall Islands; and a Mr. Jose Villagomez said he overheard a similar conversation." The same Jesus Salas was interviewed by Fred Goerner. Salas told Goerner a different story. He said: "A white woman had been put in the cell next to his in the old Garapan jail in 1937. She was kept there only several hours. He saw her briefly but did not talk with her because he did not speak English. The guards told him the woman was an American pilot the Japanese had captured."

Goerner also talked with Villagomez in 1963. "Japanese officers spoke to me of one American woman flier and one man captured near Marshall Islands before the war," Villagomez told him. "They were found somewhere near Jaluit Atoll, but I do not know what was done with them. It is possible they were brought to Saipan. I told this two years ago to Mr. Patton, the secret policeman for the United States Government."

Although Agent Patton questioned the reliability of Salas in his report, there is also the notation, "According to the Sheriff, information he (Salas) gave in 1944 about the location of the remains of two American military pilots he had buried proved to be correct." Is it possible that Patton was covering up the actual burial/exhumation of Earhart and Noonan by implying they were American military pilots?

The Patton report emphasizes that there were few reliable informants on the island of Saipan. None had ever heard of a so-called crash landing occurring in Tanapag Harbor in 1937. No one knew of an execution of two white people. And Commander Bridwell, ComNav Saipan, who was quite familiar with Goerner's interviews of Saipanese locals, told Agent Patton: "It is my opinion that Goerner's investigation was slanted, and that he reported information as fact which he had received as hearsay evidence from informants who are not considered reliable by persons who have been on Saipan for many years and are acquainted with the island and the Chamorros living there."

The final paragraph of Patton's nine-page report reads as follows:

A preponderance of hearsay evidence, and the statements of persons who were in the area in 1937, failed to indicate that Subject crash landed her airplane at Saipan, or that she was buried at Saipan. The hearsay evidence that was advanced by two informants set forth supra; Jesus SALAS and Jose VILLAGOMEZ, tended to indicate that the Japanese at Saipan had known at least the approximate location of Subject's crash to have been in the Marshall Islands. The hearsay evidence given by Mrs. Antonia BLANCO indicated that Subject may possibly have been brought to Saipan by the Japanese military.

It is telling that Patton's report carries the title "EARHART, Amelia; information ref: location of grave of."

Only once in his nine pages does Patton mention a grave. He discusses various cemeteries and adjoining roads, and mundane things like roadside signs and fishing huts, but there is nothing about the location of Amelia's grave. We can only imagine that originally his report did perhaps discuss a specific grave, and subsequently those key pages were purged. But the file name was never altered.

What happened to the Earhart remains after they were shipped out of Saipan? Ross Game's CIA contact eventually relented ever so slightly and said to him, "I can't take you by the hand, but why don't you look in the most logical place?"

Ross Game and Fred Goerner spent the next several weeks focusing on Arlington National Cemetery. They went through every record, every name, and every burial from 1944 through 1965, below ground and above. Their conclusion: "Unless they were 'unidentified' there was no Amelia Earhart and no Fred Noonan listed at Arlington." It seems, then, that Amelia and Fred did make a return to their home country, but the mystery remains as to where they rest today.

Part Five: The Trail of Witnesses

Chapter 10

Conspicuous Communications

Dorothea's Diary

It would have been an enormous undertaking involving many, many local folks to join together and fabricate the common threads that make up the mystery of Earhart and Noonan making it to the Marshalls.

—Bill Prymak, noted Earhart researcher

Japanese in the Marshalls

The United States was aware of Japan's possible militarization of the World War I-mandated islands even before the threat of Pearl Harbor. For various reasons, however, including the immediate objective of overcoming America's economic recession and the reality of relying on Japan for foreign trade, the United States did little other than to question the matter from afar.

In 1939, during hearings on Japanese activity in the mandated islands, the Senate Committee on Naval Affairs investigated rumors that the Japanese government was militarily fortifying the islands, which were supposed to be used solely for agriculture and fishing purposes as stated by the Treaty of Versailles. After the hearings, the Senate Committee met several times with the State Department, but no definitive information was forthcoming and the proceedings were kept confidential. The State Department issued the following statement: "With regard to the questions whether the terms of the treaty have been violated by Japan . . . the Government of the United States has at no time raised any question with the Japanese Government in regard to the Japanese mandated islands."[1] With regard to the Japanese government's denial of US Navy vessels to visit the harbors and waters of the mandated islands, the Secretary of State responded, "Regret was expressed that the Japanese authorities were unable to give consent to the proposed visits." This information was not made public until June 7, 1944.[2]

Although Allied ships traversing the waters around the Marshall Islands provided tidbits of information and occasional sailing captains reported on what they might have seen, the Japanese maintained that any construction on the islands was either for the well-being of their people or for open commerce and trade. It was not until November 27, 1941, just days before Pearl Harbor, that US Army Air Corps Gen. Hap Arnold ordered a photo reconnaissance mission. Though it is likely that there were other such missions, they never were publicly acknowledged other than in the Australian *Smith's Weekly* following the disappearance of Amelia Earhart.[3]

Japanese officials categorically denied any military preparations in the mandates. Gen. Masatake Okumiya of the Japanese Air Defense Force boldly proclaimed that Japan had never fortified the islands.[4] Nevertheless, it was no secret that from 1934 through 1941 there was considerable construction activity in the Japanese island possessions. Capt. Hidemi Yoshida of the Imperial Japanese Navy, who was intimately connected with naval construction in the mandates, stated that the construction program was primarily for "cultural and industrial facilities," including ramps and runways for aircraft, wireless stations, direction finders, meteorological stations, and lighthouses, which Yoshida claimed were necessary for "safe navigation, promotion of commerce, and other peaceful pursuits."[5]

Knowledgeable Marshallese subsequently reported that the construction activity was confined to certain key islands. Alfred Capelle, former president of the College of the Marshall Islands and Marshallese ambassador to the United Nations, noted that by the mid-1930s, "the Japanese plan had been put into action."[6] Older Marshall Islanders later told him (and history confirmed) that "the most desirable pieces of native land had been condemned in order to build docks, airfields, barracks and the like."[7]

Robert Reimers, head of Robert Reimers Enterprises, a Marshall Islands-based importer of building and construction materials, told Earhart researcher Bill Prymak during an interview in 1990 that "the Japanese would permit outside visitors to see only what they, the Japanese, wanted them to see. They could, for example, visit Jabor, the principal business center of Jaluit Atoll. However, they were prohibited from getting anywhere near Emidj, ten miles up the lagoon, where we delivered many tons of construction material for the huge seaplane base and accompanying facilities."[8]

The Japanese began preparations in the Marshall Islands for a military build-up as early as 1933. Mili Atoll was designated to become a major base, and Roi Namur, adjoining Kwajalein, would feature the largest airfield in the Marshalls. Maloelap, Eniwetok, Emidj (also spelled "Imiej"), and Wotje saw great concentrations of construction. Dredging and deepening harbors, bulldozing airstrips through jungle and coral, and building hangars, seaplane ramps, operational buildings, mess halls, and barracks required huge amounts of labor. The islanders were a natural local resource. Many were conscripted into forced labor and mistreated by the Japanese. Men were separated from their families and moved from island to island. Thousands of other laborers were brought in from Japan and Korea.

The fate of Amelia Earhart and Fred Noonan did not begin to emerge until seven or eight years after their disappearance, when the US Navy and Marines landed on Majuro in the Marshall Islands and at Saipan in the Marianas, and the natives came forward with their stories. Many recounted their stories to US troops and repeated later to American researchers and tourists. A stalwart group of Earhart enthusiasts and researchers who spent years trying to determine the truth compiled the stories for their records.

When asked by Bill Prymak for any information on the mystery of Amelia Earhart and Fred Noonan, Robert Reimers responded: "It was widely known throughout the islands by both Japanese and Marshallese that a Japanese fishing boat first found them and their airplane near Mili. They then transferred them to a larger boat. They were brought to Jabor where Bilimon treated them. [Bilimon Amram was a successful Marshallese businessman. In 1937 he was a medical corpsman working for the Japanese.] They were then taken to Kwajelein, and from there to Truk, and then Saipan. There was no mystery, everybody knew it."

Reimers also related to Prymak how the islanders were brutally treated by the Japanese and were deathly afraid of them. Heads were lopped off for the slightest mistake or incident. He explained how an intrusion into the islands was considered a serious offense and that there was "great cover and secrecy" in the Earhart case: "It is difficult for the Americans to know the fright and fear of my people during the war. These fears did not die easily after the war. There are some old-timers who still think the Japanese may come back. It would not be wise to discuss things deemed secret during the war."[9]

As with so many legends and mysteries, the documentation is incomplete. But one thing is certain: these stories are compelling. And for those who believe that Amelia survived, there will be no turning back.

Records Revealed

Dorothea Garsia, wife of Nauru Island administrator Rupert C. Garsia, kept a personal diary during her husband's six-year tenure from 1933 to 1938. Her diary entries recorded official news and local gossip on the Pacific outpost, formerly known as Pleasant Island. At the end of 1938, Garsia's post was not renewed and the couple relocated to Australia. During World War II, Garsia served as a captain in the Royal Australian Navy.

Nauru Island was under German control until after World War I, when the League of Nations took over and appointed an Australian commissioner. The Germans returned in December 1940, sank four merchant ships off the coast, and heavily shelled the island. In 1942, the Japanese attacked Nauru, forcing its surrender in August and the deportation of twelve hundred Nauruans to Truk (now the State of Chuuk).

Mrs. Garsia died in Canberra on May 16, 1968, at the age of seventy-five. Her husband predeceased her by fourteen years. Her diary was donated to the National Library of Australia.[10] Sprinkled among reports of local society events such as raisings of the flag, welcoming the passing Bishop, cocktail parties, bachelor dances, bridge contests, golf outings, and parades of the Boy and Girl Scouts are the following entries related to the Earhart-Noonan flight:

July 2, 1937
Mrs. Putnam essayed her flight from New Guinea (Lei) [sic] to Howland Island. We had notified her of weather, lights, etc. We picked up her wireless at 6 p.m. but though increasingly loud, we could not make out the speech. She was due near or over Nauru at 9:40 p.m. but though we watched she did not come near.

July 3, 1937
Clowstons to bridge—Mrs. Putnam failed to reach Howland Island. We heard their wireless calls clearly, but again could not make out any word.

July 4, 1937
Church—heard Mrs. Putnam calling again.

These brief notes indicate that Amelia's Lockheed Electra was more or less on course and headed for Howland Island. Noonan likely followed radioman Harry Balfour's recommendation from Lae to pass close enough to Nauru to utilize the island's phosphate mining lights as an aid to navigation. Nauru radio had confirmed that the mining lights would be turned on for Amelia.

The July 3 entry (July 2 on Howland because of the International Date Line) likely referred to Amelia's hourly calls to the *Itasca* throughout the early morning. From the *Itasca*'s logs, we know that there were very few messages broadcast by Amelia until she attempted a final approach about one hundred miles away from Howland. As the Electra neared Howland Island—more than one thousand miles from Nauru—its radio signal would have become weaker to Nauru ears and static likely would have obscured the transmissions.

Because she wrote most of her diary entries in the evenings, Mrs. Garsia's July 3 diary entry was probably recorded in the evening of the day of Amelia's disappearance. The words do not reflect what surely must have been the considerable anxiety of those listening to Nauru radio messages.

The July 4 entry (July 3 on Howland) is the most significant writing, because it comes the day after Amelia supposedly disappeared. The July 4 commercial radio log of Amalgamated Wireless in Sydney also noted, "the report from Nauru sent to Bolinas radio at 6:31, 6:43 and 6:45 p.m. Sydney time today on 48.31 meters, fairly strong signals, speech not intelligible, no hum of plane in background, but voice similar to that emitted from plane in flight last night between 4:30 and 9:30 p.m."[11]

These records, both from a personal diary and from a commercial radio log, reported that Amelia's voice was heard after she and Fred Noonan supposedly ran out of fuel, crashed, and sank. The note of the voice without the hum of the engine in the background clearly confirms that she did not crash in the Pacific. She had to have been somewhere dry to use the radio. Several of Mrs. Garsia's diary entries indicate that radio communications at Nauru Island were generally good to excellent. For example, on the evening of May 12, 1936, she wrote, "We listened to the coronation [of George VI] broadcast heard perfectly." Such statements reinforce the credibility of messages heard in Nauru and their records in both personal and professional capacities.

They also lend credence to other reports: Walter McMenamy and Karl Pierson's "positive identification" of July 3, 1937, being "from the plane but poorly sent;" the HMS *Achilles* radio report of the same date; the written reports from Pan Am radio stations at Wake and Midway Islands and Makapuu Point, later seized by Naval Intelligence; and the 281 wireless message received by US Naval radio in Hawaii.[12] Although Earhart and Noonan may never have reached Howland Island, it

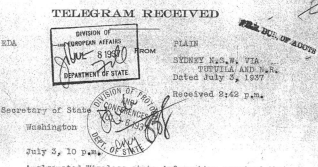

TELEGRAM RECEIVED

EDA

PLAIN

SYDNEY N.S.W. VIA
TUTUILA AND N.R.
Dated July 3, 1937

Received 2:42 p.m.

Secretary of State

Washington

July 3, 10 p.m.

.. Amalgamated Wireless state information received that
report from ~~Peru~~ *"NAURU"* was sent to Bolinas radio "at 6.31, 6.43
and 6.54 p.m. Sydney time today on 48.31 meters, fairly
strong signals, speech not intelligible, no hum of plane
in background but voice similar that emitted from plane
in flight last night between 4.30 and 9.30 p.m."
Message from plane when at least 60 miles south of Nauru
received 8.30 p.m., Sydney time, July second saying "a
ship in sight ahead". Since identified as steamer MYRTLE
BANK which arrived Nauru daybreak today. Reported no
contact between Itasca and Nauru radio. Continuous watch
being maintained by Nauru radio and Suva radio.

DOYLE

KLP:WWC

Telegram to the Secretary of State from officials in Sydney, Australia.
(Courtesy National Archives)

is clear that they survived their flight from Lae, New Guinea—they simply had a different destination than originally intended.

Message in a Bottle

Bottles that wash ashore along a stretch of sandy beach have an intriguing aura. Inside, they might contain a desperate SOS or a time capsule of information from the past.

In November 2003, students at Oak Ridge Middle School in Naples, Florida, wrote messages about themselves and their lives and inserted these messages into the bottles. Their teachers sent the bottles to the National Oceanic and Atmospheric Administration in Miami, where officials took them aboard a research vessel and launched them into the ocean. By 2006, only one of the bottles had made it across the Atlantic. It washed up on the beach at Malpica, Spain, some four thousand miles distant.

In the case of the disappearance of Amelia Earhart and Fred Noonan, two bottled messages have surfaced. One was a definite hoax, but the other seems to offer a genuine plea . . .

The Acapulco Sham

Amelia's husband, George Putnam, received hundreds of telephone calls, letters, and telegrams after Amelia vanished. Quite a few of these messages were from friends and fellow mourners. Many more were from people who were simply caught up in the Amelia mystique and mania. Some were clairvoyants claiming psychic abilities and suggesting where Putnam should search for his missing wife. Many of these folks had dreams or premonitions of a latitude and longitude where Amelia could be found. There were also ham radio reports that interfered with US Government search efforts and confounded legitimate Navy and Coast Guard radio operators. For Putnam, it was a nightmare.

There were hoaxes, too. George P. Shaw, the American Consul in Mexico City, forwarded the letter reproduced below to the US Department of State on May 31, 1940, with the attached covering memo regarding a bottle that reportedly washed ashore at Acapulco. The letter from the Acapulco bottle read as follows:

Friday, July 2, 1937
We are down in the water. We hit hard! The plane is still afloat, but the starboard gas tank is ruptured and taking water. We hit the water

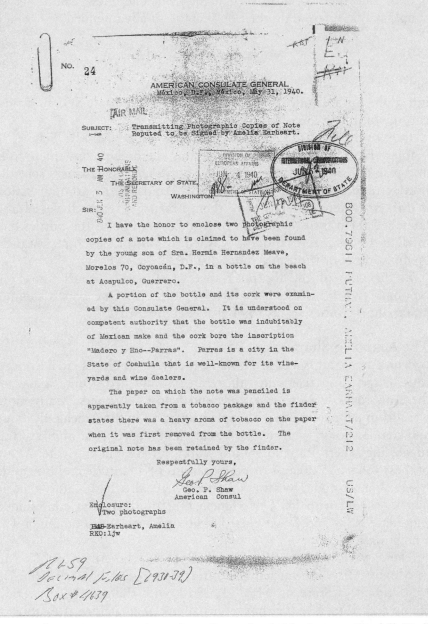

AMERICAN CONSULATE GENERAL
México, D.F., México, May 31, 1940.

AIR MAIL

SUBJECT: Transmitting Photographic Copies of Note
Reputed to be Signed by Amelia Earheart.

THE HONORABLE
THE SECRETARY OF STATE,
WASHINGTON.

SIR:

I have the honor to enclose two photographic
copies of a note which is claimed to have been found
by the young son of Sra. Hermia Hernandez Meave,
Morelos 70, Coyoacán, D.F., in a bottle on the beach
at Acapulco, Guerrero.

A portion of the bottle and its cork were examined by this Consulate General. It is understood on
competent authority that the bottle was indubitably
of Mexican make and the cork bore the inscription
"Madero y Hno--Parras". Parras is a city in the
State of Coahuila that is well-known for its vine-
yards and wine dealers.

The paper on which the note was penciled is
apparently taken from a tobacco package and the finder
states there was a heavy aroma of tobacco on the paper
when it was first removed from the bottle. The
original note has been retained by the finder.

Respectfully yours,

Geo. P. Shaw
American Consul

Enclosure:
Two photographs

Earheart, Amelia
RKO:ljw

*Letter from American Consulate General of Mexico to Cordell Hull,
Secretary of State.* (Courtesy National Archives)

at 8:57 a.m. We have been in the water now for 8 minutes. I have pulled myself to the front of the plane and am holding Amelia in my arms. I think my back is broken. I can't say for sure. Amelia is dead. Her chest was pushed in on impact. She never spoke to me after we hit the water. She just died as I held her. As I looked at her she looked into my eyes. I thought, why didn't the cutter answer us? Why! We went back and forth up to 7500 kc. I can't think. I just can't think. My head hurts. Okay! I'm dumping out the distilled water Amelia has in this bottle. She had the water for her eyes. This note will go into one of the two bottles. I hope that some soul will find them soon, or some day. I'm so afraid now. I'm holding Amelia as I write. I have to keep writing. Amelia is so beautiful, she looks so royal. Even more so now. I'm looking at the damn empty gas gauges. Forgive me, Father in Heaven! Clumsy man that I am, forgive me for my trespassing against you. And, my trespassing against my fellow man. And for dear Amelia, please take her now. Take her into your bosom please. I'm not so afraid now. I don't need a drink. I thought I did. No, please God, let me drink it new in your Kingdom! I will seal this second note in the bottle. I think I can get it out the cockpit hatch door. My legs, I can't feel them. I can't even get out on the port wing. We are going in slowly on the starboard side. The sun is coming through now. We will both be okay. I can't find Amelia's good luck bracelet! I'm sure I just saw it.

Goodbye now. And to my new wife, think of me and what happened on our wedding night. I'm so clumsy, but what memories! And I will love you with a love that will never die! Goodbye. AE and Fred Noonan

P.S. GB, [author's note: the writer should have written "G.P."] the engines ran beautifully. But low oil pressure on the starboard. Oil on the wind-shield. The time is now 9:39 a.m. I'm sorry George. I did my best. Amelia did her best, too.

Goodbye. F. N.

The files indicate that State Department personnel had a good laugh over this letter from a supposedly injured Fred Noonan, who was unable to extract himself from the slowly sinking plane as he cradled a dead Amelia in his arms.

However, another message in a bottle found on a beach on the western coast of France legitimizes a possible fate for the two fliers and has far-reaching implications.

Geneviève's Discovery

The date was October 30, 1938. The place was the beach of Soulac-sur-Mer, Gironde, France, a quaint, seaside resort town serving the major wine-producing region around Bordeaux. Located on France's western coast south of the Gironde River's entrance from the Atlantic and nine kilometers below Pointe de Grave, Soulac-sur-Mer has been a fashionable vacation resort since the early twentieth century. Had our little bottle not washed upon the beach of Soulac-sur-Mer, it may well have been swept into the swift waters of this great river to become marooned unceremoniously among the mud and assorted river-bank vegetation of the inland river, never to be found.

The time on this particular fall afternoon was about 5 p.m. While strolling along the beach, thirty-seven-year-old Geneviève Barrat spotted something bobbing in the shallow surf. It appeared to be a small bottle, and it was being pushed shoreward by the incoming tide. High tide that evening was at 9:35 p.m., according to the French Naval Hydrographic and Oceanographic Office. She took a few steps into the shallow water and plucked the bottle from the waves. Examining the contents, she could see several small pieces of paper along with a lock of light brown hair. The bottle was about 10 centiliters in size (about 6 cubic inches, or perhaps 3.5 inches high including the neck and 1.75 inches in diameter). This small bottle had been sealed with a cork and coated with wax, suggesting that someone had gone to a lot of trouble to protect the items inside. The neck of the glass bottle was wrapped and glued in aluminum foil. On the underside of the bottle was the imprint "V.B.2."

Overcome by curiosity, Geneviève stripped away the foil covering

Beach at Soulac-sur-Mer, France, where a small bottle washed ashore. (Photo by Robert Stenuit)

Interpretation of Geneviève Barrat finding the bottle in the surf. (Illustration by Elizabeth Whelan)

and freed the cork stopper to expose the contents it had so admirably protected. Ever so gingerly, she extracted first one piece of tightly rolled paper and then a second and a third. She unfolded one of them and read:

HAVE BEEN A PRISONER AT JALUIT (MARSHALLS) BY JAPANESE. IN PRISON OF JALUIT HAVE SEEN AMELIA EARHART (AVIATRIX) AND IN ANOTHER JAIL HER MECHANIC (MAN) AS WELL AS OTHER DETAINEES . . . BRING THIS MESSAGE IMMEDIATELY TO THE GENDARMERIE SO WE SHALL BE SAVED.

Geneviève Barrat had just become the first person in the Western world to learn the fate of Amelia Earhart and Fred Noonan.

The barracks of the brigade of the Soulac-sur-Mer gendarmerie nationale was only a few blocks away. Geneviève turned in her find and signed off on the bottle and its contents. As she reported in her official statement shortly afterward, "I saw a bottle floating in the waves. Inside there were three pieces of paper and a lock of hair. Since one of these papers specified that the Gendarmerie should be notified, I am giving all of this to you."

Forty-year-old Felix Dourthe was the designated official on duty when Geneviève arrived at the Gendarmerie door. He became the second Westerner to learn the truth.

It would be Gendarme Dourthe's responsibility to officially

document Geneviève's discovery in the *Proces-Verbal no. 139 de la Brigade, du 30 Octobre 1938*. The time of the report was 7:15 p.m.

The first item Dourthe viewed was a handwritten note in his native French language. Studying the small, square pieces of paper, he carefully read for a few moments. Most of the words were printed quite neatly. Puzzled, he looked up at Geneviève. Neither she nor Dourthe had ever heard of Jaluit or the Marshalls, but both immediately recognized the name of Amelia Earhart.

Glancing back at the mysterious message, he began reading faster, and later made note of the following entries in his report:

> Further proof: A lock of hair.
> May God guide this flask, I entrust in it my life and that of my companions in misery.
> [In ordinary writing as translated from the original French. Recto/Front:] Have been prisoner at Jaluit (Marshalls) by Japanese. In prison of Jaluit have seen Amelia Earhart (aviatrix) and in other jail her mechanic (man) as well as other detainees, for so-called spying on the gigantic fortifications which are built in the atoll. EARHART and companion have been fished up by Japanese seaplane, will serve as hostages have said Japanese. Myself have been prisoner for have disembarked at Milatoll. My yacht "Veveo" sunken, crew massacred (3 Maoris), the boat (26 T), sailing boat, was fitted with wireless set (continuation on verso).
>
> [Verso/Back:] After having made a long stay in Jaluit as prisoner, was forcibly enrolled as coal-trimmer seaman, being fed only, on board "Nippon Name"? Sailing Europe. Shall escape as soon as cargo vessel nears the coast. Bring this message immediately to the Gendarmerie so that we shall be saved.
>   This message has probably been thrown off Santander, will surely arrive in Vendée around September or at the latest October 1938. Continuation in the bottle attached to this one Message no. 6.
>
> [In stenography around the main text:[13]] To have more chances of liberating Miss Amelia Earhart and her companion, as well as the other prisoners, it would be better that policemen should arrive incognito at Jali. I shall be with joy among them if I succeed in escaping . . . because if one asks the Japanese to liberate the prisoners, they will certify they have no prisoners at Jali. It will therefore be necessary to be cunning. I have sent other messages to save the prisoners of Jali at the risk of my life, and I shall send more.
>   This bottle serves as a float for a second one containing the story of my life and my curriculum vitae and some small objects having

belonged to Miss Amelia Eart [sic] for her last voyage around the world. These documents attest to the veracity of this story in ordinary words and shorthand that I have approached Amelia well after her pseudo-death.

The second flask contains also a report on the voyage that my yacht made from the Mar [abbreviation believed to be "Marquesas"] to the Mars [believed to be "Marshalls"—ink splotches partially obscure the stenography]. I am writing this in steno for I have very little paper . . . The finger prints were taken by the Nipponese police, another with a thumb.

This message #6 is written on board the Nipponese cargo [freighter].

The French typist, not being familiar with Jaluit Island, made an error in spelling it "Jalint" in the French gendarmerie report. In fact, there are numerous typing, spelling, and punctuation errors in the report, whereas the hand-printed pages of the message are remarkably clear and readable. On both sides, notes in shorthand in the margins around the main text are a continuation of the French printed text, and obviously were inserted after the main narrative. This combination of written text and steno was clearly intended to take maximum advantage of the limited amount of paper available to the writer of this unusual SOS.

The message refers to Vendée, which is on the southwest coast of France. This coastal province is located north of La Rochelle and the Île de Ré, or some 120 kilometers north of Soulac-sur Mer, where the bottle ultimately washed ashore.

The French gendarmerie report indicated, "These objects were seized and handed over to the Office of the Public Prosecutor. The second bottle was not found." It is regrettable that the second bottle disappeared, and with it Amelia's "small objects" and the curriculum vitae of the message writer. It would certainly have clarified the story of the yacht *Veveo* and other obscurities within the message text.

Felix Dourthe's typed report (including its mistakes in spelling, etc.) reached the desk of the directeur général of the Sûreté Nationale (the French Interior Intelligence Service and the equivalent of our FBI) at the ministère de l'Interieur (Ministry of the Interior) in Paris. The file of the bottle message was retained about two months at the Sûreté Nationale before copies of the Gendarmerie report, in French, and photos of the front and back of the original handwritten messages were forwarded to the US Embassy in Paris by the ministère des Affaires Étrangères (Ministry of Foreign Affairs). A copy of these official documents now resides safely in the National Archives at College Park, Maryland.[14]

Geneviève Barrat and Felix Dourthe both signed the originals of the recorded documents at Soulac-sur-Mer. Slightly more than two months later, on January 5, 1939, Amelia Earhart was declared dead at the request of her husband. If only Barrat and Dourthe had known that the answer to one of the greatest mysteries of the twentieth century was staring them directly in the face! Other than a few diplomatic exchanges between France and the US, however, their discovery would remain largely unreported. The official account stated that Amelia and her navigator, Fred Noonan, had run out of fuel and disappeared in the waters of the Pacific. Who could have imagined that the sweetheart of America, a national heroine of the greatest country in the world, was believed to be dead but possibly still alive in the hands of the Japanese in absolute violation of international law?

Efforts to contact Geneviève Barrat's living relatives yielded no additional information, with the exception of this reply from Madame Helene Barrat of Hourtin, France, a small town in Gironde fifty kilometers from Bordeaux and thirty-seven kilometers from Soulac-sur-Mer:

> Dear Sir,
> I found your letter intriguing. The event which you mentioned has been told to me by my parents. The person who interests you was a distant parent of my father. I know no more. One of my uncles to whom I have forwarded your letter also has heard about that event. Neither he nor I are able to locate the person in question in our family. My grandmother had the regrettable habit of quarrelling with parents and step-parents . . .

The small, insignificant bottle that drifted ashore at Soulac-sur-Mer, France, could very well be proof that Amelia Earhart and Fred Noonan came down in or near the Marshall Islands, were taken by the Japanese, and were held and treated as spies. At that particular time—a little more than a year after the fliers had disappeared—no one other than the Japanese could have identified Jaluit Atoll or any other Japanese-mandated island as a place of confinement for the two missing aviators. In 1937 and 1938, no hoaxer could have possibly picked out such an unlikely atoll as Jaluit as the site of his story or make the claim that "Earhart and companion have been fished up by Japanese seaplane" unless he knew something about their actual situation—unless he were there himself.[15]

The actual message survives today in the form of two excellent photographic copies of its front and back (recto and verso). The message apparently was written on strong but not very thick paper, since a number of ink spots have leaked through and are visible on both sides. The surface on both the front and back appears smooth. A thin, black vertical margin (probably an original element of the paper, not made by the author of the message) appears on the left side on the back. Vertical and horizontal creases indicate that the document was folded in four sections after it was written, presumably in order to roll it in order to fit in the very small flask. The paper was white or of a very light color.

The square of paper is of a size that may well have been used for fingerprinting. The paper measures 13.5 centimeters by 13 centimeters, or 5¼ inches by 5³⁄₁₆ inches. The ink stains demonstrate the paper's absorbency. The thin vertical black line on the left could have been the demarcation for placement of the inked fingertips, with the section on the right possibly reserved for a photograph, ID, serial number, or other method of identification.

Geneviève Barrat admitted that she took time to open the bottle before taking it to the Soulac-sur-Mer gendarmerie headquarters. The *proces-verbal* records her declaration as follows: "Today the 30th approaching 17 [5:00 p.m.], I had gone on a stroll on the beach in front of La Pergola. I saw a flask in the breakers of the waves. Seeing that it was hermetically sealed, I wished to be aware of its contents."

Apparently, the Sûreté Nationale photographed only the written

La Pergola, a beachfront café located on the upper section of beach off of Rue Barriquand, Soulac-sur-Mer, France, in 1938. (Photo by Robert Stenuit)

The gendarmerie where Geneviève Barrat turned in the small bottle that washed ashore at Soulac-sur-Mer, France, on October 30, 1938. (Photograph by Marcel Delbey)

contents and not the bottle itself or the lock of hair. The hair and the bottle remained in France along with the original documents until the German invasion, when thousands of files and records of every description disappeared. On May 16, 1940, officials gave a direct order at the Ministry of Foreign Affairs to incinerate all archives. The incineration was undertaken hastily and on a large scale. It was probably at this time that the original messages, the bottle, and the lock of hair were lost forever. Only the photograph of the handwritten message containing the shorthand script reached the US State Department accompanying the official Embassy cover documents.

The loss of the lock of hair is not as devastating as it first might appear. Though it would be helpful from a historical standpoint to compare its color with Amelia's, DNA analysis today would not be possible because the lock comprised a bunch of cut pieces.[16] DNA is only present in the bulb, or root, of the hair, and not in cut strands.

Ultimately, the Soulac-sur-Mer gendarmerie transmittal found its way through administrative channels to Henri Hoppenot, the sous-directeur d'Europe at the Ministry of Foreign Affairs. It was Hoppenot who appropriately summoned Edwin C. Wilson, Interim chargé d'affaires at the American Embassy in Paris.[17]

"The chances were ninety-nine to one that these messages were

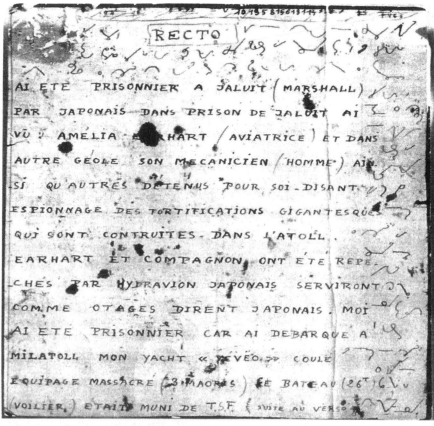

Photograph of recto of original bottled message found at Soulac-sur-Mer.
(Courtesy National Archives)

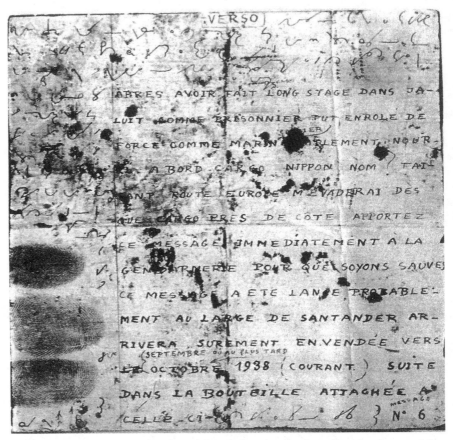

Photograph of verso of original bottled message found at Soulac-sur-Mer.
(Courtesy National Archives)

a hoax, the work of an impostor or someone out of his senses," Hoppenot suggested in his cover letter (see Exhibits at the end of the chapter). "On the other hand there was always an outside chance they might contain an element of truth," stated Wilson. "For this reason he thought it desirable to hand them to me."

Wilson was a "take charge" manager and immediately asked Lt. Cdr. Roscoe H. Hillenkoetter, assistant naval attaché at the Embassy, if he would interview Eric de Bisschop, a well-known French sailor who had spent several years in the Pacific studying ocean currents.[18] He hoped that de Bisschop might shed some light on the mystery of the lost aviatrix as well as on the discovery of the bottle message. De Bisschop had recently delivered a most interesting lecture to the French *Société de Géographie,* which Wilson attended. In the course of his remarks, de Bisschop mentioned having stopped at Jaluit Atoll in the Marshall Islands, where the local Japanese authorities "found his presence, even momentarily, quite undesirable."[19] He described the Japanese as wearing expressions of grave concern when he mentioned having passed by Mili Atoll. As a result, both de Bisschop and his boat endured "a particularly severe inspection" before the Japanese finally released him.[20]

Commander Hillenkoetter met with Eric de Bisschop at de Bisschop's home on Avenue Mozart in Paris on January 7, 1939. He wrote a three-page summary of his interview but uncovered little additional information about Amelia Earhart. De Bisschop had met some of the top US Navy brass while in Honolulu in 1937 and enjoyed dropping a few names, such as Admiral Yarnell, Commander Kilpatrick, Admiral LeBreton, and Cdr. C. D. Leffler.[21] He also volunteered what information he could on the Japanese military construction he had seen.

Though de Bisschop was unable to glimpse any of the building activity at Mili, he was able to learn that there was considerable dredging being undertaken on Jaluit Atoll: "It is held so closely confidential that even Japanese merchant ships are not allowed to visit there. Coal, munitions (three-inch shells and dynamite sticks), and other supplies are brought to Jaluit by regular Japanese merchant vessels; there, they are transshipped to a small navy transport (about 1,000 tons) manned by regular officers and men of the Japanese Navy, which carries the supplies from Jaluit to Mili Atoll."[22]

De Bisschop described to Hillenkoetter which harbors and channels were being dredged at Jaluit. He confirmed that the Japanese had new hydrographic charts of entrance channels and approaches but that they were being kept confidential. He had seen shells for three-inch guns, but did not see the guns themselves; he recognized the construction of seaplane ramps, hangars, and small shops at Emidj. He learned that there were a number of radio transmitting and receiving sets spread throughout the islands. He related that there was an especially tall antenna station at Jabor, the main harbor of Jaluit Atoll.

As to the story about Amelia Earhart and other people kept as prisoners, de Bisschop indicated that it was much more likely to hear of someone accidentally drowned than of someone being held by the Japanese. Natives told him that before his visit, a white man who had stopped at Jaluit was found drowned shortly thereafter, with indications that he had been struck over the head first. Releasing Amelia and Fred would have been unthinkable to the Japanese. The Americans immediately would have told the world about the Japanese fortifications under construction, their poor treatment of foreign individuals, and the uncivilized practice of holding prisoners without trial.

Hillenkoetter's interview with de Bisschop concluded with the Frenchman describing his plans for completing another boat similar to the large outrigger canoes sailed by the Polynesians.[23]

Roscoe Hillenkoetter. (Courtesy National Archives)

Eric de Bisschop.

It is interesting that the American Embassy's Edwin Wilson volunteered his own views on some of these developments in his cover letter with his submission to the US Department of State:

> It is perhaps not without interest to point out the disquieting attitude of the Japanese authorities as regards those persons which the hazards of navigation bring too close to the Marshall Islands where there are certainly constructions of the highest importance to Japan and which that country is most anxious not to have known.
>
> It is difficult not to connect this incident and the details contained in the note in the bottle thrown overboard by an unknown sailor, a note which gives certain information concerning the disappearance of the American aviatrix Amelia Earhart and her mechanic.
>
> These details, however strange they may seem, appeared a great deal less strange after hearing M. Eric de Bisschop's lecture; in any case they appear worthy of attention.[24]

It thus seems plausible that the writer of our message had been navigating in the Marshall Islands' waters and came ashore at Mili Atoll. Because of what he may have seen, he was apprehended, searched, interrogated, and imprisoned at Jaluit, the regional Japanese headquarters. He most likely was French, because the message was written in French, and he was familiar with the currents along the French coast. Alternatively, he could have been a French-speaking Kiwi, which would account for his Maori crew. Or, he could have stopped in New Zealand for repairs and picked up a change of crew. But what was he doing in that part of the world at that particular time? A loner yachtsman on a twenty-six-ton sailboat would not likely have had such a large crew except to facilitate around-the-clock watch standing. He could have been a French secret agent, ordered into the Marshalls for a specific purpose.

When the Japanese exited from the League of Nations in February 1933 after invading China in 1931, the coming menace appeared obvious. The Japanese boldly flaunted their indifference to the concerns of other nations about Japan's imperialistic plans throughout the Pacific. French colonial authorities, somewhat isolated in the Polynesian Islands (the Society Islands, comprised of Tahiti, Tuamotus, and Marquesas, among others), were monitoring the increasing Japanese belligerence and were uneasily aware of Japan's fortifications in the Mandated Islands.

After an expensive and exhaustive three-year global search, I could not track down any single vessel named *Veveo* or any other sailing craft spelled similarly with a TSF radio transmitter and receiver. Although the Embassy typist mistakenly spelled the yacht's name as *Viveo,* the original message in French clearly shows it to be *Veveo.* The possibility that *Veveo* might not be the name of a yacht at all could force a change of research direction and open an entirely new avenue of maneuvers and intrigue.

Few reports exist in which French intelligence operations in the South Pacific are confirmed. There were even fewer living French Intel operatives who were willing to speak with me. With perseverance, however, a few ex-intelligentsias provided a smile or nod to questions that acknowledged the possibility that *Veveo* might have been a code name.

The French Secret Services responsible for gathering intelligence came under the famous Deuxième Bureau of the Services de Renseignements (SR). The services de transit de Shangai (Shanghai) (STS) was a special naval surveillance operation concerned with the Pacific far-East region. The STS was responsible for the entire Pacific west of Hawaii, which included all of the islands mandated to Japan after World War I. In far-removed French colonial territories, there was a considerable reliance on volunteers for assistance in data gathering. These volunteers, designated as honorable correspondents, could be retired SR French Intelligence officers, patriotic French commandos, naval officers, or other former military personnel who chose to reside on one of the many idyllic Pacific French islands.[25] Certainly, the author of our bottle message could have been an agent of the French intelligence services, most likely on a volunteer basis—and the name of his boat, *Veveo,* could have been his pseudonym or the code name for his mission. The fact that he specifically asked that the message be brought "immediately to the gendarmerie" instead of to the police is also telling, because the gendarmerie is a military body under the authority of the French Ministry of Defense, whereas the French police force is simply a civilian body. Only the Ministry of Defense would be able to recognize the name *Veveo* and identify the message's accompanying fingerprints.

If the Japanese were sufficiently provoked to massacre the three Maori crew members, scuttle the French sailor's twenty-six-ton sailboat because a radio transmitter and receiver were aboard, and to throw the man in jail for "a long time" at Jaluit before deploying him aboard a Japanese freighter as a coal stoker, then the offense must have been serious. Though the writer did not state for how long he was in prison, he must have entered the prison either sometime shortly before Amelia's disappearance in July 1937 or immediately after. If he did, in fact, come in contact with Amelia while jailed on Jaluit and received "a few objects having belonged to Amelia Earhart" that he placed in a separate bottle "containing the story of my life," which served as a float to the bottle that survived, the question of what happened to him still remains. Of course, the Japanese were known to be extraordinarily suspicious of outsiders who might have been spies. After the war, Marshallese natives described numerous Japanese atrocities. Many other islanders, who were warned to keep quiet during those pre-war days, remained terribly afraid that the Japanese might return.

The French sailor who wrote the message clearly knew that the Japanese freighter on which he'd been impressed was headed for Europe. He also had to be deeply concerned about his ultimate fate upon conclusion of the voyage. He possessed local knowledge of the waters around France and Spain, because he knew—or at least believed—that he was off the coast of Santander when he threw the bottle into the sea. And he had knowledge of the winds and currents of that region based on his estimate of the time it would take his bottle to "arrive in Vendée," a province 120 km north of Soulac-sur-Mer.[26] He conveyed a definite impression of being a versatile seaman, and perhaps a good swimmer, as he was quite confident that he would be able to escape "when his ship is near the coast," although he did not share his plan for escape. He surely would have known that the water temperature in that region of the Bay of Biscay in late October hovers around fourteen degrees Celsius (fifty-seven degrees Fahrenheit). Even a very good swimmer, well-nourished and in good health, would not last long in such cold water.

Did the originator of the bottle message live to escape his fate as a slave stoker on a Japanese ship? He never gave his name or identified himself, other than through the fingerprints on the message. There is no indication he was ever heard from again, even though he stated, "At the risk of my life, I shall send further messages." Did he leap from the ship one dark night to swim toward the lights on a distant shore, only to drown or be eaten by sharks? Or did he remain shackled to his post as an enslaved coal stoker and ultimately starve to death on a Japanese tramp steamer? Unfortunately, to date we do not know who this mysterious messenger was or where he ended up.

After receipt of the Wilson and Hillenkoetter reports from the US Embassy in Paris, Commander Creighton, Office of the Chief of Naval Operations, dictated the following memo on February 8, 1939:

OP-16-B-11
A4-3 / Earhart, Amelia

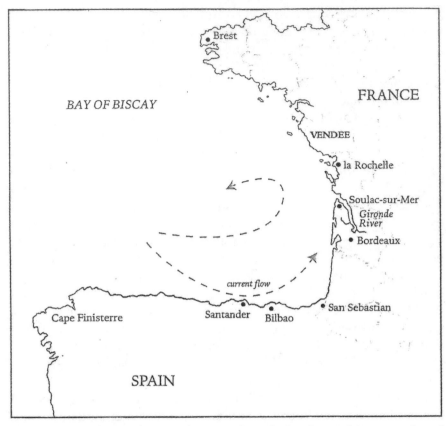

Map of current flow in the Bay of Biscay, where the bottle was thrown overboard. Surface sea currents flow in a counter-clockwise direction, northward and westerly. The average speed of a small object caught in this directional flow would be about a half-knot per hour. A knot being the equivalent of one nautical mile (6,080 feet), the bottle's drift rate would have averaged twelve miles during a twenty-four-hour period. (Map by Elizabeth Whelan)

Serial No. 1007
From: Director of Naval Intelligence
To: Naval Attaché, Paris
Subject: Report of Amelia Earhart as Prisoner in the Mandate Islands
Reference: Paris Report dated 7 January 1939
1. It is desired that the attaché secure from M. de Bisschop an accurate outline of his former voyages to the Mandate Islands, giving a sequence of ports visited and the dates of arrival and departure. The reference does not state clearly how many times M. de Bisschop has been to the Mandates, nor when nor whether he visited any harbor other than Jaluit.

As a matter of general interest, M. de Bisschop is quoted as saying he turned over information to Admiral Yarnell in Honolulu in 1937. Admiral Yarnell was detached from the Fourteenth Naval District on the 7th of October, 1936, and departed for an Asiatic Station promptly thereafter.

There is no indication in the files that the naval attaché obtained any additional information. Nevertheless, the US Navy was apparently still attempting to gather information on the fate of Amelia Earhart more than a year and a half after she disappeared. We already have learned that US Navy intelligence officers continued to seek information on Amelia's fate as late as 1960. And, let's not overlook the significance of Father Arnold Bendowske's 1977 deposition of various Chamorro women who testified under oath that they had seen or had some contact with a Caucasian woman who was being held by the Japanese before World War II.

The authenticity of the gendarmerie report as an official French document detailing the discovery of a message in a bottle at Soulac-sur-Mer has never been questioned. When shown a copy of the original report dated October 30, 1938, the present-day Soulac Brigadier, along with a group of his fellow gendarmes, agreed that every administrative term was correct, and there was nothing that might imply any kind of fabrication. Other than some minor changes in terminology over the years, the 1938 report was determined to be official and proper.

The text of the message was evaluated at all administrative levels in France and later at the US Embassy. Edwin C. Wilson, the interim chargé d'affaires in Paris, didn't question why the original French report dated October 30, 1938, at Soulac did not reach him in Paris until January 3, 1939. Perhaps he knew that the French intelligence services were taking the contents of the message seriously. His cover letter simply said, "The details appear worthy of attention." There is every indication he conveyed his concerns to the US Department of State.

Remaining Questions

A few important questions remain to be asked with regard to the discovery and analysis of the bottled message. First, we must consider whether the first line of numbers on the front of the message designates a message in cipher.

As can be seen from the photograph, the first line on the recto of the message consists of a list of numbers, which may be in cipher. This grouping of single and multiple numbers has never been mentioned by other Earhart researchers, few of whom have viewed the message itself. All of the numbers and digits were precisely formed and neatly drawn, apparently using the same pen and ink with which the message was prepared. These digits and numerals could be the key to unlocking this entire mystery.

Though some of the numbers appear to be crossed out by thin horizontal lines, the line reads:

94^2 96^{52} 9077 V 10 135 815613114 X 6 / 75 2865

A code is a table that unlocks the meaning of certain digits or letters in front of syllables, words, nouns, numbers, or expressions. In French, the word "code" conventionally applies to a list containing between one thousand and ten thousand substitution groups. When all of the elements of the words and the groups are listed in alphabetical order, the code is known as being "ordinate." One table allows both ciphering and deciphering. If the coded groups are in an arbitrary or incoherent order, the code is known as being "disordinated." In this case, two tables are necessary: one for ciphering where plain words are found in alphabetic order and one for deciphering where corresponding words appear in front of the ordinated code groups. Within the Deuxième Bureau and their various Cipher Sections, code dictionaries and ciphering tables were modified frequently for precautionary purposes. Canceled codes were immediately incinerated, and certification of such destruction was confirmed by formal letter to the appropriate Cipher Section. In the files inspected, all that is left today are cover letters referencing codes that had been cancelled and had disappeared in smoke. There was, however, one exception. It consisted of copy number eleven of the Dictionary CODE KG. It had belonged to the French Naval Attaché to the Embassy in Washington, DC, from 1932 to 1939. It was found in its original sealed envelope stamped SECRET and marked "PLI KG." Accompanying instructions stipulated when the envelope should be opened and the code used for secret communications: "Tension in France, tension in the Pacific, mobilization, war in France, war in the Pacific." Two groups of five letters joined together would constitute a ten-letter word. In a telegram the text often would consist completely of letter-words, with either the first five or last five letters being the actual coded word. Some examples follow:

An example of a 1900s French cipher correspondence dictionary.
(Photograph by Robert Stenuit)

prisoner	=	mytsy
japan	=	wofli
japanese	=	jispu
yacht	=	cumva
cipher	=	hevlu

In the Code KG, the five-letter groupings of words were identical in their make-up. They contained a consonant, vowel, consonant, consonant, and vowel. In the search for the yacht *Veveo*, similar words appeared: VERVO, VESWO, VETZO, VEVBO, VEVCU, VEVDY, etc. No groups beginning with VEVE existed—there was nothing between VAVDY and VEVTA. It did not take long to determine CODE KG was not the Code Group for *Veveo*, which ends in two vowels. According to the Code KG, 9077 refers to the Islands of the Bahamas, 1013 means "connecting rod," and 2865 means "shining." In addition, the groups of numbers are of varying lengths, which is unusual because generally only groups of four or five are used.

One person in France has the background, security clearances, and status to shed some light on the ciphered first line of the bottled message: Général Ribadeau-Dumas, president of the Association des Réservistes du Chiffre et de la Sécurité (Association of the Reserve Officers of the Cipher and of Security). He was, in his glory days, a cipher specialist and a former Chief of the Cipher Section of the Deuxième Bureau of the War Department. At age ninety-three, the general is one of the last survivors of the French cipher community that operated in the late 1930s. He has a clear mind and a good memory and is poised, reserved, and very guarded when answering questions.

The general opined that the message in a bottle could be authentic ("a well-considered yes, I would say") and that it "doesn't seem impossible" that its author was an agent working for some division of the French *Service de Renseignements,* "perhaps" as an honorable correspondent. He observed that this particular message is "too short to allow decipherers to apply their usual method of interpretation, which is based on statistical analysis of the repetitions of the digits or groups." He acknowledged that some systems were simple enough to use from memory, but did not see any usable clues in this particular set of numbers. The code word "Veveo" appeared to mean nothing to him. He recommended following up with the Cipher Museum in Rennes, Brittany, where, unfortunately, little additional information was available.

Some super-sleuthing and a little inside assistance from former French Naval intelligence sources indicated that the code that was needed was Marine Code RD, which was widely in use from 1937 to 1939. In spite of an intense search of French records, no dictionary for Marine Code RD could be found. The absolute rule of incineration had been accomplished. Unless a misplaced copy can be found, as was the case of Code KG, the meaning of the word *Veveo* will never be known. The twenty-six-ton sailing vessel may have been named for a stream of ocean currents running through the Solomon Islands that is also called Veveo.

Next, we must ask whether there was a Japanese cargo vessel named *Nippon "something"* bound for Europe in September or October 1938.

Japanese shipping and shipbuilding had been in decline after the end of World War I. Japan's invasion of Manchuria in 1931 encouraged a war economy and an increase in foreign trade. It soon became evident that the Japanese government was directing a large portion of its civilian and military fleet to its needs in China, which reduced the number of Japanese vessels available for foreign trade in other regions. By 1937, Japan faced a severe shortage of ships. The government took over all ship construction. As a temporary solution to the problem, a cartel of leased "tramp ships" came into being. These were under the control of the Japanese government but were registered in foreign countries.

In a letter dated October 26, 1938, four days before our message in a bottle was discovered, the French consul in Bilbao, René Castéran, wrote to his minister:

CONCERNS: WAR SUPPLIES SENT TO JAPAN
I have just been informed that a rather important traffic is reported to have happened for the last few weeks between Bilbao and some harbours of Japan. Ships loaded with war supplies (shells and hand grenades) are said to have been sent to that country.

This notice would appear, at first sight, as unbelievable. However, the reasons for it which were given to me appear to justify it. Indeed, such war supplies would be paid by Japan in foreign currency and in gold, of which nationalist Spain has more than ever the most pressing need. Finally, this could explain why the heavy steel making industry and the war equipment factories in Viscaya, which last month had slowed down their production because of an accumulation of stocks, have started again this month at an accelerated rhythm.[27]

Another official memo, written on June 17, 1939, by D. J. Rogers, the consul general of Great Britain in Barcelona, to the British ambassador in San Sebastian, reported: "Sir, I have the honor to report that my French colleague informs me that he learnt from very reliable authority that the arms factory Laguna de Rins in Zaragoza is making munitions for Japan. The articles being made include: collimators, telemeters, shell parts, and rockets to explode on contact or with delay. It is possible that these goods are being shipped to Naples on Italian boats via Tarragona."[28]

The British ambassador in San Sebastian, Sir Maurice Peterson, transmitted this information when responding: "Information has also reached me to the effect that a large number of shell cases found in Madrid on the capture of the city are being shipped to Japan after removal of the high explosive."[29]

A later dispatch from Consul Casteran also related the following:

General Franco's government continues to suffer from a lack of foreign currency as very frankly stated by General Jordana, Minister of Foreign Affairs. Nationalist Spain not only has heavy charges imposed on it by its foreign purchase of war supplies, but must also face increasing needs for importing products necessary to sustain its own trade and industry. Spanish exporters are obliged to deliver to the government all foreign currency obtained through their sales abroad, yet the government reimburses for such foreign currencies in pesetas at a discounted rate.

This significant circular letter went out to all of Lloyd's agents in Spain, written by the Spanish Minister of Industry and Commerce, dated October 7, 1938:[30]

1. From now on, and during the actual circumstances, you will abstain from remitting to your central office in London any information on movements of national merchant shipping as well as the change of names of vessels, etc.

2. Prior to reporting about merchant shipping, all Lloyd's agents from now on must apply first to the Navy commander of the maritime province before transmitting any such information.

This directive is quite clear. Franco's Spain was operating secretly with Japan and other countries and was happy to accept gold (which Spain badly needed) for payment of what was now to Franco excess arms and munitions of war (which Japan was busily stockpiling in preparation for war against the US and Western colonial powers). This scenario makes it all the more plausible that the author of the bottle message was forcibly enslaved on a tramp steamer chartered by and under the strict control of the Japanese government. This control purposely enabled false registrations or none at all, vessel name and flag changes as desired, questionable cargo and tonnage reports, and reduced shipping fees, all of which combined to keep the ship from being a known, active listing among the merchant shipping trade.

It is also interesting to note that the Japanese government had recognized the Franco government as early as January 1937. An official chargé d'affaires for Japan was situated in Burgos, Spain, by January 1938.[31]

What could not be found in official Japanese shipping records was documentation of their extensive clandestine trips and cargoes. In the six months from September 1937 through February 1938, 239 registered cargo vessels were recorded by harbor police at Shanghai, with an additional 102 showing no registration number. In addition to the large number of vessels trading with China without registration numbers, the manner in which cargoes were disguised is also telling. Cargo number 184, for instance, appeared once aboard the ship

Bandung Maru. The next listing appeared under the name *Padan Maru*. Alternatively, a registration number of 116 appeared a second time as 416, accomplished via two strokes of a paintbrush.[32]

This is evidence of prolific and illicit activity by non-registered vessels. Their captains ignored international shipping laws and such "impractical" requirements as safety regulations, maximum load capacities, crew well-being, harbor access, and tonnage fees for the purpose of trading under the table with China and other countries while bypassing assorted regulatory burdens to which the international maritime fleets normally conscribed. One last piece of Japanese deception was their exportation of gold, which at the time was strictly regulated and forbidden.[33]

So, while no records exist of a Japanese vessel entering Spanish harbors during the timeframe in question, any ship belonging to the Government of Japan, and carrying (for all practical purposes) no "official" trade, would have no local Spanish agent or port authority announcing its arrival or departure. The Japanese and Spanish governments would be loath to have any publicity of their affairs, especially if the cargo consisted of questionable goods. This appears to be the exact the situation of our missing *Nippon something*.

The next important question that remains to be addressed is whether the fingerprints on the message can be identified. There was no name attached to the bottle message, only a partial set of fingerprints. Whose prints were they? Were the Frenchman's prints on file in his country of residence? More importantly, could these prints be traced today?

Although fingerprinting was invented in France around the turn of the century, the Soulac-sur-Mer gendarmerie could not perform technical studies such as fingerprint comparison and identification. Such work would have to have gone to a specialized central office in Paris.

The fingerprints inked on the note appear to be the imprint of the left-hand thumb (indicated by two arrows, and described in shorthand), followed by the forefinger and middle finger. Shorthand text above and to the right of the fingerprints read, "Fingerprints taken by Nipponese policemen." Underneath, with arrows pointing to the bottom print, another line read, "Other with thumb." The forefinger print appears small, a size consistent with a woman's slender hand, as does the middle finger. Somewhat fainter but readable prints appear in the upper right corner on the front side and the upper left corner of the back side. These could have been made by accident during the fingerprinting process if the paper were held between two inked

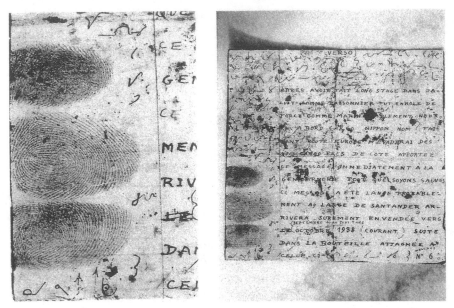

Enlargement of fingerprints stamped on bottled message. (Courtesy National Archives)

fingers. The paper may simply have been discarded by the Japanese police as a bungled effort and quickly retrieved by the message writer because it was his only source of writing material.

Another possibility is that it could have been the message writer's identification papers, sacrificed as a clue for the gendarmerie. The fact that the writer of the message did not say whose prints they were or identify them in any way may indicate they not only belonged to him but would serve to identify him. If this was the case, he certainly could have been a French secret agent because he would have been fingerprinted as part of his file documentation. The only other people fingerprinted in France at the time were persons convicted of a crime or being held for trial. Some illiterate French people were also allowed to be fingerprinted for the purpose of identifying themselves via their passports, but the message writer was clearly not illiterate. Of course, any records of his fingerprints—if they ever existed—were most likely incinerated in the early days of WWII.

Alternatively, the prints could have been Amelia's. After the Lindbergh kidnapping and the ensuing wave of national intrigue, a California newspaper advocated a campaign for the fingerprinting of all children. Amelia readily endorsed this program and was photographed on the Los Angeles Courthouse steps when her

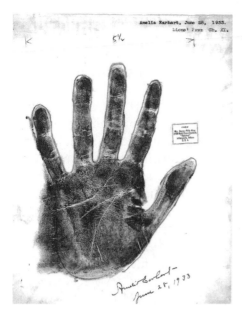

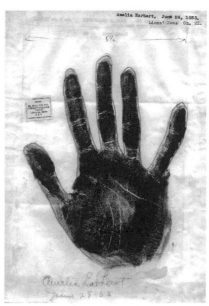

Imprint of Amelia's left hand.
(Courtesy National Archives)

Imprint of Amelia's right hand.
(Courtesy National Archives)

fingerprints were taken as part of the promotional effort. Imprints of Amelia's palms had been made in 1933 in order to appear with handprints of other celebrities in a book composed by Nellie Simmons Meier, an American palmist. High-quality photos of the imprints are now located in the manuscript division of the Library of Congress.

Fate Kirby, a former handwriting and fingerprint expert in the US Army Criminal Investigative Division, worked to identify the prints.[34] Only two of the fingerprints proved sufficiently legible to be compared with the palm prints, and he was unable to make a definitive conclusion.

A former FBI chief hostage negotiator with a private practice in security matters recommended having a scientist review the best possible computer enhancements of the palm prints. At the same time, the top fingerprint analysis experts of the Laboratoire de la Police Scientifique in Lyon agreed to examine the prints. Their conclusion was that "None of the few exploitable B prints corresponds with any of the few exploitable A prints. Since there is no possible correlation, A and B are two different persons." The FBI's former chief latent fingerprint examiner reported that "the thumb and little fingers appearing on the palm print were illegible and could not be used for comparison purposes," and that "the fingerprints on the message in the bottle were not identical with the remaining fingerprints of Amelia Earhart."

If the fingerprints were not Amelia's, it is all the more likely that they belonged to the writer of the message and that this was his method of identifying himself. Unfortunately, any record of his prints has disappeared.

Now, we must ask where this leaves us. At the US Naval Historical Center, located in the Washington Navy Yard compound along the Potomac River, there is a voluminous collection of documents from a variety of official government sources concerning the disappearance of Amelia Earhart. The Center historians make their collection available to journalists, authors, researchers, and Earhart enthusiasts. They have carefully documented every clairvoyant letter, every psychic revelation, and every ham radio operator's statements of the time and frequency in which they intercepted Amelia's voice SOS or Noonan's Morse code radio messages. Their files are replete with Navy and Coast Guard official responses to every devotée's contact. There is even a memorandum written by J. Edgar Hoover, director of the FBI, summarizing to Naval Intelligence what was heard through a Philippine hotel wall by two members of the American armed forces. Apparently, before Pearl Harbor, two Japanese were heard talking in English about Amelia Earhart being alive and held in Tokyo.

There is no end to the hundreds of files the US Government is happy to allow visitors to review about Amelia Earhart. And yet, amidst this entire assortment of Earhart documentation, there is no reference whatsoever to the message in a bottle that washed up at Soulac-sur-Mer. That, to me, is most curious.

Was it because the truth was too awful and its political implications too enormous for the Roosevelt administration? We know that President Roosevelt was notified of the Soulac-sur-Mer gendarmerie report by the State Department via memo of January 3, 1939, from Sumner Welles. And yet, the President's options would have been limited. The Japanese would have disavowed any knowledge of Amelia's fate, and already-fraying relations between the two countries would have further deteriorated had the President demanded an explanation. Ultimately, the file was stamped "Confidential" and buried.[35]

There is one last remaining question to be considered: this is a fantastic story, but is it really true? Could it have been a hoax?

Certainly, I have done my best to document everything that could be documented. For a long while, I had wondered if President Roosevelt was privy to this intriguing information. When my research

```
                                    DEPARTMENT OF STAT
                                       WASHINGTON

                                    January 3, 1939



My dear Mr. President:

     I have received today a personal letter from

our Chargé d'Affaires in Paris of which I am enclos-

ing a copy for your information.  I believe you will

find it of interest.

          Believe me

                         Faithfully yours,




Enc.




The President,

     The White House.
```

Copy of note from Under Secretary of State Summer Welles to FDR regarding the discovery of the bottle. (Courtesy Franklin D. Roosevelt Library)

came across the attached informal note from Under Secretary of State Sumner Welles, there was no longer any question. FDR did know about Amelia and Noonan's capture and imprisonment by the Japanese. This subject probably became a major topic of discussion behind closed doors at the White House for a period of time.

Affirmation of Theory

With regard to this bottled message, Bill Prymak, founder and president of the Amelia Earhart Society of Researchers, had this to say:

> Dave Horner's research into this particular message in a bottle is pivotal toward solving the greatest aviation mystery America has ever known: the disappearance of Amelia Earhart. Dave has more staying power, tenacity, and correct directional ability than any researcher I have known in my twenty-five years of attempting to unravel this mystery. After reading his discourse, I came away unable to find fault or deficiency in his conclusions, to wit:
>
> 1. The key issue is the triangle of perfectly-spelled words: *Jaluit, Marshalls,* and *Amelia Earhart.* Nobody in 1937 could have linked these three entities together without actually having been there . . . that is the key. In the mid-thirties, geography books barely even recognized the Marshall Islands, describing them as scattered spits of sand and brush tightly controlled by a little known feudal empire called Japan who denied all access to these islands. Hoaxers did not have knowledge of the name "Jaluit."
> 2. The author of the message in the bottle is a very capable and well-educated man, judging by the excellence of his writing skills and knowledge of sea currents off France. He even knows that the fortifications (Emidj, the big naval seaplane base) are *in atoll,* where the naval base lies, eight miles up the lagoon away from Jabor, the main town and harbor entrance to the lagoon. A small point, but very poignant, which could be known only to those who had been there. My personal research places the construction of these seaplane ramps and hangars beginning in 1936, or earlier.
> 3. His description of the murder of his three crewmen fits perfectly with the character of the Japanese military at that time, as described to me by elderly natives during my three expedition visits to the Marshall Islands, notably to Mili and Jaluit. I have personally interviewed several elderly witnesses on these atolls who alluded to seeing or hearing about the lady American pilot who came down in these waters and was captured by the Japanese. These are sincere, genuine people, not hoaxers.
> 4. In summation, I am totally convinced that the message in the bottle is genuine.

Chapter 11

Memories from the Marshalls

Prior to World War II, few of the Marshallese had ever seen an airplane or encountered a white person. Yet, the islanders shared stories of a shiny silver airplane crashing in the Marshall Islands with a Caucasian man and woman emerging from the wreckage long before the name Amelia Earhart was familiar to them. Sometimes, these verbal accounts originated with the personal recollections of older islanders who were present at the time; they often embellished their tales for the intrigue of outsiders, especially if money was offered. The stories persisted, and, embellished or not, they began to show a pattern in the order of events, although few considered them to be historically significant.

The Marshall Islanders were well aware that the secretive Japanese did not like outsiders coming into their territory, and they dreaded their brutality. If word spread about a plane crash and Japanese

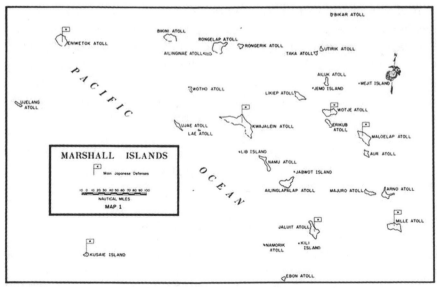

Map of the Marshall Islands. (Map by Elizabeth Whelan)

soldiers taking away two white strangers, the islanders knew to mind their own business. These oral traditions persisted in the hearts, minds, culture, and lore of the Marshall Islander. Due to the novelty of the situation, they issued postage stamps in 1987 celebrating the fiftieth anniversary of the crash landing there.

Years after the war, when people came to the islands and asked questions about the twin-engine silver airplane and the woman who flew it, the islanders drew upon their memories and related the stories told by their parents and grandparents. Many of them took pride in sharing their history with others who were interested in those bygone days.

In 1983, for example, Oscar "Tony" de Brum, then first secretary to the president of the Republic of the Marshall Islands, told T. C. Brennan, author of *Witness to the Execution,*

> I remember distinctly when I was going to school on Jaluit Island, about the first grade. It would have been in 1937. My father came home one day and informed us that an American lady pilot had been captured and she was being taken to the Japanese command office and people were not permitted to go close to her or come anywhere near where she was captured and taken to the office. He did not say whether he actually saw her but the information he passed on to the family I recall distinctly.[1]

If the multitude of stories were the result of just one person's recollection, the telling of them would not carry much meaning. Of course, skeptics worry that "the Marshallese are gentle people. They want to make friends. They want to be helpful and likeable. They listen to the questions, answer the inquiries, and tell the Americans, the British, and other researchers and tourists what they want to hear."[2] Such skeptics also point, not unreasonably, to the absence of any wreckage where the Electra went down, the fact that the US Government has never confirmed anything, and the general lack of hard evidence. However, there is not just one story of the crash—there are many.

Local Lore and Legend

Queen Bosket of Mili related to Oliver Knaggs in 1979, "the Japanese not only captured the American pilots but went to great extent to seize the Lockheed Electra." There always has been the question of how they could maneuver a barge or vessel large enough into reef-strewn waters to transport a twin-engine airplane. Bill Prymak related an interesting story he picked up from a Mili native elder known as Joro, who described the creative maneuver accomplished in such shallow water:

> The barge was eased in toward the shallow water reef at high tide. An aft corner section of the craft's bilge was flooded with sea water, which lowered its freeboard. Flotation devices were attached to the plane to give it some buoyancy. With the backside of the barge flooded and thus lowered, the plane was then dragged aboard the deck of the purposely sunken barge which then pumped its bilges, emptying the seawater. The now lighter barge floated clear of the reef and was towed into deeper water with the Electra safely secured by lines of hemp. This salvage was an effort of monumental proportions. It required some forty men with rope and winches to get the plane on the barge.
>
> The two Americans were being held in the nearby village of Port Rhin. When the patrol boat successfully cleared the reefs with the barge, that rig was secured directly to a Japanese Naval vessel waiting in deeper water offshore. The American fliers were then brought aboard and transported directly to Jaluit Atoll. Joro made it clear that the Mili natives were threatened with death by beheading if they ever spoke about this event to anyone.[3]

Mili Atoll is a semi-rectangular stretch of coral islands twenty miles long, with a coral-studded lagoon reaching about ten miles on its longitudinal axis. Barre Island, the legendary splash-down location, is positioned just inside Jobenor Island pass. Tokowa Channel and the village of Port Rhin are situated five miles to the west. The Mili airport (formerly the old Japanese military air base) was on the southwestern corner of Mili Atoll. Enajet Island, a skinny, five-mile strip of coral and sand, supports the southeasterly corner. Chickens, goats, and pigs outnumbered human occupants, but when Amelia and Noonan splashed there, the Japanese rounded up sufficient laborers to salvage the Electra. It still might be possible to locate some part of the Electra's broken wing or other scattered parts of the airplane lost at the time the aircraft was dragged over the shallow Barre Island reef and placed on the barge for transport.

The most consistent trail of evidence for a Marshall Island landing traces the Americans and their airplane from the reef of Mili Atoll to the harbor of Jabor, Jaluit Atoll, the southeastern

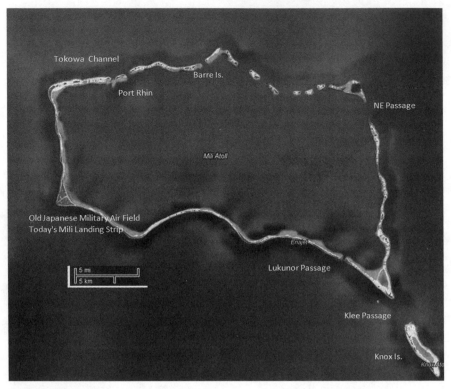

Mili Atoll.

regional headquarters of the Japanese military establishment. On this atoll, Emidj Island constituted a major construction project. A seaplane base was being built on the eastern side with ramps extending into the huge lagoon. Extensive barracks and a medical facility also represented major construction projects. The small town of Jabor was the primary port and anchorage in that section of the Marshalls. It was in the harbor of Jabor where Bilimon Amram treated Noonan's wounds while he and Amelia were on the Japanese ship that brought them there.

According to a number of local natives, Emidj Island also was famous for its executions, with numerous beheadings having occurred there. The writer of the bottled message found on the beach of Soulac-sur-Mer referred to "Amelia and her mechanic having been held there" for a period of time. This hand-printed message offers original and documented confirmation of what happened to Amelia and Noonan in that little known part of the world.

That Earhart and Noonan were fished up by a Japanese seaplane relates to statements made by Marshall Island natives, as does the statement that the "two were accused of supposed spying." The fact that the writer of our bottle message had the bad luck to put into Mili Atoll where his yacht *Veveo* was destroyed and his Maori crew massacred was actually confirmed to Oliver Knaggs by Queen Bosket of Mili in 1979.

The consistent native lore next notes the transfer of the Americans from Jaluit to Kwajalein and from there being flown by seaplane to Saipan. Some leads suggest that the seaplane stopped for refueling at Ponape or Truk. Regardless of their route to Saipan, Amelia and Noonan most certainly did not fly their Electra to that Japanese island. They were brought there by Japanese military, as in concordance with Office of Naval Intelligence special agent Joseph M. Patton in 1960, and held for an undefined period of time, at first in the old Garapan jail.[4]

These stories confirm the statements and documents from high-ranking US military officers that indicated that there was knowledge of Amelia's presence on Saipan. While the actual cause of her death still is uncertain—either by execution or dysentery—until Amelia's Lockheed Electra is found and identified on the bottom of the sea, an island jungle, or a junk yard, the evidence of government documents corresponding with witness memories is firm.

As the years pass, there remains an undefined fascination that lingers in the cloudy haze of the Earhart-Noonan disappearance. Both were in the height of their careers and heading towards a long and prosperous career.

Alfred Capelle

One such testimony is that of the research of Alfred Capelle. Capelle and his parents knew a number of Marshall Islanders who were involved to varying degrees with the Earhart mystery. Key speaker at the May 2002 Amelia Earhart Society Symposium in Oakland, California, the former president of the College of the Marshall Islands and later Marshallese Ambassador to the United Nations said the following:

> I have no doubt that Ms. Earhart and Mr. Noonan were in the Marshall Islands. Bilimon Amram and several other Marshall Islanders saw them with their own eyes in 1937 on Jaluit. There are several theories about where they finally ended up. But, it's a fact they came down in the Marshall Islands after crash landing somewhere at or near Mili Atoll. I suspect when Bilimon saw Amelia Earhart and Fred Noonan he probably didn't think much about the incident until later when he met up with some of the researchers in Majuro and heard from them the story. That's probably when it clicked in his mind who these people were.

Capelle later added in a personal email: "Why a Marshallese would even bother to invent such a story is beyond me. I really don't see why Bilimon would want to fabricate the story if he truly hadn't seen a woman and a man that fit the descriptions of Amelia and Fred. The man was telling the truth and the truth is congruent with the history of what happened and the characters involved in the event."[5]

He summed up his conviction by saying,

> There appear to be quite a few Marshallese of that generation who seem to have had some knowledge of Amelia's presence in the Marshalls. They either had heard of the incident from the Japanese themselves, or were told by fellow Marshallese who reported having seen the white woman and man. The question I'd like to ask is: why would these simple Marshallese want to attest to something they had no vested interest in at all? It would have been much easier and simpler to dismiss the matter and say, "No, I don't know what you're talking about. I've never heard of any white woman flyer who had been picked up by the Japanese and brought to Jaluit," and just left it at that.[6]

Oliver Knaggs

What about the landing near Mili Atoll that Capelle mentioned? South African Oliver Knaggs had already become a credited author when he became intrigued by the mysterious disappearance of Amelia Earhart. Two trips to the Marshall Islands and subsequent research in the US, France, and Saipan provided sufficient information for him to write a book containing interesting interviews with selected Marshall Islanders and, most significantly, Knaggs's discovery of the remains of Fred Noonan's small tin case to which Amelia referred in the context of efforts to clean out the plane and lighten their load: "All Fred has is a small tin case which he picked up in Africa. I notice it still rattles, so it cannot be packed very full."[7]

On his first expedition to the Marshalls in 1979, Knaggs interviewed Queen Bosket of Mili Atoll. When asked about the lady pilot who crashed on or near Mili, the Queen told him, "I heard it from Lijon. Lijon said he had seen the silver plane landing next to the island of Barre and had watched while a man and a woman from the plane buried something. Then the Japanese soldiers came to take them away. When they took the Americans, they took the plane away as well."[8] Queen Bosket went on to describe how Lijon slipped away when he saw the Japanese coming.

Lijon was a Mili Atoll native who was fishing near the entrance to the lagoon when Amelia's plane came down. He was alone at the time of the crash, but he later described the event to Queen Bosket as well as to another Mili native named Lorok. Before Knaggs could go to Barre Island, it was necessary to obtain permission from the island owner. This is still the rule in the Marshalls, and if any excavation is considered, authorized government archaeologists must be present. At the time of Knaggs's visit, Lorok owned Barre and other islets nearby. Lorok related to Knaggs the story Lijon had told him:

I was maybe 11 years old. I remember Lijon coming home with his news.

Illustration of discovering the crashed plane. (Illustration by Elizabeth Whelan)

Lorok, owner of Barre Island, related the story of Lijon, who witnessed the crash. (Courtesy Norma Knaggs)

He had been fishing in the lagoon near Barre when he saw this big silver plane coming. It was low down and he could tell it was in trouble because it made no noise. Then it landed in the shallow water next to the small island. He pulled in his fishing line and went quickly to the island to see if he could help. When he got there he saw that these were strange people, and one was a woman. He hid then because he was frightened; he had not seen people like these. He watched as they buried something in the coral under a Kanal tree. He could tell the man was hurt because he was limping and there was blood on his face and the woman was helping him. He waited there in his hiding place until he saw the Japanese coming and then he left. Later we were told they were Americans . . . Nobody at that time was allowed on Mili. The Japanese were making ready for war. They didn't want anyone to see their fortifications.[9]

Lorok gave Knaggs permission to search the island. The search was grueling because of the thick jungle foliage and intense heat. Knaggs carried a metal detector in one hand and swatted voracious mosquitoes with the other.

There was a large trunk of a rotting tree that could have been a Kanal and there was also a small Kanal growing nearby. I scanned the area with the detector and almost immediately got a response. The Marshallese began to dig away the soil. About 50 centimeters down we came to a hard knot of soil that appeared to be growing on the root of the tree. Cutting into it, we discovered a mass of rust and what looked like a hinge of sorts.

I can only say that at the time I did not believe we had uncovered anything of significance. It must be remembered that we were dog-tired, mosquito-bitten, and operating under extremely hot and humid conditions. In my mind I had envisioned a much more substantial

Barre Island, part of Mili Atoll. Native lore suggests that Amelia's Electra came down on a partially submerged reef to the left. A portion of a wing broke off in the crash. Noonan suffered a head wound and a deep cut in his right leg above the knee. (Courtesy Norma Knaggs)

Alfred Capelle sharing his testimony.

Oliver Knaggs holds part of the small metal box that he unearthed near Barre Island. (Courtesy Norma Knaggs)

Queen Bosket of Mili. (Courtesy Norma Knaggs); *Oscar "Tony" de Brum.* (Courtesy Norma Knaggs); *Amata Kabua.* (Courtesy United States Department of the Interior)

piece of evidence. If the canister had rusted, I expected to find at least something like the remains of a logbook inside it.[10]

Knaggs brought the hinge and rust clump back to South Africa for metallurgical analysis. It is a shame that his inexperience as an archaeologist prevented more careful handling, cleaning, and preservation of the encrusted metal conglomerate. The University of Cape Town Department of Metallurgy and Materials Science analyzed the rusted mass and found that the microstructures were consistent with a fine, clean, low-carbon steel with a carbon content of approximately 0.05 percent, indicating good technology in its manufacture. Possible uses of this metal would have been "for material subject to drawing and pressing such as stampings, automobile body steel, rivets, nails, and tin plate."[11]

According to Knaggs, he and his team thoroughly searched the remainder of the island but discovered nothing else. The corroded hinge and rusted remains could very well have been Noonan's small tin case to which Amelia referred and the item that Lijon witnessed being buried after the airplane came down.

On that first trip to the Marshall Islands in 1979, Knaggs met Amata Kabua, then the *Iroij,* or president of the Republic of the Marshall Islands, as well as Tony de Brum, then foreign secretary. Both men had heard Amelia's story from other Marshallese as well as from some Japanese who were personal friends and acknowledged that the airplane came down on Mili and that the Americans were then taken to Jaluit: "Ultimately they were shipped off to Saipan . . . but what happened thereafter, I have no idea."[12]

Bilimon Amram, Tatios Tatios, and Paul Amram

Knaggs also met Bilimon Amram, who had a pivotal role in debunking the Earhart mystery. In 1937, Bilimon was a sixteen-year-old medical corpsman working for the Japanese at an old German hospital in the town of Jabor on Jaluit Atoll. He was being trained by a Japanese doctor, and one day the two were summoned to the harbor to treat the wounds of a white man who was on board a Japanese naval vessel. "He was very different from any person I had seen before," Bilimon told Knaggs. "He was a tall, thin man with dark hair and blue eyes." Bilimon had never seen blue eyes before. He also noticed a white woman sitting on deck. He recalled she was wearing trousers "like a man, and had short, blondish hair." She appeared very tired, but was otherwise unhurt. The man had a head wound above the forehead and a badly cut knee. Both injuries were infected. The head wound required only a bandage. "I could not stitch but used paraply on the knee."[13]

Bilimon related to Knaggs, as he later did to others, that the Japanese told him the two fliers were American and that "their airplane exhausted its fuel and crash landed at Mili."[14] He said that it was a shiny, silver plane and it had been picked up with straps and positioned on the stern of the Japanese ship. He added, "One of the wings was broken." The Japanese were amazed that the pilot was a woman. There was a lot of talk about it on the island. According to Bilimon,

> Then one day the news came. "You remember that woman pilot? She and the man were found guilty of spying. The man was put to death with the sword, and she has gone to prison to be starved to death." This was not a story put out for the benefit of the people. The people were not supposed to know anything about her. It was a simple statement of fact, an end, a conclusion, if you like, of something that happened on the island.[15]

Bilimon introduced Knaggs to a man named Tamaki Myazoe who, back in 1937, had been ordered to load coal one evening from a lighter barge onto the Japanese seaplane tender *Kamoi*. Tamaki volunteered what he knew of the Earhart saga: "I was called out during the night, together with the rest of my shift, to go and load coal on this ship, the *Kamoi*. We were told to hurry because they had to go and pick up an airplane and some Americans at Mili. They heard on the wireless there was an American airplane crashed there. We worked like machines. It was very hard. Then the ship left quickly."[16]

Bilimon repeated his story to Bill Prymak and Joe Gervais when they met with him in 1990.[17] He elaborated that a Japanese officer on board the vessel told him the white man and woman were Americans. They were flying from Lae, New Guinea, to Howland Island but flew into a huge storm and were set far north of their intended course and missed Howland. Because of low fuel, they turned northwest to try and reach the Gilbert Islands. They sighted land about the time their fuel was exhausted, and came down in shallow water near a beach. They were not sure where they were. The officer indicated that they would be sent to Saipan. According to Bilimon, "the crew called the lady pilot 'Meel-ya.'" Bilimon also identified Amelia Earhart and Fred Noonan from photos that Prymak and Gervais showed to him.

Like Bilimon Amram, Tatios Tatios was a medical corpsman working for the Japanese. While Tatios did not have direct contact with Amelia Earhart or Fred Noonan, he told Alfred Capelle that he "not only saw a white woman and white man at about the same time

Bill Prymak with Bilimon Amram in 1990. (Courtesy Bill Prymak)

One of the last pictures taken of Amelia Earhart and Fred Noonan before leaving Lae, New Guinea. The unidentified woman on the left, believed to be the wife of Tommie O'Dea, holds what is believed to be a pearl ring given to Amelia before her departure. Continuing from left to right: *L. J. Joubert, manager of Bulolo Gold Dredging, Ltd.; Mrs. Eric Chater; Mrs. Joubert; Mrs. F. C. Jacobs; Amelia; F. C. Jacobs, manager of New Guinea Goldfields, Ltd.; and Fred Noonan.* (Courtesy Woody Peard)

Section enlargement of previous photograph, showing hands holding pearl ring. (Courtesy Woody Peard)

frame as Bilimon, he also heard from a Japanese they were Americans." Similarly, before the war, Kanki Amlej was a Marshall Islander working for the Japanese as a laborer at Emidj on Jaluit Atoll in 1940. Capelle related Kanki's story: "A Japanese with whom Kanki had gotten acquainted told him that previously two Americans were brought to Jaluit for interrogation. The two, including their airplane, were captured after their plane went down near Mili Atoll."[18]

Paul Amram was Bilimon's younger brother. A year after Bilimon's death in 1996, Bill Prymak visited with Paul, who had prepared a written statement in English and presented it to Bill as a testament to Bilimon's integrity. According to Prymak, the statement added the following significant detail: "One of the Americans wanted to give him [Bilimon] a ring or something. He said the lady was calm, but the man seemed excited."

Prior to Amelia and Noonan's final takeoff at Lae, New Guinea, for the flight to Howland Island on July 2, 1937, there was a brief photo session at the aerodrome. Among the well-wishers on hand to watch the historic flight of Earhart and Noonan commence were executives and family members from the Bulolo gold mining operations. In the photograph, the woman on the left standing next to L. J. Joubert, the manager of Bulolo Gold Dredging, Ltd., appears to have a small, simple ring in her hands. From her stance, the expression on her face, and the manner in which she is holding the ring in front of her, it appears that she is presenting the ring to Amelia.[19]

Tokyo

On that same 1990 trip, Prymak and Gervais interviewed one of the workers brought to the Marshalls from Japan for the construction efforts. He was known among the Marshallese as "Tokyo." He was brought to the island of Emidj in 1935 to supervise crews pouring concrete on what would become a huge seaplane facility. With the assistance of the local pastor (for translation purposes), Tokyo related the following story:

> There was a great flurry of excitement one day as the weekly barge came up from Jabor. The barge normally carried construction materials off-loaded from larger ships in Jabor harbor, but on this day the barge carried no ordinary cargo. All work was suspended for the day and the entire work force was kept off base. [I] could see from a distance that a silver land airplane, partially covered by a canvas tarp, was being off-loaded by bulldozers with winches and dragged to a remote area where it was promptly fenced off and camouflaged.[20]

Tokyo went on to describe how the few supervisors who witnessed this unusual event were absolutely agog. There was little or no talk among the civilian workers prior to the aircraft being moved ashore. The islanders knew that the Japanese had no tolerance of loose

Emidj Island, Jaluit Atoll, at eighty-three hundred feet before the US bombing of the seaplane base on April 21, 1944. (Courtesy National Archives)

tongues. According to Tokyo, the aircraft he saw brought ashore at Emidj had a broken wing. He also said that the plane remained behind the operations building for the entire time that he worked in the Emidj military complex.[21]

Prymak noted,

> Years later, we came across a U.S. Air Force reconnaissance photo taken in 1943 at an altitude of 8300 feet over Emidj. It was a pre-bombing picture with all the targets to be hit identified. Sure enough, behind what once was the Japanese operations building, just as old Tokyo described it, you can see the silhouette of an airplane with a broken wing. After getting the dimensions of the "Emily" Japanese bombers pictured on the ground, which had wing spans of 125 feet, I was able to scale down and measure

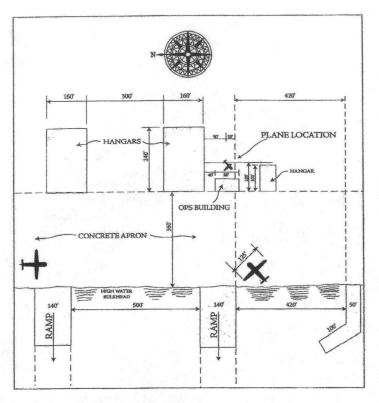

Japanese seaplane base at Emidj Island, Jaluit Atoll. Two Emily bombers pictured here have 125-foot wingspan compared with Electra's 55-foot wingspan, shown behind the Operations building.

that airplane behind the ops building. Indeed, the wing measurements came out to approximately 55 feet, the wing span of Amelia's Lockheed Electra. How many other places could you go in the Marshalls to find an airplane with a broken wing and a span of 55 feet?[22]

The possibility is very real that the Japanese disposed of Amelia's Electra by barging the aircraft to the seaplane ramps at Emidj. They certainly could not have left the airplane in full view on Jabor Harbor's beach. At Emidj, the Electra could have been winched up the seaplane ramp and pulled to an inconspicuous location where Japanese engineers could inspect every nut and bolt as well as Lockheed's latest radio and direction-finding technology.

Prymak also added this tantalizing story. While he was walking down a dirt road in the village of Jabor in 1997, a Japanese teenager

Bomb-damaged seaplane ramp at Emidj Island. (Courtesy Bill Prymak)

Seawall at Emidj showing bomb damage, with new development in the background.

Old Japanese Army barracks at Emidj converted to Modern Housing Facility. (Courtesy Bill Prymak)

Bombed and burned former Japanese headquarters building on Emidj. (Courtesy Bill Prymak)

Rusted airplane parts on a section of Emidj beach. (Courtesy Bill Prymak)

Emidj Island jungle overpowers a former Japanese gun emplacement. (Courtesy Bill Prymak)

Japanese bunker in the midst of Emidj jungle. (Courtesy Bill Prymak)

came up to him and, speaking in near-perfect English, asked what Prymak was doing in Jaluit, since tourists there are a rarity. Prymak said that he was searching for some evidence that Amelia Earhart might have been there many years ago. The boy, named Ichiwata Lamae, offered to introduce Prymak to his eighty-five-year-old grandmother, who lived on the outskirts of the village. Prymak found an alert, bright-eyed Japanese lady, whose name was Ana. The boy translated her story: "In 1937 my husband came home one evening very excited. He was a cook at the Japanese naval base. He told me that the Japanese had just captured an American lady pilot and her mechanic. The two were being held in the post office. 'Don't dare tell a soul,' he threatened. 'It is very secret. They would chop off our heads if they thought we knew anything about this.'"

United States Military Witnesses

Second Lt. Alvan Fitak
Second Lt. Alvan Fitak came ashore at Majuro in 1944. With three other marines, he landed a small boat on the island at night to reconnoiter the area prior to the approach of a major task force. These men were part of the First Anti-Aircraft Battalion of the Fifth

Amphibious Force. Their orders were to determine the strength and number of Japanese on the island. Fortunately for Fitak and his men, there were only a few Japanese, and they were no threat.

The lieutenant was on Majuro for a period of nine months. During that time, he met a native Marshallese named Mike Madison who spoke English. Madison told Fitak that he had served as a cook on an American freighter and had lived for a while in San Francisco before returning to the islands. Madison looked to be about forty-five years old and took pride in speaking English. According to Fitak, "He had a friendly, educated air about him, and you could tell he had been around and had seen something of the world."[23]

Madison told Fitak about a female American aviator with a male companion who had crashed not far away on a beach near shallow water. They were picked up by the Japanese and brought to Majuro several years before the war. "The woman wore an aviator's suit and had short, curly, brown hair," he stated. "There was a tall, dark-haired, white man with her. He had a bloody bandage on his head. The natives reported that the man had disappeared by the next morning, probably having been killed. The woman was kept there for some days before being taken away supposedly by submarine. The Japanese believed the pair was on a spy mission."

Fitak wrote a summary report on Madison's story that was filed with the Navy Department in Washington. However, he was never contacted by anyone for more details and "thought it was strange nothing had ever come of his information, and that Earhart and Noonan were still officially considered to have vanished at sea."[24]

Lt. Eugene Bogan

Lt. Eugene T. Bogan also came ashore at Majuro in 1944. During his stay there he too talked with Mike Madison, who became his principal interpreter and intermediary. He also met Elieu Jibambam, an educated Marshallese native and schoolteacher in his early thirties who was extremely helpful to US forces as a scout and informant. Elieu told Bogan this story, which Bogan later passed on to embedded press accompanying the occupying forces: "A Jap[anese] trader named Ajima told me that an American woman pilot came down between Jaluit and Ailinglapalap Atolls, and that she was picked up by a Japanese fishing boat. The trader heard that she was taken to Japan."[25]

What Lieutenant Bogan didn't say to the press in 1944 was revealed in a letter dated January 8, 1970, to Fred Goerner. On his Washington, DC, law firm stationery, Bogan wrote:

> When I asked Elieu about Ajima, he told me that Ajima had been a storekeeper on one of the islands on the Majuro Atoll—the one we had renamed as Rita. This was the island which contained a number of Japanese buildings and where the Japanese had a ramp for sea planes. Seaplanes from this little base, I later learned from rumor, had been used for scouting in connection with the Pearl Harbor attack. Elieu had worked for Ajima in Ajima's store. Ajima journeyed to other atolls periodically. He had left the Atoll when the Japanese evacuated— sometime before we arrived . . . I had tried to elicit from Elieu what facts he knew that would come only from him.
>
> Shortly after we took over Majuro Atoll on January 31, 1944, it was decided to establish a harbor entrance control post on Calilin Island. This island is about ten miles from the headquarters island at a point where there is a deep passage through the Majuro reef to serve as a fleet entrance to the huge lagoon. That lagoon was to be set up as an anchorage for the entire Pacific Fleet.

As it turns out, Elieu and one or two other native households were living on Calilin Island and it was decided they should be evacuated to the island at the other end of the lagoon, about twenty miles away. The Island Commander, Navy Capt. Vernon Grant, directed Lieutenant Bogan to take an LCT (Landing Craft Tank) up to Calilin Island and evacuate the native families.

> I duly arrived one afternoon and beached the LCT and arranged the evacuation. We loaded the LCT with all the household gear of these families and even took the new thatched roof off of Elieu's house and put it on the LCT together with the pigs and chickens. The idea was that the following morning we would take these people twenty miles down the lagoon to the large native village and resettle them. We spent the night on the island. During the evening at a big campfire over which we cooked supper the Earhart story developed.
>
> I remember asking somebody to let me do some innocent questioning around the campfire, and I put a number of questions to Elieu, carefully avoiding anything that would suggest answers or facts. That's when Elieu stated the facts I related earlier: that a Japanese storekeeper named Ajima had told him about a plane coming down near Jaluit Atoll containing one white man and one white woman. A Japanese boat had taken them to Jaluit, administrative headquarters for the eastern Marshalls.

Elieu Jibambam (right) *enjoys a coffee with Dwight Heinie.* (Courtesy Norma Knaggs)

The next morning I delivered my natives plus pigs and chickens and household gear to the big island at the other end of the lagoon, unloaded them and got back to the headquarters island long after dark. I went into the headquarters tent and found Captain Grant talking to several newspapermen from the carrier Lexington which was now anchored in the lagoon. They were starving for news. I reported completion of the evacuation mission and mentioned the Earhart clues as just an incident. I very well remember that scene as this was the first time Grant and island headquarters had a word of the story. The newspapermen got quite excited and kept peppering Grant and me with questions. I held my responses down to the bare simple facts. Grant made a number of fiery statements about the fact that it was impossible this was a clue to the Earhart disappearance.

According to Bogan, Elieu reportedly told another Navy lieutenant, Charles J. Toole, the same story. In 1944, on Majuro Atoll during the invasion of the Marshall Islands, Vice Adm. Edgar A. Cruise learned from a native interpreter that two American fliers, a man and a woman, had been picked up and brought to the Marshalls in 1937. Around that same time, *Pacific Islands Monthly* ran the following story:

EARHART MAY HAVE COME DOWN IN JAP[ANESE] TERRITORY

Reports from Washington, USA, on March 22, quoted two Navy lieutenants as saying that natives in captured Marshall Islands told a story of a white woman who crashed in a plane there several years ago. The natives said that the woman had been taken to Japan by Nipponese who picked her up.

It has been many times suggested that Earhart and her navigator, Fred Noonan, when they left Lae, New Guinea, in 1937 for Howland Island (Central Pacific), got astray and came down in Japanese territory and were "liquidated" as spies. If the American fliers failed to locate Howland—a tiny dot with a vast empty ocean beyond it—they almost certainly would have turned away northwestward knowing that, if they had enough fuel, this would inevitably bring them over the widely spread and innumerable atolls of the Gilbert (British) or Marshall (Jap[anese]) archipelagoes.[26][end extract]

Maj. Joseph C. Wright, USAF

Former Air Force Maj. Joseph C. Wright was on temporary duty at Guam in 1967.[27] While visiting a relative on Majuro Atoll, he was reading Fred Goerner's book and was struck by Goerner's conclusion that Earhart and Noonan probably had crashed near Mili Atoll.

Wright took the time to visit that section of the Marshall Islands. Near the southern side of Mili is Inajet Island. It was there that Major Wright became acquainted with an elderly Marshallese who told him through an interpreter about the "flying machine" he saw land in the lagoon years ago. He described how two white people exited from the wrecked airplane. One was a man who had a towel wrapped around his head. The other was a woman with short hair who wore trousers like a man.

Wright said that the old man had no way of knowing who the pair was. He had never seen white people before and wasn't sure what to do. The Japanese were very careful not to allow the local islanders near the couple. The aged islander reckoned that it was about thirty years earlier when all of this happened, which would have dated the year as being 1937.

The Air Force veteran confirmed information passed on to him by the Marshall Islanders of the often brutal treatment dished out by the Japanese who had little patience with their prisoners or with locals who didn't follow their orders. A Marshall Islands woman who tried to befriend the white couple after the Japanese soldiers told her to stay away was beheaded.

Pilot Jack Ralph and Lt. Steve Stevens

Jack Ralph was a B-24 Heavy Bombardment Air Group pilot. In 1943, he was stationed on Guadalcanal in the Solomon Islands. In July of that year, he and his flight crew received a two-week rest and recreation leave in Auckland, New Zealand. At a social center maintained by the City of Auckland and the American Red Cross, Ralph's navigator, Lt. Steve Stevens, met a young woman who had previously lived on Nauru Island. Her father was a senior official responsible for the management of a number of Pacific islands under British possession in that part of the Pacific. After the attack on Pearl Harbor, the mother and daughter evacuated to New Zealand. When Lieutenant Stevens met her in 1943, she still did not know the fate of her father.

On Stevens's last evening in Auckland, the young woman and her mother told him about listening to Nauru radio the night that Amelia Earhart passed near the island and how some months later an outrigger canoe with Marshall and Gilbert Island natives appeared at Nauru carrying a handwritten note signed by Amelia Earhart. According to the two women, the note said that Amelia had landed in the Marshall Islands and that she and her navigator had been taken prisoner by the Japanese. She was praying that her note would be swiftly conveyed by friendly natives to a place that might send help.[28]

Upon returning to his duty station, Lieutenant Stevens reported the incident to his Group Intelligence Officer. After the war, Jack Ralph wrote the Pentagon, but received only "an unconcerned reply saying there was no record of such an incident . . . As time passed we concluded the Allies were intent on making good and dependable friends of the Japanese and didn't want to open old wounds with bad publicity. We wrote the whole thing off as diplomatic expediency and figured the story would forever be suppressed."[29]

John Heine

John Heine, a notable attorney in Majuro whose parents were missionaries on Jaluit, was a schoolboy at Jabor during the summer of 1937.[30] His recollections of the events at the time were told to Bill Prymak and Joe Gervais:

> One day in the middle of July, 1937, we were in school. Suddenly the schoolmaster took us outside, gave us all little Japanese flags, and told

us to parade down to the harbor wharf. Leaving school in the middle
of the day was an exciting event for us, and when we arrived at the
waterfront, a ship had just pulled into the harbor. Behind it was a
barge, and on the barge was a big silver airplane with two motors, held
secure by slings coming from the aft boom of the ship. The next day
the barge was moved via the lagoon to the naval base at Emidj.

After the war broke out, Heine's grandfather, Carle Russell Heine,
was beheaded by the Japanese on Emidj Island for being a missionary.
His father and mother were later seized by the Japanese and beheaded
as spies for having a typewriter in their home. Young John was taken
by Japanese soldiers and was being held in an air raid shelter until
one of the soldiers guarding him told him to run to the beach and
escape while he shot over John's head:

> It was a miracle I wasn't killed along with my parents. I recall that
> the Japanese soldier was not much older than I. He must have been
> a Christian for he seemed to be having a hard time trying to decide
> what to do with me. It was just about dark when he suggested I run
> for the beach. You better believe I took off like a scared rabbit and
> never looked back. Swimming in the dark to a nearby island I lived off
> coconut crabs and small amounts of rain water for quite awhile.

There is more to the Heine family story. A mysterious piece of
evidence occurred in an article by his grandfather in *Pacific Islands
Monthly*. The article reported on an unclaimed letter for Amelia
Earhart, submitted by Mr. Carle Heine, special correspondent,
Marshall Islands, Jaluit Atoll, March 17, 1938. The letter was
addressed as follows:

> Miss Amelia Earhart (Putnam)
> Marshall Islands (Japanese)
> Ratak Group. Maloelap Island, (10)
> South Pacific Ocean

Carle Heine discovered the letter in the Jaluit post office on
November 27, 1937. The return address was the Hollywood-
Roosevelt Hotel, Hollywood, California, and the postmark was Los
Angeles, California, October 7, 10 p.m. Amelia's personal assistant,
Margot DeCarie, was living at the Hollywood-Roosevelt Hotel at
the time of Amelia's disappearance. The letter was unopened. Heine
speculated that it could have been just a hoax, since by October it

Sketch depicting John Heine's testimony of students watching the silver airplane being towed by the Koshu. (Illustration by Elizabeth Whelan)

was well known that Amelia had been given up for missing, although he notes in the article that the writer of the letter "displays a little more geographical knowledge of these parts than one would expect of the average individual." His article stated:

> It is conceivable that Amelia Earhart may have told some trusted friend in America, before setting out on her ill-fated journey, that she intended to take a look-see at the Marshalls en route or that she might possibly do so if in any danger as she passed by. And it is possible that this hypothetical friend in Hollywood might think that Amelia had reached this group, and might be lying low for some reason or other at Maloelap. It seems curious that anyone without specific interest in the group should know the name of that particular atoll which is of no great importance.

I have made an earnest attempt to evaluate the benefits and detriments of the many tales told in order to eliminate the most skeptical and bring forth those with the most meaningful and logical data. At the same time, I have tried to use caution in measuring the value of a given story until it was corroborated, or at least acknowledged by others to have been possible. The significant number of people who have stepped forward and made their statements also is impressive.

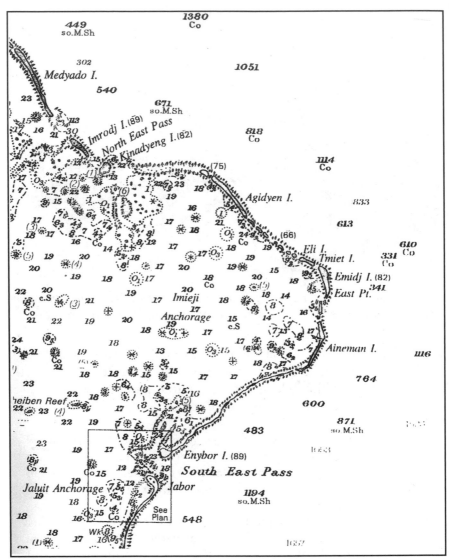

Map of southeastern section of Jaluit Atoll showing Emidj Island, where the large Japanese seaplane base had been established. (Courtesy US Government Printing Office)

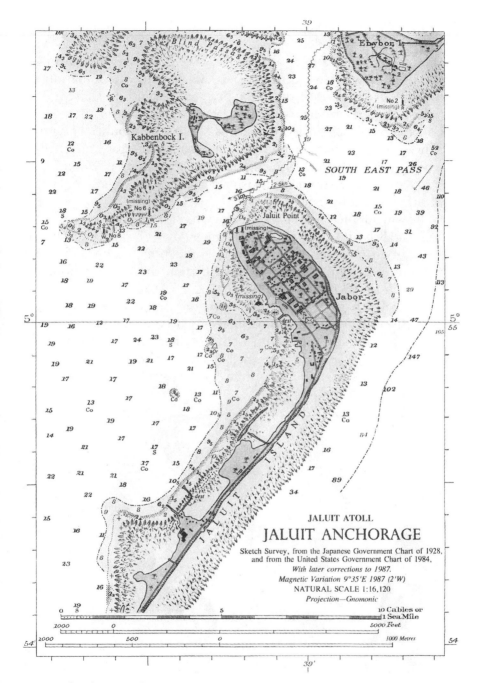

Map of Jaluit Anchorage of Jaluit Atoll, featuring the Southeast Pass.
(Courtesy US Government Printing Office)

After more than a decade of research, it would seem to me that any degree of initial skepticism on my part has reasonably given way to probability. This is not to imply that we have all the answers—we don't. But what we do have is a wonderful accumulation of testimonies from a deserving populace that should be shared with the world. I hope readers will appreciate my contribution.

Can the truth be learned if there is reasonable doubt? How can we know for certain that one person's story has more merit than another? It is important to recognize fact from fiction. When hard evidence or direct testimony just isn't available, one must rely on the most believable information.

In drawing upon our ability to judge what may have taken place in the Marshall Islands and Saipan as Amelia and Fred are concerned, we need to develop our curiosity. At the same time, we need to apply a measure of common sense to make certain that we are honestly weighing all the factors involved.

It is likely that these islands still hold some answers to our questions. Unfortunately, today there are few around who might voluntarily provide them. But we have their letters, stories, and memories. Their eyes have seen, their minds, remembered. The hearts of these islanders have sought out a way to share their past, and that honesty is undeniable.

Chapter 12

Saipan Sightings

Willard Price, a notable author, wrote of numerous sources who stated that Earhart and Noonan were brought from the Marshall Islands to the military headquarters on Saipan and died there, Earhart in prison and Noonan executed. He observed, "Since their statements are made by responsible people they are probably true."[1] The many stories told by residents of Saipan after WWII are meaningful, and those that follow here are some of the more believable.

Robert E. Wallack

Through various sources and witnesses, it has been possible to construct what might have happened on July 2, 1937. To add to the credible testimony is Robert E. Wallack's story.[2] His discovery on Saipan offers concrete evidence of Amelia's presence there.

Wallack was seventeen when he joined the US Marine Corps. On his eighteenth birthday, he walked up the gangway with a heavily loaded sea bag to board a troop transport headed for Hawaii. Before long, he was a designated machine gunner with C Company, First Battalion, Twenty-Ninth Marines, destined to come ashore on the right flank of the invasion landing at Chalan Kanoa, Saipan, on June 15, 1944. Wallack was in the second wave to attack the beach, riding in a steel-tracked landing vehicle known as a Buffalo. Though he took some mortar shrapnel in his hand, he was grateful he wasn't in the first wave: "Most of those guys were floating in the waves or lying on the beach when we got there. It was the most horrible sight I'd ever witnessed. Not only were we taking heavy fire from the Japanese, but many of the kids had been dropped too soon and they stepped into water over their heads. They drowned before they could get out from under all the gear carried on their backs."

Fighting continued for twenty-three days as Marines pushed across the island. Wallack's job was to haul a 135-pound, 30-caliber, water-cooled machine gun wherever it was needed. After holding off a massive charge by thousands of Japanese, most of the heavy fighting was over and clean-up operations began.

"We had to be alert and careful at night because there still were some renegades up in the hills that would try to take advantage of any careless Marines that might get caught off guard," Wallack stated. "But during the daytime we did some mopping up and souvenir hunting."

It was on one of those patrols that Wallack wandered into a bombed-out Japanese administration building in the town of Garapan. In the midst of the rubble, he discovered an old safe that the bombing had not destroyed. "One of our guys was a demolition expert," Wallack said. "The door of the safe was about three feet by three feet. Some explosive gel was appropriately placed and in no time he had the thing blown open. When the smoke cleared I was the first one to see what was inside. Grabbing a leather briefcase with a flip-top, I hustled outside to see if I'd become a millionaire in Japanese yen."

There was no money. But he has remembered what was there for the rest of his life. In that briefcase were charts, fly-over permits, visas, and assorted papers and documents with Amelia Earhart's name on them—part of her documentation for entering and leaving countries along her around-the-world route in her Lockheed Electra with Fred Noonan in 1937. "What's more," he said, "There was no evidence of salt water on the briefcase or the documents. Ink signatures on important permits were not blurred. There were no salt stains on the case or the papers inside it. Our Government's word that she crashed into the Pacific Ocean is baloney."

After spending a day enjoying his discovery, Wallack decided to turn over the leather case to someone in authority. He located a naval officer who seemed to be in the center of activity. The officer was dressed in khakis with no insignia, but Wallack could tell that the man was senior in rank by the gold on the visor of his cap.

I don't know if he was an intelligence officer or not, but he seemed very interested in my find. In fact, he told me he'd return the briefcase if it was not deemed important. Of course, that was the last I saw of it. The officer did give me a receipt that I placed in my money belt which included a waterproof pouch my mother had given me. That receipt stayed there along with my rosary. As best I can remember, the small slip of paper stated, AMELIA EARHART'S BRIEFCASE— NON MILITARY—and the date. I never knew the man's name. He signed my receipt with just his service I.D. number. I wrote my mother shortly afterwards and told her about my discovery, urging her to be on the lookout for an Earhart story, but no such story ever appeared.

The war was moving fast at that time, and soon afterward Wallack was on his way to Guadalcanal to prepare for the invasion of Okinawa, where another heroic battle took place. After he took a bullet in his upper leg, medics cut away his pants with his money belt where his receipt was stored. His receipt for Amelia's personal belongings disappeared, but he remains certain about what he found in the safe and firmly believes that Amelia died on Saipan. He also talked with several local women before being shipped out to Guadalcanal. "They pointed to the graveyard and told me that two white people, a man and a woman, were buried there. This was an important statement. There were few, if any, white people on Saipan at the time Earhart disappeared."

Bob Wallack's friend Erskine Nabers was a radio-deciphering technician assigned to the Eighth Marine Communication Platoon. He told Wallack about having unscrambled a coded message that came in one morning through the field radio. The message reported that Earhart's plane had been discovered in an old hangar at Aslito Field. A day or so later, Nabers described how he watched other Marines set the aircraft on fire. "Erskine Nabers was a good Marine," said Wallack. "He watched my briefcase being put in a mail bag headed for Hawaii."[3]

Wallack agreed with Thomas E. Devine, who had also been on Saipan in 1944 serving as a sergeant in an Army postal unit. In his book, Devine described having seen an airplane being pushed by Marines from a hangar at Aslito Airfield. He believed the plane was Amelia Earhart's Lockheed Electra. Devine watched as it was set on fire and destroyed under order of Navy Secretary James Forrestal. Wallack noted glumly,

> The U.S. Government continues to say that Earhart and Noonan crashed and died in the Pacific. In my opinion they didn't tell the truth from day one and they still haven't. It would have been a huge embarrassment to President Roosevelt if the American people had learned Amelia was taken by the Japanese who believed she was a spy, and America didn't do anything about it. So many years have now come and gone that even if our Government wanted to divulge the Earhart secret they would be unable to do so. Such a decision would likely have a negative impact on the excellent foreign trade and international relationship enjoyed today between Japan and the United States.

In June 2002, Wallack told his story to Gary Solis, lieutenant colonel, USMC, ret., and chief of the oral history unit, Marine Corps Historical Center, Washington, DC. Colonel Solis made a two-hour tape of their interview.

"Getting my story about finding Earhart's briefcase into the Marine Corps archives meant an awful lot to me," Wallack said. "It records an accurate account of what I found, touched, and opened that day so many years ago on Saipan. I really wanted to hold on to that briefcase. But my buddies urged me to do the right thing and turn it in. I knew it was my duty to report it. In looking back I'm glad I did, but it sure would be great to know what happened to that briefcase before I pass on. Probably it's gathering dust in some Government basement inside the Beltway."

After seeing Wallack on a History Channel program, another marine wrote the editor of the *Cincinnati Post-Journal*: "I don't believe Amelia Earhart and Fred Noonan disappeared near Howland Island. Why? Because I believe more in the honor and integrity of a fellow combat marine on Okinawa than I would any bureaucrat in Washington."

Wallack's son, William C. Wallack, has this to say about his father: "If my Dad's views tend to support a so-called conspiracy theory evolving around the disappearance of Amelia Earhart, so be it. Certainly, I have every reason to trust he's telling the truth. Why

Amelia Earhart's briefcase. (Drawing by Bill Wallack)

This is to confirm to Dave Horner that I found a briefcase after the battle of
Saipan containing documents and charts belonging to Amelia Earhart. This briefcase was
turned over to a U. S. Navy officer who gave me a receipt which was subsequently lost.

Robert E. Wallack 5-17-07
Robert E. Wallack   Date

*Robert E. Wallack's confirmation of having found a briefcase with
documents and charts with information related to Amelia Earhart's world
flight.* (Courtesy Robert Wallack)

Loading valises at Massawa, Eritrea, Africa, picturing Amelia's briefcase. (Courtesy Purdue University Libraries)

would he fabricate a story like this? He's not only my Dad, he's a twice-wounded United States Marine who fought in the horrific battles of Saipan and Okinawa. He doesn't need to make up stories."[4]

General Shoup, chief of staff for the Second Marine Division during the invasion of Saipan, related to Fred Goerner: "He [Wallack] heard that some property—artifacts or something—belonging to Earhart was recovered on Saipan after the invasion. But he was so damn busy trying to win the battle he didn't pay much attention to the information."[5] This is a qualified reference to the Wallack discovery, and supports what Bob Wallack told me personally.

In addition, Ed T. Jones, a fellow marine, endorsed Wallack's memory: "I was a combat Marine with Bob Wallack on Okinawa. We got to know each other as we both lived in the outskirts of New Haven, Connecticut. He was a good Marine and a good friend of honor and integrity. Bob told me in detail about his experiences on Saipan, just as he told Dave Horner. I can wholeheartedly endorse what he said about finding Amelia Earhart's briefcase with the navigational charts and permits. There's no question in my mind that Amelia and Noonan died on Saipan. Case closed."

Joe Artero

Twenty-two-year-old Joe Artero was an employee of the US Department of Commerce on the island of Guam in 1937.[6] He and a cousin visited friends on Saipan in July. They stayed at the home of a friend of Artero's father, Mariano Pangelinan, who lived in Garapan, a town of twenty-nine thousand later reduced to rubble during World War II bombings.

The boys were restricted to the Garapan town limits and were not allowed to drink alcohol. Artero learned from a police detective

Pacific Daily News

GUAM, WHERE AMERICA'S DAY BEGINS

VOL. 1 NO. 310 AGANA, GUAM, THURSDAY, NOVEMBER 19, 1970 TEN CENTS

Amelia Killed In Saipan

Visiting Guamanian Was Told In Saipan In 1937

By Janet Go

Famed aviatrix Amelia Earhart and her navigator, Fred Noonan, were executed on Saipan, a Guam man was told during a short visit to Saipan only days after Earhart's aircraft crashed in 1937.

Joe Artero, an employee of the Department of Commerce, Government of Guam, said in an interview Tuesday that while he was visiting friends on Saipan on July 16, 17 and 18, 1937, a police detective Jesus Guerrero, told him that the flyer and her navigator had just been executed

but he did not reveal where the execution took place.

Although travel to the Japanese Mandated Islands had been restricted since 1936, persons could get clearance from Tokyo for visits to relatives. Artero then 22 years old, and his cousin had obtained a visa to visit Saipan for three months and had booked passage on the Japanese copra schooner Mariana-Maru for July 13, 1937. However, his trip was delayed two days because the Japanese fleet was having maneuvers around Saipan,

Artero said. In fact, he thinks that officials with the Japanese fleet probably went to Saipan to witness Earhart's execution.

The Mariana Maru docked at the pier near Garapan, Saipan around 5 p.m. on Thursday, July 16, Artero said. He and his cousin went to stay with Mariano Pangelinan, a friend of Artero's father, in Garapan, a city of 29,000 which was reduced to rubble during World War II. The boys were restricted to the city, at worst in Saipan as also, and were not allowed to drink alcoholic beverages, he said, although the Japanese had beer and sake to drink.

The next day, Jesus Guerrero who lived near the Pangelinan's, told them about the execution. Guerrero is known to have worked with the Japanese police before and during World War II. His responsibility was to keep the Saipanese in line and his methods were reputedly not gentle.

Sunday morning, July 18 Artero attended Catholic Mass and while kneeling in the church, someone told him that he had to leave the island an hour on the Mariana Maru Artero left the church and returned to Pangelinan's house where he found his suitcase waiting at the door.

The Japanese were suspicious

IOE ARTERO

Pacific Daily News *article featuring Joe Artero and his visit to Saipan.*

named Jesus Guerrero, who lived near Pangelinan, that the American female aviator named Amelia Earhart and her navigator had been captured by the Japanese and executed. Guerrero was known to have worked with the Japanese military and, when necessary, to keep local Saipanese in line. His methods were not always gentle.

On Sunday, July 18, Artero attended Catholic Mass, where a friend told him it was important for his own safety to leave the island immediately. Artero left the church and headed for the Pangelinan home, where he found his suitcase waiting at the door.

Artero left on the *Mariana Maru*, headed for Japan. After spending some time in Japan, Artero arrived in Guam on Saturday, August 26.

That Monday morning he was summoned by a US Navy commander, whose name he later forgot, and questioned about Saipan.[7] Artero told the Navy authority that the island of Saipan was being fortified and a substantial submarine base was under construction on Saipan's south side. Artero emphasized to the commander that the Japanese were making preparations to capture Guam. As far as Artero knew, his warnings were never investigated. He also told the commander about hearing that Amelia Earhart and Fred Noonan had been executed on Saipan. The commander laughed at this, saying that Noonan could not have made a thousand-mile error in navigation.

Matilde Fausto San Nicholas Arriola

Fred Goerner spoke with Matilde San Nicholas Arriola in June 1960, when she was in her early thirties.[8] Matilde's story is one of the more engaging witness tales. With the help of Father Sylvan Conover, a

Interpretation of pre-war photo of the Kobayashi Ryokan Hotel, Garapan, Saipan, where Amelia was reputedly seen. (Courtesy S. Viviano)

priest of the Capuchin order, Goerner extracted some amazing details from Matilde. Originally from Brooklyn, New York, Father Sylvan had been on Saipan for about ten years when he agreed to assist Goerner with interviews of several local Chamorros in the village of Chalan Kanoa. Those interviewed had confided in the priest earlier about having seen a white man and woman in Japanese custody before the war.

Matilde had originally lived in Garapan, where her father was a tailor. Their home was next to the Hotel Kobayashi Ryokan, where the Japanese housed political prisoners and others who were held for questioning. In 1937, Matilde, then in her early teens, had seen the white woman whom the Japanese referred to as "flier and spy."[9] She described the woman as "tall and very thin. She had not much hair for a woman. It was cut short. When I first saw her she was wearing a man's clothes, but later they gave her a woman's dress." She told how the Japanese guards kept a close eye on the woman, but allowed her to walk around the yard of the hotel. On several occasions, Matilde said she gave the woman some fruit: "On one day she came out in the yard looking very sick and sadder than usual. I gave her a piece of fruit and she smiled. Then she gave a ring from her finger to my sister Consolacion. The next day one of the police came and got some black cloth from my father. He was told the lady had died of dysentery and they were going to bury her."[10]

Matilde testified that when her sister got sick, Consolacion loaned the ring to a younger cousin, Trinidad. The ring featured a single pearl set in white gold.

Father Arnold Bendowske, OFM captain of Saipan.

Goerner showed Matilde pictures of various American women. After studying them for a few moments, she did not hesitate to pick out Amelia. "This is the American woman," she acknowledged. "I'm sure of it. But she looked older and more tired."[11]

In November 1977, Father Arnold Bendowske of Saipan interviewed a number of Chamorros, including Matilde. Matilde told this priest much of what she had said to Goerner years earlier. She

Connie and Len Kaufer. (Courtesy Len and Connie Kaufer)

explained that she didn't know who the white woman was back in 1937 when she first saw her. She said she would see her out in the yard when she walked to the outside toilet facility of the old hotel. From time to time, she offered the lady some broiled breadfruit, and she usually would eat a little.

She appeared to have a problem with diarrhea and often looked sickly. She went to the toilet a lot. One day I noticed what looked like burn marks on her face and hands. Another time she walked near the house. I was studying my geography lesson and she sat beside me. She took my pencil and said something in English, pointing to an island, and suggested I should put the name down there. I don't know where that book is now.

She usually wore something that looked like a nightgown. Her hair was cut short and appeared brunette. Her face was that of a very strong woman. My mother said she was an American. Although she was allowed to walk around the yard I knew that she was being guarded and for that reason I was afraid of the Japanese. They had spies everywhere. My husband later told me she was the woman pilot who survived the plane crash.[12]

During my research, I had the pleasure of becoming friends with Connie and Len Kaufer on Saipan. Connie is the niece of Matilde Fausto Arriola and was named for Matilde's sister, Consolacion, who originally received the ring from the "foreign white woman." In an email dated January 23, 2009, Connie wrote to me:

I can attest that the ring was given by my aunt Consolacion to her sister Matilde (my aunt, Nan Tilde) who in turn gave it to my eldest sister, Trinidad (Trini). When I was about eleven years old (1956), my sister Trini gave me the ring. She did not lose it as some others have said when she went for teacher education studies in Truk. I wore the ring regularly until the time when Father Sylvan, OFM, came with a man who said, "he wanted to see Amelia Earhart's ring." My recollection is that this happened when I was a sophomore in high school. When I went to get the ring from the box where I kept it in my bedroom it was not there.

Like all houses built after the war on Saipan, the floor of our house was supported by pillars several feet above the ground. The individual floor boards were spaced apart at set intervals, unlike tongue and groove. Our first thought was that the ring may have fallen through one of these openings to the ground below. Although we crawled under the house below my bedroom and searched carefully we could not find the ring.

Because I wore the ring regularly for several years, I remember it well. It was made of white gold, and had a single white pearl mounted like a crown above an opposing set of claws or clasps. The upper body of the ring band below the pearl was done in a kind of open filigree work on both sides. On the inside of the ring's band was an inscription of some kind.

I hope this helps you in your quest for answers to questions about the final days of Amelia Earhart.

The story of Consolacion and Matilde's ring has unique and special

Felix Umberto Flores, Bishop of Guam.

significance. In her last photo from Lae, it seemed that Amelia was given a ring that fit that description. From the many photos taken of Amelia during her momentous journey and ports of call, she was not pictured wearing a ring or any other jewelry. It certainly would have been in keeping with Amelia's gentle personality, however, to give the ring to the young girl who befriended her just before she died. Of course, it is also fitting that the ring would be lost without a trace, just as Amelia supposedly was.

It is also significant to note that these interviews were undertaken at the request of Adm. Kent J. Carroll through Guam's Catholic Bishop, Felix Umberto Flores. Admiral Carroll formerly had been a commanding officer on Guam. Bishop Flores was responsible for the translation from Chamorro to English. Though they interviewed a number of local witnesses, they selected four testimonies for translation to allow the Bishop to personally transport these sworn statements on his forthcoming trip to Washington. William H. Stewart, former Deputy Administrator of the US Trust of the Pacific Islands, secured a copy of the original testimony from the Saipan Division of Historic Preservation. These documents confirm the facts of Goerner's documentation as well as the truth of Earhart and Noonan's fate.

Josephine Blanco Akiyama

Riding her bicycle along the Beach Road of Tanapag Harbor in 1937, eleven-year-old Josephine Blanco was taking lunch to her brother-in-law, Jose Matsumoto, who worked at the Japanese Navy base. As she arrived at the gate, she saw a crowd of people gathered around a large seaplane. In the midst of this crowd of military and civilian workers were two white people. She watched as they were taken away and later learned that they were Americans. She had never seen

The old Japanese hospital, now Garapan's Historical Museum. (Courtesy Saipan Museum of History and Culture)

white people or Americans before. One of them was a woman who wore pants and had hair cut short like a man.

When Josephine returned home and told her mother what she had witnessed, she described the white people and said that the man seemed to have hurt his head some way. After learning that the pair had been taken to the Japanese Police Headquarters at Garapan for interrogation, Josephine's mother impressed upon her the importance of not telling anyone what she had seen. "It could cause our family big trouble!" she emphasized. Later, when her mother saw the two Americans on display in front of the police station and labeled as spies, she reiterated the need for silence.

In 1945, after Saipan had fallen and the war was over, Josephine worked as a dental assistant for a US Navy doctor, Casimir Sheft, on the recently established US base in Saipan. Dr. Sheft was cleaning the teeth of a Navy pilot when the subject of Amelia Earhart came up. "At that point," said Dr. Sheft, "Josephine came into the conversation and told us about having seen two American fliers, a man and woman, on Saipan before the war."[13]

Fred Goerner tracked down Josephine, who had moved to California in 1957, and Dr. Sheft at his practice in New Jersey. Dr. Sheft told Goerner that Josephine always had been reliable and that he believed her story. "She couldn't have had any reason for inventing such a story back in 1945," he explained.[14]

Josephine's story was the reason for Fred Goerner's original trip to Saipan in 1960, which led to other witnesses and contributions to discovering the fate of Earhart and Noonan. Also in 1960, special agent Joseph M. Patton, Office of Naval Intelligence, interviewed Josephine's mother, who confirmed what her daughter had witnessed back in 1937. Patton interviewed other Saipanese as well but tended to discount as hearsay most of the information he gathered. However, he concluded his confidential report by saying that Amelia Earhart and her navigator may possibly have been brought to Saipan by the Japanese military. That this comment came from the Office of Naval Intelligence signifies the verity of the information.[15]

The Museum Curator

The ruins of an old hospital facility have been converted to a historical museum located not far from the old Japanese jail near Garapan. It was in this jail that the Japanese reportedly held Amelia Earhart and navigator Fred Noonan in 1937. Today, the museum features pottery, illustrations, views of Saipan's history, and artifacts from the treasure galleon *Concepcion*. A museum curator who requested to remain anonymous reported that, in 1937, his father witnessed a slender white woman and a tall white man wearing flight-type uniforms being marched by this prison.[16]

Judge Gregorio Camacho

Gregorio Camacho was seventy-six years old when Oliver Knaggs interviewed him on Saipan in 1979. A former judge and deacon of the San Roque Church, he married the sister of Josephine Akiyama, the young dental assistant. He was also the uncle of Monsignor Tomas Camacho, Bishop of Saipan. Because his uncle's command of the English language was limited, the Monsignor assisted as an interpreter.

After Knaggs explained that he was interested in learning about Amelia Earhart and her navigator, he began by asking whether the Americans were definitely on Saipan.[17] Gregorio, somewhat surprised by the simple questions, replied, "Oh yes. They were brought here by the Japanese and held in the Garapan prison."

Knaggs indicated he thought they were held in some sort of hotel. "No, they were held in jail," responded Gregorio. "The woman often was taken to the big three-story building of the Japanese [the Kobayashi Ryokan Hotel] for questioning." When Knaggs asked

Former Saipan judge Gregorio Comacho with his nephew, Bishop Tomas Comacho. (Courtesy Norma Knaggs)

Oliver Knaggs inspecting Amelia's reputed cell in the old Garapan jail in Saipan. (Courtesy Norma Knaggs)

about the man, Gregorio said, "He did not behave himself. The Japanese brought him some *misu* soup—a favorite breakfast food—and he insulted them by throwing it back in their faces. He was instantly beheaded. He had committed a grave insult. The Japanese could not tolerate a prisoner doing that."

When Knaggs expressed disbelief, Gregorio responded, "I am sure. The Japanese talked about it openly for weeks. The woman was taken to the big house for questioning. He was executed soon after they arrived in Saipan."

Knaggs was shocked but asked what had happened to Amelia. Gregorio said that she also was executed. Knaggs said that he thought she had died of dysentery, and the judge shrugged. "She might have had dysentery, but she was killed. She and her navigator were brought here as spies. They were paraded in front of the people who were told they were American spies. I don't think there would have been any trial."

Knaggs said that he had heard that Amelia might have been shot, but Gregorio shook his head and said, "No. The Japanese did not shoot people sentenced to death. They beheaded them. The prison guards were given orders to execute her and they did it the only way they knew how. Women were nothing to the Japanese."

Knaggs knew that Gregorio had been questioned some years earlier by Fred Goerner, and he asked what Gregorio had said at the time. "I cannot now remember what I said to him, nor the questions he asked," said Gregorio. "But had he asked me what happened to Miss Earhart, I would have told him what I have told you, for there is only one truth about it."

The Muña/Cabrera Family

T. C. Buddy Brennan, author and businessman, traveled to the Marshall Islands in 1987 looking for restorable Japanese Zero airplanes. His book, *Witness to the Execution,* opened with a quote from a man named Tanaki, a sixty-three-year-old Marshall Islander living on Majuro, who told Brennan, "You want old airplane. You find airplane American lady crash in." This simple statement switched Brennan's focus from World War II Zero airplanes to the likely fate of Amelia Earhart. (Author's note: "Tanaki" is the very same Tamaki Myazoe, the coal handler whose story appears earlier in this section.)

Brennan described how local contacts on Saipan helped him

Amelia in front of the Electra. (Courtesy Purdue University Libraries)

find some interesting witnesses. One of these was Manuel Muña, a former senator and local historian, who worked for the CIA in radio communications after the war and also assisted Fred Goerner in 1962. Muña's sister, Joaquina Muña Cabrera, had worked part-time for the Japanese at Garapan Prison. She remembered Amelia being there and indicated that Amelia had shown kindness to her. Joaquina, then twenty-five or twenty-six years old, also worked in the laundry of the old Hotel Kobayashi Ryokan, where she said the American lady pilot had been lodged for a while on the second floor.

Joaquina reported her memories to Fred Goerner as a testament to

Amelia's presence on Saipan. She related how a white man and woman were present one day when she arrived at work. The Japanese gave Joaquina the woman's clothes (pants and jacket) to clean, although she did not clean the jacket as it was leather. Joaquina noted how she saw the man only one time but remembered that his head was bandaged—this detail corresponds with other testimonies of Fred Noonan's presence on the island. Joaquina described the woman as being thin, tired, and somber, although she smiled at Joaquina and, she imagines, thanked her. Joaquina noted that the woman was hurt or bruised. The last Joaquina heard was, "one day . . . police said she was dead from disease."

The Muña family also directed Brennan to seventy-year-old Nieves Cabrera Blas. After being assured that Brennan was not from the police or in any way connected with the CIA (which had a major training center on Saipan), Mrs. Blas told her story, which Brennan characterized as "prompt, complete and concise:"

Before the war one day there is great excitement. It is said that the Japanese have captured two spy people. They are holding them in

Tommy Brennan with Nieves Cabrera Blas and Joaquina Cabrera's grandaughter, Rosa, in the area where Nieves remembered the execution taking place. (Courtesy Tommy Brennan)

Illustration of Amelia's execution. (Illustration by Elizabeth Whelan)

town. Many of us go there to see the two spies. I saw them in the square where the Japanese police building was. The Japanese guards made them take off all their clothes, everything they had on.

It is then that we can see one of the spies is a woman. Both of them were wearing trousers and I believed both had been men. I had never known before a woman who wore men's trousers. The man seemed to be hurt and had a bandage on his head. The woman was wearing a watch, and some rings and some kind of medal. They take these and then put her back in the cell. We learn in the village the woman's name is Amelia Earhart and she was a flyer and an American spy.

One day I am working on the farm and I see three Japanese motorcycles. Amelia Earhart is in a little seat on the side of one motorcycle. She is wearing handcuffs and she is blindfolded.

I ran from that place so the soldiers do not see me. Later, I go back
to see if they bury her, and they had.[18]

According to this testimony, Amelia wasn't executed until just
prior to the US invasion in 1944. This is contrary to other statements
that indicate that she was held only a short while before being killed
or dying from dysentery. However, it is important to note that no
matter the outcome, Amelia existed for a time and then was gone and
not seen again.

Mrs. Blas directed the Brennan team to the burial site, where they
eventually got permission to excavate but found only a piece of black
cloth, which Mrs. Blas identified as the blindfold that had covered
Amelia's face.

Manny Muña also related to both Fred Goerner in 1962 and
Don Wilson in 1991 that he had known Gregorio Sablan, who was
recognized as one of the most learned men on the island. In addition
to Chamorro, Sablan spoke Japanese, German, Spanish, and English.
Before dying of tuberculosis in 1945, Sablan confided in Muña that
he had been summoned by the Japanese to be the interpreter at the
time Earhart and Noonan first appeared on Saipan. After being
taken from a seaplane that landed at Tanapag Harbor, the pair was
escorted to military police headquarters at Garapan. According to
Sablan, the interrogation lasted three or four hours. The woman then
was taken to Garapan Prison. A short while later, she was removed
to the old hotel. The man was taken to the Muchot point military
police barracks.

Jae Hong Lee

The fact that the previous account by Mrs. Blas has merit is further
supported by the words of Jae Hong "Jimmy" Lee. Today a real
estate businessman on Saipan, Jimmy had been a longtime friend
of William H. Stewart. For a quarter of a century, Stewart lived
and worked on Saipan, arriving in 1970 as deputy director of the
Department of Resources and Development at the headquarters of
the US Trust Territory of the Pacific. This huge territory comprised
the Mariana, Marshall, and Caroline Islands after they came into
America's possession upon conclusion of World War II.

A friend of Lee's confided some important information regarding
Earhart's destiny on Saipan. Lee wrote:

William H. "Bill" Stewart, a US Department of State foreign service officer and former economic adviser to the high commissioner of the Trust Territory of the Pacific Islands, primarily the Northern Marianas, Chuuk, and Palau. (Courtesy William Stewart)

Today I was able to talk to my friend again. His mother talked to old Japanese man at Puerto Rico, Saipan in 1986. The Japanese old man mention to my friend mother:

Japanese soldiers brought EMELIA [sic] EARHART from one of island in MICRONESIA (Palau) to here in SAIPAN before the World War Two.

After three days later, he got to order from Japan Army headquarters to kill EMILIA EARHART ASAP.

He was a Japanese soldier and NO 3 high ranking at SAIPAN Japanese Army.

In 1986, when he came to SAIPAN that time, he was 82 years old and my friend mother was 79 years old. They talk in Japanese language.

He want to tell the truth about EMILIA EARHART before he died.

He strongly asked my friend mother to do your best to find out family of EMELIA EARHART and explain everything what he did to her.

The Garapan prison where Amelia Earhart and Fred Noonan were temporarily incarcerated, according to Saipan locals. (Courtesy Norma Knaggs)

An improved and expanded Garapan Prison. (Courtesy David Celis)

He said to detail information like which room EMELIA EARHART stay, (only 3 days in SAIPAN) and how he killed her and where they bury her.

Before the day of killed her, all of Japanese soldier and prisoner moved from GARAPAN to CHALAN KANOA and came back to GARAPAN one day later.

My friend mother was died in the 2006.

Mr. Bill [STEWART] would you please refer to PRYMAK all above information. I will inform you right away if I get another information.

Respectfully, Jae Hong Lee [signed in Japanese][19]

In talking further with Bill Stewart and Jimmy Lee, I became even more convinced of the authenticity of Lee's written statement. He made it very clear that the elderly soldier's sole purpose in returning to Saipan was to tell the truth and confess his sin before he died. He didn't know how to reach an Earhart family member to whom he might apologize. He also said the body was buried three to five feet deep behind the old Saipan jail and near the old Japanese hospital on Middle Road.

Francisca Sablan Celis

Francisca Sablan Celis, "Nan Kai." (Courtesy David Celis)

In 1986, a Japanese cruise ship, *Oriental Queen,* called at Saipan. Among those who disembarked were two elderly Japanese men. They began walking down the road to the home of Francisca Celis.

"I remember seeing that ship in the harbor because every day I go to my mom's house to check on her," stated David Celis Jr., a retired dental technician on Saipan. During his first interview with me, he recollected:

The two men were former Japanese military stationed here before the war. They wanted to locate a cave they remembered which was hidden on a bluff near the port area, and had been walking over two hours in the hot sun on the road leading to our home. Upon encountering my mother they inquired about the cave, asking if she knew the location. She replied that she did know the cave because she was here on Saipan during the war and her family had hidden there when the bombs began falling.

According to Francisca's son, the two men engaged his mother in a fairly extensive conversation in the Japanese language. They made one comment that troubled her for many years. Her son presented the question to me just as his mom apparently had received it. It was simple, direct, brutal: "Do you remember the American lady flyer we killed before the war for spying? We didn't want to kill her but were ordered by Tokyo to do so. Her plane had come down in islands of Micronesia and she was brought to Saipan as a spy. I tell you this because I am ashamed of my behavior and wish to apologize to her family. You are the first person I have met here and I beseech you to help me find the family of the American lady pilot."

David told me that his mother was so stunned by the comment that she did not know how to respond. "Of course she did not know, or could not recall the name of the female flyer, and she certainly had no knowledge of the whereabouts of her family. I do remember Mom describing how the old man wept uncontrollably as he told his story. He was clearly remorseful."

David Celis points to Amelia's reputed burial site behind the old Garapan prison. (Courtesy David Celis)

This Japanese Army officer who was doing most of the talking had apparently taken part in Amelia's execution, as he volunteered specific details on her death, some of which were confirmed in Jimmy Lee's testimony: "She was executed immediately behind the old Garapan jail and buried there after dark around midnight. I am the only person still alive who knows about this. The soldier who dug the hole for the grave and helped bury her died in the war. I have never felt proud about my action. Many nights I have not slept. Many nights I have endured nightmares. I am now old and do not care what happens to me."

I asked whether he remembered the name of the officer. "He introduced himself to my mom," David responded. "I have tried to help her remember, but she could not. The only fact she could recall was that the old soldier told her he was the third highest ranking officer on Saipan at the time." The rank of the officer corresponds with that of Lee's letter.

His mother worried for years whether or not to go to the authorities with this information. He finally took her to the Historical Society after making arrangements for them to tape his mom's testimony. Francisca died in 2006 at age ninety-four.

David M. Sablan

Saipan businessman David Sablan assisted Buddy Brennan in his quest to find Amelia in the mid-1980s. "Buddy and I spent an hour or so at the ranch of Nieves Cabrera Blas," he told me in an email dated October 14, 2008.

Yes, Nieves saw an execution, but was it Amelia? As I understand the story, Nieves was about 300 yards away from the scene looking westerly toward the port area where someone was beheaded and buried at the same spot.

Buddy and I also called on Mr. Herman Guerrero, an elderly man who used to be a police officer during the Japanese occupation of Saipan. Herman told us that the person Nieves probably saw was not Amelia, but was an American. Mr. Guerrero had the remains exhumed and taken to the Catholic cemetery in Lizang area, and then later transferred to Chalan Kanoa.

Sablan said that Judge Camacho had been gone a long time, but he knew his eldest son, Luis. "Luis had heard opinions expressed by his father about the execution of a tall lady with blond hair in the same location where Nieves Cabrera Blas said she saw someone executed."

David M. Sablan. (Courtesy David Sablan)

When Dave Sablan was asked if he really believed that Amelia had been held on Saipan by the Japanese, this was his guarded answer: "It is just too coincidental that a tall, blondish haired woman would be seen here and later disappears with no one knowing where she went. At the same time I cannot help but feel that some of these stories might be exaggerated."

Pedro Sakisag

Pedro Sakisag was a native of Guam who was working at Tanapag as a stevedore in the 1930s. He witnessed the white man and woman being removed from the seaplane and taken away. He later told his priest, Msgr. Oscar Calvo, how he had been unloading food from a ship when the big plane splashed down along the beach and the two people were removed. He commented to his co-workers, "I'll bet you anything that lady in custody of the Japanese is an American!" She had light brown hair cut short. I had seen other Americans on Guam and recognized the clothes and the look. I was in shock wondering how the Japanese could keep an American lady there![20]

Jesse Boyer

Jesse Boyer was a farmer living in San Roque. He confirmed to Fred Goerner that he saw two white people in 1937, one a man and the other a woman dressed like a man. "I was working at Tanapag and I remember the lady well. Her face, arms, posture . . . all looked American. She was wearing a bandana and her hair was cut short like a man's. The Japanese held them because they were suspicious. It was kept very secret."

Antonio Diaz

Antonio Diaz was a chauffeur for the Japanese commanding officer of the Tanapag Chico Navy Base. He overheard lots of comments from his high-ranking passengers. He told Goerner, "The woman pilot was brought to Saipan. It is possible her plane also was brought here. Do not believe anyone who tells you she flew that plane to Saipan. The Japanese one day unloaded it from a ship at Tanapag, and they took it on a big truck to Aslito Field. The officers talked about it as being her plane. It was a two-motor plane of silver and some other color I had not seen before." Diaz later became a member of the Saipan legislature.[21]

Vicente Sablan

Vicente Sablan, a Chamorro, spoke with Fred Goerner: "The woman you look for, along with a man, were picked up by the Japanese in the Marshall Islands. I heard this from Japanese officers. Many of us knew this. They were brought to Saipan from the Marshalls. They did not fly their plane here."[22]

Michiko Sugita

When Joe Klaas and Joe Gervais published a book in 1970 claiming that Amelia Earhart had survived and returned to the United States under a false name, a Japanese newspaper printed an article about the book highlighting the authors' unusual hypothesis. Upset over that claim, forty-four-year-old Michiko Sugita of Katsushika Ward telephoned the *Tokyo Shimbun* and declared the statement to be a falsehood.[23] The Tokyo newspaper sent an interviewer to Sugita's home to report her story. Prior to the war, Sugita had lived on Saipan for ten years. Her father, Mikio Suzuki, was a section police chief at Garapan.

Though she had been told by her father never to say anything about this subject, she felt it was time for the truth to be told. Michiko related how she remembered an event that took place in 1937. She was eleven years old and preparing to enter junior high school.

As police chief, her father often entertained Japanese military policemen at his home. These parties sometimes involved fairly heavy drinking, and it was easy for Michiko to pick up pieces of conversation. At more than one such event, she overheard guests talk about the American aviatrix captured for spying and brought to Saipan to be put to death.

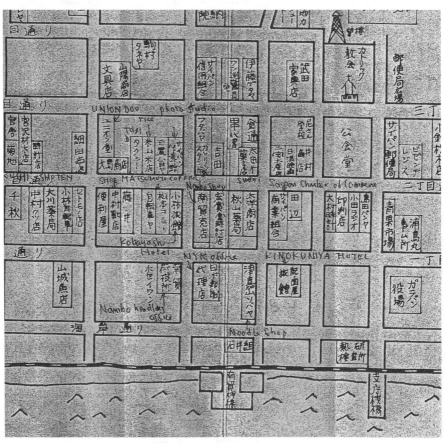

Map of pre-war Garapan, Saipan. (Map by Marie Castro and David Sablan)

Amelia Earhart Shot, Tokyo Housewife Says

Amelia Earhart, the American aviatrix lost in the Pacific during a round-the-globe flight in 1937, was shot to death by Japanese military police in Saipan, claimed a 44-year-old Tokyo housewife and a former resident of the island in an interview with The Japan Times Thursday.

The housewife, Mrs. Michiko Sugita of Katsushika Ward, made the disclosure at her home after reading in a Japanese paper about the book just published in the U.S. that claimed that the aviatrix was alive.

"I couldn't believe it and phoned Tokyo Shimbun to make it sure," she said.

Mrs. Sugita is the second daughter of a deceased section chief of police, Mikio Suzuki, in Saipan. The Suzukis lived in Garapan in the central part of the west coast of the island for nearly 10 years. Mrs. Sugita said that her father used to invite his friends, including military policemen, at home to hold drinking parties. During one of the parties, she, then 11, overheard their conversation that an American aviatrix who flew alone for spying was captured and shot to death, she said.

However, she said that she did not hear where her airplane was shot down and where she was killed.

Military policemen at the party seemed impressed with her since she flew there alone, she said. Mrs. Sugita said that many attendants at the party said that she was a beautiful woman.

According to Mrs. Sugita, her father later asked her if she heard the conversation. When she said "yes," he told her not to tell it to anybody else. And she kept the promise—until Wednesday when she phoned in what she knew.

Her father, she said, was disgusted with the murder and told her that they killed the woman pilot in spite of the Geneva Convention, which banned the murder of any captive.

Similar conversations were repeated every night for a while whenever her father's friends visited the home, she said.

Asked about the approximate time of the incident, she could not recall it since similar tropical weather prevailed on the island all through the year. All she could remember was that the incident happened before she took an examination to enter a junior high school in March 1938.

Mrs. Sugita returned to Japan in January 1947, with her mother, younger sister and younger brother. Her elder sister committed suicide when Saipan was occupied by the U.S. military forces in July 1944. Her father was killed when he was captured by the U.S. military forces.

Mrs. Sugita's story goes opposite to Joe Klass and Joseph Gervais's contention that Miss Earhart still survives as Mrs. Irene Bolam in New Jersey.

The contention was stated in the book "Amelia Earhart Lives," published by McGraw-Hill. Mrs. Bolam denied publicly Tuesday that she was Amelia Earhart.

Negro GIs Mob MPs in Okinawa

NAHA (Kyodo)—Some 60 angry Negro GIs mobbed a U.S. military police station here Wednesday after one of several Negro soldiers was taken into custody for beating a Caucasian GI in Koza, central Okinawa.

Reports reaching the Ryukyu police headquarters said that at about 9:30 p.m. the Negro soldiers set upon the white GI in a street frequented by Negro servicemen.

Military police sent to the scene, fired several shots in the air and apprehended a Negro who was taken to a military police station.

Shortly afterward some 60 Negro soldiers surrounded the station shouting abuse. At one stage the situation became alarming and military police headquarters and Ryukyu police headquarters dispatched men to the aid of the MPs manning the station.

U.S. military authorities refused to comment on the incident.

Japanese Times article of November 13, 1970, featuring Michiko Sugita's testimony.

Michiko said that the military policemen were impressed with Amelia because she was a pilot and a beautiful woman. Her father was disgusted over the murder of Amelia. He told his daughter it was against the Geneva Convention to kill a captive. When he learned that she had listened to the Japanese military and police discussions, he ordered her not to tell anybody, as it could cause him trouble if word got out. Michiko's father was killed after US troops invaded Saipan in July 1944.

Father Everett F. Briggs

Father Everett Briggs, who died in 2005 at the age of ninety-nine, was an extremely intelligent person and a published author. Briggs was assigned to Japan in 1932 as a Catholic Maryknoll missionary. With financial assistance from Catholics in the United States, he founded Saint Mary of the Lake Catholic Church in Otsu City, which was the first Catholic Church built in Japan since the sixteenth century. Briggs overheard an intriguing conversation on a Tokyo street corner in 1937:

> I had become disoriented in Tokyo on a hot July day in 1937. I came on a number of Keio University male students involved in heavy conversation as I approached this street corner. There was much animation and excitement. They didn't notice this foreigner as I stood near them, listening with interest. And even if they had seen me they wouldn't have guessed I understood every word they spoke.
>
> Their conversation concerned an American airplane that had reportedly crashed within the Japanese mandated islands. The news being conveyed was that the pilot was a woman. They couldn't believe it and were in awe over the fact an American woman was piloting an airplane so far away from her country of origin.
>
> There was some talk about her being a spy, and what might happen to her. Probably they would bring her to Saipan or Tokyo, was the consensus.[24]

In reflecting on Amelia's life, prominent author and syndicated columnist of the *New York Herald Tribune,* Walter Lippmann, wrote after her disappearance:

> The world is a better place to live in because it contains human beings who will give up ease and security, and stake their own lives in order to do what they themselves think worth doing . . .
>
> The best things of mankind are as useless as Amelia Earhart's adventure. They are the things that are undertaken, not for some definite, measureable result, but because some-one, not counting the costs or calculating the consequences, is moved by curiosity, the love of excellence, a point of honor, the compulsion to invent, or to make or to understand. In such persons mankind overcomes the inertia which would keep it earthbound forever in its habitual ways. They have in them the free and useless energy with which men alone surpass themselves . . .
>
> And what they prove to themselves and to others is that man is no mere creature of his habits, no mere automaton in his routine, no mere cog in the collective machine, but in the dust of what he is made there is also fire, lighted now and then by great winds from the sky.[25]

Part Six: The Legend and the Legacy

Chapter 13

The Theories Abound

Over the decades, the myth surrounding Amelia and Fred has inspired some interesting theories, some more realistic than others. The desire to find the lost plane has incurred numerous searches in various parts of the Pacific Ocean. The following hypotheses with regard to Amelia Earhart and Fred Noonan's fate have yet to be proven:

A. Elgen Long and David Jourdan's "Crashed and Sank" Theory
B. TIGHAR's Nikumaroro Island Speculation

A. Elgen Long and David Jourdan's "Crashed and Sank" Theory

Most Earhart researchers are realists and consider Amelia's disappearance unproven until her missing Lockheed Electra has been found. Certainly, locating and identifying the lost airplane would accomplish much, essentially ending most of the debate as to what really happened on July 2, 1937. Both the US Navy and Coast Guard stated unequivocally that Amelia Earhart and her navigator, Fred Noonan, ran out of gasoline while searching for Howland Island. Their Lockheed Electra crashed and sank in the deep Pacific, within fifty to one hundred miles northwest of Howland.

Many Earhart enthusiasts agree with this view. Two of the propagators of this hypothesis are professional pilot Elgen Long and David Jourdan, president of Nauticos, LLC, a deep-ocean search and recovery company, the assets of which were acquired by Oceaneering International, Inc. Let's examine why they think that Amelia's Electra lies on the bottom of the sea northwest of Howland.

Long's forty thousand hours of worldwide flying experience coupled with his understanding of the relatively primitive avionics equipment of the Noonan-Earhart day (without radar, LORAN, or GPS), helped him to convince Dave Jourdan of the likelihood that they could find Amelia's lost Electra on the bottom of the Pacific. In fact, Long seemed to be a walking encyclopedia on the subject, as he had been so immersed in the multitude of facts and information relating to the airplane's disappearance. All that Jourdan had to do, Long suggested, was raise a couple million to get the job done. They would then sail to his secretly designated site in the far Pacific, find the lost airplane, and become famous. Jourdan went out and raised the funds for the search. He and Long and a specialized team sailed for the South Pacific in 2002.

These points were basis for their ocean-floor search northwest of Howland:

- Elgen Long's experience, who had calculated the Electra's supposed position of sinking
- Collins Radio scientific analysis of the Electra's radio transmissions
- California Tech University's aeronautical analysis of Electra's fuel consumption
- Reconstruction of Noonan's navigational techniques
- Nauticos's proprietary deep-ocean sonar equipment (NOMAD) and previous successes

The Nauticos expedition employed the 175-foot research vessel *Davidson*, equipped with the latest multi-beam sonar to provide high-quality bathymetric deep-water data. Long and Jourdan directed the survey ship, crew, and thirty-four specialists, including radio-analysis technicians, navy oceanographers, still- and motion-picture photographers, and a host of sonar- and depth-recording professionals. The team covered a deep-water search of some six hundred square miles of never-before-viewed Pacific Ocean seafloor until a serious equipment failure forced a regrettable retreat. Upon regrouping four years later, another expensive search in 2006 turned up nothing other than some fantastic sunsets and more charted ocean bottom. The principal contributor of funds for this effort was Ted Waitt of the Waitt Institute for Discovery. Both of these expeditions used the navigational data analysis of Elgen Long and the deep-sea search techniques of David Jourdan and his Nauticos team. Experts from Rockwell Collins also carefully evaluated studies of radio signal strength.

Long had meticulously examined the records of volume and weight of aviation gasoline that the Electra carried. He factored in the aircraft's extreme weight overall, its climbing speed, and the time and fuel used to reach the ten-thousand-foot cruising altitude. He considered the total mileage flown, adverse wind conditions, and

NOMAD technology. (Courtesy Nauticos)

other aspects of the flight that an experienced pilot would intuitively consider. Having studied the *Itasca* radio logs and the Rockwell Collins sound-sensitivity calibrations in an effort to measure the distance of Amelia's transmissions, Long and Jourdan felt that they could determine the general area in which the Electra fell into the sea. If Amelia and Noonan really did crash and sink northwest of Howland shortly after radio contact was lost, Elgen Long and David Jourdan likely would have located the lost airplane on the bottom of the Pacific and achieved a well-deserved place in the history books.

The facts are that after not one, but two, expensive expeditions to the far Pacific with many hundreds of square miles of ocean floor meticulously searched and more than $5 million expended, no Electra has been found. What is significant about this is the fact that Jourdan and his team of deep-sea technicians are extremely good at what they do and that Long's experience lends itself to credible calculations. If they couldn't locate a specific wreck in a specific area of the ocean, nobody could.

Technical Measurements

Elgen Long made the point that average reported headwinds over the route flown by Amelia were 26.5 mph. This wind velocity was correct for a certain period of time, but not for the entire flight. He also stated in his book, *Amelia Earhart: The Mystery Solved,* that "Earhart flew at airspeed of 160.5 mph . . . and the 160.5 mph fuel endurance works out to 20 hours and 34 minutes . . . a confirmation that Earhart ran out of fuel at 0843 IST [*Itasca* Standard Time]."[1]

However, that may not be quite accurate. While Amelia did report at 7:18 a.m. GCT that "wind was 23 knots" (26.5 mph), it was not reported as such for the entire flight. There is no way to know for certain or to accurately reconstruct the average headwind velocity that Amelia faced during the entire twenty hours from Lae to the Howland region other than to estimate. It is highly unlikely that she and Noonan faced constant headwinds of this strength for the entire flight. Certainly, the early four to five hours of the flight with the plane so heavily loaded with fuel would, without a doubt, have severely curtailed the Electra's true ground speed.

The log of the Coast Guard cutter *Itasca* indicated that wind velocity during the early morning hours of July 2, 1937, in the vicinity of Howland was recorded at Force 2, which translates to 4 to 6 knots (7 mph). While this reflects surface wind conditions and not wind aloft, surface winds remained at Force 2 throughout that day and evening. That is a huge reduction from the hypothetical 23 knots stated by Long for the evening before. Furthermore, if Amelia had been flying at an average airspeed of 160.5 mph as Long states, that would have been in direct conflict with what she was taught by Lockheed's executive vice president, C. L. "Kelly" Johnson, and Lockheed's president, Robert Gross, whose opinions certainly must be considered.[2]

Lockheed's president discussed the potential range of the Electra in a letter dated March 5, 1936, to George P. Putnam:

> When you were here before, we gave you our informal assurances that a range of 4,500 miles was possible with 1,050 gallons of gasoline. We still believe it is possible, but in order to achieve this range, the conditions would have to be perfect and the mixture control operation during the flight would demand the utmost care and attention. For our own protection, therefore, we feel it advisable to submit our guarantees on the basis of the extra fuel as well as the 1,050 gallons if the 4,500 mile range is essential.[3]

The standard Lockheed 10E model carried 350 gallons of fuel and weighed about 10,500 pounds. With the added gasoline in Amelia's plane, the aircraft at takeoff would have weighed between 14,700 and 15,000 pounds. On this long flight of approximately 2,556 statute miles, she would not have achieved the standard model fuel-consumption level until well more than halfway to Howland. At this point, most of the fuel overload would have been used. While Kelly Johnson's recommendations included many parameters, such as power settings and altitudes, his report to Amelia on optimum fuel consumption in a fully loaded condition was as follows:

Optimum Fuel Consumption:

First hour	100 gallons per hour
Next three hours	60 gallons per hour
Next three hours	51 gallons per hour
Next three hours	43 gallons per hour
Remaining hours	38 gallons per hour

If Amelia managed to adhere to this recommended schedule, she would have burned a hypothetical 562 gallons after ten hours of flying. The weather report that reached Lae just after her takeoff indicated that she would have faced 26 mph headwinds as the flight progressed. We do not know for how long that condition prevailed, but if she did achieve the 38-gallon average fuel burn rate for the last ten hours of flight, she then would have consumed a total of 951 gallons when reaching the Howland area at 8:43 a.m., leaving a theoretical 149 gallons remaining from the original 1,100 gallons at the start of the flight. (The Electra's fuel capacity was 1,149 gallons, but the 102-gallon take-off tank of 100-octane fuel was reported only half full at the time of takeoff.) Nevertheless, the gallons-per-hour fuel burn rate translates very well to the Plan B "turnaround" to the Gilberts.

Views of Lockheed Executives and Other Advisers to Amelia

Kelly Johnson had made a number of training flights with Amelia in a full fuel capacity. He constantly expressed the importance of mixture control and good fuel management. In addition to the fuel consumption chart, he discussed and wrote procedure for takeoff with full fuel, landings, and constant fuel management. There is every indication that he considered Amelia a competent pilot. She had flight-tested the Electra to achieve maximum full-fuel performance in his presence. He stated several times that his fuel consumption chart for Amelia allowed for a twenty-five percent safety margin of fuel for the range of the flight, assuming zero wind conditions and that Amelia would have "23.0 hours of conservative flight time."

Robert Gross stated that Amelia should have had a "4,000 mile range (assuming zero head winds) and average TAS (True Air Speed) of 145 mph; with 1,100 gallons fuel available average fuel burn rate would be 41.75 gph for total flight time of 26.35 hours."

Art Kennedy, Amelia's mechanic, based on his Pratt & Whitney engine test-cell work, stipulated, "Amelia would have 26.5 hours flying time," as illustrated to Bill Prymak and Joe Gervais in Portugal in December, 1992, and reported to the Amelia Earhart Society in its newsletter of November, 1998.

Amelia's original around-the-world flight began on March 17, 1937, from Oakland to Honolulu with a documented 947 gallons of gasoline on board. With a crew of three, Amelia took off into a 14 mph headwind and utilized nineteen hundred feet of runway. This flight of approximately twenty-four hundred statute miles and fifteen hours forty-eight minutes' duration (a new record, assisted by a tailwind of 10 to 12 mph) burned 38.97 gph, which compared favorably with the Lockheed and Kennedy calculations. Nevertheless, they still would have had more than four hours of fuel remaining, good for another six hundred miles. Amelia even stated that she had throttled down to 120 mph (indicated airspeed) so as

LAST FLIGHT RADIO TRANSMISSIONS FROM KHAQQ

TIME		RADIO COMMUNICATIONS FROM ELECTRA
GMT & ELAPSED	LOCAL	(UP TO 10:30 GMT, TWO-WAY WITH LAE RADIO; AFTER 10:30 GMT, ONE-WAY TO HOWLAND ISLAND & USCGC ITASCA.)
00:00	10:00am	TAKEOFF FROM LAE/CLIMB TO 10,000 FEET ALTITUDE.
05:00	3:00pm	REPORTED DESCENT TO 7000 FEET.
07:20	5:20pm	REPORTED POSITION CALLED THE "FIX"—741nm FROM LAE.
10:30	—	"A SHIP IN SIGHT AHEAD"—HEARD AT NAURU ISLAND.
14:18	2:48am	"...CLOUDY AND OVERCAST...." (VERY FAINT)
15:15	3:45am	"OVERCAST. WILL LISTEN ON HOUR AND HALF-HOUR ON 3105 [KILOCYCLES]...."
16:23	4:53am	"...PARTLY CLOUDY...." (VERY FAINT)
17:44	6:14am	REQUESTED BEARING ON 3105 kc ON HOUR. "...WILL WHISTLE IN MIKE."
17:45	6:15am	"ABOUT 200 MILES OUT—APPROXIMATELY—WHISTLING NOW." (FAIR RECEPTION)
18:15	6:45am	"PLEASE TAKE BEARING ON US AND REPORT IN HALF-HOUR. I WILL MAKE NOISE IN MICROPHONE—ABOUT 100 MILES OUT." (GOOD RECEPTION)
19:12	7:42am	"WE MUST BE ON YOU BUT CANNOT SEE YOU BUT GAS IS RUNNING LOW. BEEN UNABLE TO REACH YOU BY RADIO. WE ARE FLYING AT ALTITUDE 1000 FEET." (VERY FAINT)
19:28	7:58am	"WE ARE CIRCLING BUT CANNOT HEAR YOU. GO AHEAD ON 7500, EITHER NOW OR ON THE SCHEDULE TIME ON HALF-HOUR." (VERY LOUD)
19:30	8:00am	"WE RECEIVED YOUR SIGNALS [ITASCA SENT A SERIES OF THE LETTER A IN MORSE ON 7500 kc] BUT UNABLE TO GET A MINIMUM. PLEASE TAKE BEARING ON US AND ANSWER 3105 WITH VOICE." (SENT LONG DASHES ON 3105 kc FOR FIVE SECONDS OR SO)
20:14	8:44am	"WE ARE ON THE LINE OF POSITION 157–337...WE WILL REPEAT THIS MESSAGE ON 6210 kc. WAIT—LISTENING ON 6210 kc. WE ARE RUNNING NORTH AND SOUTH." (VERY LOUD)

Log of radio transmissions from KHAQQ on its last flight. (Courtesy Lockheed Martin)

not to arrive in darkness. "We are burning less than 20 gallons of gas at 10,000 feet."

Dave Jourdan and Elgen Long were not the first to seek the whereabouts of the Earhart Electra. In 1999, pilot and sailor Dana Timmer led an expedition with the assistance of Williamson & Associates, a Seattle-based ocean engineering firm, to search for the Earhart aircraft. A six-hundred-square-mile area was covered with side-scan sonar some sixty miles northwest of Howland Island. Timmer reported on this search effort at the 2002 Amelia Earhart Society Symposium held at the Western Aerospace Museum in Oakland, California. He indicated to those attending the Symposium that he found two targets deserving a closer look, but he never reported a return visit to the area. In view of the failures of Timmer and the two Nauticos expeditions, one could consider the area to have been thoroughly searched. Not everyone felt that way, however.

Ted Waitt's Search

Having had his appetite whetted through his major participation in the Nauticos failed endeavors, Waitt became seriously infected with Earhart discovery fever. He had learned enough from his association with the Nauticos group and was convinced that he could do a better job, as he had the money, contacts, and wherewithal to return to the northwestern section of Pacific ocean beyond Howland Island, where experts of every category calculated that the Earhart Electra could be found.

He undertook his secret deep-water search for the missing Electra in February 2009. The Waitt Institute for Discovery in La Jolla, California, also solicited participation from the Harbor Branch Oceanographic Institute of Fort Pierce, Florida (a division of Florida Atlantic University), as well as from a team from Woods Hole Oceanographic Institution in Massachusetts. There is no question that the entire combined effort was a class act.

These three scientific groups led by Ted Waitt operated from the research vessel *Seward Johnson*. A total of sixteen crew and thirty-two specialists, including sonar technicians, AUV (Autonomous Underwater Vehicle) operators, and a multifaceted support team, sailed from Pago Pago, American Samoa, under the expedition name Catalist 2.

After reaching the region of Howland Island, it took a while to get a handle on the immense project of working in seventeen thousand to twenty thousand feet of water, searching for the relatively small target of the Electra three miles down. Computer software difficulties of the two AUVs, known as Mary Ann and Ginger respectively, took two weeks to resolve. In the final analysis, the team thoroughly searched more than two thousand square miles of Pacific Ocean floor. The AUVs completed eighty missions recording ocean-floor data the size of Delaware. They found unique rock formations, towering underwater mountain ranges, and unknown species of fish and marine life but spotted no airplane of any type. Ted Waitt summarized it well: "We are loathe to come home only to be able to say we know where she was not."

However, some important information came out of the Catalist 2 expedition that can still assist in determining the Electra's fate. Ted Waitt himself reported that he could not see Howland Island clearly from the air in his helicopter at a distance of ten miles. "It was indistinguishable from sunspots or cloud shadows." Both Waitt and Tom Sharp, his chopper pilot, agreed that from one thousand feet altitude, one would have to be within at least eight miles to make a positive identification of the island. Even at a distance of five miles at 9 or 10 a.m., "shadows looked like islands and sun spots looked like reefs."

These comments further confirm that Amelia and Noonan truly could have been within ten miles of Howland and not seen the island. Waitt determined that those on the *Itasca* or on Howland Island in 1937 could not have seen or heard the airplane at eight miles. They also believed that the smoke blown by *Itasca* would have camouflaged the island and precluded visibility of that landmark, since the smoke tended to hang near the sea's surface instead of rising in the air.

The Electra's overall fuel burn rate calculations are not conclusive, but they are the primary data we have with which to work in recreating Amelia's situation after more than seven decades have passed and technology has advanced. While many of us have driven a car or flown a plane all day or all night, we have generally had the benefit of a pit stop or two. We most certainly didn't have the degree of noise and vibration from pounding engines and the constant smell of aviation fuel throughout the cabin as Amelia would have had. Given Amelia's competitiveness and can-do attitude as well as Noonan's superb navigational qualifications with many years and miles of seamanship and flying, it is hard to visualize their wasting precious fuel by flying up and down a hypothetical sun line, hoping at the last minute to locate Howland Island or see the Coast Guard ship blowing black smoke. When this pilot and navigator recognized that they had used all of their search-for-Howland time, they did what any sensible pilot and navigator would have done—they headed for a place they knew existed to put the airplane down.

The distances involved in this vast Pacific Ocean region are huge. There is no land to the north and east of Howland for many miles. About four hundred miles to the southeast are the Phoenix Islands, McKean and Canton being the closest. Gardner, Hull, Bimiel, and Enderbury are an additional fifty-plus miles distant.

In the Gilbert Island group to the southwest are Beru, Nukunau, and Arorae lying some 450 nautical miles from Howland. Farther west are Makin, Marakei, Tarawa, Nonouti, and Tabiteuea as major island landmarks. Next to the Phoenix group, these are the most likely island landing choices in the southerly and westerly quadrants.

To the northwest, Knox Reef and Mili Atoll on the lower southeasterly reach of the Marshall Islands are some 750 to 800 statute miles distant from Howland Island. One might visualize how Fred Noonan may have made a decision to turn northwesterly, especially if he suspected that the Electra had been set north of his track to Howland. In this case, he would have tuned in from habit during his Pan Am days to his previous old standby radio station located on Jaluit Atoll. From that station's signal, he could have gotten a direction-finder bearing and established a reliable course to likely islands with dry land along the Electra's desperate salvation and rescue route.

Elgen Long wrote that the Lockheed could not have made it to Mili. "To begin, we know that Earhart ran out of fuel . . . and further, 8 gallons vented overboard because of the 88-degree day time temperature at Lae."[4] Lockheed's Roy Blay agreed with that possibility.

The *Itasca* log indicated winds from the southeast at 4 to 6 knots (Force 2) on July 2, from midnight until daylight and throughout the entire day. Clearly, the equatorial front that had battered the plane and its occupants through the afternoon and evening of the previous day had passed through the Howland area and had begun to improve. The following summary of weather conditions from *Itasca*'s records reflects this improvement, although it should be noted that reference was made to a heavy cumulus cloud bank some forty to sixty miles to the northwest of Howland. If Amelia and Noonan had drifted fifty miles north of their track, they easily could have been within the grasp of this cloud bank.

Amelia reported low fuel to the Coast Guard cutter *Itasca* at 7:42 a.m. on July 2 as the Electra approached Howland Island. The actual wording of radio log No. 1, staffed by radioman third-class Bill Galten, read: "KHAQQ CALLING ITASCA. WE MUST BE ON YOU BUT CANNOT SEE YOU BUT GAS IS RUNNING LOW. BEEN UNABLE TO REACH YOU BY RADIO. WE ARE FLYING AT 1000 FEET." Radio Log No. 2, staffed by radioman third-class Tom O'Hare, reported at 7:40 a.m.: "EARHART SEZ RUNNING OUT OF GAS. ONLY ½ HOUR LEFT. CANT HR US AT ALL. WE HR HER AND ARE SENDING ON 3105 AND 500 SAME TIME CONSTANTLY AND LISTENING IN FOR HER FREQUENCY . . . "

Note that Galten on radio log No. 1 made no reference whatsoever to running out of gas. His notes were that "gas is running low." Furthermore, log No. 1, which he staffed, represented the primary log between the Coast Guard ship and the airplane. O'Hare on Log No. 2 was supposed to be monitoring other traffic.

It is only the O'Hare log that indicated that Amelia had only a half-hour of fuel remaining. Galten reported exactly what he heard

Hour	Wind		Barometer	Temperature		Weather	Clouds	Visibility (miles)	Sea Conditions
	Direction Force		Height (inches)	Air	Water				
1 a.m.	E	2	29.82	82	83	Calm	—	8	1
2 a.m.	E	2	29.82	81	83	Calm	—	8	1
3 a.m.	E	2	29.82	81	83	Calm	—	8	1
4 a.m.	E	2	29.82	81	83	Calm	Cumulus	8	1
5 a.m.	E	2	29.82	81	83	Calm	Cumulus	9	2
6 a.m.	E	2	29.83	81	83	Calm	Cumulus	9	1
7 a.m.	E	1	29.84	81	83	Calm	Cumulus	9	1
8 a.m.	E	1	29.87	84	83	Calm	Cumulus	9	1
9 a.m.	E	2	29.88	83	83	Calm	Cumulus	9	1
10 a.m.	ESE	2	29.88	83	83	Calm	Cumulus	9	1
11 a.m.	E	2	29.88	84	83	Calm	Scat. Cum.	9	2
12 p.m.	E	2	29.85	85	83	Calm	Scat. Cum.	9	2

Weather conditions at Howland Island on July 2, 1937, per USCG cutter Itasca.

with no additional information. This messy report has led many researchers down the wrong road. More than three decades later, *Itasca* radioman Bill Galten confirmed to Fred Goerner that perhaps the half-hour of fuel comment was not the case at all.

Elgen Long combined the two log reports in his book: "At 0742 IST, she reported that she should be on them but could not see them. Her gas was running low and she had only one half hour left." Long stretched excessively to note that Amelia was running out of fuel at the time of her last transmission to further accommodate his view of crashing in the ocean. Most experts who have calculated Amelia's

Letter from Fred Goerner to Leo Bellarts indicating possible misinterpretation of radio logs. (Courtesy David Bellarts)

likely remaining fuel estimate an approximate four hours remaining.

With this estimation of overall flight time available, the Coast Guard, even taking into consideration the stiff headwinds and the long climb to cruising altitude, recognized that there should have been ample fuel reserve available to allow the fliers an hour to search for Howland before pursuing a retreat to a different location. Although Long has contributed significant research, his contention that the 8:43 a.m. to 8:44 a.m. transmission was the last message because the Electra had exhausted its fuel and crashed into the Pacific must be inaccurate. Facts to prove the contrary come from Lockheed itself.

According to Lockheed Fuel Analysis Report 487, the fuel analysis tables calculate that 1,100 gallons of fuel should have provided the fully-fueled Electra, weighing an estimated 16,500 pounds, a range of 3,886 statute miles overall with zero headwinds. With a 25-mph headwind, after approximately twenty hours (if this was the case, as Long implied) they would have had fuel sufficient for another 500 miles of flight at 150 mph. Even so, Lockheed calculations suggest that they had fuel for another 692 statute miles. A lesser headwind, such as 10 mph, would have burned only 200 miles' worth of fuel, thus freeing up even more potential fuel availability for the survival flight to the Marshall or the Gilbert Islands.

The Lockheed report, which provides distance calculations for several hypothetical gross weights of the airplane, indicated that only a slight increase in speed would be necessary to offset a 20-mph headwind, requiring a fuel burn rate of an additional 6 mpg. So, even if Amelia had increased her airspeed to compensate for the 20-mph headwind, it would not have consumed that much more additional fuel. Amelia stated that her Electra, fully fueled, weighed a little more than 15,000 pounds. Consequently, this report (based on weight of 16,500 pounds fully loaded) provided data from Lockheed that reinforced its executives' commitments to Amelia and her husband and presented evidence that the Electra would not have run out of fuel unless it was managed poorly, of which Amelia had been trained in the opposite.

The Electra flown by Amelia Earhart and Fred Noonan from Lae, New Guinea, to Howland Island could have made it to the lower Marshall Islands. It was Lockheed's executive vice president, Kelly Johnson, who reported, "Amelia should have had sufficient fuel to fly another 1500 miles after reaching Howland." Since his calculations were in zero wind conditions, even after subtracting the estimated 500 miles of fuel to offset the 26-mph headwinds reported by Long, there could have remained sufficient reserve to fly another approximate 1,000 miles based on Lockheed's own numbers. To the southeast of Mili Atoll, Knox Atoll lies approximately 725 nautical miles west-northwest of Howland Island—an easy distance with room to spare, in terms of the proposed fuel capacity.

In May 1937, Dick Merrill and Jack Lambie had flown a similar Lockheed, the 10E Daily Express, 3,546 statute miles from New York to London in twenty-one hours and two minutes, carrying only 1,060 gallons of fuel at an average speed of 168 mph. This distance was almost a thousand miles more than Amelia's flight to Howland Island—proving that the Electra did have a substantial long-range capability.[5]

Today, current Federal Aviation Regulations require only three hours of extra fuel reserve for propeller-driven airplanes flying over water where there is no alternate airport (FAR 121.641). The estimated four to six hours of reserve fuel that Amelia and Noonan carried theoretically should have enabled them to reach the lower stretch of the Marshall Islands if they missed the Gilberts.

Among the authorities stating how much fuel the Electra carried and how much flight time Amelia and Noonan might have expected was the US Coast Guard. In its message on July 5, 1937, Coast Guard San Francisco reported to *Itasca*: "LAE VERIFIED EARHART TOOK OFF WITH 1100 GALLONS GAS. ESTIMATED FLIGHT TIME 24 TO 30 HOURS."

After *Itasca* got under way that fateful morning at 10:40 a.m. to search for the missing plane, weather conditions remained similar to early log reports. Surface air temperature built up to eighty-nine degrees at 5 p.m. before dropping back to eighty-one degrees during late evening hours. Sea conditions remained calm, clouds were a scattered cumulus most of the day, and visibility was good. It was obvious that the heavy weather reported the previous afternoon and evening had passed through the region by midnight at Howland. Because of slackening headwinds and a much lighter airplane, I am convinced that Noonan's navigation was virtually on the money. The exhausted fliers just missed visually sighting Howland Island because of cloud cover and weary eyes.

Ann Pellegreno retraced the Earhart flight thirty years later in 1967. She noted that even with excellent navigational equipment and crew competency, she was virtually on top of Howland and still found it difficult to see and recognize among the whitecaps of the sea and the shadows cast by the overhanging clouds.

> My navigator (Bill Polhemus) was using the same technique Noonan had, shooting a sun line of position with the sextant. Even with our superior equipment, we as yet had not located the strategic island. Exhausted from having left Lae, New Guinea, at 6 a.m. the day before, flying all day and all night with only a fuel stop at Nauru Island, we saw nothing but scattered rainstorms. Circling at 1000 feet, we looked for the island, mistaking as that other crew might have done, every cloud shadow for that speck of land. My navigator informed me over the interphone we have only enough fuel for another twenty minutes. Then we'll have to go.
>
> But we HAD to find Howland! We had come too far to give up.

As the twenty-minute deadline neared, Lee Koepke, owner of the Lockheed 10, tapped the shoulder of copilot William R. Payne: "I think I saw something that looked like an island." In describing this dramatic adventure, Ann recalled: "They probably had been 10 to 12 miles north of the island when it was first glimpsed."

The plane circled the island and descended to fifty feet for Ann to drop a wreath of red, green, and yellow leaves in honor of Amelia. The first objective of the flight having been achieved, she and her crew flew another 420 miles to land at Canton Island. After resting, the world-flight team proceeded to Honolulu, Oakland, and Denver amid much acclaim and fanfare.

Sooner or later, the final answer to Amelia's flight will be before us. If that answer displays the Electra being successfully retrieved from the deep sea, I will be among the first to congratulate the salvors. Until then, theorists should consider this research and the multitude of facts, statements, and depositions compiled here that suggest that the Electra is not on the ocean floor.

B. TIGHAR's Nikumaroro Island Speculation

The International Group for Historic Aircraft Recovery, also known as TIGHAR, proposes in their Earhart Project the supposition that Amelia and Fred continued flying on their southeasterly sun line course of 157° to reach Gardner Island, now known as Nikumaroro. Executive Director Ric Gillespie and his supporters theorize that after the Electra crash-landed on that island's coral beach, the plane subsequently was swept off by breaking surf and settled into deeper water. Twelve publicly funded expeditions to "Niku" over a twenty-four-year time frame since November 1988 have occurred, with little verified success.

A 2010 expedition was expected to initiate an underwater search for signs of wreckage beyond the reef but failed. TIGHAR manages to keep its hypothesis and modus operandi alive by continuing to quote from a Navy document that stated that search planes from the USS *Colorado* flew over the island a week after Amelia's disappearance and reportedly saw "signs of habitation." Although Lieutenant Lambrecht, then in charge of the fly-over, stated continuously that he had not referred to modern habitation, each Gillespie (and TIGHAR) expedition to Niku has returned with an assortment of flotsam and jetsam that "might be from the Earhart plane."[7]

Located a little more than four hundred miles southeast of Howland, this island certainly could have been a last-ditch choice for Amelia and Fred, although McKean Island of the Phoenix Island group would have been closer and Canton Island (also of the Phoenix group) was known to have wide sand beaches. Canton Island also had a cache of gasoline and oil stashed there by British and American scientists who gathered on the island a month before to witness an eclipse of the sun, though Amelia may not have known that.

Gillespie and company make their case for the Niku coral flat being the crash-landing site by reminding enthusiasts that this island lies on the general magnetic compass heading that Amelia and Noonan last reported they were flying, 157°-337°. Assuming the fliers proceeded southeasterly on 157°, this would be an accurate assumption. But other islands and reefs also are positioned nearby and in fact are aligned more closely to a course of 157° from Howland.

Pilot and navigator Gary LaPook made an enlightened navigational judgment about Gillespie's reference to Fred Noonan's sun line course of 157° intersecting with Nikumaroro Island:

> The 337-157 sun-line line of position (LOP) was derived by an observation of the sun when the sun's azimuth was 67 degrees true since the LOP is at right angles to the azimuth to the celestial body. When the sun rose in the vicinity of Howland Island on July 2, 1937, its azimuth was 67 degrees true. It would stay at 67 degrees until an hour after sunrise. Noonan would have computed the same 337-157 LOP from any sight taken during this one hour period. As he approached the LOP he would have taken several sights, then more after the interception to ensure staying on it.

In other words, because Nikumaroro was more than four hundred nautical miles from Howland Island and because Amelia likely was flying at about 150 mph, she would not have found Howland simply by staying on a course of 157° until sufficient time elapsed to cover the four-hundred-mile distance—she and Fred would have had to alter their course.

Gillespie refers to the Pan American Airways direction-finder bearings that passed through the vicinity of Nikumaroro Island to support his case. That bearing reported by Pan Am's manager at Wake Island also passed through the lower section of the Marshall Islands, in particular through the area of Mili Atoll. From a measurable standpoint, Mili's location would have been much closer and therefore more likely to have been accurate. Wake Island's Pan Am manager at the time of Earhart's flight, R. W. Hansen, stated: "From 1223 to 1236 GCT on July 5 a very unsteady voice modulated carrier was observed. I was able to get an approximate bearing of 144°. At the time I believed this bearing to be reasonably accurate, and I am still of that opinion."

In October 1937, three months after the Earhart disappearance, Henry E. Maude and a team of British surveyors landed on

Nikumaroro and investigated both the island and lagoon. Absolutely nothing was found that would have linked the missing fliers to that piece of land. The following year, a joint New Zealand and British team known as New Zealand Pacific Air Survey (NZPAS) and headed by E. A. Gibson, landed on the island, surveyed it for an airfield, and cleared obstructions in the lagoon. The purpose was to claim Nikumaroro for Great Britain and to prepare the island for defense in the event of a Pacific war.

In 1939, Henry Maude returned to Nikumaroro with the first contingent of settlers from the Gilbert Islands. The island was continuously inhabited until the end of 1963 with as many as sixty-eight men, women, and children. They built a village in the area originally designated for the airfield. They planted hundreds of coconut palms. The colony even established its own Nikumaroro post office. During all of this activity—for all of those years—they found nothing that could have been connected with Amelia Earhart and Fred Noonan. It seems strange that with all of Henry Maude's work on this island and the continuous human presence for almost three decades, Gillespie did not mention him or his work on Nikumaroro and continues to propagate his questionable hypothesis.[7]

Also in 1939, the US Navy ship *Bushnell* surveyed the island for defense purposes and took a number of aerial photos. No mention of Earhart evidence ever appeared.

Following Pearl Harbor and the onset of the Pacific War, the US Coast Guard constructed a long-range navigation (LORAN) station on Nikumaroro in 1943. The station was manned around the clock until 1947. Coast Guard personnel reported that every inch of the island had been explored, since there was nothing else to do except for watching the evening movie.

In his book, Gillespie referenced a telegram sent in September 1940 by Gerald B. Gallagher, officer in charge of the Phoenix Islands settlement scheme. To Resident Commissioner Barley of the Gilbert and Ellice Islands Colony, Gallagher messaged: "Some months ago working party on Gardner discovered human skull. This was buried and I only recently heard about it. Thorough search has now produced more bones (including lower jaw) part of a shoe, a bottle, and a sextant box." Gallagher indicated that the skull had some teeth intact but he had not exhumed it. He noted, "The bones look more than four years old to me but there seems to be very slight chance that this may be the remains of Amelia Earhardt [sic]."

He fails to reason that the skeleton could also have been remains from any of the *Norwich City* shipwreck of 1929 and the survivors who were marooned and subsequently died there. By that year, the island also would have contained an assortment of debris from the Maude's colonists, Gallagher's survey crew, the Coast Guard LORAN crew, various other surveying crews, and occasional vagabond sailors stopping for some crabs and coconuts. In short, the skeleton could have belonged to any number of search teams, inhabitants, or marooned sailors.

TIGHAR's 2010 expedition was scheduled to include an underwater search beyond the reef for wreckage of the Earhart aircraft. When their primary underwater detection unit encountered unexpected difficulties, they stopped their search. Except for the recovery of some miscellaneous small bone chips, evidence of camp fires, fish bones, and a pocket knife, no word from TIGHAR was released as to success or failure of the 2010 expedition. There was a reference to the possibility of the bodies of Amelia and Fred having been consumed by giant hermit crabs.

Regardless of the lack of previous successes, in April 2012 the US Department of State announced their support of TIGHAR's anticipated forthcoming expedition in recognition of the seventy-fifth anniversary of the disappearance of Amelia and Fred. Flanked by Secretary of State Hillary Clinton and flush with $2.2 million from anxious contributors, Ric Gillespie proudly announced his latest expedition to repeat the journey from Hawaii to Nikumaroro to find the Earhart plane.

With a great degree of hoopla and fanfare, the 2012 expedition was scheduled to depart from Hawaii on July 2, the date of Amelia's disappearance. Loaded with sophisticated underwater robotic detection equipment, a team of experts ready to dive and photograph the virgin depths off of Nikumaroro, and Discovery Channel videographers standing by to document the excitement, several last minute problems forced a delay. When the ship and team finally reached the island, the group's readiness and experience was overshadowed by numerous complications, including equipment limitations and failure, hazardous currents, and rugged undersea terrain. With nine earlier trips to Nikumaroro spanning more than two decades, one would think that the TIGHAR team would have been able to plan ahead for those challenges. Instead, they based their success on analysis of the high-definition video and sonar targets and, of course, a future expedition.

Regardless of their lack of success, Gillespie's group deserves credit for their ability to keep the Earhart torch burning for so long and encouraging interest at various levels. Although no basis for belief of Amelia or her airplane ever being there has been found, TIGHAR has built an interesting sales pitch and library referencing anything and everything to do with Amelia Earhart.

Chapter 14

Curious Conjectures

Quite a few people became convinced of Amelia Earhart's survival long after she disappeared, though their reasons for belief were rather untenable. Their stories are worth telling, if only to show how Amelia and her world flight morphed from reality to legend to fantasy.

The Right Reverend Monsignor James Francis Kelley was equally convinced that a beautiful friend named Irene Bolam, who graced his social circle in retirement, was the famed Amelia Earhart in disguise—despite the lady's contradictory physical and social attributes.

In his old age, Lt. Jim Hannon, who died in 2007, firmly believed that a very ill woman whom he had assisted during the liberation and evacuation of a Japanese internment camp in 1945 and who may (or may not) have died in a plane mishap, was Amelia Earhart.

And last but certainly not least, Australian engineer David Billings steadfastly believes in an interesting tale about an Australian Army patrol during WWII that stumbled upon the jungle-covered wreck of a twin engine aircraft heavily camouflaged by dense vegetation and resembled Amelia's Lockheed Electra.

Their convictions inevitably persisted and spread among other enthusiasts. To have proven any of them right, of course, would have crowned the researcher with glory. To date, no researcher has found definite proof that Amelia survived eight years in Japanese custody, that she was spirited back to the United States to live as Irene Bolam, or that the New Guinea jungle wreck is her airplane. Telling the story of Amelia Earhart's destiny is not complete without the views of these men, whose faith demonstrates the extent of Amelia's legend as well as illuminates the variety of tales that have sprung up in her absence. It proves that the truth remains in the hard evidence surrounding her disappearance.

Rt. Rev. Msgr. James Francis Kelly and Irene Craigmile Bolam

The Right Reverend Monsignor James Francis "Doc" Kelley

(1902-96) rode high on the social currents of his time, elbow to elbow with movie stars, golfers, and literary figures as well as august dignitaries of the Church. He was president of Seton Hall (from 1936 to 1949), twenty-five year pastor at Our Lady of Mount Carmel Church of Ridgewood, New Jersey, and the recipient of numerous recognitions, medals, and patriotic service awards. His fixation on Amelia Earhart appears now to have been a flight of fancy, as very little about the New Jersey woman named Irene Bolam corresponds with known facts about Amelia Earhart—her physical build, her family connections, and even her personality. Bolam was thrice married (to men who were not G. P. Putnam) and was the mother of a son whose indignation over the rumors is a matter of record.

Irene Bolam had an aunt who had once done some legal and accounting work for Amelia Earhart. This aunt was a patient in a New Jersey nursing home and tended regularly by a nurse named Gertrude Hession. Gertrude was Monsignor Kelly's sister. To a suggestible old man accustomed to basking in the glow of celebrity, perhaps something dropped in casual conversation and made its way through his memories to erroneously associate Earhart with Bolam.

Grasping for Attention and Approval

When the Monsignor hinted that he had entertained the lost Amelia at his retirement home in St. Croix and actually ministered to the famous pilot mental, physical, and spiritual rehabilitation after her ordeal in Japanese custody, word spread. Coincidental with this announcement came Joe Klaas and Joe Gervais's release of their book, *Amelia Earhart Lives*. The book's last chapter dealt with Gervais's efforts to induce Irene Bolam into admitting that she was the long-lost Amelia Earhart. These incidents combined to start an international media barrage on Bolam and her family. The resulting melee ended in a lawsuit as she tried to affirm her individual identity. Although she won the lawsuit, for many years Gervais and others continued to hold to the view that Irene Bolam was really Amelia Earhart. It did not matter that plenty of people disagreed. All kinds of investigations persisted—handwriting and voice comparisons with Amelia's (no match), invasions of her personal life, and reports of her pilot's license and awards. That she was four or five inches shorter than Amelia did not bother zealous believers in the least.

In 2002, I met with Marilyn Munson, Gertrude Hession's daughter, and Adrian "Red" McBride, the Monsignor's nephew. The two had kindly traveled to my home to have lunch and discuss the facts of the case. Marilyn was aware of the controversy about her mother's friend Irene Bolam as the supposed female pilot. In fact, contentions even had made their way among Bolam's personal friends. Gertrude had told Marilyn never to bring up the Amelia subject in the presence of Irene, because it always upset her. "That lawsuit placed considerable stress on Irene," Marilyn emphasized. "The Earhart-Bolam controversy was forbidden territory as long as my mother was alive."

Marilyn had brought an assortment of photographs taken during several travel trips of her mother and Irene. In looking over the photos I asked Marilyn how tall Irene was. "About five feet three inches or five feet four," she responded. "See, in this picture she's about the same height as my mom." Amelia was five foot eight inches tall, and although humans shrink as they age, a five-inch height difference is considerable. Marilyn continued, "And the photo of Irene with her third husband, Guy, in *Amelia Earhart Lives* pictures a slightly hefty woman. Amelia may well have become more matronly with age, but I have difficulty accepting that picture as the same person who befriended my mother and Doc Kelley."

I asked Red McBride if he had ever heard his uncle talk about Amelia. Watching him reflect on my question for a long, serious moment, I detected a wry smile as he answered.

Dave, I loved my uncle. He was a great man, a good priest, had a lot of important friends, and I wouldn't say this if he was alive today. But he was absolutely the biggest bull-shooter in New Jersey. The older he got, the more vociferous he became. Each yarn he concocted would see the malarkey improve in its degree of exaggeration. Although I don't recall him ever saying anything to me about knowing Amelia, it's hard to tell what he might have said to others. I do know that he considered Irene Bolam a friend.

Doc was not a drinker, but he liked to socialize. If drinks were being poured and everyone was having one, Doc would too. It wouldn't take long for him to get pretty loose as he wasn't accustomed to much alcohol. As he aged his memory and eyesight began to fail. These physical disabilities were hard for him to accept. In his heyday he had mixed with many important people. I took him several times to Carnegie Hall to see the incomparable Hildegarde. I think Doc was in love with her. He loved the lady golfers too. I accompanied him to a number of events where he'd follow gals like Sandra Palmer, Janie Blalok, Nancy Lopez, and Amy Alcott. If any one of them was having a bad day, he'd ease over to her, give her encouragement, or say a little prayer. That's the way he was.

Jackie Gleason was a big buddy, as was June Taylor. Other friends were Helen Hayes, Bowie Kuhn, and Guy Lombardo. Pat O'Brien actively assisted Doc in teaching "True Americanism" at Seton Hall. During his later years most of those celebrities had passed on. He apparently felt it necessary to reinvent his assortment of VIP connections. Perhaps Amelia Earhart was his badly needed tonic, his miracle Viagra that bolstered his aging ego.

Dave, I hope these thoughts clear the air on some of the confusion and misrepresentations from the past. The crazy part of all this is people tend to believe that because Doc was a priest, everything he said simply had to be true.

In addition, several priests knew Doc Kelley quite well and commented on his character. When I asked Father Stephen F. Duffy of Long Branch, New Jersey, about Doc's strengths and weaknesses, he gave me an example of both:

> At the end of World War II, the government made available excess war materiel to colleges to market and raise funds to assist returning men and women from the armed services. Doc jumped on this program and was successful in disposing of all kinds of stuff. I think he raised some $15 million for the benefit of Seton Hall. That was a definite strength.
>
> On another occasion, Doc managed to secure an entire railroad car load of Navy rubber sea boots. This was quite a conquest, but it became his Waterloo when he turned around and sold the Navy boots back to the Navy! The press got wind of that little maneuver and it led to his downfall. I don't know if the Monsignor structured the deal himself, or if it was the aggressive result of some well-meaning volunteers. But the resulting negative publicity necessitated a special meeting of the Seton Hall Board, who asked for his resignation.

Rev. Msgr. Francis R. Seymour, archdiocesan archivist of Newark, New Jersey, was very helpful in directing me to Seton Hall source material. In answer to some questions about Monsignor Kelley, he responded: "He had a very vivid imagination and tended to exaggerate. He may or may not have met the individuals cited in your letter, but I seriously doubt that he had a close personal relationship with any of them. I was with him on several occasions when he dropped names of people whom he claimed had just left him and he asked if I had run into them. Of course, I had not."

Another close friend of Kelley's was Rev. Msgr. Thomas P. Ivory, Pastor of St. Joseph's Church of West Orange, New Jersey. Monsignor Ivory had been a regular visitor of Kelley's during his final days and gave the homily at Doc Kelley's funeral mass. In a letter dated May 28, 2004, he wrote: "At times it's difficult to separate fact from fantasy in some of his memoirs. He did speak of knowing Amelia

From left to right: *Msgr. James Francis Kelley, Irene Bolam, a friend, and Gertrude Hession.* (Courtesy Marilyn Munson)

Earhart, but I never met her in Monsignor Kelley's company."

Upon receiving the report of handwriting expert and former CID agent Fate Kirby, who attempted to determine if the note was in Amelia's handwriting, I reviewed the findings with Marilyn Munson. As she graciously expressed her appreciation in keeping her updated on my research, she suggested that I speak with Larry Heller, Irene Bolam's son with her second husband. In asking Heller, he responded, "Yes, I am the son of Alvin Heller, Irene's second husband. She later married a third time to Guy Bolam." In describing his mother's height, he noted that "she was not a tall person, nor was she short. I'm guessing that she was at the most 5 feet, 5 inches tall." Suggesting a connection between his mother and Amelia Earhart, he promptly replied.

Dave, I'm fed up with all the hogwash tied to my mother's name . . . from the ridiculous conspiracy stories, to her being smuggled back to this country under a protected witness program. So, I'll tell you. My mother was NOT Amelia Earhart! She was unduly pestered and harassed for years because of the controversy from the Klass-Gervais book. Frankly, I'm sick and tired of it myself. My mother was well traveled, had lots of friends, had her own pilot's license and flew an airplane for a short period back in the thirties. She lived a good life . . . but she was not Amelia! Let me say it one last time, my mother was not Earhart and Earhart was not my mother!

Larry's comments to me were confirmed in the *Woodbridge (NJ) News*

Tribune. A series of articles published in 1982 included an assortment of photographs of Irene Bolam from her days as a young girl through three marriages. "I swear on my life, my mother was not Amelia Earhart," Larry stated several times to the newspaper. "I can say this in all honesty that mother was not Amelia. She just liked the publicity."

Alvin Victor Heller, the flight instructor who taught Irene to fly, later became her second husband and Larry's father. He also was adamant about the rumor. "There is no possible resemblance between the two women. Their bone structure, shape, size and personality were entirely different. I feel certain Irene never met or knew Amelia Earhart."

Eventually, the Monsignor's story sank under the weight of things that could not be explained away. In any case, Irene Bolam's family clearly has stated a number of times that Bolam was not Amelia Earhart and vice versa—Bolam liked the possibility of having been Amelia, but they were in fact two distinct individuals.

The Weihsien Telegram

By the 1970s, rumors and memories of rumors about Amelia Earhart's fate still circulated. Survivors of a Japanese internment camp at Weihsien, China, and even the crew that liberated them at the end of WWII, heard stories that Amelia had been captive among them. The camp was liberated in 1945, just before the Japanese surrender and eight years after Amelia's Electra disappeared.

Lt. Jim Hannon, whom I was privileged to call a friend, was in every way an American war hero. Originally a platoon leader of the 509th Parachute Battalion, he was captured by the Germans in Italy in 1944, escaped from a concentration camp in Poland, and was rescued by the USAAC in Romania in early 1945. As military careers go, Hannon's was one of the highest in adventure and most brilliant in associations.

After returning to Washington and being interrogated at length by his superiors (including a Sunday brunch with Gen. and Mrs. George C. Marshall), Hannon was promoted to first lieutenant and assigned to a special intelligence section, the Air Ground Aid Service (AGAS, an airborne intelligence unit). Shortly after, he volunteered to undertake a secret mission on the opposite side of the world to rescue internees at what the Japanese called the Weihsien Civilian Assembly Center in what was known as Operation Duck.

Hannon became part of an elite six-man OSS team that parachuted into the heavily guarded Japanese internment camp in northeastern China. Some fifteen hundred men, women, and children were held there, seven hundred miles behind enemy lines. Full of heroic efforts, the team successfully liberated the camp and evacuated the internees.

The Telegram

On August 24, 1945, a telegram was sent via US Naval Radio to the Secretary of State in Washington, DC. The State Department later processed approximately two hundred individual letters, dated August 28, 1945, from American internees held at Weihsien to their families back home. The Navy allowed each internee or family to send one brief wire with a limited number of words.

Buried deep inside a State Department Special War Problems file at the National Archives and Records Administration, the government kept a copy of one such telegram.[1]

TO: MR. G. P. PUTNAM
10042 VALLEY SPRING LANE
N. HOLLYWOOD, CALIFORNIA

Following message received for you from Weihsien via American Embassy, Chungking:

Camp liberated; all well. Volumes to tell, love to mother(*).
*Signature omitted

There was no such name listed as Amelia Earhart or Mrs. G. P. Putnam on the official records of American internees at Weihsien as of July 31, 1945. Could Amelia have been there incognito under a pseudonym?[2]

This telegram remains to this day an object of speculation that has nothing to do with Jim Hannon's recollections. It is worth mentioning in connection with Hannon and his memories that any physical or documentary evidence that Amelia Earhart actually was there, eight years after going down somewhere in the Pacific, has yet to be discovered. Hannon's tripod of clues will forever be missing its third leg.

An important question to quell the rumors is to know who at Weihsien knew the precise address of George P. Putnam in Hollywood, California, at Toluca Lake. Earhart researcher Ron Bright believed that it could have been a person listed on the internment records as A. Kamal. Kamal's mother lived in the Los Angeles area, and Kamal's son claims that his father talked with George Putnam about publishing a book he had been writing about India. He also asked Putnam to keep an eye on his elderly mother. Kamal sent a telegram from Weihsien to a New York publisher saying that his manuscript was ready. If so, how could he have sent

DGE—?
(9—4—43)

WASHINGTON 25, D.

SPEEDLETTER

In reply . . . .

SWP 740.0011 SA PW/—2145

Date: August 28, 1945

SPEEDLETTER

To:
Mr. G. P. Putnam,
10042 Valley Spring Lane,
North Hollywood, California.

Following message received for you from Weihsien via American Embassy, Chungking:

"Camp liberated: all well. Volumes to tell. Love to mother (*)."

Eldred D. Kuppinger
Assistant Chief
Special War Problems Division

(*) Signature omitted.

SWP:WWaters

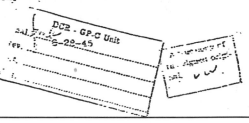

DC2 - GP-C Unit
8-29-45

Telegraph to G. P. Putnam from an internee at Weihsien, signature omitted.
(Courtesy National Archives)

a second wire to Putnam, since only one per internee was allowed? And how, after all that time had passed, could anyone, non-related in family or business, possibly recall the precise Hollywood address of Putnam and Earhart?

I asked Jim Hannon about the one telegram allowed per internee. He couldn't say whether anyone sent more than one wire, but he did pose a key question: "Why would Mr. Kamal not have sent that one telegram direct, himself, to his own mother?"

Bright contended that Kamal did manage to send two messages out of Weihsien. One went to Scribner & Sons, the New York book publisher. The telegram to Putnam is so similar, Bright pointed out, as to likely have come from the same source. "As I recall," explained Bright, "Kamal's son said his father was acquainted with Putnam, having met him in Los Angeles. He asked Putnam to keep an eye on his mother when Kamal decided to return to China in 1939." Bright said that Kamal related these Weihsien events to his son prior to the father's death in 1982.[3]

Hannon's Recollections

As a licensed pilot, Jim Hannon had a certain professional interest in Amelia Earhart and her feats. He had little reason to question the US Government's deduction that she ran out of fuel and sank in the Pacific.

A 1949 *Los Angeles Times* interview caught Hannon's eye and caused him to reconsider the events on that little compound in China, in whose history he was so deeply involved.

Amelia's mother, Amy Otis Earhart, was seventy-nine when she granted an interview to the *Times* on the occasion of Amelia's fifty-second birthday, July 24, 1949. Among other things, she told the interviewer:

> Amelia did not die in the ocean. She died in Japan. Amelia told me many things but there were some things she couldn't tell me. I am convinced she was on some kind of government mission, probably on verbal orders.
>
> She landed on a tiny atoll—one of many in that general area of the Pacific—and was picked up by a Japanese fishing boat that took her to the Marshall Islands, then under Japanese control.
>
> I know she was permitted to broadcast to Washington from the Marshalls, because the officials on the island where she was taken—I can't recall the name of it—believed she was merely a trans-ocean flier in distress.
>
> But Tokyo had a different opinion of her significance in the area. She was ordered taken to Japan. There, I know, she met with an accident, an "arranged accident" that ended her life.

Hannon recounted some of his recollections of his time liberating the Weihsien camp:

> There was an ill, semi-comatose, American woman at Weihsien. A British doctor had called her "the Yank" and the name stuck. She was housed in a former stable, along with two other sick women, in separate stalls. They had no contact with other internees, but a British nurse, one Sister Marian, brought meals to the Yank. The food was very poor. A Japanese consular representative administered morphine to her and seemed to be in charge of her.
>
> One day a Japanese Betty Bomber with large, red, rising sun markings landed at the airstrip. The Japanese flight crew was under command of a US Marine officer, a Major Kramer. As history will relate, he had commandeered the plane and crew at Tsingtao. Almost simultaneously with the arrival of the Japanese aircraft, an Agent Ingersoll in British battle dress had driven up in a Ford coupe. Equipped with ID from the NRRA, and claiming to be from the Swiss Embassy, his mission was to deliver the woman they called "the Yank" to the hospital in Tsingtao.[4]
>
> Distracted by all the activity, I asked my medic, Sergeant Hanchulak, to take Ingersoll to our Jane Doe. After a short while the two men brought her to the automobile, propping her up in the right seat. It was there I saw her for the last time. Her eyes were looking straight at mine, but I could sense she did not see me. It was during that fleeting glance, through her blank and wistful gaze, that I recognized who she might be.

According to Hannon, Sister Marian was instrumental in getting "the Yank" a private hospital room after she already had been taken to a public ward. When he finally arrived in that northeast China port city escorting his array of evacuees from Weihsien, Hannon headed for the hospital to inquire about the Yank.

> In the airfield operations complex near the hospital, the duty officer was a US Army Air Corps person. He pointed to the window, gesturing for me to look. There was an airplane at the end of the runway going through pre-flight checks. We watched as it began moving at first slowly, then faster and faster, and liftoff. The officer turned to me and smiled. I know why you're here, Lieutenant. You're looking for the American woman. She's on the plane that just took off—destination Shanghai.

Later that evening, the same Army Air Corps officer telephoned Jim Hannon at his hotel. Hannon remembered him saying: "Lieutenant, I thought you'd like to know . . . we received a mayday from that airplane. And it was not on a Shanghai course. They went down in the Yellow Sea. It seems they actually were headed for Korea or Japan." Hannon commented on this amazing turn of events: "Whether that phone call and story was cooked up to throw me off her trail, I just don't know. But that unknown American woman sure got VIP treatment."

I asked Jim Hannon if he was ever able to speak with his Jane Doe in that four-week period he was at Weihsien. He noted,

> On several occasions, Sister Marian and I attempted to converse with "the Yank." We both tried to document what she was mumbling. I would get on my knees beside the cot on which she was lying and try to communicate. Most of the time we heard just syllables. Occasionally, a word would be whispered. Once I thought I recognized something like, "Ted," "Fred," or "Ned." Another time, Marian noted the expression "Howan." And I had jotted down "Tassa." These mutterings meant nothing to us. Later, after I had been studying facts of the Earhart disappearance, I began to wonder if "Tassa" could have meant *Itasca*. And maybe "Howan" possibly meaning Howland Island. I'm virtually certain the "Ted" or "Ned" we heard was "the Yank's" attempt to say "Fred," as in Fred Noonan.

As to the mysterious incident of the Japanese bomber arriving unannounced at the Weihsien airstrip, OSS Chief Adm. Milton Miles documented the period surrounding the Japanese surrender. Admiral Milton Miles, OSS chief in China and senior naval officer under Fleet Adm. Ernest J. King, directed then-Maj. Vincent R. Kramer, to get to Weihsien any way he could. Miles later stated, "He heard Kramer did all the things he had been told to do in getting to Weihsien." Miles related how he sent Marine Maj. Vincent R. "Dutch" Kramer, who was in charge of a secret intelligence camp in Shensi Province near Sian, to the Japanese controlled airfield at Tsingtao. He was to show his orders to the Japanese commander and try and get his hands on an aircraft.

It has not yet been clarified as to what "Kramer did all the things he had been told to do" and "Quick and unauthorized run down the airfield" signified. Had Major Kramer been asked to rescue an ill American woman at Weihsien and get out as fast as he could? Were the British pilots "who knew Taku Bar and the river to Tientsin" just a handy subterfuge, covering for the real purpose of Kramer's flight to Weihsien? Noted Earhart researcher Joe Gervais spoke with Vincent Kramer twenty years after the fact. He related that "Colonel Kramer acknowledged that he did fly a woman wrapped in a blanket on a litter out of Weihsien in a Japanese Betty, but he didn't know who she was."

Other Weihsien internees absolutely deny any likelihood of Amelia having been a secret prisoner in that crowded little compound. Mary Taylor Previte told me, "Mr. Hannon has discussed this with me several times—face to face and by telephone. Other members of the Duck mission rescue team—Stanley Staiger, Jim Moore, Tad Nagaki—dispute this story. When I asked Jim Hannon if he could recall where on the camp map this person was held, he told me he was unable to recall."[5]

Pamela Masters and her British parents and two sisters found themselves at the wrong place at the wrong time. Taken from their Tientsin home by the Japanese, they were thrown into a huge mixture of Allied Nationals and taken to the Weihsien internment camp. Fifty years after-ward, she published her teenage recollections of "the horror, the humor, and the humanity that made survival possible for both prisoners and captors alike." Pamela told me:

JAMES JESS HANNON

WAR DEPARTMENT
The Adjutant General's Office
Washington, 25, D.C.

CITATION

1ST Lieutenant James J. Hannon, 0-1300319, Inf. Army of the United States, is awarded the Soldier's Medal for heroic actions and services performed during the period 17 August to 29 August 1945. As a member of a humanitarian team formed at the request of the Commanding General, United States Forces, China Theater, for the purpose of locating and repatriating Allied personnel interned in Japanese Prisons in the vicinity of WEIHSIEN, SHANTUNG PROVINCE, China, this Officer was flown deep into enemy territory where he parachuted into the midst of heavily fortified and garrisoned installations. At this time there was no assurance that American personnel would not receive hostile treatment from the Japanese, yet Lieutenant HANNON readily accepted these dangers to bring aid to the many Allied prisoners and to assist in their early repatriation. By his willingness to risk his life in a gallant effort to bring comfort and assistance to Allied Prisoners of War, this Officer performed a service which reflects the highest credit upon himself and upon the Armed Forces of the United States.
(Signed) Owen Elliott
Adjutant General

Lt. Jim Hannon's citation for honorable service. (Courtesy Jim Hannon)

My sister, Margo, was a nurse's aide in the hospital at Weihsien. She was pretty positive she knew "the Yank," a family friend who suffered an extreme nervous breakdown while in camp. Our "Yank" was flown out with the first flight of patients. As long as Jim Hannon insists on his story about his "Yank" being flown out in a Betty bomber four weeks after our liberation I can add nothing further. Just one more point, we can find no British nun by the name of Marian, Mary Ann, or anything similar on our list of prisoners. Sadly, Major Staiger passed away last year. He lived in Reno, almost next door to where I live, and we kept in contact, calling each other occasionally. He laughed every time that story came up.[6]

Langdon Gilkey had been teaching at Yenching University near Peking when he was rounded up by the Japanese and sent to the civilian concentration camp. Serving as a kitchen manager, he knew personally almost everyone at Weihsien. He asserted, "I don't believe for a minute that Amelia Earhart was in the camp at Weihsien." He recollected that "The most complaints always came at meal time. There was so little food the internees were constantly pleading with me for more. Don't you think if Amelia had been kept here they'd have to feed her? I would have known about it. The place was so small it would have been impossible to have kept such a secret. There's no way she was at Weihsien!"[7]

With the greatest respect for Jim Hannon, I stand on my belief that Amelia Earhart's story was over long before the war ended and even before it began.

The New Guinea Jungle

After the mysterious disappearance of Amelia Earhart, some voices of supposed discovery were shaped primarily by passion or desperation, not hard facts. Until the aircraft is found, everyone is operating on fragmentary speculation and hearsay evidence. One of the fascinating aspects of this tremendous study, however, is the community of people from all walks of life and from countries all over the world who have shared their hypotheses as to the truth of the matter.

One such case is that of Australian aircraft engineer, David Billings, who pursued the location of unidentified aircraft wreck first reported by an Australian Army patrol in 1945. A twenty-man reconnaissance team seeking the location of Japanese troop concentrations stumbled upon the wreck of an unknown twin-engine airplane partly buried in the mud and heavy vines on New Britain Island in Papua, New Guinea.

Though covered by tree debris and foliage, what remained of the aircraft was quite a mess. One engine was found attached to part of a wing and a small metal tag was removed. Another engine and fuselage frame was located about thirty yards away. Both wreckages were covered by heavy vines and broken trees.

The patrol submitted a report along with the engine tag, which displayed the number "C/N 1055." Billings checked with Lockheed and later reported that C/N 1055 translated to "Constructor's Number 1055, the 1055 meaning Model 10, 55th built," and that it did relate to the airframe number of Amelia's

10E Lockheed. Amelia's engine serial numbers were 6149 and 6150.[8]

Because of the extremely thick jungle in this out-of-the-way region, Billings believes that a helicopter magnetometer survey would likely be the most efficient searching procedure and claims it can be done for $100,000, though he has not yet procured the funds to conduct the reconnaissance. A magnetometer search by air might produce results in the dense jungle terrain; if Billings could just put his hands on that little, long-lost airframe tag accompanying the Australian Army report, it would be the proof in the pudding to confirm its authenticity.

How much might a 1936 muddy, corroded, 550 horsepower, S3H1 Pratt & Whitney Wasp engine be worth today? With either of Amelia's engine serial numbers, such a discovery would certainly solve the mystery and enjoy world-wide publicity. Billings now has some competition. A group of New Guinea upstarts recently entered the picture as a contender in finding lost airplanes. A news article early in 2011 momentarily revived interest in the missing Electra. The *Papua (New Guinea) Post Courier* described the excitement of locals who were reportedly guarding an area of reefs off Matsungan Island near Bougainville where an unidentified sunken airplane was discovered partially covered with coral. No identification had been disclosed, but the Minister for Culture and Tourism immediately stated that the Autonomous Bougainville Government would remain the legal custodian. During World War II, Japanese military had constructed an airfield near Buka. That area witnessed considerable air traffic and fighting until the Japanese retreated to Rabaul. Whether that particular airplane is the Electra has yet to be determined, but in any case, it most likely will provide an important WWII artifact.

The sunken plane reportedly remains resting in a depth of 70 meters, about 240 feet or 40 fathoms. Such a depth would be dangerous for basic scuba diving on compressed air without the ability for decompression. The local government's claim to all rights on the submerged wreck is not the only deterrent. The last word was that the sunken plane was being protected by very strong tides, fierce currents, a group of armed men, and a six-meter sea snake.[9]

In any case, neither the Electra nor any other plane has turned up in the far jungle or coral reaches of Oceania, although the revived interest is inspiring. Amelia Earhart, though long gone, remains in the forefront of local legend and intrigue.

Epilogue

Her dream was to ennoble the aspirations of the young, and to her renown was but a means to this end. None who have known her will forget the quality of her presence or her sweet and gracious modesty
—The Times, July 22, 1937

The circumstances and testimonies presented in previous chapters point to what we would rather not believe but have desired to know for decades. Whether Amelia Earhart and Fred Noonan survived for a week after the Electra went down or for a year or several years, there is no doubt that she did not simply crash into the ocean. Japanese treatment of presumed spies would have been the same in 1937 as during the war, and outstanding circumstances prevented our government from sharing the candid truth.

Amelia Earhart was a woman working outside of her social strata. Without reservation, she pushed herself past her limits, inspiring other women to do likewise. The nation idolized her, and the press mythicized her.

Establishing a plausible theory about what happened to Amelia Earhart and Fred Noonan must address those theories not so plausible that persist as conventional wisdom. The fanciful nature of some forms of evidence does not always prove that it is untrue. Conversely, the reasonable answer is not always the right one. Of the claims that she crashed and sank or was marooned on a distant island, the lack of concrete data leaves holes in their hypotheses.

I have attempted to demonstrate by elimination and by positive evidence a constructed history of the final flight and its aftermath, much of which has never before been presented to the public. Amelia, Fred Noonan, and the Electra did not sink in the Pacific without a trace. They were interrogated as Japanese prisoners. The traces are many and irrefutable.

Amelia Earhart and Fred Noonan died in Japanese custody. After landing in the Marshall Islands in the likely vicinity of Mili Atoll,

Amelia and Fred and the Electra were found by fishermen and apprehended by Japanese military. The Japanese naval vessel *Koshu* picked them up and delivered them to Jabor harbor on Jaluit Atoll. They were held on Jaluit for an unknown period of time before being moved to Saipan, where they eventually died.

Queen Bosket of Mili related to Oliver Knaggs, "When they took the two fliers they took the plane as well." John Heine told subsequent researchers that he saw a ship in the port on that glorious day when he was allowed out of school early to observe the Japanese ship with a silver airplane hanging over its stern. Sixteen-year-old Bilimon Amram, training to be a medical corpsman, treated an injured white male who had a head wound and a bad gash in his right knee, accompanied by a white female sitting in the waist of the ship who had been the pilot of the airplane secured to the vessel's aft end. Bilimon identified the white man and woman from photos as being Fred Noonan and Amelia Earhart.

These facts correspond with the stories of the Marshallese and Saipan witnesses. On Saipan, personal interviews of Chamorro families, including a videotape of an eyewitness, add another layer of credibility to archival evidence that is stunningly clear. State Department memos provide equally clear indications that Amelia and Noonan died on land as prisoners of the Japanese. My work moves this latter theory past rumor and surmise into the strongest probability, and it is reinforced by personal statements of respected American military officials and war heroes. In all of this, my intention is to apply common sense to counter imaginative speculation and preserve an accurate memory of Amelia Earhart's last days.

The documentation speaks for itself. There are letters, memos, audiotapes, videotapes, radio transcripts, eyewitness reports, US Naval and Coast Guard records, reports from the Amelia Earhart Society, a variety of published and un-published works, and more. However, the most earnest and enjoyable data has been provided through the special people who were either on the scene at the time of Amelia's flight or had parents or friends of merit present. Their expressions of events that happened, descriptions of what they saw and felt, and their simple words of encouragement have inspired the faith to prove that this path is the right one. Such wonderful testimonies could never have been contained within the words of any kind of government report or official document.

Amelia presented herself to the public as an open, honest, passionate aviator in the forefront of a developing field. Given the course of history, she would have wanted her truth to be told and explored for the benefit of solace to her family and misinterpretation of the general public.

Fred Goerner reported that by 1968, two years after his book was published, people in Congress began to ask questions of certain governmental departments, which previously had denied the presence of classified records of any kind that dealt with Amelia Earhart. However, by 1987—fifty years after Amelia's disappearance and more than twenty after Goerner's initial publication—Goerner reported that there were more than twenty-five thousand pages of classified records dealing with Earhart's military or governmental involvement.

Fred Goerner made it clear that he did not believe Amelia was any kind of spy. He believed that Amelia cooperated with certain equipment testing and other helpful aspects of "white intelligence" while in parts of the world closed to our military and government.

"I think it is a supreme salute to Amelia that, 50 years after her disappearance," Goerner stated, "we are still concerned about finding the truth. Records that have been released reveal unequivocally that Amelia was cooperating with her government at the time of her disappearance. That does not mean she was a spy. I have had conversations with Clarence Kelly Johnson at Lockheed Aircraft, the real technical advisor for her final flight, and he has convinced me that Amelia was not on an overt spy mission."

It does appear, however, that Amelia was encouraged by US Government persons to change her original flight plan by flying easterly around the world instead of westerly as originally planned. Amelia was the civilian reason for construction of the airfield at Howland, which later could have served military use. By keeping an open eye and mind to weather and radio conditions, runway lengths, fuel supplies, and other details, she would be providing a valuable service to her country.

On June 16, 1995, on the occasion of the fiftieth anniversary of the climax of the Second World War, the Honorable G. V. "Sonny" Montgomery made a presentation to the US House of Representatives honoring some forgotten heroes who were among the earliest victims of that difficult war. He mentioned the first victim of the Pacific theater, purportedly poisoned by the Japanese for spying in 1923, was Col. Earl Hancock "Pete" Ellis. He saluted another veteran, Navy carrier pilot Winfield Scott Cunningham, commander of Wake Island at the time it was captured by the Japanese, and Gen. Claire Lee Chennault, who entered the war against Japan as commander of the Chinese Air

Force under Madame Chiang Kai-shek's direction. At the end of his presentation, he stated,

> The last two veterans I would have you recognize and honor, if the government will admit that any honor be due, were perhaps the second and third casualties of the Pacific war, namely Amelia Earhart and Fred Noonan, who disappeared on their famous around the world flight. In light of the tons of evidence, and entire lifetimes spent by researchers on the subject, there seems to be little doubt that these two people were working in some sort of espionage role for the U.S. government when they disappeared on that mission. The Amelia Earhart story, in my opinion, sets a world record for the most duplicity, the most lies, many of them in the highest places, the most "fishy" identities of people, the most people claiming to do one thing and then doing another, from her husband George Putnam to the President of the United States, that it honestly, as stated by Admiral Nimitz, "staggers the imagination."

George Putnam ended his book, *Soaring Wings: A Biography of Amelia Earhart* (1939), by describing an evening near dark when he and Amelia were returning home in their car from the Sperry Gyroscope plant in Brooklyn, New York:

> An old man, rugged, weary, pale—stepped out from the curb. He had been old a long time. It was evident he was used to being hungry, yet as evident that it was difficult for him to ask people for money for food.
>
> Before he could quite get the words out, and though my hand was already on the way to a pocket, the lights changed and our car was being impelled with the stream. Words which had been so hard in coming floated after us. "It's hard to get old . . . so hard . . ." The man spoke simply without bitterness.
>
> At the next corner, saying nothing, Amelia swung her car out of the line of traffic, off Flatbush Avenue into the side street, around the block and back into traffic just about where the old man had stepped out.
>
> But the evening crowds were thickening, and though she looked all along the sidewalk where he had been, she couldn't see him.
>
> We went home, and nothing more was said about the old man through dinner or the evening. But later, when the world was closed down and still, Amelia said, "It is hard to be old—so hard. I'm afraid I'll hate it. Hate to grow old."
>
> She was quiet for some minutes.
>
> And then, as one who may be imagining or simply comprehending a fact, she said slowly, "I think probably, G. P., that I'll not live . . . to be old."

Appendix A

List of Witnesses, Authorities, and Persons of Interest

From the Marshall Islands crash-landing to Saipan—if any of these people could talk with us today about the fate of Amelia Earhart and Fred Noonan, what a story they might tell!

The following pages summarize the important players connected to Amelia Earhart and her disappearance along with those who testified to have seen her on the Marshall Islands and in Japanese custody after July 2, 1937. No matter how Amelia died, the fact that she and Noonan were seen and identified on Saipan and later no longer observed tells us all we really need or want to know.

Pre-WWII

Baruch, Bernard. Adviser to FDR.

Bendix, Vincent. CEO of Bendix Electronics. Furnished the Electra with a RDF.

Black, Richard. Admiral of the US Navy. Prepared Howland Island for Amelia's intended arrival.

Gibbons, Robert. Under-secretary of the Treasury under FDR.

Grew, Joseph C. Ambassador to Japan.

Gurr, Joseph. Lockheed radio technician.

Hansen, R. W. Wake Island Pan American Airways station manager.

Hull, Cordell. Secretary of state under FDR.

Johnson, Clarence L. "Kelly." Executive vice president for Lockheed Corporation.

Kennedy, Art. Amelia's mechanic and friend.

Mantz, Paul. Amelia's technical adviser.

Morgenthau, Henry. Secretary of the treasury under FDR.

Price, Willard. Author of *America's Paradise Lost.*

Swanson, Claude A. Secretary of the Navy under FDR.

Vidal, Eugene. Director of the Bureau of Air Commerce, 1933-37. Friend of Amelia Earhart.

Westover, Oscar. Major general of the US Army Air Corps.

Yau Fai Lum. Colonist ham radio operator on Howland Island.

Post-WWII

Military Officials
Bogan, Eugene T. Lieutenant, USMC. Came ashore at Majuro in 1944 during the American invasion of the Marshall Islands. While there, he met two enlightened islanders, Mike Madison and Elieu Jibambam. Both spoke English and reported stories of the American female flier.

Bridwell, Paul. Commander, USN, ret. Was involved in the US invasion of the Marshalls. Was Naval commandant of Saipan during the war. He was quoted by Goerner as saying, "I don't believe Earhart and Noonan flew their plane to Saipan. You'll find they went down near Majuro, Alilinglapalap and Jaluit in the Marshalls. A supply vessel was used to take them to Yap in the western Carolines. A Jap[anese] naval seaplane then flew them to Saipan. You'll find the proof you need in the radio logs of four US logistic vessels in 1937 . . . the Gold Star, Blackhawk, Chaumont (later named Oglala) and Henderson, supplying and providing radio listening and relays for the Far East fleet in 1937."

Carroll, Kent J. Vice admiral, USN. Requested the Bishop of Guam, Felix Umberto Flores, to testify in Washington on statements provided by Saipan parishioners who had some contact with

Amelia Earhart: Matilde Fausto Arriola, Anna Villagomez, Sister Remedios Castro, Maria Roberto DelaCruz.

Cruise, Edgar A. Vice admiral, USN. Learned from a native interpreter that two American fliers, a man and a woman, had been picked up in the Marshalls in 1937.

Erskine, Graves B. Brigadier general, USMC, ret. Admitted to Goerner, "We did learn that Earhart was on Saipan and that she died there."

Green, Wallace M., Jr. commandant, USMC, ret. To a twelve-question letter submitted by Goerner, Green essentially responded, "The Marine Corps takes no position on these questions."

Nimitz, Chester. Admiral, commander of the Pacific Fleet. Initially told Fred Goerner, "I remember hearing during the war some things had been found that belonged to her." Shortly before he died, Nimitz asserted: "I want to tell you Earhart and her navigator did go down in the Marshalls and were picked up by the Japanese."

Schmidt, Harry. Major general, USMC. Agreed to meet with Goerner at the request of Admiral Nimitz. When Goerner showed up for the meeting, Schmidt had changed his mind: "he was sorry but there was nothing he could say about Amelia Earhart."

Watson, Thomas E. Major general, USMC, ret. Confirmed the presence of Earhart and Noonan on Saipan before the invasion.

Marshall Islanders

Amram, Bilimon. Was one of the first Marshall Islanders to see the two Caucasians and later identified them from their photographs. Recorded his thoughts to Bill Prymak and Joe Gervais.

Cabrera Blas, Nieves. Related her story to Buddy Brennan of how Amelia lived and died on Saipan.

Capelle, Alfred. Former president of the College of the Marshall Islands, later Marshallese Ambassador to the United Nations. Told the 2002 Amelia Earhart Society Symposium in Oakland, California, "I have no doubt that Ms. Earhart and Mr. Noonan were in the Marshall Islands . . . Why a Marshallese would even bother to invent such a story is beyond me."

de Brum, Oscar "Tony." First Secretary of the Republic of the Marshall Islands. Testified that the airplane landed at Mili and the Americans were taken to Jaluit.

Diklan, Bosket. Queen of Mili Atoll. Related to author Oliver Knaggs in 1979, "Lijon had been fishing and saw the silver plane coming down next to the island of Barre. He saw two white people get out. When the Japanese came to take them away they took the plane as well."

Heine, John. A notable attorney at Majuro after the war whose parents and grandfather were beheaded by the Japanese. He recollected viewing the Japanese ship in the harbor at Jabor with a twin-engine silver airplane in a sling on the stern.

Jibambam, Elieu. Taught English in the local high school at Majuro. A scout and guide for American troops when they came ashore in 1944. He also had some information about Amelia given to him by a Japanese trader.

Kabua, Amata. President of the Republic of the Marshall Islands. Acknowledged that the airplane came down at Mili and the Americans were taken to Jaluit and ultimately shipped off to Saipan.

Reimers, Robert. CEO, Robert Reimers Enterprises. Imported building construction materials. Related to Earhart researcher Bill Prymak, "It was widely known throughout the islands by both Japanese and Marshallese that a Japanese fishing boat first found them and their airplane near Mili . . . there was no mystery, everybody knew it."

"Tokyo Joe." A concrete foreman brought to the islands in 1935 by the Japanese to help build the huge seaplane base on Emidj. Told a memory to Bill Prymak that may identify the location of Amelia's Lockheed Electra airplane.

Saipanese

Akiyama, Josephine Blanco. Observed the plane and the Americans exiting the ship at Tanapag Harbor at Saipan.

Camacho, Gregorio. Former judge. Originally interviewed by Oliver Knaggs in 1979. Revealed stunning details to Knaggs describing the end of the life of Amelia Earhart: "Amelia and Noonan were not the only people brought here as spies. There were others. Amelia and her navigator were the first foreigners to be executed here, which is why I remember them. I did not witness it, so I cannot swear to it. This is what I was told, and it is what the Japanese would have done. Everyone who was there at the time saw the Americans. The American government should make a proper enquiry. There are many people who will testify that Miss Earhart and the man were on Saipan."

Fausto San Nicholas Arriola, Matilde. Lived in Garapan next to the Kobayashi Ryokan Hotel, where the Japanese housed political prisoners. In 1937, Matilde first saw the white woman whom the Japanese referred to as "flier and spy." She said, "My family gave her some fruit and one day she gave a ring to my younger sister, Consolacion. The next day we were told the white lady had died of dysentery." She was given the ring in turn, but it disappeared under the floorboards of her house.

Muña, Manny. Assisted Fred Goerner in 1962.

Muña Cabrera, Joaquina. Manny's sister. Worked at the old hotel and had seen and identified the two American fliers. Personally cleaned Amelia's leather jacket.

Sablan Celis, Francisca. Died in 2006 at the age of ninety-four. Responsible for hearing the testimony of two Japanese military who executed an American female flier.

Sugita, Michiko. Daughter of Saipan pre-war police chief Mikio Suzuki. Overheard Japanese military officials who discussed capturing and executing an American aviatrix for spying.

Appendix B

Timeline of Amelia Earhart's Life and Career

1897 *July 24.* Amelia Mary Earhart, first daughter of Edwin and Amy Otis Earhart, is born in Atchison, Kansas.

1908 At age eleven, Amelia examines an Iowa State Fair airplane with her father.

1920 Amelia convinces her father to pay for a ten-minute flight with pilot Frank Hawks at Rogers Field in Los Angeles.

1921 Amelia takes her first flying lesson from Neta Snook in a Canuck. *July.* Amelia purchases Bert Kinner's Airster and promptly wrecks it in a stall.

1922 *October 22.* Amelia sets an altitude record of fourteen thousand feet at Rogers Field.

1923 *May 16.* Amelia earns her pilot's license, Flying Certificate #6017, from the Fédération Aéronautique Internationale.

1924 Amelia's mother and father divorce. Amelia sells her Kinner airplane and purchases a bright yellow Kissel automobile known as her "Yellow Peril," in which she drives to Boston with her mother.

1925 Answering a social worker ad in the newspaper, Amelia begins working at Boston's Denison House, a settlement for immigrant workers and their families.

1927 Amelia receives the memorable telephone call from H. H. Railey asking if she would like to be the first woman to cross the Atlantic by airplane.

1928 *June 17-18.* Amelia becomes the first woman to fly across the Atlantic as a passenger in a tri-engine Fokker with Bill Stultz as pilot and Lou Gordon as mechanic.
Amelia moves into George Putnam's Rye, Long Island, home and writes about her adventure, which later became her book *20 Hrs., 40 Min: Our First Flight in the Friendship.*

1929 Amelia enters the Women's Air Derby race from Santa Monica to Cleveland and takes third place.

1930 Amelia helps organize the Ninety-Nines and becomes their first president; it officially registers in 1932.

July. Amelia sets a speed record of 181.18 mph over three kilometers.

1931 *February 7.* Amelia marries George Palmer Putnam.

April 8. Amelia sets an autogiro altitude record of 18,451 feet.

1932 *May.* In her Lockheed Vega, Amelia becomes the first woman to fly the Atlantic solo in fourteen hours and fifty-six minutes from Harbor Grace, Newfoundland, to Londonderry, Ireland.

August. She sets a non-stop US transcontinental flight record of nineteen hours and five minutes from Los Angeles to Newark. Amelia received the following awards: Distinguished Flying Cross by the US Congress; National Geographic Society Gold Medal, presented by Pres. Herbert Hoover; the Harmon Trophy for America's Outstanding Airwoman; the Cross of Knight of the Legion of Honor, awarded by the French Government.

1933 *July.* Amelia breaks her transcontinental speed record by two hours. As a guest of the Roosevelts, Amelia spends the night at the White House.

She wins the Harmon Trophy for the second time.

1934 Amelia wins the Harmon Trophy as Outstanding Airwoman for a third year.

1935 *January.* Amelia becomes the first person to fly solo from Honolulu to Oakland (2,408 miles) in seventeen hours and seven minutes.

April. She becomes the first to fly solo to Mexico City from Los Angeles, California in thirteen hours and twenty-three minutes.

May. She becomes the first person to fly from Mexico City to Newark, New Jersey, in fourteen hours and nineteen minutes. She was named a visiting counselor to women at Purdue University and the Harmon Trophy winner for the fourth consecutive year.

1936 As a result of her position at Purdue, the University finances a twin-engine Lockheed Electra aircraft to be customized for Amelia's purposes as a "flying laboratory." Planning begins for her around-the-world flight.

1937 *March.* Amelia and her crew set a record of fifteen hours and forty-seven minutes for the first leg of her world flight. During takeoff at Honolulu for Howland Island, Amelia ground loops the Electra, considerably damaging the aircraft.

June 1. Following repairs, Amelia leaves from Miami for a second attempt at a world flight.

July 2. Amelia Earhart and Fred Noonan leave Lae, New Guinea, headed for Howland Island. They do not reach their destination. The enigma begins.

Appendix C

International Collections of Earhart-Era Documentation and Evidence

Australia

Missionaries of the Sacred Heart, Kensington, New South Wales. Valuable for research with relation to Eric de Bisschop's note of an Australian missionary on Jaluit and the three Maoris that reputedly were slain by the Japanese.

National Archives of Australia, Canberra, Australian Capital Territory. Instrumental in efforts to find the yacht *Veveo*.

Belgium

Archives générales du Royaume, Brussels, Belgium. Helpful in the search to find the *Veveo* through the use of their extensive archives.

Canada

Library and Archives Canada, Ottawa, Ontario. Public Archives include lists of sailing vessels with radiotelegraphy.

France

Archives diplomatiques, Ministère des Affaires Étrangères (le Quai d'Orsay), Paris. Foreign Archives with a plethora of military, political, and commercial documents and registrations with regard to maritime activity in the Japanese and Oceanic waters and harbors.

New Caledonia

Museum of Maritime History, Noumea. Collection of artifacts from shipwrecks used to search for *Veveo*.

New Zealand

Alexander Turnbull Library, National Library of New Zealand, Wellington, New Zealand. Informative registry of ships and yachts as well as newspapers of the 1930s.

United Kingdom

National Maritime Museum, Greenwich. Houses huge maritime library used to track down marine activity.

Guildhall Library, London. Contains Lloyd's Register of British and Foreign Shipping and Yacht Register.

United States

Amelia Earhart Birthplace Museum, Atchison, Kansas. The place of Amelia's childhood, it is now a museum dedicated to Amelia's life and work.

Amelia Earhart Collection of Muriel Morrissey. Schlesinger Library. Radcliffe College, Cambridge, Massachusetts. Holds some of Amelia's sister's records about Amelia, pre- and post-disappearance.

Carl B. Allen Papers. West Virginia University Library, Morgantown, West Virginia. Contains correspondence, scrapbooks, newspaper clippings, documents, photographs, and other papers of Carl B. Allen, Army Air Corps officer, aviator, and newspaper writer, who covered Amelia's career.

Colonization Islands Collection. Bernice P. Bishop Museum, Pacific Scientific Information Center, Honolulu, Hawaii. Contains records and documentation of colonists and the colonization project on the Pacific islands.

Eugene Vidal Collection. American Heritage Center, University of Wyoming, Laramie, Wyoming. Holds the papers and correspondences of Eugene Vidal, friend of Amelia and director of the Bureau of Air Commerce during Amelia's heyday.

Fred Goerner Collection. National Museum of the Pacific War, Fredericksburg, Texas. Houses documents regarding Amelia's flight and disappearance as well as the United States' role in World War II, especially in relation to Japan.

Fred Goerner Papers. Special Collections, San Francisco Public Library. Contains Goerner's personal papers, letters, and records about his research into Amelia's life and disappearance.

George Palmer Putnam Collection. Purdue University Library, West Lafayette, Indiana. Documents the life and career of Amelia through personal papers and mementoes.

Pan American Airways Collection. University of Miami Library, Miami, Florida. Houses all papers and files of the records of Pan American Airways, including technical and administrative files regarding Amelia's Electra.

Seaver Center. Natural History Museum of Los Angeles County, Los Angeles, California. Holds California newspapers through 1940, including those that document Amelia's flights.

Smithsonian National Air and Space Museum Library, Washington, DC. Houses a premier history of aviation and aerospace collection; gives context to Amelia's role in aviation.

University of Hawaii Library, Honolulu, Hawaii. Contains extensive archives of native Pacific history, including the islands destined for US colonization.

Appendix D

Exhibits

Chapter 7
The following are copies of the Marshall Islands surrender documents at the end of World War II.

JALUIT

Date of Surrender: 5 September 1945 aboard the USS McCONNELL (DE-163).

Japanese Commander: Rear Admiral Kisuke Masuda.

Japanese Garrison:

At time of surrender:

| Army 637 | Navy 1191 | Civilian 75 | Total | 1903 |

At time of isolation:

| Army 719 | Navy 1401 | Civilian 85 | Total | 2205 |
| | | | Total loss | 302 |

Losses (approximate) due to:

Figures not yet available.

Progress of Surrender Terms:

The McCONNELL remained at Jaluit as guardship to oversee the carrying out of surrender terms, until relieved by the USS THORNHILL (DE-195) on 13 September 1945.

All conditions of the Instrument of Surrender have been accomplished except minesweeping (Condition #4). Compliance by the Japanese has been very good. They began carrying out their requirements well before the surrender and had accomplished most of the conditions by 30 August. At conferences with the Japanese on 29 and 30 August to arrange for the surrender signing on 5 September, rosters, charts and inventories were ready and all information the Japs had concerning sea mines. The collecting of ammunition, arms, etc., and removal of land mines had already been started and was completed by 7 September. In the disposal of ammunition the Japs used 9 trucks and a working party of 800 men. With the exception of minesweeping, for which the Japanese had no equipment, all conditions were accomplished by 14 September when the segregation of the natives was finished.

We intend to start minesweeping about 20 October 1945.

Health:

The Medical officer with the surrender party reported 71 hospital cases of which 4 were serious. Many of these were suffering from wounds and burns resulting from bombing and shelling. There is a moderate number of severely mal-nourished but portly ambulatory patients. The natives are relatively in better condition with very few ill patients.

385

JALUIT (CONT'D)

Facilities and Equipment:

There is no airfield on Jaluit. The concrete seaplane ramp remains in good condition. Hangars were demolished by bombings. The dock on Emidj Island is in fair condition.

A radio station was still operational.

A few very small boats, mostly without power, are still in existence.

Military Government:

By 14 September all natives (about 1280) had been segregated from the Japanese. They were established among the islands in the northern portion of the atoll. Proclamations and ordinances have been posted and explained to the natives; temporary appointment of native officials made; relief supplies distributed, preliminary census made; yen collected, and arrangements made for trade stores and the revival of the handicraft industry.

War Crimes:

Reports have been received of the alleged beheading of American personnel on Jaluit during the war. These reports will be investigated in the war crimes investigation in the Area.

Chapter 8

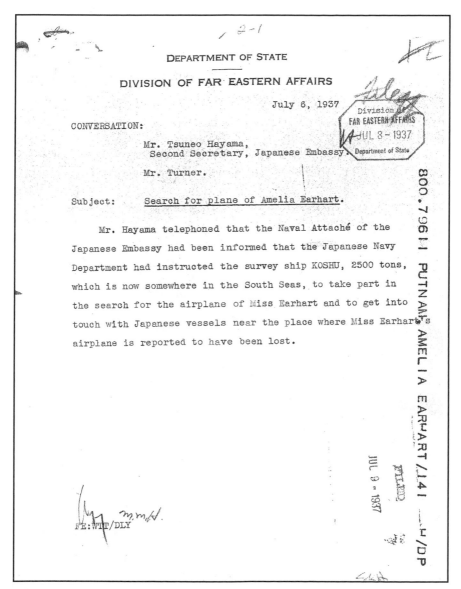

DEPARTMENT OF STATE
———
DIVISION OF FAR EASTERN AFFAIRS

July 6, 1937

CONVERSATION:

    Mr. Tsuneo Hayama,
    Second Secretary, Japanese Embassy.

    Mr. Turner.

Subject: Search for plane of Amelia Earhart.

    Mr. Hayama telephoned that the Naval Attaché of the Japanese Embassy had been informed that the Japanese Navy Department had instructed the survey ship KOSHU, 2500 tons, which is now somewhere in the South Seas, to take part in the search for the airplane of Miss Earhart and to get into touch with Japanese vessels near the place where Miss Earhart's airplane is reported to have been lost.

FE:WTT/DLY

This telegram of July 6, 1937, from Joseph Ballantine of the Division of Far Eastern Affairs, confirms Tsuneo Hayama's report from the Japanese Embassy that the Japanese were sending the Koshu, *a coal-fired survey ship, to assist in the search for Amelia Earhart.*

```
                          TELEGRAM SENT
        LMS                                  GRAY

                                             July 12, 1937

                                             2 p. m.


        AMEMBASSY

             LONDON  (ENGLAND).


             RUSH.

             289.

             Navy Department requests authorization for aircraft

        squadrons from USS LEXINGTON to search Gilbert Islands

        for Amelia Earhart if necessary.  Expedite reply.


                                             HULL
                                              (RS)



        PC:SBS:JMD    EU
```

Telegram dated July 12, 1937, from Secretary of State Cordell Hull to the American Embassy of London, requesting authority to search in the Gilbert Islands.

```
        JR                          GRAY

                                    London

                                    Dated July 13, 1937

                                    Rec'd 9 a.m.


        Secretary of State,

             Washington.


             RUSH.

             463.  July 13, 1 p.m.

             Department's 289, July 12, 2 p.m.

             Foreign Office advises authorization granted.


                                    BINGHAM

        KLP:DDM

        Searching of Gilbert Islands for Amelia Earhart
        by aircraft from USS LEXINGTON.
```

Telegram dated July 13, 1937, granting the United States authorization to search the Gilberts by aircraft from the USS Lexington.

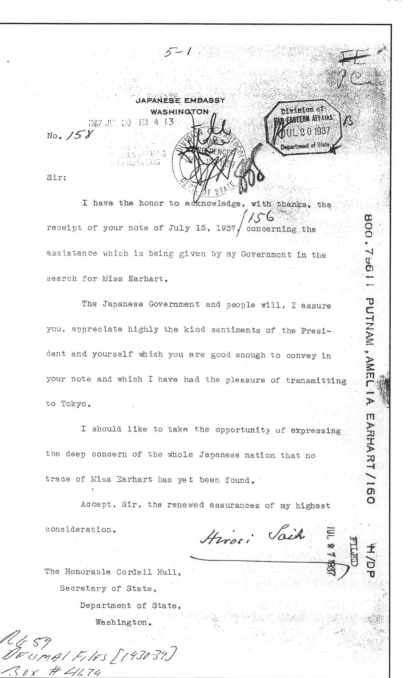

5-1

JAPANESE EMBASSY
WASHINGTON
1937 JUL 20 PM 4 13

No. *158*

Sir:

I have the honor to acknowledge, with thanks, the receipt of your note of July 15, 1937, concerning the assistance which is being given by my Government in the search for Miss Earhart.

The Japanese Government and people will, I assure you, appreciate highly the kind sentiments of the President and yourself which you are good enough to convey in your note and which I have had the pleasure of transmitting to Tokyo.

I should like to take the opportunity of expressing the deep concern of the whole Japanese nation that no trace of Miss Earhart has yet been found.

Accept, Sir, the renewed assurances of my highest consideration.

Hirosi Saito

The Honorable Cordell Hull,
    Secretary of State,
        Department of State,
            Washington.

Telegram dated July 20, 1937, from the Japanese Embassy in Washington to the Secretary of State, conveying concern over Earhart's disappearance.

August 5, 1937

MEMORANDUM FOR   SUMNER WELLES

        With reference to the postscript, is
there anything that I could write or tell
Mr. Putnam?

                    M. H. McINTIRE
                Secretary to the President

Enclosure   mhm/tmb

Let. to MHM from Geroge Palmer Putnam, 2 West 45th Street, New York, N. Y.
7/31/37 thanking MHM for his trouble re finding Amelia Earhart.
Postscript "Is there any way of ascertaining what the Japanese actually
are doing -- especially as regards a real search of the eastern fringe
of the Marshall Islands? That is one of the most fruitful possible locations
for wreckage."

An interesting telegram reflecting G. P. Putnam's suggestion to search the eastern Marshalls.

TELEGRAM SENT

RB

GRAY

August 2, 1937

8 p. m.

AMEMBASSY

LONDON (ENGLAND)

333.

Department's 328, July 30, 7 p. m.

With reference to the request that a boat from the Gilbert Islands make a thorough surface search for Amelia Earhart at Mr. Putnam's expense, the latter now urges that an immediate search be begun of the following position: 174 degrees ten minutes east longitude two degrees 36 minutes north latitude. This is only 85 miles from Tarawa on Making Island bearing thence 106 degrees true. Mr. Putnma believes he has apparently authentic information from former commander copra vessel substantiated by reliable American that uncharted reef exists at that point which is frequently visited for turtles eggs, et cetera, by older Gilbertese natives. He believes that Captain I. Handley of Tawara knows about it. Please expedite reply.

HULL
SW

EU: PM:VAS

Telegram dated August 2, 1937, from Secretary of State Cordell Hull to the American Embassy of London, requesting assistance for a private search by Putnam.

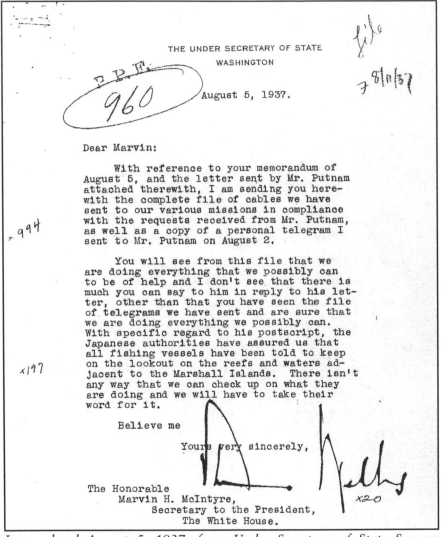

THE UNDER SECRETARY OF STATE

WASHINGTON

P.P.F.

960

August 5, 1937.

Dear Marvin:

With reference to your memorandum of
August 5, and the letter sent by Mr. Putnam
attached therewith, I am sending you herewith the complete file of cables we have
sent to our various missions in compliance
with the requests received from Mr. Putnam,
as well as a copy of a personal telegram I
sent to Mr. Putnam on August 2.

You will see from this file that we
are doing everything that we possibly can
to be of help and I don't see that there is
much you can say to him in reply to his letter, other than that you have seen the file
of telegrams we have sent and are sure that
we are doing everything we possibly can.
With specific regard to his postscript, the
Japanese authorities have assured us that
all fishing vessels have been told to keep
on the lookout on the reefs and waters ad-
jacent to the Marshall Islands. There isn't
any way that we can check up on what they
are doing and we will have to take their
word for it.

Believe me

Yours very sincerely,

The Honorable
    Marvin H. McIntyre,
        Secretary to the President,
        The White House.

*Letter dated August 5, 1937, from Under Secretary of State Sumner
Welles to Marvin McIntyre, FDR's personal assistant, explaining the State
Department's efforts to assist Putnam.*

TELEGRAM

The White House
Washington

8WU. RA. 57-D. L. 3:25 p.m.

Burbank, California, August 24, 1937

Marvin H. McIntyre.

Unless wired contrary will phone you tonight ten o'clock EST after three weeks state department apparently unable secure reply or cooperation British on small specific search financed by me. Please help getting action at least information. Also anxious head off threatened story by newspaper which knows situation same likely hurtful all concerned and internationally embarrassing.

George Palmer Putnam, Union Air Terminal.

Telegram dated August 24, 1937, from George Putnam to Marvin McIntyre, expressing anxieties over permissions for his private search.

sent at 3:48 PM

August 24, 1937.

GEORGE PALMER PUTNAM, ESQUIRE,

BURBANK, CALIFORNIA.

Following telegram just received from Embassy London: QUOTE Foreign Office advises High Commissioner at Suva has telegraphed that United States vessels visited all Gilbert Islands and that Captain Handley left by cutter on August 10 for position mentioned in Department's telegram of August 2.

Signed Sumner Welles

Eu:PM:ASD

Telegram dated August 24, 1937, from Sumner Welles to George Putnam, confirming that US vessels left on August 10 to search the area designated by Putnam.

Telegram dated August 31, 1937, from Cordell Hull to George Putnam, advising that Captain Handley returned without finding any trace of the turtle reef or the plane in the area that Putnam specified.

Chapter 9

Upon the conclusion of World War II, several members of the US Congress pressed the Japanese for full disclosure in an effort to bring the persistent Earhart rumors to some settlement. On August 4, 1949, a G-2, General Headquarters memo reports the results of this investigation by the Japanese, in which, according to those in Japan responsible for the research, an exhaustive effort was expended. The following is a translation of a document received from the Liaison Office, Foreign Ministry:

G-2, GHQ
INTER-OFFICE MEMORANDUM
INFORMATION CONCERNING AMELIA EARHART
We are unable to find any Japanese Navy records pertaining to Amelia Earhart.

The following is a compilation of what has been recalled concerning the search carried out by the Japanese Navy by those who were connected with it at the time:

Upon receipt of the information that Amelia Earhart's plane was missing, an order was sent by the Navy Ministry to the Twelfth Squadron which was in the Marshall Islands at the time to the effect that they should send the seaplane tender, *Kamoi*, Commanding Officer Kosaka Kanae, and large-type flying boats in search of said plane.

Using the sea to the south of Jaluit Island as a central point, the *Kamoi* and its flying boats carried out their search but no traces of the plane were found.

Later, the surveying ship, *Koshu*, Commanding Officer Captain Hanjiro

Tagaki, was also ordered to search for the lost plane. This craft carried out a search in the sea southeast of the Marshall Islands, but no traces were found.

Miss Amelia Earhart was not taken to the Marshall Islands and no broadcast was made from the Marshall Islands to Washington.

This 1949 report may have at least one detail incorrect. The seaplane tender *Kamoi* did not participate in the search for Earhart and Noonan—it was anchored at Saipan the day the Electra disappeared. *Kamoi*'s log indicates that the vessel sailed the following day for Ise Bay, Japan. The survey ship *Koshu* appears to be the only official Japanese naval vessel involved in the search. Based on comments from credible sources on Jaluit, it was the *Koshu* on which both Amelia and Fred were seen in custody of the Japanese and later identified by photos. The *Koshu*'s log does not reflect picking up two downed American pilots. The Captain of that ship, Hanjiro Tagaki, also denied any contact with Amelia Earhart.

Another G-2 Report was issued the following day by the Japanese Police:

REPORT ON AMELIA EARHART
Report of a former official of the South Sea Government: Former Assistant Chief, General Affairs Section, Jaluit Branch Office, Nakajima Yoshitaka.

Nakajima, who was an official of the Jaluit Branch Office that was in charge of the area in which Miss Earhart's plane was purported to have fallen, reports as follows:

a. At that time, the Police Affairs Section Branch Office was in contact with the main office of the South Sea Government in regard to this matter. I heard that the Japanese Navy had sent warships to search the areas and that the two companies, Nanyo Trading Co. Ltd. and Taino Co., which owned small seacraft, were asked to notify the main office of the South Sea Government if they came across any clue as to Miss Earhart's whereabouts.

b. Sometime later, I heard that an employee of the Jaluit Branch Office called Morita Kuzo [name partially blurred] had seen a red horseshoe-shaped lifebuoy inscribed NEW YORK adrift on the sea near Radak Island and that he thought the lifebuoy may have been Earhart's. Morita was later transferred to Saipan as an aide in a hospital and, after the outbreak of the Pacific War, to Guam where he was required to work for the Japanese Military Government. After the war he returned to Japan but I do not know his present address.

Broadcasting by the South Sea Government: Radio broadcasting was begun in the summer of [unreadable copy—probably 1935] when tower facilities were completed there. [Report incomplete.]

TELEGRAM SENT

PREPARING OFFICE
WILL INDICATE WHETHER
Collect
Charge Department
OR
Charge to
$

Department of State

TO BE TRANSMITTED
CONFIDENTIAL CODE
NONCONFIDENTIAL CODE
PARTAIR
PLAIN

Washington,

August 31, 1937.

GEORGE PALMER PUTNAM, ESQUIRE

BURBANK, CALIFORNIA.

I regret to inform you that Foreign Office
London advises us that High Commissioner at Suva
has telegraphed that Captain Handley has returned
from the position *you specified* without finding any
trace of reef or plane.

CORDELL HULL

Secretary of State

Eu:PM:ASD

Enciphered by _____

Sent by operator _____ M., _____, 19___,

D. C. R.—No. 50   I—1402 U. S. GOVERNMENT PRINTING OFFICE

Telegram dated July 2, 1936, from Department of State Chief of Protocol to Eleanor Roosevelt.

THE COMPANY WILL APPRECIATE SUGGESTIONS FROM ITS PATRONS CONCERNING ITS SERVICE

WESTERN UNION

SIGNS
DL = Day Letter
NM = Night Message
NL = Night Letter
LC = Deferred Cable
NLT = Cable Night Letter
Ship Radiogram

R. B. WHITE PRESIDENT   NEWCOMB CARLTON CHAIRMAN OF THE BOARD   J. C. WILLEVER FIRST VICE-PRESIDENT

The filing time as shown in the date line on full-rate telegrams and day letters, and the time of receipt at destination as shown on all messages, is STANDARD TIME.

Received at 708 14th St., N. W., Washington, D. C.   1937 JAN 8 AM 6 10

SA71/2/21 =

WITH ENTIRE SITUATION STOP PLEASE FORGIVE TROUBLESOME
FEMALE FLYER FOR WHOM THIS HOWLAND ISLAND PROJECT IS KEY
TO WORLD FLIGHT ATTEMPT=

      AMELIA EARHART UNION AIR TERMINAL.

THE COMPANY WILL APPRECIATE SUGGESTIONS FROM ITS PATRONS CONCERNING ITS SERVICE

WESTERN UNION

SIGNS
DL = Day Letter
NM = Night Message
NL = Night Letter
LC = Deferred Cable
NLT = Cable Night Letter
Ship Radiogram

R. B. WHITE PRESIDENT   NEWCOMB CARLTON CHAIRMAN OF THE BOARD   J. C. WILLEVER FIRST VICE-PRESIDENT

The filing time as shown in the date line on full-rate telegrams and day letters, and the time of receipt at destination as shown on all messages, is STANDARD TIME.

Received at 708 14th St., N. W., Washington, D. C.   1937 JAN 8 AM 6 10

SA71 206 1/185 NL XC=WG BURBANK CALIF 7

HONORABLE FRANKLIN D ROOSEVELT=

    THE WHITE HOUSE WASHDC=

JUST BEFORE YOU LEFT FOR SOUTH AMERICA I WROTE YOU ABOUT
MY PROPOSED ROUND THE WORLD FLIGHT THIS SPRING AND HOPED
FOR NAVY COOPERATION IN REFUELLING WEST OF HAWAII WHICH WAS
SUBSEQUENTLY KINDLY ARRANGED BY ADMIRAL STANDLEY STOP SINCE
THEN THE NECESSITY FOR SUCH DIFFICULT AND COSTLY MANEUVERS
HAS BEEN OBVIATED AND INSTEAD I HOPE TO LAND ON TINY HOWLAND
ISLAND WHERE THE GOVERNMENT IS ABOUT TO ESTABLISH AN
EMERGENCY FIELD STOP COMMERCE APPROVES MY PLAN INTERIOR
VERY COOPERATIVE COAST GUARD DITTO ALL DETAILS ARRANGED
STOP CONSTRUCTION PARTY WITH EQUIPMENT DUE TO SAIL FROM
HONOLULU NEXT WEEK STOP AM NOW INFORMED APPARENTLY SOME
QUESTION REGARDING WPA APPROPRIATION IN AMOUNT THREE
THOUSAND DOLLARS WHICH COVERS ALL COSTS OTHER THAN THOSE
BORN BY ME FOR THIS MID PACIFIC PIONEER LANDING FIELD WHICH
PERMANENTLY USEFUL AND VALUABLE AERONAUTICALLY AND
NATIONALLY STOP REQUISITION NOW ON DESK OF A V KEENE BUREAU
OF BUDGET TREASURY DEPARTMENT STOP UNDERSTAND ITS MOVING
REQUIRES EXECUTIVE APPROVAL UNDER CIRCUMSTANCES COULD YOU
EXPEDITE AS IMMEDIATE ACTION VITAL STOP WILLIAM MILLER
BUREAU OF AIR COMMERCE DELEGATED BY ROPER AND JOHNSON TO
WORK WITH ME IS FAMILIAR=

*Telegram dated January 8, 1937, from Amelia Earhart to President Roosevelt, re-
questing assistance in expediting WPA funds for a Howland Island landing strip.*

UNITED AIR SERVICES, Ltd.

EXECUTIVE OFFICES

BURBANK, CALIFORNIA

April 26th 1938.

Mrs. Franklin D. Roosevelt,
The White House,
Washington, D.C.

Dear Mrs. Roosevelt:

The writer acted as technical advisor to Miss Earhart and made the flight with her to Honolulu which was climaxed by her accident on the take-off.

I received a letter from Miss Jacqueline Cochran the other day requesting that I answer a great many questions regarding my opinion and actual messages that were received and tied together with the times in relation to the take-off.

I have often wanted to make up a complete report in detail on this situation in order to determine whether or not a search would be practical, even at this late date. In order to do so would like to have a copy of the official report of the "Itasca" which is on file at the Coast Guard Headquarters in Washington. I saw this report in San Francisco at the time Miss Earhart was first reported missing but made no notes and if you could arrange to have a copy sent to me I would in turn furnish you a detailed report and theories for your own personal use - but not for publication.

I have attempted to draw up this information ever since last August but just this morning I was advised by Mr. F. K. Johnson of the U.S. Coast Guard, San Francisco, that the official report was on file in Washington and could not be released except through certain channels.

Letter dated April 26, 1938, from Earhart adviser Paul Mantz to Eleanor Roosevelt asking her help in obtaining a copy of the Itasca log.

Mrs. F. D. Roosevelt   -2-

       I feel that all of us who were so close to Miss Earhart should at least make a certain amount of effort along the lines I know she would follow if the situation were reversed.

       Would deeply appreciate it if you could have the above information forwarded and in turn you will receive a report which I am sure will answer any question of doubt that may be in your mind.

                Yours very truly,
                UNITED AIR SERVICES, LTD.

APM:S   A. Paul Mantz, President

THE WHITE HOUSE
WASHINGTON

May 10, 1938

Dear Henry:

A little while ago Floyd Oldham
and his wife, Jacqueline Cochran, were at
the White House when she received the Harmon
Trophy for aviation. She told me they all
felt that not enough search had been made
amongst certain islands where Amelia Earhart
might be. I told her to send me a memo on
the Islands and the reasons why they felt
this, and I would transmit it to you and to
the Navy Department at once. Now comes this
letter which is evidently inspired by Miss
Cochran. I do not know whether you can send
the man these records, but, in any case, I am
sending you the letter and let me know whatever
your decision may be.

Affectionately,

THE WHITE HOUSE
WASHINGTON

Mr. Morgenthau says that he can't give
out any more information than was given
to the papers at the time of the search
of Amelia Earhart

It seems they have confidential information which would completely ruin the
reputation of Amelia and which he will
tell you personally some time when you
wish to hear it.

He suggests writing this man and telling
him that the President is satisfied
from his information, and you are too,
that everything possible was done.

Letter dated May 10, 1938, from Eleanor Roosevelt to Secretary of the Treasury Henry Morgenthau, asking how to answer the Cochran letter. Morgenthau's undated response to Mrs. Roosevelt indicated that there was confidential information that could ruin Amelia's reputation.

May 14, 1938

100

My dear Mr. Mantz:

I have made inquiries about the search which was made for Amelia Earhart and both the President and I are satisfied from the information which we have received that everything possible was done. We are sure that a very thorough search was made.

Very sincerely yours,

Mr. A. Paul Mantz
United Air Services, Ltd.
Burbank, California

S:DD

Letter dated May 14, 1938, from Eleanor Roosevelt to Paul Mantz, indicating that she now is able to provide a copy of the Coast Guard log to Mr. Mantz, and an undated letter from Morgenthau to Roosevelt confirming the availability of the Itasca log.

aen 7-5

THE SECRETARY OF THE TREASURY
WASHINGTON

Dear Eleanor:

We have found it possible to send to
Mr. A. Paul Mantz a copy of the log of the
ITASCA, which I think will supply him with all
the data he asked for in his letter of June
21st.

Sincerely,

Henry

Mrs. Eleanor Roosevelt,

The White House.

Franklin

file
private

PSF
Astor

Nourmahal

Dear Franklin:—

Kermit has
been with me on this
whole cruise, and
is leaving tomorrow at
Honolulu to go back
to work. He has had
hardly anything to
drink — and then only
beer and sherry — and
is in the best shape in
years. When you see
him, I think you will

*William Vincent Astor's notes from the Nourmahal regarding his
Pacific cruise, the Marshall Islands, and Japanese activities.*

agree.

The information gathering side of our cruise has proved interesting, instructive, and, I hope, will be helpful.

On my return, I shall of course make a proper report to O.N.I. However, in the remote possibility of trouble between now and then, you might consider the following conclusions of mine concerning the Marshall Islands worth forwarding to Naval Operations + O.N.I.

Nourmahal

First. I did not
visit any Japanese Island
(Sounds fairly cowardly
after the arrangements
you made!)

A letter received at
Suva from the Jap.
Consulate General in N.Y.
led me to believe that an
application to visit their
Territory would be
favourably considered.
(This was probably a
successful leg pull on
me) So I made my
application through the

N. y. Consulate to the
minister of Overseas
Affairs — Tokyo —
To enter at Jaluit.
Permission was ~~withheld~~
withheld not only for
this, but to go anywhere
else in the Marshalls.
(The radio correspondence
is quite instructive)

I happened to have
learned what happened
to the two latest British
Intelligence efforts, and
it seemed evident that
any attempt to get in
would produce zero

Nourmahal

in useful results, and about a 100% probability of making serious trouble for you, + the State + Navy Depts.

So I spent my time circulating amongst the neighboring to Ellice + Gilbert Islands picking up all I could.

Here are the results in Brief. They are not guaranteed as ~~exact~~ facts, but are conclusions which I

believe to be substantially
correct.

1. <u>ENIWETOK</u>, and
not Jaluit or Wotje
has been, and will be
the principal naval
base in these islands.
A large dock with deep
water alongside has
been built on PARRY
island.   In 1935 ~~some~~
large naval units were
observed in lagoon, the
dock being then still
under construction.
Large fuel stores
reported but no evidence

④

Nourmahal

which was not conclusive
to me.

2. _BIKINI_. Probably
their second string bone,
now ~~their~~ being prepared.
"Out of Bounds" to
all visiting natives,
and hence no information
obtainable, except that
supply ships are known
to proceed there often.

3. _WOTJE_. There
deffinitely is an airplane
landing field (on the
islet of Wotje) By

March 1931, the space
had been cleared of
trees, and one or two
houses (huts?) demolished.
There is some evidence
that a corner (or edge) of the
lagoon is being filled
in. Within last year
10 motor trucks (also
tractors?) were landed.

Apparently the cargo
handling and pier
facilities are very
poor, and there is no
evidence of their being
improved. Lighters are
used. In spite of

Nourmahal

this, 5000 Tons of Coal
(Briquettes) were landed
last summer, slings
from the lighters and
manual power being
used. (The trucks had
a bad time.)
Six to (?) submarines +
a tender have been
observed in Wotje lagoon,
the submarines always
being alongside the ship
when in port.
There is a good fresh water
supply from a fresh water
pond about 2 acres

in extent & 12 feet
deep in center. The
British impression is
that Wotge will be
used as a base for
submarines, and
Commerce raiders.
(The coal suggests that
too, $\frac{1}{2}$ re coal burning
raiders)

Some large concrete
platforms have been
constructed. As there is
no evidence of guns, these
might $\neq$ well be intended
for ware house floors!

Nourmahal

Some underground
tanks are being dug;
— the Japanese state for
fresh water storage.
However, as there
appears to be a fairly
ample natural water
supply (from the pond)
there might be intended
for oil.

JALUIT   I don't
believe that there is
much of military
importance here, although
the terminal of the air

line to Ponape Etc.

Jaluit is essentially
the administrative ~~seat~~ seat
of the islands, is the
port of greatest commercial
importance, and is the
center of propaganda
efforts. This last
activity is quite a story
in itself.

Fortifications.

I feel moderately
certain that there are
none in the Marshalls.

Searchlights, and
Observation balloons:- YES

Honolulu

Nourmahal

We have just arrived. Please forgive the lack of continuity and the many failings of this report. I meant to improve it, but the ship has been overrun with everything from reporters to friends. (Plus Leis!)

I do hope I see you on getting home. Affectionately and Respectfully. Vincent

Chapter 10
The following are copies of the official messages sent regarding Geneviève Barrat's discovery of the bottle at Soulac-sur-Mer.

Enclosure #7 to Despatch No. 3522
dated January 4,1939,
from the Embassy in Paris.

Bordeaux, November 21,1938.

The Prefect of the Gironde

To the Minister of the Interior
    (General Direction of National Safety)
    (Cabinet of the General Director)

    I have the honor to transmit herewith a dossier concerning the discovery, on the beach of Soulac-sur-Mer, of a bottle containing messages whose sender claims to be a former fellow-captive of Miss Amelia Earhart, the American aviatrix who disappeared during an attempted round the world flight.

    This dossier was sent to me by the Public Prosecutor at Lesparre for such action as might be deemed advisable.

    I can only leave to your judgment as to the propriety of submitting this matter to the Minister of Foreign Affairs.

Enclosure No. 2 to Despatch No. 3590
dated January 4, 1939
from the American Embassy, Paris.

COPY.

Bordeaux, le 21 novembre 1938

Le Préfet de la Gironde,

à Monsieur le Ministre de l'Intérieur

(Direction Générale de la Sûreté Nationale)
Cabinet du Directeur Général)

J'ai l'honneur de vous transmettre, sous ce pli,
un dossier relatif à la découverte, sur la plage de
Soulac-sur-Mer, d'une bouteille contenant des messages
dont l'expéditeur se dit ancien compagnon de captivité
de miss Amelia Earhardt, l'aviatrice américaine
disparue au cours d'une tentative du Tour du Monde.

Ce dossier m'a été adressé par M. le Procureur
de la République à Lesparre à toutes fins utiles.

Je ne puis que vous laisser le soin d'apprécier
s'il convient d'en saisir M. le Ministre des Affaires
Etrangères.

EMBASSY OF THE
UNITED STATES OF AMERICA
Paris, January 4, 1939.

No. 3590

~~UNCLASSIFIED~~
~~CONFIDENTIAL.~~

Subject: Miss Amelia Earhart.

GROUP 4
Downgraded at 3 year
intervals; declassified
after 12 years

- UNCLASSIFIED

The Honorable

The Secretary of State,

Washington, D.C.

Sir:

I have the honor to enclose herewith copies in
French and office translation of certain documents which
were handed to me on January 3 by M. Hoppenot, Chief of
the Far Eastern section of the Foreign Office, when at
his request I called upon him on that date.

These documents have to do with a report made by the
Gendarmerie Brigade at Soulac-sur-Mer, Department of the
Gironde, regarding the discovery on the beach at Soulac
on October 30, 1938, of a sealed bottle containing what
purports.......

- 2 -

purports to be messages concerning the disappearance
and alleged whereabouts of Miss Amelia Earhart. I also
enclose two photostatic copies of portions of these
messages which were also given me by M. Hoppenot.

M. Hoppenot said that of course the chances were
ninety-nine to one that these messages were a hoax, the
work of an imposter or of someone out of his senses; on
the other hand, there was always an outside chance that
they might contain some element of truth and for this
reason he had thought it desirable to hand them to me.
He offered no explanation why the report, dated October 30,
1938, and transmitted to the Ministry of Foreign Affairs
by the Ministry of Interior on December 2, had been
communicated to me only on January 3,1939.

The last document of the attached papers, dated
November 26,1938, refers to a conference on the previous
day by M. de Bisschop, a French explorer, at the
Geographical Society in Paris, in which M. de Bisschop
mentioned certain aspects of his recent visit to the
Marshall Islands which might possibly have some bearing
on the information given in the papers found on the beach
at Soulac-sur-Mer. The Assistant Naval Attaché of the
Embassy has ascertained that M. de Bisschop is absent
from Paris for a few days; he will endeavor to interview
M. de Bisschop on the latter's return.

Respectfully yours,

Edwin C. Wilson
Chargé d'Affaires ad interim

Enclosures....

- 3 -

This message was probably thrown off Santander, and will surely arrive at the Vendée towards September or at the latest in October 1938, remainder in the bottle tied to this one, Message No.6."

In shorthand.

In order to have more chance of freeing Miss Amelia Earhart and her companion, as well as the other prisoners, it would be preferable that policemen should arrive incognito at Jalint ? I shall be with JO........eux and if I succeed in escaping.........for if the Japanese are asked to free the prisoners they will say that they have no prisoners at Jalint. It will therefore be necessary to be crafty in order to send further messages to save the prisoners of Jalint. At the risk of my life, I shall send further messages.

This bottle serves as a float to a second bottle containing the story of my life and........empty, and a few objects having belonged to Amelia Earhart. These documents prove the truth of the story in ordinary writing and shorthand and that I have approached Amelia Earhart......... believed to be dead.

The second bottle doesn't matter.

I am writing on my knees for I have very little paper, for finger prints taken by the police. Another with thumb.

Message written on the cargo boat, No.6."

These objects were seized and handed to the

Office...........

- 4 -

Office of the Public Prosecutor.

The second bottle in question was not found.

1st copy to the Public Prosecutor at Lesparre.

2nd copy placed in the archives.

Done and sealed at Soulac-sur-Mer, October 38, 1938.

Enclosure No. 1 to Despatch No.
dated January 4, 1939,
from the American Embassy, Paris.

COPY.

Paris, le 2 décembre 1938

P.A. N° 13.038/V
Le Ministre de l'Intérieur
(Direction Générale de la Sûreté Nationale

à Monsieur le Ministre des Affaires Etrangères
(Cabinet)

a.s. de la disparition de
l'aviatrice Amélia Earhardt.

J'ai l'honneur de vous adresser sous ce pli,
en le signalant à votre attention, un rapport en
copie de M. le Préfet de la Gironde du 21 novembre
dernier et annexes concernant la découverte sur la
plage de Soulac, le 30 octobre 1938, d'une bouteille
contenant un message dont l'expéditeur se dit ancien
compagnon de captivité de Miss Amelia Earhardt,
l'aviatrice américaine disparue, croit-on, au cours
d'une tentative de raid autour du monde, mais qui
serait prisonnière des autorités japonaises dans les
Iles Marshall, suivant les dires de l'auteur de ce
message ci-joint en photographie.

Vous voudrez bien trouver également ci-annexée
une note en copie de mes services relative à une
Conférence donnée le 25 novembre 1938 par un naviga-
teur bien connu, M. Eric de Bisschop, à la Société de
Géographie, 10 Avenue d'Iéna, sous la présidence de
M. le Général Perrier, de l'Institut, Président de la
Société.

M. de Bisschop a relaté notamment les cir-
constances dans lesquelles il a été soumis à un

interrogatoire ....

- 2 -

L'inscription sur les divers papiers est la
suivante:

    1°- Autre preuve mèche de cheveux

    2°- "Que Dieu guide cette fiole, j'y confie ma
vie et celle de mes compagnons de misère".

    3°- En écriture ordinaire:

    RECTO "Ai été prisonnier à Jalint (Marshall)
par Japonais, dans prison de Jalint; Ai vu: Amelia
Earhart (aviatrice) et dans autre geôle son mécanicien
(homme) ainsi que d'autres détenus, pour soi-disant
espionnage des fortifications gigantesques, qui sont
construites dans l'Atoll.

    EARHART et compagnon ont été repêchés par
hydravion japonais, serviront comme otages dirent
Japonais. Moi ai été prisonnier, car ai débarqué à
MILATOLL. Mon yatch "VEVEO" coulé, équipage massacré
(3 Maoris) le bateau (26 T) (Voilier) était muni de
T.S.F. (suite au verso).

    VERSO : Après avoir fait long stage dans JALINT
(ou JALUIT) comme prisonnier, fût enrôlé de force comme
marin soutier, simplement nourri, à bord "Nippon Nom?
faisant route Europe, m'évaderai dès que cargot près
de côte. Apportez ce message immédiatement à la
gendarmerie pour que nous soyons sauvés.

    Ce message a été lancé probablement au large de
SANTANDER, arrivera surement en Vendée vers septembre
ou au plus tard octobre 1938 (courant) suite dans la
bouteille attachée à celle-ci Message n° 6".

    En sténographie

    Pour avoir plus de chance de pouvoir libérer
Miss Amelia Earhart et son compagnon, ainsi que les
autres prisonniers, il vaudrait mieux que les policiers
                      arrivent ....

- 3 -

arrivent incognito à Jalint ? Je serai avec JO.....
eux et si j'arrive à m'évader .....car si on demande
aux Japonais de libérer les prisonniers, ils diront
qu'ils n'ont aucun détenu à Jalint.   Il faudrait donc
ruser pour l'envoi d'autres messages pour sauver les
détenus de Jalint.   Au péril de ma vie, j'en enverrai
d'autres.

Cette bouteille sert de flotte à une deuxième
contenant l'histoire de ma vie et .... vide et quelques
objets ayant appartenu à Amelia Earhart.   Ces documents
prouvent la véradté du récit en écriture ordinaire et
en sténographie et que j'ai approché Amelia Earhart...
pseudo-mort.

La deuxième fiole m'est égal.

J'écris sur mes genoux car j'ai très peu de
papier, pour empreintes digitales qu'ont pris les policiers.   Autre avec pouce.

Message écrit à bord du cargo n° 6.

Ces objets ont été saisis et remis au Parquet.

La deuxième bouteille en question n'a pas été
trouvée.

Ière à Monsieur le Procureur de la
République à Lesparre

Deux expéditions:

2ème aux Archives

Fait et clos à Soulac s/mer le 30 octobre 1938

Enclosure #10 to Despatch No. 3590
dated January 4, 1939,
from the Embassy in Paris

Paris, November 26, 1938.

On November 25 of this year, M. Eric de Bisschof,
wellknown French navigator, gave at the Geographical
Society, 10 avenue d'Iéna, Paris, under the presidency of
General Perrier of the Institute, President of the
Society, a very interesting lecture on his last voyage
in the Pacific: "Six Years of adventure in a Chinese
junk and a Polynesian canoe".

In the course of his remarks, M. de Bisschof
mentioned that, having stopped off at the Marshall Islands,
he was very cordially received by the local Japanese
authorities until he mentioned passing by Mila Atoll.
He suddenly saw their faces change and take on a distinctly
hostile expression.

Suspected of spying, he was immediately made to undergo
very close questioning and he soon learnt that his
boat had been submitted to a particularly severe inspection.
Naturally nothing was discovered and he was released.

The next day M. de Bisschop received a basket of
magnificent fruit from the Japanese authorities who
sent it with marks of the most exquisite politeness.
But remembering, perhaps in time, he said, the
celebrated verses of Virgil "I fear the Greeks even
bringing gifts", he preferred to abstain from touching

this............

- 2 -

this fruit which he really needed very badly because
of the critical situation in which he found himself
on board his modest boat. Twenty-four hours later
very suspicious spots appeared on the outside of the fruit
and he hurriedly threw it all into the sea.

It is perhaps not without interest to point out the
disquieting attitude of the Japanese authorities as regards
those persons which the hazards of navigation bring too
close to the Marshall Islands where there are certainly
constructions of the highest importance to Japan and which
this country is most anxious not to have known.

It is difficult not to connect this incident and
the details contained in the note in the bottle thrown
overboard by an unknown sailor, a note which gives certain
information concerning the disappearance of the American
aviatrix Amelia Earhart and her mechanic.

These details, however strange they may seem,
appeared a great deal less strange after hearing M. Eric
de Bisschop's lecture; in any case they appear worthy of
attention.

The American naval authorities may possibly find it of
interest to make this parallel and perhaps ask M. de
Bisschop for further details concerning his eventful call
at the Marshall Islands.

It should be noted that the lecturer alluded in his
account to the passage of the American aviatrix Amelia
Earhart in these waters of the Pacific during her attempted
round the world flight.

ECW/FP

Enclosure No. 5 to Despatch No. 3570
dated January 4, 1939
FROM THE AMERICAN EMBASSY, PARIS.

COPY.

P.A. N° 13.022/V   Paris, le 26 novembre 1938

a.s. de la disparition de l'aviatrice américaine Amélia Earhardt.

     Le 25 novembre courant, M. Eric de Bisschop,
navigateur français bien connu, a donné à la Société de
Géographie, 10 Avenue d'Iéna à Paris, sous la présidence
de M. le Général Perrier de l'Institut, Président de la
Société, une très intéressante conférence sur son dernier voyage dans le Pacifique : "ö années d'aventure en
jonque de Chine et pirogue de Polynésie".

     Au cours de son exposé, M. de Bisschop a mention-
né que s'étant arrêté aux Iles Marshall, il fut l'objet
d'une réception extrêmement cordiale de la part des
autorités japonaises jusqu'au moment précis où il vint
à faire allusion à son passage devant "MILATOLL". Il
vit soudain les visages se renfermer et prendre une
expression nettement hostile.

     Soupçonné d'espionnage, il fut aussitôt con-
traint de subir un interrogatoire très serré et il ne
tarda pas à apprendre que son bateau était soumis à une
visite particulièrement sévère. On ne découvrit
évidemment rien et on lui rendit la liberté.

     Le lendemain, M. de Bisschop reçut une corbeille
de fruits magnifiques de la part des autorités japonaises qui les lui envoyaient avec les marques de la plus
exquise politesse. Mais se souvenant peut-être à
temps, dit-il, du célèbre vers de Virgile "TIMEO DANAOS
et DONA FERENTES" il préféra s'abstenir de toucher à

ces ....

- 2 -

ces fruits dont il aurait eu cependant grand besoin dans
la situation critique où il se trouvait à bord de son
modeste bateau.   Vingt-quatre heures après, des taches
très suspectes apparaissaient, en effet, à leur surface
et il s'empressa de jeter le tout à la mer.

Il n'est sans doute pas indifférent de signaler
l'attitude inquiétante des autorités japonaises à l'égard
de ceux que les hasards de la navigation poussent trop
près des Iles Marshall où se trouvent certainement des
ouvrages de la plus haute importance pour le Nippon et
que ce pays tient essentiellement à ne pas faire connaître.

Il est difficile de ne pas faire un rapprochement
entre cet incident et les détails contenus dans la note
lancée dans une bouteille par un matelot inconnu, note
qui donne certains renseignements sur la disparition de
l'aviatrice américaine Amelia Earhardt et de son mécanicien.

Ces précisions, si étranges soient-elles, l'ont
paru beaucoup moins, après avoir entendu la conférence
de M. Eric de Bisschop; elles paraissent en tout cas
susceptibles de retenir l'attention.

Les autorités navales américaines trouveraient
vraisemblablement un certain intérêt à faire ce rapprochement et peut-être à demander des précisions à M. de
Bisschop sur son escale mouvementée aux Iles Marshall.

Il est à noter que le conférencier a fait allusion
dans son récit au passage de l'aviatrice américaine Amelia
Earhardt dans ces parages du Pacifique au cours de sa
tentative de raid autour du monde.

Enclosure #5 to Despatch No. 3590
dated January 4,1939.
from the Embassy in Paris.

Paris, December 2,1938.

The Minister of the Interior,
   (General Direction of National Safety)

To the Minister of Foreign Affairs,
   (Cabinet)

Re the disappearance of the aviatrix Amelia Earhart.

I have the honor to send you herewith, in calling
your attention thereto, a copy of a report, with its
enclosures, from the Prefect of the Gironde, dated
November 21 last, concerning the discovery on the beach
of Soulac, on October 30,1938, of a bottle containing a
message whose sender claims to be a former companion of
captivity of Miss Amelia Earhart, the American aviatrix
who is believed to have disappeared during an attempted
long-distance flight around the world, but who is reported
to be a prisoner of the Japanese authorities in the
Marshall Islands, according to the statements of the
author of this message, a photograph of which is transmitted herewith.

You will also find enclosed a copy of a note from
my office concerning a lecture given on November 25,1938,
by a wellknown navigator, M. Eric de Bisschop, at the
Geographical Society, 10 avenue d'Iéna, under the
presidency of General Perrier of the Institute, President
                                             of..............

- 2 -

of the Society.

M. de Bisschop related in particular the circumstances under which he was subjected to very close
questioning by the Japanese authorities who found his
presence, even momentarily, quite undesirable in the
vicinity of the Marshall Islands, over which the American
aviatrix, Amelia Earhart is reported to have flown before
disappearing.

Chapter 12

The following samples are testimonies transcribed from interviews of Father Arnold Bendowske, November, 1977.

EXHIBITS

Original Testimony taken by Father Arnold Bendowske, O.F.M. Cap. of Saipan, from Chamorro natives in November, 1977 (19 pages).

I once had an opportunity to ask Father Arnold about peoples' remembrance of the "foreign white woman" seen by various people in the Garapan area of Saipan before the war. He told me that he was acquainted with the people who testified about this matter, and knew all of them to be truthful people.

As a pastor on Saipan for many years, Father Arnold spoke fluent Chamorro, and was the single most universally respected and revered public person in the Northern Mariana Islands.

Leonard J. Kaufer, Ph.D.

TESTIMONY OF

MATILDE FAUSTO ARRIOLA

ANNA VILLAGOMEZ

SISTER REMEDIOS CASTRO

MARIA ROBERTO DELA CRUZ

TESTIMONY OF MATILDE FAUSTO ARRIOLA

Father Arnold: First of all, you recall that you told Fred Goerner about the story on Amelia Earhart?

Matilde: I don't know, Father, what the name of that man was.

Father Arnold: First of all, on this tape, Admiral Carroll, through Bishop Flores, asked me to make this interview by tape. He was in Guam before but he is now in the States.

Matilde: The Admiral?

Father Arnold: Yes, the Admiral. He used to be in Guam but now he is in Washington, D.C.
The Admiral has the tape which probably would be given to the CIA, the tape that I made in English after our meeting at the rectory in Chalan Kanoa the last fourth of July when I narrated what I knew about the Amelia Earhart story.
I mentioned to the Admiral at that time your name because you saw Amelia Earhart yourself.

Matilde: I did not know her name when I first saw her. She did not mention her name nor who she was.

Father Arnold: What year was this?

Matilde: I believe it was 193-

Father Arnold: Was it 1937 or 1938? Do you recall?

Matilde: At the moment I don't seem to be able to pin down the exact year. You know, I was sick recently and maybe that has impaired my memory my powers of memory.

Father Arnold: What is your name?

Matilde: Matilde is my name.

1

Father Arnold: Matilde...

Matilde: Matilde Arriola.

Father Arnold: How old were you at the time?

Matilde: At that time?
                 (there was quite a bit of time involved here
                 for Matilde to try to remember how old she was
                 at the time)

Father Arnold: When you saw this woman, were you already
                 married? Did you see her and what did she look
                 like?

Matilde: That woman came to our house and sort of peeped
                 from the outside when she was coming from or
                 going to the outside toilet and that was how
                 she used to pass by our house, because we were
                 located between the short distance of the place
                 where she was staying, called a hotel, and the
                 outside toilet.

                 (this is a repeat of some parts)
                 That woman came to the house and she used to peep
                 into the house because she was going to the out-
                 side toilet and our house was near, so she used
                 to peep in and then she would come back again and
                 for just a brief moment. But she came back again.

                 Then when she came again, my brother Felipe was
                 at the house. He just came home from school. They
                 met at the door and I saw them talking when they
                 were at the door but I didn't know what they dis-
                 cussed. I didn't know what the topic of conversa-
                 tion was.

                 My mother knew English because she learned from her
                 father, so she knew what they discussed.

                 At the Sister's place we were taught a little En-
                 glish but it was only for three months. I learned
                 a little English from my mother when I heard her
                 talk. But I did not talk to the woman.

                 At the house there was broiled breadfruit and we
                 offered her to try the breadfruit. She ate a
                 little.

                                         2

Then I believe there was a third time she came
to the house. I was studying my lesson. Then
I was writing something, doing my homework about
the islands of the Marianas and the rest of
Micronesia and stories and geography and history.

I opened the map. She sat right next to me and
as I was writing on the map she took my pencil;
then she pointed out to me the islands that I
should note on the map. Afterwards, she helped
me with my geography homework. We offered fresh
fruits from the kitchen. She did take some fruit
but she had to go to her house.

I thought probably she had some kind of problem
with diarrhea. Then she came back again that
same evening and when she left my mother said:
"That woman looks sickly". There was on one side
of her body something that looked like burns from
cooking by oil. She got burnt. It was on one
side of her and her hand had burn marks. The
woman did look sick to me. My mother said the
same thing.

And she talked with my mother and then she met with
my brother who was leaving the house, bringing his
textbook materials; probably to study with his
classmate. Then the servant of the hotel came to
our house asking for fruits but didn't say whom
the fruits were for.

My father got some fruits from the ranch-pineapple,
mangoes, and "laguana"-so we sent the fruits to the
hotel where the woman was staying.

That woman knew my sister, Consolacion, when she
was going to the school with the Sisters. She
gave Consolacion a ring and then also some kind of
balsam that smelled good. She gave her that and
the ring.

Father Arnold: What kind of ring?

Matilde: Father, the stone was white stone and I believe it
was white gold, the setting which she gave my
sister. There was a stone in the ring. And when
she came to the house she gave my sister...and when
my sister was sick, she took the ring off of her
finger and gave me that ring and I took care of that

3

ring until after the war. And then Trinidad, the daughter of my brother, borrowed the ring when they went to Truk and it was lost there.

Father Arnold: Was the ring white?

Matilde: Yes, the stone was white, too.

Father Arnold: Was there anything written or inscribed on the ring?

Matilde: I didn't notice.

Father Arnold: What was that book? Did she write in the book or did she indicate something in that book?

Matilde: She took the pencil and indicated to me some place. She said something in English which I did not understand and she signalled I ought to put the name there.

Father Arnold: Where is the book? Did she write in the book?

Matilde: No, she did not write in the book.

Father Arnold: I thought that there was a book that was sent to the States. Did they give it back to you?

Matilde: No, it hasn't been returned to me.

They took two books from me and I asked where those books were because they were a souvenir of when I was still a single girl. The woman took the pencil, pointed it down and told me where those islands were I was trying to figure out for my homework.

Father Arnold: How long was she here?

Matilde: I saw her many times because we were neighbors and she used to come to the house.

Father Arnold: What was she wearing? What kind of dress was she wearing?

Matilde: She was wearing something like a nightgown, something that was long. Looked like a duster, that color.

Father Arnold: What was the color of her hair? What did her

4

hair look like?

Matilde: It looked brunette to me.

Father Arnold: Short or long?

Matilde: No, it wasn't long. It seemed to me like it was a man's hair cut, a little longer, and her face was that of a very strong woman.

Father Arnold: Thin?

Matilde: No, she was not very thin.

Father Arnold: Did Fred Goerner show you her picture?

Matilde: Yes, he showed me some pictures to identify and it seemed to me that the hair I saw in the picture was very, very short but when the woman came to the house, it appeared longer.

Father Arnold: Do you know what year that was?

Matilde: I think it was 1937 or '38.

Father Arnold: Do you know what month?

Matilde: That was a time when the fruits were in season.

Father Arnold: What kind of fruits?

Matilde: There were pineapple, mangoes, laguana.

Father Arnold: What month is that?

Matilde: It could be July. June probably.

Father Arnold: So it would be around that time? Do you know if there was some man with her?

Matilde: No, I didn't hear about it.

Father Arnold: Whatever happened to this woman?

Matilde: After she stopped coming to the house, the servant came and asked us to make a wreath.

A lot of times we were asked to make wreaths.

5

Then the servant asked us to make a wreath. He asked us for two wreaths.

I asked him who died. He said the big "koo koo". He didn't say European. He just said big "koo koo". Not an English woman, not a German, not Spaniard. I believe she was an American because the servant said a big "koo koo".

The servant said she was not European.

Father Arnold: Was the woman who came to your house European?

Matilde: My mother said she was an American. Just a little bit of a mestiza according to my mother. Very, very little.

When the servant came asking for wreaths, he came back to take the wreaths and I asked him who died. He said the American woman. I said,"What happened to her." And he said, "ameba", which is Japanese for dysentery, diarrhea. It is true that that woman, Father, went to the toilet a lot and after that she would go to our house.

I didn't know what she was saying because I didn't know English. Felipe, my brother died. He would have understood. He died during the war. My mother died just before the war.

And I said, "How do you know she died?" And the answer was that they found her other gown on the bed stained with the effects of dysentery. He took the wreaths. He paid for the wreaths. We made some artificial paper flowers and there was no black ribbon so the wife of the ship of the port, half-English, got the black ribbon for the wreaths, for the two wreaths.

Father Arnold: But you don't know where she was buried?

Matilde: I do not know because I was then going to school. Most of the day I was out. Then after that I didn't see her come to the house at all. Then when I asked my mother, my mother said she died because the climate did not agree with her. She had dysentery or diarrhea.

She and my mother talked a lot.

6

Father Arnold:	Were they guarding the woman?
Matilde:	Sometimes somebody came to our house but at that time policemen used to come to our house when some other visitors came to us and they were kind of snooping at that time. Yes, it is true that they were guarding her.
Father Arnold:	Ana said that she used to do the laundry for her. She said that she was living across the street and they were neighbors.
Matilde:	You didn't have to get out to the streets because they were all close by and you could see when she left the house or came in.
Father Arnold:	Good. I will give the Bishop your statement and he will transcribe it.
	Thank you very much.
	Did she tell you that she had a husband?
Matilde:	I believe that she said she had a husband. My mother wasn't too sure whether he was her husband or whether she had a boyfriend.
	That woman looked to me like she wanted to talk but she was always in a hurry.
Father Arnold:	Why? Because she was afraid of the Japanese?
Matilde:	I don't know, Father, because she didn't say. My brother talked with her quite often. My brother was supposed to go to Japan to enter the seminary. I went to Japan before the war to visit him and he told me that the times were dangerous so I had to tell Father Tardio about this.
Father Arnold:	Have you ever heard their names mentioned?
Matilde:	No, I didn't know their names. I don't know what they called them.
Father Arnold:	Do you know what work she was involved in? Did she say what she did? or why she came to Saipan?
Matilde:	We couldn't communicate because she did not know Chamorro and I didn't know English and I didn't ask

her if she spoke Spanish because I was beginning
to learn Spanish but my mother really knew a lot.

Father Arnold: Your mother was born in Guam?

Matilde: Yes, my mother was born in Guam, went to school
                  there and knew English and Spanish. My brother,
                  too, knew a little Spanish and English. He went
                  to school.

Father Arnold: Okay, thank you and I will give this thing to the
                  Bishop.

Matilde: It seems to me that she said she had a family.

Father Arnold: I knew that.

Matilde: That, of course, was the knowledge I got, I over-
                  heard from my mother. I understood when we talked
                  about family. The English word for family, that
                  much I knew, the English word family, it's familia
                  in Spanish. When she spoke long enough, I could
                  gather some of the Spanish words that I understood.

                  I knew that she was being guarded and for that
                  reason I was afraid because you know these Japanese.
                  They had spies all over.

                  When she left for the last time, she held my hand
                  very tightly. And that was her last visit because
                  she got sick and I figured out she died when the
                  wreaths were ordered. She held my hands very tightly.

Father Arnold: Again, thank you very much. This statement of yours
                  will be translated and sent to Washington.

                  Now I will interview Mrs. Baltazar. I think her
                  husband knew something but not much.

Matilde: Is her name Maria Baltazar?

Father Arnold: Yes.

Matilde: Maybe she knows something. I heard that some woman
                  came and it was a woman who came, traveling and then
                  I was so involved in school work that when I came
                  home I studied again and worked at home, did domestic
                  duties because my mother was very strict.

8

Father Arnold: Do you remember when Fred Goerner came and he
                  asked you what you knew about Amelia Earhart
                  and then you came to the rectory and you told
                  me what he had said?

Matilde: I didn't know whether the gentleman was talking
                  about this island or Ponape.

                  My husband came back from Japan in 1937, the
                  month of July, and I don't recall now whether
                  my husband was telling me about the woman who
                  came down from Ponape or one of the islands.
                  He said something happened. There was a plane
                  crash and the pilot was a woman. She was a very
                  brave woman because she piloted the plane. Even
                  the Japanese admitted that this white woman was
                  courageous to do such a thing and I was told that
                  the plane crashed.

Father Arnold: Did your husband and the Japanese say this woman
                  was strong?

Matilde: Yes, they were very startled because she was
                  piloting the plane.

Father Arnold: Did they say where that plane crashed?

Matilde: My husband said that the Japanese said it crashed
                  to the southwest of us. That's what I heard.
                  That it fell somewhere in the southwest.

9

TESTIMONY OF ANA VILLAGOMEZ

Father Arnold: First of all, what is your name?

Ana: My name is Ana Villagomez Benavente.

Father Arnold: When this woman came here, did you see her?

Ana: Yes, Father. She was a beautiful woman. As
                 the days progressed, I noticed that she was
                 such a charming woman. She smiled and she
                 asked me from the place where she was staying
                 to wash her clothing for her.

                 I said, yes, I would like to help her and I
                 wanted to because I was going to be paid for it.
                 The woman and I did not get into some long con-
                 versations because she was upstairs on the
                 veranda and I was downstairs and then there were
                 some house orders restricting visitors. The land-
                 lords were the ones giving me the clothing to wash.
                 The clothing was not Japanese made but European.
                 The clothing was beautiful. They were all marked.
                 They were dresses.

Father Arnold: Were they woman's dresses?

Ana: Yes, they were women's dresses.

Father Arnold: What was the appearance of the woman?

Ana: She was white, beautiful. Not too slim, not too
                 fat. Regular. Just an attractive, the right size
                 and attractive. Her hair was red...

Father Arnold: Long or short hair?

Ana: Not too short, not too long. She had curly or
                 wavy hair.

Father Arnold: Did you see her? Did you speak often to her?

Ana: I saw her but I did not speak often to her. When
                 she left the house it was in the car that belonged
                 to the house where she was staying.

Father Arnold: Where was the woman at the time? Was she at this
                 hotel?

10

Ana:	Yes. It was at this house or hotel. I washed her clothes for one month. After that, I wasn't called over to pick up the clothes.
Father Arnold:	Was your house on the other side of the road, across the street?
Ana:	Yes, it was like this (demonstrating), we were on the north and they were on the south side of the street. That is why it was so visible because of the short distance, like right now you can see the students just across the street.
Father Arnold:	Was there a veranda in the house?
Ana:	Yes, there was a veranda. It was a two-story house. The poor people lived in small houses. The owner to the house lived up near the front because the house was pretty big but the woman was upstairs.
Father Arnold:	Was she upstairs?
Ana:	Yes, she often used the veranda.
Father Arnold:	You didn't speak to the woman?
Ana:	Only when she asked me to do the laundry for her.
Father Arnold:	Who owned the house?
Ana:	Some Japanese.
Father Arnold:	What ever happened to that woman? You said she was there for one month?
Ana:	Yes, she stayed for one month and after that I didn't know what ever happened or where she went. I don't know. What I heard was that she was taken to some place, either to be imprisoned or watched. I don't know.
Father Arnold:	Then you never saw her after that?
Ana:	No, then I never saw her after that.
	I don't know whether you heard of Josefina Blanco. At that time she was working for Nanbo where they were taking passengers on the busses. Nanbo had a

11

i

big car there. A branch store there and Josefina
was driving the bus and I believe that she also
saw the woman.

Father Arnold: Have you ever talked to Matilde about this?

Ana: No, I never talked to her about this.

                 I hear that Matilde was given a ring but I don't
                 know why she was given a ring by the woman. At
                 that time I was not interested in knowing about
                 it. I was fearful because the times were getting
                 dangerous and the Japanese were saying they were
                 soon going to fight against the Americans. They
                 said by 1941 and there were at the time quite a
                 bit of Japanese ship movements. It is true that
                 I didn't know how long after I got married on
                 June 24 when that woman came. Neither did I take
                 note of her disappearance.

Father Arnold: Do you know if some man was with her? Or was she
                 alone?

Ana: I did not know because I never saw a European man
                 then.

Father Arnold: Do you know what kind of work she was doing?

Ana: No, I didn't. They weren't talking about it. All
                 I understood, all I knew, was that she was staying
                 in a hotel. What I heard and what I saw was that
                 she was piloting a plane and the Japanese brought
                 it here after the crash.

Father Arnold: Did you hear about this woman? Where did you know
                 that this woman was right in the plane?

Ana: From the people who talked to her. When they first
                 came here they were taken by the police.

Father Arnold: Were they guarding the woman at the hotel all of
                 the time?

Ana: I can't tell you because I didn't see her under
                 surveillance all the time.

Father Arnold: You said she was taken by the police, who took her?

12

Ana:	It must be the Japanese. The head of the Chief of Police. I didn't quite understand his role. But I didn't know whatever happened to the woman.
Father Arnold:	Did you ever come to the hotel when she was there?
Ana:	No.
Father Arnold:	But her clothing was taken to your house?
Ana:	Yes, they called me and I took the clothing. But she didn't have too many clothing that I had to wash.
Father Arnold:	Was the woman sickly the time you saw her.
Ana:	No, she was pretty energetic.
	If my brother Juan were here, he would know who that woman was, who was being imprisoned but he is now dead.
Father Arnold:	Which brother?
Ana:	Juan.
Father Arnold:	So you didn't know whatever happened to the woman?
Ana:	I didn't know.
Father Arnold:	What about her physical appearance?
Ana:	Not thin, not fat. Red head and not exactly a man's haircut.
Father Arnold:	What were her features, facial?
Ana:	Kind of elongated head but not that long. Her face was beautiful. She wasn't wide at all, broad faced, no. But she had classic face.
Father Arnold:	What do you think was her age?
Ana:	I would say she could have been in her 20's.
Father Arnold:	Just that?
Ana:	I wouldn't think she would be older than early 20's. That's how she appeared to me.

13

Father Arnold: Have you ever heard her name?

Ana: No, I never heard her name mentioned.

Father Arnold: Have you ever heard where she came from.

Ana: No never. Because I didn't think of speaking
                 to her. I knew that she was a foreigner other
                 than a Japanese because of her looks. As a
                 matter of fact, the powder she was using was not
                 Japanese powder. It was different, like the
                 American powder lady. She was not using the
                 Japanese powder. That powder and lotion were
                 of another kind.

Father Arnold: But you didn't know where she came from.

Ana: No. I wasn't sure whether she just came here or
                 whether some Japanese brought her here. I didn't
                 know. I knew that she came to Saipan and was
                 brought to the hotel. I did see her, however.

Father Arnold: Thank you very much and I'll see if I can have
                 Sister Remedios because she probably knows some-
                 thing.

Ana: Josefina said that she was brought to the school
                 playground where the Japanese had programs and
                 all their feasts days in honor of the emperor.
                 That's where the children celebrated their dancing
                 and atheletic games.

Father Arnold: I know that the prison was above, not on that play-
                 ground. The prison was not too far from the hospi-
                 tal in Garapan. You passed by the prison to go to
                 the playground.

                 You have to pass by the prison on the way to the
                 hospital.

Ana: If my brother Juan were alive today, he would know
                 it very well. He was imprisoned.

Father Arnold: But Juan is already dead.

Ana: That house that I was referring to was set north-south
                 The roof was of galvanized iron and part of the
                 sidings were also of galvanized iron but there was
                 a veranda to the house. The main door was on the

                                   14

east side. Those who were imprisoned in those days were kept from public view. Nothing like that today.

Father Arnold: Did you see the woman in the jail?

Ana: Yes, as I said, I saw her. She was dressed beautifully. I saw the woman but I couldn't take closer and longer looks because the policemen were always guarding her. I, too, was always followed by policemen.

Father Arnold: Do you know whether it was actually she or not?

Ana: I know that it was a woman. Later I saw her in that same hotel.

Father Arnold: When you visited Juan did you see the woman?

Ana: Yes, the woman was there. But later when I visited Juan, the third day he was in prison, the woman was still there. Juan was transferred to another place then where greater punishments were given. Then on the east side (the other building) as I now remember, they (prisoners) stayed there for five days before sentence was passed. There they awaited the verdict whether they were guilty or not guilty. My brother, Juan, who was in prison was transferred to the larger prison for bigger offenses, like stealing, murder, etc. They were all put there together for at least four days.

Father Arnold: Was that the place where you saw the woman, the other place for lesser offenses?

Ana: Yes and I looked at her several times but I did not have a chance to be real close to her because the Japanese were constantly watching me. I was afraid because the Japanese can really give some punishment.

Father Arnold: Was this woman an American?

Ana: Yes, she was an American.

Father Arnold: Did you see her so that her face was very clear to you?

Ana: Clear enough. When I saw her, she was combing her hair and powdering her face. What I am sure of is that her hair was red.

15

Father Arnold: Did you notice her dress?

Ana: It was something like nightgown. Had a low neck-
                 line. It is something like a kimona or pajama.

Father Arnold: Was she wearing that dress in jail?

Ana: Yes. It was a printed type of dress. Beautiful.

Father Arnold: How many times did you see her? Just once?

Ana: No, I saw her at least three times. When my
                 brother was transferred to the other jail I was
                 never allowed to enter the building.

Father Arnold: Then you didn't know what happened to her?

Ana: I didn't know what happened to her because my
                 brother was no longer in the same place.

Father Arnold: Is there anything else you know about the woman?

Ana: This is all I know, Father.

Father Arnold: Next Monday I will send your statement to the
                 Bishop and he will translate it into English. I
                 don't know whether the FBI wants to know something
                 about this.

Ana: Are they still looking for the woman?

Father Arnold: Yes, the Admiral who was on Guam is very interested
                 on the fate of Amelia Earhart. He asked the Bishop
                 to have some statements taken this time. The
                 Bishop said that if need be, we can go and testify
                 in Washington. But maybe it is better if they send
                 somebody to Saipan who would further follow up these
                 interviews.

Father Arnold: Thank you very much.

Ana: You are very welcome.

16

TESTIMONY OF SISTER REMEDIOS CASTRO

Father Arnold: Do you know anything about Amelia Earhart?

Sister Remedios: I heard about that name. I did hear that she was in Saipan and was said to be a spy.

Father Arnold: What year was that?

Sister Remedios: I was already in the convent - 1947. No, no, I don't mean '47. That was the year I left for Ponape. I heard more about it in the years '44, '45, but when I heard about this woman coming to Saipan, I was already in the convent.

The war broke out in 1941. It could be 1939 or something like that when I first heard about the woman. I heard that there was a woman spy who came to Saipan but they said she was most likely killed. But I did hear that an American woman was caught spying. I also heard that her name was Amelia but that was already the year 1941.

Father Arnold: The war started December 1941.

Sister Remedios: Yes, about 1939. We were already preparing for war. It was around that time when I heard more about the woman but I didn't know much about it. All I knew was what I heard.

Father Arnold: This was Sister Remedios Castro who made this very brief testimony.

17

TESTIMONY OF MARIA ROBERTO DELA CRUZ

Father Arnold: You are Maria Dela Cruz?

Maria: Yes.

Father Arnold: When were you married?

Maria: I was married to Baltazar in 1928, August 1928.
                  No, 1927.

Father Arnold: You came from Japan in the month of June? 1938?

Maria: Yes, because we were getting ready to go to Ponape.

                  There was news at the time that some incident of
                  that nature (a plane crash) took place but it was
                  not clear in my mind where. I didn't know whether
                  it was Ponape or some place else.

Father Arnold: I came from Ana Benavente Mannibusan. She said she
                  saw an American woman. She washed, laundered her
                  clothing and she said that her brother saw her, but
                  not she, herself.

                  Was it the year '38 that they brought her here?

Maria: I believe so. That time her hair had grown so it
                  did not look like her picture with short hair.

Father Arnold: The Bishop wants me to talk to you about something
                  you may have firsthand knowledge of, namely, Amelia
                  Earhart. You will make your statements in Chamorro.
                  He will himself translate them into English. He
                  wants the tape done before he leaves next Tuesday
                  for Washington, D.C.

Maria: I recall hearing about a plane that crashed, the
                  topic of conversation in Saipan. I remember going
                  to Church to see Father Dionisio. At that time, I
                  lit a candle for my husband, Baltazar. I wanted to
                  light a candle because a battleship was scheduled to
                  come into the port about 10 o'clock in the morning.
                  The plane was exhibited in front of the house of the
                  Blancos and that was when the Japanese made an announce
                  ment to all the people that those who wanted to see an
                  airplane may come and see it at that place. That was
                  the year 1937 or 1938. Felipe was still alive as I

18

had mentioned to you before, Father Arnold. I
remember when he came to see me sometime ago
about information you were going to give Fred
Goerner, I believe.

Father Arnold: I recall you saying that your husband remarked
about this very courageous American woman because
she happened to be piloting the plane.

Maria: That is right. There were talks about the plane
having fallen down in the island south of us in
Micronesia. That fact was well concealed. But I
know of a ring that belonged to that woman. I
don't know whatever happened to it.

Father Arnold: Yes. But I heard that Trinidad Arriola was given...

Maria: That ring?

Father Arnold: My understanding was that it was given to Felipe,
Trinidad's brother.

Felipe, at the time Amelia was very sick, gave the
ring that was given to him to his sister. She was
wearing that ring.

Did you ever see that ring?

Maria: They were talking about it, Father. There was a
ring, according to statements I heard, but no one
knows where it is right now.

Father Arnold: Matilde said that when Amelia Earhart was at her
house she took a pencil to indicate on a map where
that island was, where the mishap took place.

Maria: She did indicate the place but did not write it
down.

Father Arnold: Matilde said that she was the one who made the wreath
when the American lady died.

That happened in what year?

Matilde: '38, I believe.

Father Arnold: So thank you very much

That was all the testimony of Maria Roberto Dela Cruz.

19

Notes

Epigraph

Reprinted with permission of Sally Putnam Chapman, from George P. Putnam, *Soaring Wings: A Biography of Amelia Earhart* (New York: Harcourt, Brace, and Co., 1939).

Chapter 1

1. From a letter Amelia wrote to her husband to be read if it was her last flight. Reprinted with permission of Sally Putnam Chapman, from Amelia Earhart, *Last Flight,* comp. George Palmer Putnam (New York: Harcourt, Brace, and Co., 1937), 134.
2. Cam Warren, "The Last Days of Amelia Earhart," *Amelia Earhart Society Newsletter* (January 1997): 27-31.
3. Mrs. Louis Joubert, telephone conversation with Fred Goerner, 23 June 1968.
4. Harry Balfour to Leo Bellarts, 1 October, 1970, copy from David Bellarts.
5. According to Pan American Airways in Miami, the trailing wire antenna, consisting of 460 feet of J1 wire and reel, weighed 8.9 pounds.
6. Earhart, *Last Flight,* 131.
7. Amelia Earhart to G. P. Putnam, cablegram, 30 June 1937, Special Collections, V111.B4, Purdue University Library.
8. Elgen M. Long and Marie K. Long, *Amelia Earhart: The Mystery Solved* (New York: Simon and Schuster, 1999) 166-67.
9. Observation about *Swan*'s radio range by Paul Rafford Jr.
10. Amelia was concerned about the details of flying the airplane. Being alone in the cockpit with Noonan positioned aft behind the fuselage fuel tanks, it would have been challenging for him to leave his navigation station and crawl forward to tend the radio when code was being transmitted. Voice communications, though not as efficient over long distances, thus were required if Amelia was going to handle them herself. Eric Chater to M. E. Griffin, Placer Management, Ltd., 25 July 1937, 8.
11. Long, *Mystery Solved,* 167.
12. Chater letter, 4.
13. 654 imperial gallons equals 785 US gallons, bringing the weight of the airplane to more than fifteen thousand pounds. The weight of the gasoline would have totaled about five thousand pounds. Chater letter, 5.
14. Bob Iredale to Fred Goerner, 28 July 1985, Victoria, Australia.
15. Earhart, *Last Flight,* 131.
16. Alan Vagg, interview by Fred Goerner, tape recording, at Vagg's home, Australia, 17 September 1988, records of Bill Prymak.

17. Iredale letter.
18. Long, *Mystery Solved,* 184.
19. Earhart, *Last Flight,* 131-33.
20. Chater letter, 7.
21. Ibid.
22. Earhart, *Last Flight,* 133.
23. Alan E. Board, "A Letter Never Before Published," *Amelia Earhart Society Newsletter* (February 1996): 6.
24. Iredale letter.
25. J. A. Collopy, report of 28 August 1937, Special Collections, Purdue University Library.
26. Lt. Arnold E. True to Harry Balfour, weather forecast, 2 July 1937.
27. Paul Rafford Jr., conversation with author, 22 April 2007.
28. Chater letter, 8.
29. Coast Guard Commander (San Francisco) to *Itasca,* radio cablegram, 26 June 1937.
30. Alan Vagg, interview by Fred Goerner, at Vagg's home, Australia, 18 September 1988, records of Bill Prymak.
31. Ibid.
32. Capt. Almon Gray, "Amelia Earhart and Radio" (paper presented at the Annapolis Seminar of the US Naval Institute, Annapolis, Md., April 1993).
33. Chater letter, 8.
34. Bill Prymak, Paul Rafford Jr., and Adm. Gene Tissot, meeting with the author, 22 April 2007.
35. Ibid.
36. Ibid.
37. Ibid.
38. Paul Cook, "USS *Ontario,*" *Amelia Earhart Society Newsletter* (June 1993): 4.
39. T. H. Cude to Dr. Francis X. Holbrook, Department of Social Studies, Fordham Preparatory School, as noted in Holbrook, Francis X., "Amelia Earhart's Last Flight." *U.S. Naval Institute Proceedings* (February 1971): 49-55.
40. Bowen P. Weisheit, USMCR, ret., *The Last Flight of Frederick J. Noonan* (2001) 19.
41. See Appendix D for a copy of *Itasca's* typed organizational responsibilities prepared by the communications officer, W. L. Sutter.
42. Frederick J. Hooven to Fred Goerner, 5 December 1966.
43. Leo Bellarts to Fred Goerner, 1 April 1962.
44. Ibid.

Chapter 2

1. White House formal communications about colonizing Jarvis, Baker, and Howland Islands began with the president asking Cordell Hull to familiarize himself with the situation relating to these islands and then "speak to me in regard to possible negotiations with Great Britain" (FDR to Cordell Hull, memo, 16 October 1934). Hull responded, recommending an executive order be issued "without communicating in the matter with the British" (Hull to FDR, memo, 18 February 1935). The next day, FDR approved an executive order placing these islands under the Department of the Interior.

2. Jon E. Krupnick, *Pan American's Pacific Pioneers: The Rest of the Story, Pictorial History of Pan Am's Pacific First Flights 1935-1946* (Missoula: Pictorial Histories Publishing Company, 2000), 523.

3. Justin Libby, "Pan Am Gets a Pacific Partner," *Naval History* (September/October 1999): 24-28.

4. Harold Gatty (1903-57) was a Tasmanian-born air navigator who pioneered South Pacific air routes for Pan Am and later Fiji Airways (Air Pacific). He also worked with Philip Weems in developing the Weems Navigation Systems.

5. Krupnick, *Pacific Pioneers*, 537.

6. Born William Thomas, William T. Miller adopted the surname of his foster mother, Mrs. Covert T. Miller, after being orphaned as a young boy.

7. E. H. Bryan Jr., *Panala'au Memoirs* (Honolulu: Pacific Scientific Information Center, Bernice P. Bishop Museum, 1974), 1-12.

8. George West journal, 1935, Kamehameha School Archives.

9. E. H. Bryan Jr., curator of collections, Bishop Museum, was a participant in this first colonization effort through his documentation work and was on board for several other cruises.

10. Bryan, *Panala'au Memoirs*, 4.

11. A larger lizard than the gecko, the skink is seven to ten inches long with a shiny body featuring smooth scales and short legs.

12. The Digest, "Airplane Island," *The Literary Digest* (18 September 1937): 18-20.

13. Bryan, *Panala'au Memoirs*, 66.

14. *Aholehole* is similar in color and taste to Sailor's Choice. *Uhu* is a parrot fish.

15. Bryan, *Panala'au Memoirs*, 102.

16. Ibid.

17. Richard Blackburn Black was born in Grand Forks, North Dakota, on August 10, 1902. He was awarded a BS in Civil Engineering from the University of North Dakota in June 1926. From 1927 to 1933, he held assorted engineering jobs and, from 1933 to 1935, participated in the Second Byrd Antarctic Expedition as a surveyor and assistant scientist. From 1936 to 1941, he was field representative for the Department of the Interior, Division of Territories and Island Possessions. As a member of the Navy Reserve, he was stationed at Pearl Harbor when the Japanese attacked. He fought in the battles of Tarawa and Saipan and was awarded the Bronze Star with Combat V.

After the war, he served as a federal aeronautics official in Hawaii, was a civilian aide in South Korea during the war there, and later was appointed an operations analyst in the Office of Naval Research. In 1955, he again returned to the Antarctic with Admiral Byrd's Operation Deep Freeze. Upon the death of Byrd in 1957, Black was named officer in charge, US Antarctic Programs, and was awarded the Antarctic Medal. He retired from the Navy Reserves in 1962 and was promoted to Rear Admiral because of his wartime service. He died on August 11, 1992, and is buried in Arlington National Cemetery.

18. Richard Black to Fred Goerner, 27 February 1968.

19. Gretchen G. Grover, captain, USNR, "The Coast Guard's Pacific Colonizers," *Naval History* 16, no. 4 (August 2002): 46.

20. James C. "Jimmy" Kamakaiwi Jr. was aboard *Itasca* when that ship first departed Honolulu for the colonization effort of March 20, 1935. He soon

was named Island Leader and held that position until returning to Honolulu on August 6, 1936. Returning to Howland on October 26, 1936, he resumed his position as leader and served until July 25, 1937. After the widespread search for Earhart and Noonan, he returned to Honolulu aboard *Itasca*.

21. Richard Black to Dennis Von Ruden, 5 March 1969.
22. Grover, "Pacific Colonizers," 46.
23. Actually, this "darkened lights and radio silence" invasion ended up quite a friendly beach party, with each group entertaining the other. Both sides recognized that jurisdictional settlement would be decided in London and Washington and that it would be futile to harbor any hostility.
24. Bryan, *Panala'au Memoirs*, 197.
25. Grover, "Pacific Colonizers," 44.
26. James L. Mooney, *Dictionary of American Naval Fighting Ships*, 8 vols., (Washington, DC: Naval Historical Center, 1959-81).
27. Thomas Bederman, "Howland Island Rescue," *Life* 12, no. 10 (March 9, 1942): 57-60.
28. Burl Burlingame, *Honolulu (HI) Star-Bulletin*, 4 April 2002.
29. Grover, "Pacific Colonizers," 47.

Chapter 3
1. Hilton H. Railey, *Touch'd With Madness* (New York: Carrick and Evans, 1938), 101.
2. Ibid., 102.
3. Ibid.
4. Ibid., 103.
5. Ibid., 106.
6. Amelia's handwritten prenuptial agreement to G. P. Reproduced with permission of Sally Putnam Chapman, from *Whistled Like a Bird: The Untold Story of Dorothy Putnam, George Putnam, and Amelia Earhart* (New York: Warner Books, 1997).
7. Virginia Morell, "Amelia Earhart," *National Geographic* (January 1998): 130.
8. Earhart, *Last Flight*, 9.
9. The barograph is a barometer that automatically records variations in atmospheric pressure on a revolving cylinder (Earhart, *Last Flight*, 9).
10. Earhart, *Last Flight*, 15.
11. Ibid., 22.
12. Friction grew between Mantz and Putnam as Amelia's programs and horizons progressed. There's no question that Amelia and Paul spent considerable time together. They practiced instrument flying on the Link Trainer in Mantz's hangar. Paul was responsible for specifying instrumentation in the new Electra as well as many other custom features. When Paul divorced his wife, Myrtle, there is little wonder that Amelia was named a co-respondent.
13. Paul Mantz went on to become Hollywood's most celebrated stunt pilot and aerial motion picture photographer. After World War II began, because of his motion picture connections and superb flying ability, he was promoted to major and named head of the First Motion Picture Unit of the Army Air Corps. FMPU was staffed with a number of motion picture technicians and actors including the likes of Ronald Reagan, George Montgomery, Alan Ladd, Van Heflin, and many others.

14. Don Dwiggins, *Hollywood Pilot* (New York: Doubleday, 1967), 14.
15. Born in Germany in 1897, Harry Manning took up the seafaring urge at an early age. After graduating from the New York Merchant Marine School in 1914 at the age of eighteen, he held several miscellaneous seagoing assignments before joining the United States Lines in 1921. He earned his Master Mariner's title and was named skipper of the *Roosevelt* at the time that Amelia and her two pilots were returning from their historic Friendship flight across the Atlantic. Manning later served in the US Navy from June 14, 1941 to January 31, 1947.
16. Lodesen, Marius, "Captain Lodi Speaking," in *The Greatest Tragedy,* 232.
17. Ibid., 234.
18. Because of Amelia's relationship with Purdue University, she and her husband were able to bend the ear of Pres. Edward C. Elliot, who liked the idea of a Purdue "flying laboratory." He persuaded his secretary-treasurer, R. B. Stewart, to establish the Amelia Earhart Fund for Aeronautical Research and to seek appropriate donors. J. K. Lilly (Eli Lilly), Purdue alumnus David Ross, Vincent Bendix, and other aviation-industry manufacturers were happy to oblige. The fund totaled approximately $70,000.
19. Roy Blay, "Amelia Earhart's Last Flight," *Lockheed Horizons* 26 (May 1988): 25.
20. Ibid., 26.
21. Muriel Morrissey and Carol Osborne, *Amelia, My Courageous Sister: Biography of Amelia Earhart* (Santa Clara, California: Osborne Publishers, 1988), 185.
22. At this time, mid-air refueling was uncommon in civilian aviation and highly risky even for the military.
23. We know Amelia gave her flare gun to radioman Harry Balfour prior to leaving Lae, New Guinea. It is likely she discarded the kite as well. Balfour also removed Amelia's flight covers to have them stamped at the Lae post office (*New York Herald Tribune,* 7 March 1937).
24. Competent pilots and navigators have stated that it would have been incomprehensible to have undertaken this around-the-world flight with no Morse telegraph key on board.
25. Earhart, *Last Flight,* 107.

Chapter 4

1. Art Kennedy, *High Times—Keeping 'Em Flying: An Aviation Autobiography,* ed. Jo Ann Ridley (McKinleyville, California: Fithian Press, 1992), 80.
2. Dwiggins, *Hollywood,* 102.
3. The gasoline had been trucked from Wheeler Field, and Mantz discovered it was contaminated. He proceeded to purchase 590 gallons of aviation gasoline from the military (Doris L. Rich, *Amelia Earhart: A Biography* [Washington, DC: Smithsonian Press, 1989], 243).
4. Vincent Loomis and Jeffrey L. Ethell, *Amelia Earhart: The Final Story* (New York: Random House, 1985), 65.
5. George P. Putnam, *Soaring Wings: A Biography of Amelia Earhart* (New York: Harcourt, Brace, and Co.), 283.
6. Luke Field Board of Inquiry, *Accident Report,* 23 March 1937, exhibits C-F, US Navy Archives.
7. Kennedy, *High Times,* 82.
8. Ibid., 83.

9. Ibid., 85.
10. Alex Coutts, conversation with author, Oakland, California, 18 May 2002.
11. Kennedy, *High Times,* 81-82.
12. Kelly Johnson to Fred Goerner, 22 January 1970.
13. G. P. Putnam to Stanley Meikle, Purdue Research Foundation, 12 April 1937.
14. Lodesen, *Tragedy,* 14.
15. Putnam letter.
16. Mary S. Lovell, *The Sound of Wings: The Life of Amelia Earhart* (New York: St. Martin's Press, 1989), 253.
17. Putnam letter.
18. The likely reason is that William Bendix, a huge initial sponsor of the original flight who also put up another $20,000 after the Luke Field disaster, talked Amelia and her husband into utilizing the new Bendix high-frequency direction finding equipment. There apparently was little training or calibration of radio equipment and antenna. Of the many things that could have foiled the success of this world flight, the unjustifiable belief in the untested Bendix equipment are prime candidates.
19. Lovell, *Sound of Wings,* 262.
20. Rich, *Amelia Earhart,* 260.
21. Earhart, *Last Flight,* 119.
22. Ibid., 120.
23. Maj. Joe Gervais, USAF, ret., interviewed Amelia's secretary, Margot DeCarie. Per his conversation with Margot, Joe related: "Two private meetings were held between Amelia and Baruch and Westover at which neither Margot nor G. P. Putnam was in attendance. No one knows what was discussed, but noticeably fewer bills came across her desk for payment afterwards" (Joe Gervais, conversation with author, 14 January 2004).
24. Kennedy, *High Times,* 88-89.

Chapter 5
1. Paul Rafford Jr., *Amelia Earhart's Radio* (Orange, California: Paragon Agency, 2006), 127.
2. In addition, about eight gallons of fuel most likely were vented overboard as a result of the excessive heat of the New Guinea day and subsequent expansion of the tanks (Long, *Mystery Solved,* 232).
3. Kelly Johnson to Fred Goerner, 22 January 1970.
4. Blay, "Last Flight," 33.
5. Paul Van Dyke to Fred Goerner, 28 July 1971, National Museum of the Pacific War.
6. Paul Rafford noted that Captain Blakeslee of the *Ontario* claimed that he never had any communication from the Earhart flight and went to bed, as the weather was squally and dirty. Paul also mentioned that *Ontario* could only transmit and receive on 500 kcs. Earhart could not successfully transmit for any distance on this frequency without her trailing antenna, which had been left in Miami at the start of the flight.
7. Van Dyke letter.
8. Ibid.
9. Fred Goerner, *The Search for Amelia Earhart* (New York: Doubleday, 1966), 296.

10. Frederick J. Hooven to Fred Goerner, 23 February 1975.

11. The testing of the new high-frequency DF equipment may very well have been the "special mission" that Amelia mentioned to her mechanic, Art Kennedy, prior to the world flight attempt.

12. Hooven nevertheless overlooked the political clout of Bendix. Although Earhart paid little attention to necessary details of direction-finder operation, we can only wonder whether Hooven's equipment could have brought her safely to *Itasca* and into Howland Island (Hooven letter).

13. Kelly Johnson to Fred Goerner, 13 February 1982.

14. Blay, "Last Flight," 34.

15. Kelly Johnson to Fred Goerner, 13 February 1982.

16. Johnson to Goerner, 22 January 1970.

17. Almon A. Gray to Cam Warren, 1 September 1994.

18. Gray letter.

19. Eugene Vidal, self-conducted, taped interview, 95-97, box 40, Eugene L. Vidal Collection, University of Wyoming.

20. Earhart, *Last Flight,* 35.

21. Pare Lorentz, *FDR: Day by Day,* 26 July 1937.

22. *Oakland Tribune,* 9 July 1937.

23. Stewart A. Saunders to Leo Bellarts, 13 June 1968.

24. Krupnick, *Pacific Pioneers.*

25. Leo Bellarts to Fred Goerner, 28 November 1961.

26. *Seattle Post-Intelligencer,* 1 July 1962.

27. Kelly Johnson to Fred Goerner, San Francisco, 3 January 1982.

28. A similar story was reported by Buddy Brennan. The first chapter of his book opens with the sentence, "You want old airplane, you find airplane America lady crash in." Brennan's quote was from Tamaki Mayazo, although Brennan had misspelled Tamaki's name as Tanaki in his book. Oliver Knaggs also interviewed Tamaki and related an almost identical story in his book. In Knaggs's account, Tamaki replenished the Japanese seaplane tender *Kamoi* with coal.

29. Bill Prymak, former president of AES and noted Earhart researcher, related this story to me as it was told to him by Bilimon Amram. Prymak and Joe Gervais interviewed him in 1989.

Chapter 6

1. Leo Bellarts, interview by Elgen Long, tape recording, 11 April 1973, provided by David Bellarts.

2. Ibid.

3. Yau Fai Lum to John P. Riley Jr., 2 June 1995.

4. Lt. Col. Ron Reuther spoke personally with Howard Hanzlik, who told Reuther that he was not actually an official United Press reporter but was substituting for a friend who wasn't able to make the trip.

5. Henry Lau retired as lieutenant colonel of the Army Signal Corps. He is buried in the Hawaiian Punch Bowl Cemetery. Ah Kin Leong, a stalwart of the Kamehameha colonizers, previously had served on Howland for three months, from August 1936 to October 1936. He later served six months on Jarvis Island, four months on Canton, and four months on Enderbury in 1938. From Howland Island colonists, Daily Logs.

6.   Yau Fai Lum to John P. Riley, 14 October 1994, provided by Paul Rafford Jr.
7.   Yau Fai Lum letter.
8.   John P. Riley, "The Earhart Tragedy: Old Mystery, New Hypothesis," *Naval History* 14, no. 4 (August 2000).
9.   Paul Rafford to the Amelia Earhart Society, e-mail, 25 October 2004.
10. David Bellarts, conversation with author, Atchison, Kansas, July 2006.
11. Leo Bellarts, interview by Elgen Long, 11 April 1973, provided by David Bellarts.
12. Richard Black to Dennis Von Ruden, 5 March 1969.
13. Paul Rafford, conversation with author, Melbourne, Florida, 22 April 2007.
14. Riley, "Earhart Tragedy."
15. Leo Bellarts to Fred Goerner, 1 April 1962.
16. From David M. Bellarts and David K. Bowman, "KHAQQ Calling Itasca . . ." *Wings over Kansas.*
17. Cam Warren to the Amelia Earhart Society, e-mail, 12 March 2006.
18. Fred Goerner to Cdr. Henry M. Anthony, 3 June 1989.
19. Rollin C. Reineck suggested that a possible government mission was the purpose for two meetings with Amelia after the Luke Field crash. Amelia's own mother mentioned her possible involvement in a government mission. Art Kennedy, in his memoirs, described Amelia talking about a "special mission." *Amelia Earhart Society Newsletter* 2 (February 1999): 16.
20. Laurance Safford, Cameron A. Warren, and Robert R. Payne, *Earhart's Flight into Yesterday: The Facts without the Fiction* (McLean, Virginia: Paladwr Press, 2003), 158.
21. Ibid., 168.
22. Bellarts letter.

Chapter 7

1.   Amy Otis Earhart to Neta Snook Southern, 6 May 1944, provided by Bill Prymak.
2.   Noonan also discussed with Weems the difficulties of determining the angle of drift when smoke bombs or flares were necessary with heavy wind and cloud conditions (P. V. H. Weems, *Air Navigation* [New York: McGraw-Hill, 1938], 173-78).
3.   Bowen P. Weisheit, USMCR, ret., *The Last Flight of Frederick J. Noonan* (1995), 25.
4.   Weems, *Navigation*, 394-98.
5.   Almon A. Gray to Cam A. Warren, 1 September 1994.
6.   Almon A. Gray, *Amelia Earhart Society Newsletter* 6 (June 1993).
7.   Mary S. Lovell, *The Sound of Wings: The Life of Amelia Earhart* (New York: St. Martin's Press, 1989), 259.
8.   Benjamin Dutton, commander, USN, *Navigation and Nautical Astronomy*, 10th ed. (Annapolis, Maryland: US Naval Institute, 1951).
9.   Benjamin Dutton and Edwin A. Beito, *Navigation and Nautical Astronomy* (Annapolis: United States Naval Institute, 1951), 184.

Chapter 8

1.   Fred Noonan to Mary Beatrice Passadori (his second wife), 11 June 1937.
2.   "Flier Lost," *Pacific Islands Monthly* (July 23, 1937).

3. *Amelia Earhart Society Newsletter* (September 1993): 19.
4. Upon the successful completion of the Hawaii-California flight, he received "warm recognition from the station and Miss Earhart," according to a proposal by E. H. Dimity of August 1939, attempting to raise funds for another Earhart search. At the time, Dimity had founded the Amelia Earhart Foundation, much to the dismay of G. P. Putnam and the Earhart family.
5. Palmer Bevis, "Grounds for a new search for Amelia Earhart," proposal, 3 February 1940. Much of his data came from E. H. Dimity's notes on Amelia.
6. Ibid.
7. Ibid.
8. Adm. Gene Tissot, former skipper of the aircraft carrier *Enterprise,* has the diary of a friend of his who had been aboard the *Lexington.* While the *Lexington*'s speed set a record from California to Hawaii in excess of 23 knots, for some reason her speed from Hawaii to the search area was considerably less, more like 12 to 15 knots. There also appeared to be no sense of urgency in the search effort. This contradicts the public urgency and implies that some fate was already known by those in charge.
9. Capt. Almon A. Gray, USNR, ret., "Where Did Amelia Land?," *Amelia Earhart Society Newsletter* (August 1994).
10. Ibid.
11. Capt. Almon Gray, "Are We Missing Something," *Amelia Earhart Society Newsletter* (July 1995): 4.
12. Bill Prymak, "Grounds for a Possible Search for Amelia Earhart," *Amelia Earhart Society Newsletter* (August 1994): 27.
13. From Joe Gervais's personal reports.
14. Capt. Almon A. Gray, "Amelia Earhart and Radio," *Amelia Earhart Society Newsletter* (June 1993).
15. Pan Am Station Reports relating to the Earhart flight.
16. Fred Goerner to Adm. Joseph J. Clark, USN, ret., 1 April 1971.
17. Joseph W. Ballantine to Tsuneo Hayama, July 1937, Franklin D. Roosevelt Library, 800.79611 Putnam, Amelia Earhart/140.
18. Tsuneo Hayama to Joseph W. Ballantine, 11 July 1937, Franklin D. Roosevelt Library, 800.79611 Putnam, Amelia Earhart/141.
19. Rear Adm. Joseph N. Wenger indicated to Fred Goerner that "Japan had a string of high-frequency direction finders in the Marshalls in 1937. They could track the Earhart plane far better than we could." Wenger was active in OP-20-G during the Earhart era and later headed the US Navy's crypto analysis agency during most of WWII.
20. Loomis, *Final Story,* 145.
21. Ellen Belotti, a long-term Pan Am employee, was secretary to the chief of radio communications at the Pacific Division Headquarters in Alameda, California. At the time the Navy seized the written reports, she was told not to discuss the contents with anyone. She felt that the Navy was acting improperly in confiscating these private corporate records. After reading Joe Klaas and Joe Gervais's book, she contacted Joe Gervais, told him about the Navy's actions, and provided him with a copy of the documents. Joe later shared the Pan Am records with the Amelia Earhart Society.
22. John O. Lambrecht to Fred Goerner, 29 January 1970.

23. Lambrecht letter.
24. USS *Lexington, Report of Earhart Search Operations 3-18 July 1937,* by Capt. Leigh Noyes, USN, 10.
25. US Naval Institute, "Proceedings," November 1971.
26. USS *Colorado, Report of Earhart Search,* 10.
27. Lambrecht carefully overflew Gardner Island only seven days after Amelia and Noonan disappeared (Lambrecht letter). Gardner Island (now Nikumaroro) is the scene of various Amelia search expeditions by The International Group for Historic Aircraft Recovery (TIGHAR), which has reported finding shoes, airplane aluminum siding, a sextant box, and other flotsam supposedly belonging to Amelia or her Lockheed Electra. To date, none of these finds have been authoritatively confirmed. If Amelia's airplane had come down on Nikumaroro a few days before Lambrecht reconnoitered the island, there would have been visible evidence. Nikumaroro was re-populated in October 1937 at the behest of the British Administrator of the Gilbert and Ellice Island Groups, and the TIGHAR artifacts could easily have belonged to one of the inhabitants. Henry E. Maude observed to Fred Goerner, "Gardner is such a small atoll that every inch of it must have been walked over many times since July 2, 1937. Anything out of the ordinary would have been reported and be on record. A skeleton wearing lady's shoes would have been a sensation regaled throughout the central Pacific."
28. Lambrecht letter.
29. USS *Lexington, Report of Earhart Search,* 8-9.
30. Black continued, "There were enough strange things about the whole flight arrangements and circumstances to cause me to think that Fred Goerner may have something." Richard Black to Mrs. L. K. Jordan, Sacramento, California, 19 March 1968. Black had dual responsibilities; in addition to representing the government, he also handled an assortment of Amelia's logistical needs for G. P. Putnam. He certainly had access to the center of things at Howland and aboard *Itasca.* The reference to Goerner is in regard to his view that Amelia and Fred did not crash and sink.
31. Office of the Commandant, Fourteenth Naval District, Pearl Harbor, *Report of the Earhart Search,* by O. G. Murfin, 31 July 1937.
32. Ibid.
33. Ibid.
34. Goerner's source was Don Dwiggins.
35. Richard Black to Fred Goerner, 18 March 1968.
36. *Popular Aviation* (December 1939): 11.
37. *Popular Aviation* (January 1940): 29.
38. *New York Times,* 25 July 1937.
39. Robert M. Morgenthau to H. Davey Hamilton, 27 June 2003.

Chapter 9

1. Hilton H. Railey, *Touch'd With Madness* (New York: Carrick and Evans, 1938), 109-10.
2. Sirovich had asked Swanson about a rumor that the Navy had encouraged Earhart and Noonan to fly over certain islands to determine if they were being fortified militarily. Emile Gauvreau, *The Wild Blue Yonder: Sons of the*

Prophet Carry On (New York: E. P. Dutton and Co., 1944), 173-74.

3. Richard M. Bueschel, "Japanese Electras and Gooneybirds," *Journal of the American Aviation Historical Society* 15, no. 1 (Spring 1970): 30-32.

4. Joint Committee on the Investigation of the Pearl Harbor Attack, "Orange Activity in the Mandates," *Hearings: Proceedings of the Hewitt Inquiry,* 1946.

5. Frederick J. Hooven to Walter P. Maiersperger, 2 August 1979.

6. Gauvreau, *Wild Blue Yonder,* 174.

7. The information presented in the *Smith's Weekly* article confirmed from various sources that during the air sweeps from the aircraft carrier *Lexington,* several planes flew over the Japanese-mandated Marshalls in 1937. Later details reported in Francis X. Holbrook, "United States Defense and Trans-Pacific Commercial Air Routes 1933-1941" and Joint Committee on the Investigation of the Pearl Harbor Attack, "Orange Activity," 1136-1144.

8. The Japanese foreign minister in 1937 was Mr. Kahi Hirota. Vincent Loomis and Jeffrey L. Ethell, *Amelia Earhart: The Final Story* (New York: Random House, 1985), 150.

9. For more details of the White House involvement, see Appendix D.

10. W. Brown to Grace Tully, memorandum, 9 April 1945, Franklin D. Roosevelt Library.

11. Data provided by Capt. August Detzer Jr., USN, ret., head of OP-20-GX, in Fred Goerner to Cdr. Henry M. Anthony, 3 June 1989.

12. Federal Reserve Bank of Minneapolis, *Inflation Index,* 1937-2011.

13. Fred Goerner, *The Search for Amelia Earhart* (New York: Doubleday, 1966), 221.

14. Ross Game to Tom C. Korologos, administrative assistant to Senator Wallace Bennett, 29 August 1966.

15. Fred Goerner to Keith A. Mackie, 2 March 1976.

16. Astor was the informal leader of FDR's private espionage group that met regularly at a secret apartment in New York. The *Nourmahal* was a thirty-two-hundred-ton vessel with twin screws built in Kiel, Germany, in 1928 for Astor. Customized as a deluxe, long-range cruising yacht, its specifications were as follows: length: 263'10", beam: 41'6", draft: 18'5", and speed: 13.7 knots. The Navy acquired it in March 1942 and commissioned it at the end of 1943 as an armed Coast Guard ship.

17. *The New York Times,* 20 February 1938.

18. President's Personal File, President's Secretary's File, *President's Papers,* Franklin D. Roosevelt Library; Collection of Astor, Vincent, *Copies of Correspondence with Franklin D. Roosevelt,* Franklin D. Roosevelt Library.

19. Roger Faligot, *Naisho: enquête au cœur des services secrets japonais* (Paris: Éditions La Découverte, 1997), 87.

20. Ibid., 131.

21. Ibid., 135.

22. Dean S. Jennings, "Is Amelia Earhart Still Alive?" *Popular Aviation* 25, no. 6 (December 1939): 10.

23. Palmer Bevis to Amy Earhart, Clarence S. Williams, Paul Mantz, E. H. Dimity, Walter McMenamy, and Margot DeCarie, 3 February 1940.

24. Bevis letter.

25. Amy Otis Earhart to Neta Snook Southern, 6 May 1944, in *Amelia Earhart Society Newsletter* (February 1994).

26. Goerner to Mrs. Albert Morrissey, 31 October 1961.

27. Goerner, *Search*, 288.

28. Ibid., 315.

29. Ibid.

30. The USNA classmate of 1924 likely was Edwin Thomas Layton, who wrote a book about naval intelligence and radio surveillance capabilities of the 1930s (Untitled, Goerner Collection, National Museum of the Pacific War). Ross Game indicated that Goerner was told by Mrs. Nimitz after the Admiral's death that the likely source of intelligence on the fate of Earhart was Capt. Bruce L. Canaga, another distinguished Naval Intelligence Officer closely associated with Admiral Nimitz.

31. Fred Goerner to Lt. General Albert D. Cooley, USMC, ret., 11 April 1988.

32. Ross Game, conversation with author, 14 July 2007.

33. Goerner, *Search*, 325; also, Ross Game, conversation with author.

34. Ellis Bailey to Bill Prymak, memorandum, February 1999.

Chapter 10

1. Committee on Naval Affairs, *The Decline and Renaissance of the Navy, 1922-1944*, by Senator David I. Walsh, (Washington, DC: US Government Printing Office, 1944).

2. Ibid.

3. This particular flight was acknowledged in March 1946 in testimony by Secretary of War Henry Stimson during the Joint Congressional Committee's hearing on the Pearl Harbor attack.

4. US Naval Institute, "For Sugar Boats or Submarines," *Proceedings*, August 1968.

5. Philip A. Crowl and Edmund G. Love, *United States Army in World War II: The War in the Pacific, Seizure of the Gilberts and Marshalls* (Washington, DC: US Government Printing Office, 1955).

6. Bill Prymak, interview with author, Florida, February 2005.

7. Alfred Capelle, "Remarks" (presented at the Amelia Earhart Society Symposium in Oakland, California, 18 May 2002).

8. Robert Reimers Enterprises had been conscripted to supply these military projects, as reported in Robert Reimers to Bill Prymak, interview, 1997.

9. Alfred Capelle to Amelia Earhart Society, e-mail, 12 June 2002.

10. Dorothea Garsia's diary is available to the public at the National Library of Australia.

11. K. L. Plain, to Division of Protocol, Department of State, Washington, DC, telegram, 6 July 1937. Radio Sydney out of New South Wales also reported in a telegram relayed from Nauru radio via Tutuila, "Message from plane when at least 60 miles south of Nauru received 8:30 p.m. Sydney time July 2 saying, 'ship in sight ahead.' Since identified as the steamer *Myrtle Bank* which arrived Nauru daybreak today. Reported no contact between *Itasca* and Nauru radio. Continuous watch being maintained by Nauru radio and Suva radio."

12. *Los Angeles Times*, 3 July 1937.

13. The method of shorthand utilized for deciphering the bottle message was the *Methode duploye ancienne*, a method using a distinct group of signs for a word, or monogrammatic method (as opposed to the syllabic method, which uses a

distinct group of signs for a syllable). The *duploye* method uses a complete system of logically made abbreviations, called metagraphy. Both methods are used in the bottle's message in a rare, hybrid way, which has made transcription difficult. The *Duploye* method, invented in Canada, was popular in France in the twentieth century.

14. Department of State, "Putnam, Amelia Earhart/1 (4639)," files 193-39, 800.79611, RG 59D, National Archives.

15. Queen Bosket of Mili Atoll affirmed the Frenchman's unwelcome reception and rough treatment at Mili: "There was talk about a sailing boat which the Japanese rammed and sank. I think they [the crew] were killed and the Frenchman imprisoned. It was a long time ago" (Oliver Knaggs, *Amelia Earhart: Her Last Flight* [Cape Town, South Africa: Timmins Publishers, 1983], 126).

16. A passport issued by the consulate general of the United States in London on May 27, 1932, to Amelia Earhart Putnam bears her signature and notes: "Height 5'8'"; hair light brown; eyes blue; place of birth: Atchison, Kansas; date of birth: July 24, 1898; occupation: flyer." Earhart must have been sensitive to her upcoming birthday at the time this passport was issued. Her actual birth date was July 24, 1897, a year earlier than documented.

17. Hoppenot was named sous-directeur d'Europe on October 24, 1938. He previously was the sous-directeur de Japon. Perhaps because of his previous responsibility as the ministry specialist on Japanese matters, he felt some empathy for the writer of the message as well as for Amelia Earhart. In June 1940, Hoppenot left for Lisbon to join the Free France movement.

18. Roscoe Henry Hillenkoetter was born May 8, 1897, in St. Louis, Missouri, and graduated from the US Naval Academy in 1919. After serving as a naval *attaché* in the American Embassy of Paris, he went on to become executive officer of the battleship *West Virginia* at Pearl Harbor. He became captain of the USS *Missouri* before becoming head of the Joint Intelligence Center Pacific Ocean Areas (JICPOA) and, later, the second director of the CIA (1947-50). He may have been the source of Admiral Nimitz's knowledge of Earhart's fate (Fred Goerner, *The Search for Amelia Earhart,* [New York: Doubleday, 1966], 315).

19. In the prologue of Eric de Bisschop's book, *Voyage of the Kaimiloa* ([London: George Bell and Sons, 1940], 6), he briefly describes his fifteen-day detention as a possible spy his earlier voyage on the junk *Fou Po*.

20. Similarly, the *Pacific Islands Monthly* of November 1933 carried the article "Foreigners Unwelcome." It read, "Señor Laslo, a Mexican citizen, arrived in Rabaul recently from the Mandate Islands which are under Japanese Administration. In an interview, Sr. Laslo expressed himself very bitterly concerning the treatment which is meted out to foreigners who even put their foot ashore within Japan's mandated area. He states his every movement whilst there was closely watched and every restriction was placed upon his activities by the Japanese authorities." From *Pacific Islands Monthly,* January 1936: "A German businessman named Richard Voigt, long a resident of Japan, who visited a mandated island for health reasons, complained to the League of Nations of intolerable vexatious and suspicious supervision. He said that he was watched night and day and continually interrogated by the police . . ."

21. Adm. Harry D. Yarnell was commander in chief, Asiatic Fleet, in 1937; Capt.

Walter K. Kilpatrick was district intelligence officer, Fourteenth Naval District, at Pearl Harbor in 1937; Capt. David M. LeBreton (later Admiral) was chief of staff of the US Fleet under Admiral Hepburn; Cdr. Charles D. Leffler was skipper of the submarine *Argonaut* at Pearl Harbor in 1937.

22. Eric de Bisschop, interview by Roscoe Hillenkoetter, transcript, Paris, France, 7 January 1939. For full transcript, see Appendix D.

23. For more details, see de Bisschop, *Voyage of the Kaimiloa*.

24. Edwin C. Wilson, chargé d'affaires, US Embassy, Paris, to US Department of State, 4 January 1939, Enclosure #6 to Despatch No. 3590, RG 59D, National Archives.

25. SR General Headquarters memo defining categories of their agents dispersed around the world was found in records of the French naval attaché in the Washington, DC, Embassy. The records had been shipped back to France after WWII instead of being destroyed. STS was under the direct authority of the Forces navales en Extrême-Orient (FNEO). The stated principal mission of the STS at that particular time was to study "the problems of the Pacific" concerning the rivalries among occidental powers, Japan, and Western powers and the activities of foreign fleets and air forces in the Pacific. A June 1936 report stated, for example: "The Mandate Islands are increasingly fortified to serve as a base for the Japanese Air Force. An enormous effort is being undertaken reflecting an increase of 29 wings [airplanes] half land based and the rest seaplanes . . . It is likely that we shall see in the near future a huge confrontation by the major powers in the Pacific."

26. The pilot charts of the United States Naval Hydrographic Office; the Service hydrographique et océanographique de la marine (SHOM) in Brest, France; and the United Kingdom Hydrographic Office in Taunton, England, all indicate that surface sea currents in this region tend to run in a circle and, upon approaching the coasts of Spain and France, turn in a counter-clockwise motion. This cycle is accentuated during the months of October and November. French pilot charts confirm, "Along this shore, at a distance of 5 to 6 miles, a slight current sets continuously to the northward." Beyond the latitude of Saint Nazaire, sea currents tend to move more west-northwesterly.

The average speed of these surface sea currents along the northern coast of Spain and the southwestern coast of France is a half-knot. A small bottle drifting at the mercy of the sea would cover approximately twelve nautical miles during a twenty-four-hour period. By working backwards in reverse of the drift, we can generally determine the route of the bottle with the assumption that the influence of the wind was minimal because the bottle was so small. The bottle could have been drifting, from the location at which it was thrown from the ship into the sea, for about fifteen days. (We must also assume the bottle was not left high and dry on some other section of beach awaiting the interval of the next tidal cycle—about six hours.) Since it was discovered on October 30, it was most likely launched on or about October 15.

The French Hydrographic Office, in their monitoring of coastal currents, routinely threw into the sea small, marked, buoyant plaques of plastic, *cartes-flotteurs*, and traced their floating directions. Of forty cards dropped fifteen to twenty miles off of Santander, twenty-seven were found and mapped along specific points of the French coast. For a single month of October, out of ten plastic cards dropped fourteen miles off Santander, seven cards arrived at their final destination along the coast of Vendee. Ergo, the captive message-writer's approximations were knowledgeably estimated.

27. *Affaires maritimes ou militaires d'intérêt général,* series B, box 280, file 6, Despatch No. 3590, 1936-1939. See Appendix D for copies of specific letters.

28. D. J. Rogers to Sir Maurice Peterson, 17 June 1939, PRO, UK, FO 425/415.

29. Sir Maurice Peterson to D. J. Rogers, 4 July 1939, PRO, UK, FO 425/415.

30. Office of the Minister of Industry and Commerce, 7 October 1938, Lloyd's Registry, record box 43, misc. item 20.

31. Embassy and Consular Archives, PRO, FO 185/1754.

32. Tomohei Chida and Peter N. Davies, *The Japanese Shipping and Shipbuilding Industries: A History of their Modern Growth* (London: Athlone Press, 1990) 49-53.

33. Chida, *Japanese Shipping,* 44.

34. Through his expert handwriting analysis, Kirby had proved several years earlier that Irene Bolam, a New Jersey woman, was not Amelia Earhart, as others had boldly stated.

35. Many intelligence transcripts were not necessarily shared with the President. Pre-war Magic intelligence was restricted to a handful of senior cabinet members, who were not allowed to take notes or make copies once the information had been visually reviewed. Even J. Edgar Hoover, director of the FBI, was not privy to Magic intelligence. We know, however, that FDR was aware of the bottled message discovery.

Chapter 11

1. T. C. Buddy Brennan, *Witness to the Execution: The Odyssey of Amelia Earhart* (Frederick, Colorado: Renaissance House, 1988), 98.

2. Alfred Capelle, "Remarks" (presented at the Amelia Earhart Society Symposium in Oakland, California, 18 May 2002).

3. Bill Prymak, conversation with author, Florida, April 2009. Prymak emphasized several times that he considered his discussion with Joro, a Mili elder, the most compelling research information he had ever received in his several trips to the Marshall Islands.

4. N. Horiguchi told the author that the old hotel was little more than a flop-house, but it was fully occupied when the Japanese tour ships were in port before the war.

5. Alfred Capelle to Amelia Earhart Society, e-mail, 13 June 2002.

6. Alfred Capelle to Amelia Earhart Society, 16 August 2002.

7. Oliver Knaggs, *Amelia Earhart, Her Last Flight* (Cape Town, South Africa: Timmins Publishers, 1983), 131.

8. Ibid., 124.

9. Ibid., 120.

10. Ibid., 136.

11. Ibid., 138.

12. Ibid., 36.

13. Ibid., 53.

14. Ibid., 55.

15. Ibid.

16. Ibid., 56. There is some question whether the ship was the seaplane tender *Kamoi* or the survey ship *Koshu*. We know *Kamoi* sailed from Saipan on July 3, 1937, at 6:00 p.m. for Ise Bay, Japan. Although *Kamoi* had visited Jaluit earlier on April 13 and departed on April 27 for Majuro, it is likely that Tamaki may have loaded coal at that time on this seaplane tender and simply confused it with the *Koshu*. The *Koshu* had definite orders to assist in the Earhart search, and we know the ship was in Marshall Islands waters at the time. Other Marshallese witnesses identify the ship that brought Amelia and Noonan to the Jaluit anchorage at that time as being the *Koshu*.
17. Bill Prymak, conversation with author, Florida, February 2005.
18. Alfred Capelle to Ronald T. Reuther, e-mail, 5 June 2002.
19. Woody Peard, conversation with author.
20. Bill Prymak and Joe Gervais, "The Jaluit Report," *Amelia Earhart Society Newsletter* (January 1991): 11.
21. Prymak interview, February 2005.
22. Ibid.
23. Alvan Fitak, interview by Fred Goerner, 18 September 1988, National Museum of the Pacific War.
24. Ibid.
25. *New York Daily News*, 22 March 1944, 45.
26. "Earhart May Have Come Down in Japanese Territory," *Pacific Islands Monthly*, July 1944.
27. Metrick Dockins, "Coast Minister Has a Theory on Earhart Fate," *Gulfport (MS) Sun Herald*, 3 July 1992; also, Joseph C. Wright to Fred Goerner, 21 July 1967.
28. The mother and daughter told Stevens that the local Nauru newspaper printed the story as front-page news. In fact, they had saved their copy of the newspaper and showed him the article. A day or two after the initial publication, the order came that the papers should not be distributed, and most of the papers carrying the article were recovered and destroyed, so only a few people on the Island of Nauru had an opportunity to read it. However, no copy of this particular paper has been located, and in fact there is no record of any newspaper published on the island at that time.
29. *Amelia Earhart Society Newsletter* 1 (July 1996): 22-23.
30. Heine was interviewed in 1989 by Bill Prymak, Heine's son John, and Joe Gervais. His full story appears in *Amelia Earhart Society Newsletter* (February 1996): 24.

Chapter 12
1.   Willard Price to Fred Goerner, 27 September 1980. Price also wrote, "More than a hundred of the older Saipanese testify to it. It made a deep impression upon them because, as one said, 'In 1937 it was unheard of for a woman to be a flier.' Among the witnesses are many presumably reliable persons: police investigators, church leaders, military men—Capt. Jose Quintanilla and Sgt. Edward Camacho of the Guam Police Department; Saipan law enforcement officer Sheriff Manual T. Sablan; Sgt. Tony Benavente; attorney Edward Wiles; Dr. Manual Aldon; Jesus P. Boyer of the present Saipan legislature; storekeeper Juan Guerrero Reyes; Francisco Tudela of the insular constabulary; merchant Jose Pangelinan; Brother

Gregario of the Yap Catholic Mission; and Jesus Salas, who had been imprisoned by the Japanese in the cell next to that of the woman flier."

2. Robert E. Wallack, telephone conversation with author, 9 March 2007.

4. William C. Wallack, letter to author, 29 June 2007.

5. From Fred Goerner to Jim Golden, Lockheed Aircraft representative, 10 April 1969, Goerner Collection, Nimitz Museum, Fredericksburg, Texas.

6. Janet Go, "Amelia Killed In Saipan: Visiting Guamanian Was Told In Saipan in 1937," *Pacific Daily News,* 19 November 1970.

7. The commander in question was Cdr. Benjamin W. McCandlish, head of the Naval Government of Guam from 1936 to 1938.

8. Matilde remarried many times; her last names are traced in Donald M. Wilson, *Amelia Earhart: Lost Legend* (Webster, New York: Enigma Press, 1994), 201.

9. Fred Goerner, *The Search for Amelia Earhart* (New York: Doubleday, 1966), 105.

10. Ibid.

11. Ibid., 107.

12. Oliver Knaggs, *Amelia Earhart: Her Last Flight* (Cape Town, South Africa: Timmins Publishers, 1983), 146-55.

13. Goerner, *Search,* 244.

14. Ibid., 4.

15. Office of Naval Intelligence, *Patton Report 2345,* 76.

16. Anonymous, conversation with author.

17. Knaggs, *Last Flight,* 174-79.

18. T. C. Buddy Brennan and Ray Rosenbaum, *Witness to the Execution: The Odyssey of Amelia Earhart* (New York: Renaissance House, 1988), 126-27.

19. Jae Hong Lee to William Stewart, 25 March 2008, and Stewart to Bill Prymak, e-mail, 2 April 2008.

20. Notes, Goerner Collection, National Museum of the Pacific War, Fredericksburg, Texas.

21. Goerner, *Search,* 115.

22. Ibid., 238.

23. "Amelia Earhart Shot, Tokyo Housewife Says," *Japan Times* 13 November 1970.

24. Father Everett F. Briggs to Bill Prymak, 1999, and Briggs, letter to author, 2003.

25. Walter Lippmann, "Amelia Earhart," *New York Herald-Tribune* 8 July 1937.

Chapter 13

1. Long's fuel endurance calculation alone is hardly confirmed. According to Long, the easterly headwinds averaged 26.5 mph for the entire twenty-hour flight. However, Capt. Ernest W. Humphrey, USN, ret., then assistant navigator on the aircraft carrier Lexington during the Earhart search, related: "Headwinds averaged 22 knots for first seven hours of the flight. The Electra encountered an equatorial front with heavy rain from 8 to 12 p.m. Instead of the expected tail wind during the last half of the flight, Amelia and Noonan actually encountered a seven knot crosswind from the southeast" (Paul Van Dyke to Fred Goerner, 28 July 1971, per Ernest W. Humphrey, interview by Paul Van Dyke).

2. Robert B. Gross, president of Lockheed, calculated that at 1,050 gallons of fuel, the range of the Electra would have been four thousand miles. The best cruising speed would have been 145 mph at four thousand feet altitude. The takeoff run

under optimum conditions would have required three thousand feet (which was the length of the Lae runway), and liftoff would have required 100-octane fuel with full throttle setting (Robert B. Gross to George P. Putnam, 5 March 1936, Purdue University Library).

3. Lockheed believed, without considering adverse wind conditions, not only that a four thousand-mile range was achievable but also that even greater distance was possible. The fuel, in that case, should have provided sufficient flying time not only to retrace the early morning flight path back to the Gilberts but also to reach farther into the Marshall Islands. Amelia had told Gene Vidal that she hoped to find "a nice beach on a Gilbert island that has fresh water" if she couldn't find Howland and ended up on or near Mili Atoll instead.

4. It has never been confirmed (with hard evidence) that Earhart ran out of fuel. Some few gallons likely did vent from expanding tanks. With the Lae, New Guinea, daytime temperature in the high eighties, it is probable that a little gasoline was lost, but there is no way to determine how much.

5. The two pilots earned the Harmon Trophy in 1937 for their achievement.

6. Lt. John Lambrecht told Fred Goerner that without question his "signs of recent habitation" were the crumbling walls of what appeared to have been buildings, as recorded in Fred Goerner to Ed Barnes, 11 October 1991.

7. Considering the detailed data maintained by TIGHAR on Nikumaroro, it's difficult to understand why there is no mention of Maude or his settlers, who came ashore only three months after Amelia and Fred's disappearance. If the Electra had truly crashed there, some evidence of the plane and its occupants would have been evident three months later, and Maude would have noted it in his reports of the island.

Chapter 14

1. War Problems Division, box 3588 (1945-1947), RG 59 National Archives.

2. Jim Hannon stated, "I placed her on the roster as 'Jane Doe'" (Jim Hannon to author, 7 October 2004).

3. Ron Bright to Amelia Earhart Society, e-mail, 14 August 2006.

4. The National Relief and Rehabilitation Administration (NRRA), was the outgrowth of several wartime humane organizations. It was organized in 1943 to monitor detention camps and ensure that prisoners of war were treated decently.

5. Mary Taylor Previte, letter to author, 17 September 2004.

6. Pamela Masters, letter to author, 30 September 2004.

7. Langdon Gilkey, telephone conversation with author, 5 November 2004.

8. If Billings could locate the Australian Army file describing the discovery of the wrecked twin-engine airplane and the tag itself, his story would be much more effective.

9. For the Electra to have successfully returned to New Guinea would have required sufficient fuel reserve to fly an additional two thousand miles (David Billings to Amelia Earhart Society, e-mail).

Selected Bibliography

Books

Aldrich, Richard J. *Intelligence and the War against Japan: Britain, America, and the Politics of Secret Service*. Cambridge: Cambridge University Press, 2000.

Backus, Jean L. *Letters From Amelia: 1901-1937*. Boston: Beacon Press, 1982.

Beck, Doreen. *The Book of Bottle Collecting*. London: Hamlyn, 1973.

Blau, Melinda. *Whatever Happened to Amelia Earhart?* Great Unsolved Mysteries Series. New York: Contemporary Perspectives, 1977.

Brennan, T. C. "Buddy." *Witness to the Execution: The Odyssey of Amelia Earhart*. (Frederick, Colo.: Renaissance House, 1988).

Briand, Paul, Jr. *Daughter of the Sky: The Story of Amelia Earhart*. New York: Duell, Sloane and Pearce, 1960.

Brink, Randall. *Lost Star: The Search for Amelia Earhart*. New York: W. W. Norton, 1996.

Brinley, Maryann Bucknam. *Jackie Cochran: The Story of the Greatest Woman Pilot in Aviation History*. New York: Bantam Books, 1988.

Brun, Michel. *Le Destin tragique du Tahiti-Nui*. Paris: Éditions Flammarion, 1959.

Bryan, E. H., Jr. *Panala'au Memoirs*. Honolulu: Pacific Scientific Information Center, Bernice P. Bishop Museum, 1974.

Burke, John, and Richard O'Connor. *Winged Legend: The Story of Amelia Earhart*. New York: G. P. Putnam, 1970.

Butler, Susan. *East to the Dawn: The Life of Amelia Earhart*. Cambridge, Mass.: Da Capo Press, 1999.

Campbell, Mike, and Thomas E. Devine. *With Our Own Eyes: Eyewitnesses to the Final Days of Amelia Earhart*. Athens, Ohio: Lucky Press, LLC., 2002.

Carrington, George Carson. *Amelia Earhart: What Really Happened at Howland*. Vancouver, BC: Britnav Services, 1977.

Ceillier, Rémi. *La Cryptographie*. Que sais-je, vol. 116. Paris: Presses universitaires de France, 1945.

Chadwick, Roxanne. *Amelia Earhart: Aviation Pioneer*. Achievers Biographies Series. Minneapolis, Minn.: Lerner Publishing Group, 1987.

Chapman, Sally Putnam. *Whistled Like a Bird: The Untold Story of Dorothy Putnam, George Putnam, and Amelia Earhart*. New York: Warner Books, 1997.

Chida, Tomohedi, and Peter Davies. *The Japanese Shipping and Ship Building Industries: A History of their Modern Growth*. London: Athlone Press, 1990.

Cliff, Norman H. *Courtyard of the Happy Way*. Evesham, England: James, 1977.

Cochran, Jacqueline. *The Stars at Noon*. London: Robert Hale, 1955.

Coit, Margaret. *Mr. Baruch*. Boston: Houghton Mifflin, 1957.

Davis, Burke. *Amelia Earhart*. New York: G. P. Putnam, 1972.

Daws, Gavan. *Prisoners of the Japanese: POWs of World War II in the Pacific*. New York: Quill/William Morrow, New York, 1994.

de Bisschop, Eric. *Voyage of the Kaimiloa*. London: George Bell and Sons, Ltd., 1940.

De Jaegher, Raymond J., and Irene C. Kuhn. *The Enemy Within: An Eyewitness Account of the Communist Conquest of China*. New York: Doubleday, 1952.

De Leeuw, Adele. *The Story of Amelia Earhart*. New York: Grosset and Dunlap, 1955.

de Pierrefeu, François. *Les confessions de Tatibouet*. Vol. 2, Au delà des horizons lointains. Paris: Éditions Plon, 1939.

Dietrich, Noah, and Bob Thomas. *Howard: The Amazing Mr. Hughes*. New York: Fawcett Publications, 1972.

Donahue, J. A. *The Earhart Disappearance: The British Connection*. Terre Haute, Ind.: SunShine House, 1987.

Duus, Masayo. *Tokyo Rose: Orphan of the Pacific*. Tokyo: Kodansha International, 1979.

Dwiggins, Don. *Hollywood Pilot*. New York: Doubleday, 1967.

Earhart, Amelia, *The Fun of It: Random Records of My Own Flying and of Women in Aviation*. New York: Harcourt, Brace, and Company, 1932.

———. *20 Hrs., 40 Min.: Our First Flight in the Friendship*. New York: G. P. Putnam's Sons, 1928.

———. *Last Flight*. Compiled by George Palmer Putnam. New York: Harcourt, Brace, and Company, 1937.

Faligot, Roger. *Naisho: enquête au cœur des services secrets japonais*. Paris: Éditions La Découverte, 1997.

Faligot, Roger, and Rémi Kauffer. *Histoire mondiale du renseignement*. Paris: Éditions R. Laffont, 1994.

Fehrenbach, T. R. *Franklin Delano Roosevelt's Undeclared War: 1939-1941*. New York: David McKay Company, 1967.

Fletcher, Edward. *Antiques Bottles in Colour*. Poole, Dorset: Blandford Press, 1976.

———. *Bottle Collecting: Finding, Collecting, and Displaying Antique Bottles*. Poole, Dorset: Blandford Press, 1972.

Flynn, John T. *The Roosevelt Myth*. New York: The Devin-Adair Company, 1948.

Francillon, René J. *Japanese Aircraft of the Pacific War*. Annapolis, Md.: Naval Institute Press, 1979.

Freehafer, Ruth W. *R. B. Stewart and Purdue University*. West Lafayette, Ind.: Purdue University, 1983.

Furuta, Ryōichi, and Yoshikazu Hirai. *A Short History of Japanese Merchant Shipping*. Tokyo: Tokyo News Service, 1967.

Gauvreau, Emile. *The Wild Blue Yonder: Sons of the Prophet Carry On*. New York: E. P. Dutton and Co., 1944.

Gilkey, Langdon. *Shantung Compound*. New York: Harper and Row, 1966.

Gillespie, Ric. *Finding Amelia: The True Story of the Earhart Disappearance*. Annapolis, Md.: Naval Institute Press, 2006.

Goerner, Fred. *The Search for Amelia Earhart*. New York: Doubleday, 1966.

Goldstein, Donald M., and Katherine V. Dillon. *Amelia: The Centennial Biography of an Aviation Pioneer*. Washington, DC: Brassey's, 1997.

Hill, Charles N. *Fix on the Rising Sun: The Clipper Hi-Jacking of 1938—and the Ultimate MIAs*. Bloomington, Ind.: AuthorHouse, 2000.

Hull, Cordell. *The Memoirs of Cordell Hull*. Vol. 1. New York: Macmillan, 1948.

———. *The Memoirs of Cordell Hull*. Vol. 2. New York: Macmillan, 1948.

Jerome, Kate Boehm. *Who Was Amelia Earhart?* Who Was . . . ? Series. Charlotte, North Carolina: Baker and Taylor, 2009.

Johnson, Clarence "Kelly," and Maggie Smith. *More Than My Share of It All*. Washington, DC: Smithsonian Institution Press, 1985.

Kelley, J. F. *Memoirs of Msgr. ("Doc") J. F. Kelley*. Locust, NJ: Adrian McBride, 1987.

Kennedy, Art. *High Times—Keeping 'Em Flying: An Aviation Autobiography*. Edited by Jo Ann Ridley. McKinleyville, Calif.: Fithian Press, 1992.

Klaas, Joe. *Amelia Earhart Lives: A Trip through Intrigue to Find America's First Lady of Mystery*. New York: McGraw-Hill, 1970.

Kokaze, Hidemasa. *Japanese Maritime Transport under Imperialism*. Tokyo: Yamakawa Shuppan, 1993.

Knaggs, Oliver. *Amelia Earhart: Her Last Flight*. Cape Town, South Africa: Timmins Publishers, 1983.

Krop, Pascal. *Les secrets de l'espionnage français de 1870 à nos jours*. Paris: Payot, 1995.

Lauber, Patricia. *Lost Star: The Story of Amelia Earhart*. New York: Scholastic, Inc., 1988.

Layton, Edwin T., Roger Pineau, and John Costello. *"And I Was There:" Pearl Harbor and Midway—Breaking the Secrets*. Annapolis, Md.: Naval Institute Press, 1985.

Leck, Greg. *Captives of Empire: The Japanese Internment of Allied Civilians in China, 1941-1945*. Philadelphia: Shandy Press, 2006.

Lerville, Edmond. *Les cahiers secrets de la cryptographie: le chiffre dans l'histoire des histoires du chiffre*. Monaco: Éditions du Rocher, 1972.

Libby, Justin Harris. *The Irresolute Years: American Congressional Opinion Towards Japan, 1937-1941*. Asian Studies Monograph Series. Hong Kong: Asian Research Service, 1984.

Lodesen, Marius. *Captain Lodi Speaking*. Madison, Wis.: Argonaut Press, 1984.

Lomax, Judy. *Women of the Air*. New York: Dodd, Mead, and Co., 1987.

Loomis, Vincent V., and Jeffrey L. Ethell. *Amelia Earhart: The Final Story*. New York: Random House, 1985.

Long, Elgen M., and Marie K. Long. *Amelia Earhart: The Mystery Solved*. New York: Simon and Schuster, 1999.

Lovell, Mary S. *The Sound of Wings: The Life of Amelia Earhart*. New York: St. Martin's Press, 1989.

Mansfield, Louis C. S. *The Solution of Codes and Ciphers*. London: A. MacLehose and Company 1936.

Masters, Pamela. *The Mushroom Years: A Story of Survival*. Placerville, Calif.: Henderson House Publishing, 1998.

Miles, Milton E., and Hawthorne Daniel. *A Different Kind of War: The Little-Known Story of the Combined Guerilla Forces Created in China by the U.S. Navy and the Chinese during World War II*. New York: Doubleday, 1967.

Miller, Michael Barry. *Shanghai on the Métro: Spies, Intrigue, and the French Between the Wars*. Berkeley, Calif.: University of California Press, 1994.

Morrissey, Muriel Earhart. *Courage Is the Price: The Biography of Amelia Earhart*. Wichita, Kans.: McCormick-Armstrong, 1963.

Morrissey, Muriel Earhart, and Carol L. Osborne. *Amelia, My Courageous Sister: Biography of Amelia Earhart*. Santa Clara, Calif.: Osborne Publisher, 1987.

Myers, Robert H. *"Stand By to Die:" The Disappearance, Rescue and Return of Amelia Earhart.* Pacific Grove, Calif.: Lighthouse Writer's Guild, 1985.

Nagakawa, Keiichirō, ed. *Government and Business: Proceedings of the Fifth Fuji Conference.* Vol. 5, International Conference on Business History. Tokyo: University of Tokyo Press, 1980.

Nagakawa, Keiichirō, and Tsunehiko Yui, eds. *Business History of Shipping: Strategy and Structure, Proceedings of the Eleventh Fuji Conference.* Vol. 11, International Conference on Business History. Tokyo: University of Tokyo Press, 1985.

Navarre, Henri. *Le Service de Renseignements, 1871-1944.* Paris: Éditions Plon, 1978.

Nichols, Ruth. *Wings for Life.* Philadelphia: J. B. Lippincott Co., 1957.

Parillo, Mark. *The Japanese Merchant Marine in World War II.* Annapolis, Md.: Naval Institute Press, 1993.

Peattie, Mark R. *Nan'yō: The Rise and Fall of the Japanese in Micronesia, 1885-1945.* Vol. 4, Pacific Islands Monograph Series. Honolulu, Hawaii: University of Hawaii Press, 1988.

Pellegreno, Ann Holtgren. *World Flight: The Earhart Trail.* Ames, Iowa: Iowa State University Press, 1971.

Pélissier, Jean. *Cinq hommes sur un radeau: Expédition Tahiti-Nui II et III.* Paris: Éditions de la pensée moderne, 1959.

Porch, Douglas. *Histoire des Services secrets français.* Vol. 2. Paris: Éditions Albin Michel, 1997.

Portsmouth, England. *The City Museum . . . Catalogue of Exhibition: Glass Bottles Through the Ages, Etc.* 1939.

Prange, Gordon William, and Donald M. Goldstein. *At Dawn We Slept: The Untold Story of Pearl Harbor.* New York: Penguin Books, 1982.

Pujol, Alain. *Dictionnaire de l'espion.* Paris: Éditions Solar, 1965.

Putnam, George P. *Soaring Wings: A Biography of Amelia Earhart.* New York: Harcourt, Brace, and Company, 1939.

Rafford, Paul, Jr. *Amelia Earhart's Radio.* Orange, Calif.: Paragon Agency, 2006.

Railey, Hilton H. *Touch'd with Madness.* New York: Carrick and Evans, 1938.

Randier, Jean. *Yacht-club de France, 1867-1967.* Paris: Yacht-club de France, 1967.

Rathel. *Historique des corps d'officiers de réserve interprétés et du chiffre de la marine.* 1964.

Reineck, Rollin C. *Amelia Earhart Survived.* Orange, Calif.: Paragon Agency, 2003.

Rich, Doris L. *Amelia Earhart: A Biography.* Washington, DC: Smithsonian Press, 1989.

Roessler, Walter, Leo Gomez, and Gail Lynne Green. *Amelia Earhart: Case Closed?* Hummelstown, Pennsylvania: Aviation Publishers, 1995.

Safford, Laurance F., Cameron A. Warren, and Robert R. Payne. *Earhart's Flight into Yesterday: The Facts without the Fiction.* McLean, Va.: Paladwr Press, 2003.

Scanlan, Patrick J. *Stars in the Sky.* Hong Kong: Trappist Publications, 1987.

Smith, Elinor. *Aviatrix.* Waterville, Maine: Thorndike Press, 1981.

Southern, Neta Snook. *I Taught Amelia to Fly.* New York: Vantage Press, 1974.

Soutou, Georges-Henri, Jacques Frémeaux, and Olivier Forcade. *L'Exploitation du renseignement en Europe et aux Etats-Unis des années 1930 aux années 1960: actes du colloque international tenu aux Ecoles militaires de Saint-Cyr Coëtquidan, organisé par le Centre de recherche des écoles de Saint-Cyr Coëtquidan, le Centre d'histoire de l'Europe et des relations internationales au XXe siècle et le Centre de l'Islam contemporain, Paris IV-Sorbonne, les 3 et 4 juin 1998*. Paris: Éditions Economica, 2001.

Spector, Ronald H. *Eagle Against the Sun: The American War with Japan*. New York: The Free Press, 1985.

Strippel, Dick. *Amelia Earhart: The Myth and the Reality*. Jericho, New York: Exposition-Phoenix Press, 1972.

Tanous, Peter. *The Earhart Mission*. New York: Simon and Schuster, 1978.

Thaden, Louise. *High, Wide and Frightened*. New York: Air Facts Press, 1973.

Thayer, James Stewart. *The Earhart Betrayal*. New York: G. P. Putnam's Sons, 1980.

Thorpe, Elliott R. *East Wind, Rain: The Intimate Account of an Intelligence Officer in the Pacific, 1939-49*. Boston: Gambit, Inc., 1969.

Tipton, Laurence. *Chinese Escapade*. London: Macmillan, 1949.

Van den Bossche, Willy. *Antique Glass Bottles: Their History and Evolution (1500-1850)*. Suffolk, England: Antique Collectors' Club, the University of Michigan, 2001.

Ware, Susan. *Still Missing: Amelia Earhart and the Search for Modern Feminism*. New York: W. W. Norton and Company, 1994.

Waterford, Van, *Prisoners of the Japanese in World War II: Statistical History, Personal Narratives, and Memorials Concerning POWs in Camps and on Hellships, Civilian Internees, Asian Slave Laborers, and Others Captured in the Pacific Theater*. Jefferson, North Carolina: McFarland, 1994.

Weems, P. V. H. *Air Navigation*. New York and London: McGraw-Hill, 1931.

Weisheit, Bowen P. *The Last Flight of Frederick J. Noonan and Amelia Earhart*. Millersville, Md.: Friendship Creative Printers, 1995.

Wills, Geoffrey. *The Bottle-Collector's Guide*. New York: HarperCollins, 1977.

Wills, Geoffrey. *English Glass Bottles, 1650-1950, for the Collector*. Edinburgh: J. Bartholomew, 1974.

Wilson, Donald Moyer. *Amelia Earhart: Lost Legend*. Webster, New York: Enigma Press, 1994.

Winters, Kathleen C. *Amelia Earhart: The Turbulent Life of an American Icon*. New York: MacMillan, 2010.

Wright, Quincy. *Mandates Under the League of Nations*. Chicago: University of Chicago Press, 1930.

Yanaihara, Tadao. *Pacific Islands Under Japanese Mandate*. London and New York: Oxford University Press, 1940.

Articles, Letters, Memos, Papers, Reports

Chater, Eric H. Concerning the movements of Amelia Earhart flying to and from Lae, New Guinea, written to M. E. Griffin. 25 July 1937.

Davies, Peter, and Katamaya Kunio. "Aspects of Japanese Shipping Industry." Paper presented at the Sutory and Toyota International Centres for Economics and Related Disciplines, London School of Economics, 5 May 1999.

Flores, Bishop Feliz Umberto. Interviews by Father Arnold Bendowske of Saipan listing Saipanese who recalled seeing or knowing about Caucasian pilots in Japanese custody. Catholic Church Records. Guam.

Fukiko, Aoki. "Was A. Earhart Executed?" Bungei Shunju 61 (April 1983): 392-418.

Goerner, Fred. "In Search of Amelia Earhart." *Unsolved* (Orbis Publishing Limited) 2, no. 18 (1984).

Grover, Gretchen G. "The Coast Guard's Pacific Colonizers." *Naval History* 16, no. 4 (August 2002): 43.

Holbrook, Francis X. "Amelia Earhart's Final Flight." *Proceedings* (Naval Institute Press) 97, no. 2 (1971): 48-55.

———. "United States National Defense and Transpacific Commercial Aviation Routes, 1933-41." PhD diss., Fordham University, 1969.

Hooven, Frederick J. "Amelia Earhart's Last Flight." Personal paper from Norwich, Vermont, June 1982. Held at Smithsonian National Air and Space Museum Library, Washington, DC.

Jennings, Dean S. "Is Amelia Earhart Still Alive?" *Popular Aviation* 25, no. 6 (December1939): 10-13.

"List of Yachts Equipped with Radiotelephones." *The Rudder: The Magazine for Yachtsmen* 54, no. 10 (October 1938).

Mandel, Alex V. "Amelia Earhart's Survival and Repatriation: Myth or Reality?" (2005).

Noonan, Frederick J. "A Letter from Fred Noonan to Lieut.-Comm. P. V. H. Weems." *Popular Aviation* 22, no. 5 (May 1938).

USS *Lexington. Report of the Earhart Search.* By Capt. Al Raithel. July 1937.

Riley, John P., Jr. "The Earhart Tragedy: Old Mystery, New Hypothesis." *Naval History* 14, no. 4 (August 2000): 20-29.

Roosevelt, Franklin D. Papers as President, Official File, 1933-1945. Franklin D. Roosevelt Library, Hyde Park, New York.

———. President's Personal File, 1933-1945. Franklin D. Roosevelt Library, Hyde Park, New York.

———. President's Secretary's File, 1933-1945. Franklin D. Roosevelt Library, Hyde Park, New York.

Scouters Council of Nauru. *The Nauru Scouter* (Nauru) all issues (August 1937-June 1938).

Vaeth, J. Gordon. "What Happened to Amelia Earhart?" *NOAA* (July 1977): 24-29.

Williams, J. "Secrets of Japan's Mandated Islands: The Bitter 'Undercover' Struggle in the Northern Pacific." *Pacific Islands Monthly* (June 1939): 11-14.

United States Government Records

Aviation General. Central Classified Files, 1907-1951. File 9-12-21. RG 126. National Archives II, College Park, MD.

Bowditch, Nathaniel. *American Practical Navigator: An Epitome of Navigation.* Washington, DC: Government Printing Office, 1962.

Chief of Naval Operations. Fleet Maintenance Division. Reel NRS-246-F. RG 26. Amelia Earhart Collection. Operational Archives Branch, Naval Historical Center.

Civilian Documents. Miscellaneous. Reel NRS-246-G. RG 26. Amelia Earhart Collection. Operational Archives Branch, Naval Historical Center.

Department of Commerce. General Records. Files 101232 and 83272/126. RG 40. National Archives.

Department of State. General Records. File 862i.01/333. RG 59. National Archives.

Director of Naval Intelligence. General Correspondence, 1929-1942. File A-403. Box 70. RG 38. National Archives.

Dutton, Benjamin, and Edwin A. Beito. *Navigation and Nautical Astronomy*. Annapolis: United States Naval Institute, 1951.

Federal Aviation Administration. Correspondence Records. Files 805.0, 805.3, and 835. RG 237. National Records II, College Park, MD.

Hawaiian Department. Air Officer, General Administrative. Files 1931-42, 334. Box 2. RG 395. National Archives.

Leo G. Bellarts. General papers. RG 200. National Archives II, College Park, MD.

Military Intelligence Defense. 183-Z-292, 255-1-94/45, 2657-G-774. Boxes 165, 237, 2112. RG 165. National Archives.

National Records Service. File A21-5. Reel NRS-246-B. RG 26.

Nautical Almanac Office. United States Naval Observatory. *The American Ephemeris and Nautical Almanac*. Washington: Government Printing Office, 1937.

Office of the Adjutant General. Records. RG 94. National Archives.

Office of Naval Intelligence. Naval Investigative Service, Amelia Earhart Collection. Reel NRS-246-D. RG 26. Operational Archives, Naval Historical Center.

Office of Naval Records. Fourteenth Naval District serial 095. File GU. Box 116. Reel NRS-246-A. RG 45. National Archives.

———. Fourteenth Naval District serial 17527. Amelia Earhart Collection. Reel NRS-246-E. RG 26. Operational Archives Branch, Naval Historical Center.

———. General Correspondence, 1924-1945. File A4-3. Box 22. RG 37. National Archives.

———. General Records. File A4-5. Box 146. RG 80. National Archives.

Putnam, Amelia Earhart/1-212. File 800.79611. RG 59. National Archives.

P. V. H. Weems. *Line of Position Book*. Annapolis: US Naval Institute, 1927.

Secretary of the Navy. Classified Correspondence, 1927-1939. File A21-5. Box 100. RG 80. National Archives.

United States Coast Guard. Correspondence. File 601. RG 94. National Archives.

———. Records. Reel NRS-246-C. RG 26. National Archives.

United States Customs. Closed Vessels Documentation.

United States Hydrographic Office. *Aircraft Navigation Manual, US Navy*. Washington: Hydrographic Office under the authority of the Secretary of the Navy, 1941.

United States Pacific Fleet and Pacific Ocean Areas. *Preliminary Interrogation Report 157, CinCPac-CinCPOA Translations and Interrogations No. 35, CinCPac-CinCPOA Bulletin 170-45*. Evidence Given during Interrogation. By N. Yamaga. Report prepared by Commander in Chief, US Pacific Fleet and Pacific Ocean Areas. 7 July 1945.

United States Strategic Bombing Survey. *The American Campaign Against Wotje, Maloelap, Mille, and Jaluit*. Evidence Given during Interrogation. By S. Yonemoto. Washington, DC: Naval Analysis Section, 1947. 291-92.

———. *The American Campaign Against Wotje, Maloelap, Mille, and Jaluit*. Evidence Given during Interrogation. By M. Yoshida. Washington, DC: Naval Analysis Section, 1947. 142-44.

———. *The American Campaign Against Wotje, Maloelap, Mille, and Jaluit*. Evidence Given during Interrogation. By N. Yoshimi. Washington, DC: Naval Analysis Section, 1947. 54-57.

Index